Expository Composition
Revised

Discovering Your Voice

Expository Composition Revised

Discovering Your Voice

Tony Romano ■ Gary Anderson

William Fremd High School
Palatine, Illinois

Foreword by
Naomi Shihab Nye

EMC
Publishing

St. Paul • Indianapolis

Senior Editor: Brenda Owens
Production Editor: Bob Dreas
Cover and Interior Designer: Leslie Anderson
Production Specialist: Jack Ross
Digital Production Coordinator: Steve Struhar

Copy Editor: Jennifer Anderson
Proofreader: Judy M. Peterson
Indexer: Ina Gravitz
Permissions Coordinator: Lindsay Ryan

Care has been taken to verify the accuracy of information presented in this book. However, the authors, editors, and publisher cannot accept responsibility for Web, e-mail, newsgroup, or chat room subject matter or content, or for consequences from application of the information in this book, and make no warranty, expressed or implied, with respect to its content.

Trademarks: Some of the product names and company names included in this book have been used for identification purposes only and may be trademarks or registered trade names of their respective manufacturers and sellers. The authors, editors, and publisher disclaim any affiliation, association, or connection with, or sponsorship or endorsement by, such owners.

Acknowledgments: See pages 563–566, which are an extension of this copyright page.

We have made every effort to trace the ownership of all copyrighted material and to secure permission from copyright holders. In the event of any question arising as to the use of any material, we will be pleased to make the necessary corrections in future printings. Thanks are due to the aforementioned authors, publishers, and agents for permission to use the materials indicated.

ISBN 978-0-82196-193-3

© 2013 by EMC Publishing, LLC
875 Montreal Way
St. Paul, MN 55102
Email: educate@emcp.com
Website: www.emcschool.com

Printed in the United States of America

20 19 18 17 16 15 14 13 12 11   1 2 3 4 5 6 7 8 9 10

For Maureen, Lauren, Angela, and Allie, always—T.R.

For Michele, Abby, and Grace, with thanks for your love and patience—G.A.

and

for the English Department of William Fremd High School

About the Authors

Tony Romano teaches English and psychology at William Fremd High School in Palatine, Illinois. He is a graduate of DePaul University (B.A.) and Northeastern Illinois University (M.A.). An award-winning fiction writer, Mr. Romano is the author of the novel *When the World Was Young* and the story collection *If You Eat, You Never Die*. He is the coauthor of *Psychology and You*, a high school textbook. His fiction has been produced for National Public Radio and has appeared in *The Chicago Tribune Magazine* and numerous literary journals. He lives in Glen Ellyn, Illinois. In 2010, Tony Romano was named Illinois Author of the Year by the Illinois Association of Teachers of English. You can visit his web site at TonyRomanoAuthor.com.

Gary Anderson teaches English at William Fremd High School in Palatine, Illinois, where he served as department chair from 2001-2007. He is a graduate of Wartburg College (B.A.) and Iowa State University (M.A.). An award-winning poet, Mr. Anderson has received honors from the Illinois Arts Council and other organizations, and his writing has appeared in numerous scholarly journals, literary magazines, and anthologies. He serves as an administrator on English Companion Ning, an online community dedicated to professional development for English teachers. He lives in Arlington Heights, Illinois. Visit Gary Anderson online at WhatsNotWrong.wordpress.com.

Both authors help organize William Fremd High School's annual Writers Week, a literary festival that brings together writers from around the nation to read and discuss their work with students and teachers. They also conduct professional development sessions and presentations around the country for teachers at conferences, seminars, and institutes.

Author Acknowledgments

We gratefully acknowledge the contributions of Henry Sampson, Gina Enk, James Wyman, Kevin Brewner, Antonette Minniti, Sabra Gerber, Emily Hill, Sara Holbrook, Tanya Miller, Dwaine Spieker, Nedra Segall, Naomi Shihab Nye, Tess Gallagher, Dan Sharkovitz, Amy Rasmussen, Dawn Hogue, Sheila Moore, Leslie Healey, Jeffrey Yagaloff, the staff of Arlington Heights Memorial Library, and everyone at EMC Publishing, especially Steve vanThournout, who believed in this project and supported its development; Brenda Owens, a talented and insightful editor who directed this revision; Bob Dreas, who deftly kept this project on schedule; Jennifer Anderson, who offered valuable suggestions; Cheryl Drivdahl, who posed hard, perceptive questions; Leslie Anderson, whose artistic talents helped make this book visually appealing; Lindsay Ryan, who worked tirelessly on permissions; and Ashley Kuehl, the fine editor of the original version of our book. This book is better because of their expertise and generosity.

Content Reviewers

Timothy Averill
Waring School
Beverly, Massachusetts

Michael Boyd
Illinois Central College
East Peoria, Illinois

Kevin Brewner
William Fremd High School
Palatine, Illinois

Kathleen Malone Clesson
University High School
Normal, Illinois

Ann Cox
Central Catholic High School
Bloomington, Illinois

Carol Duncan
Franklin Public Schools
Franklin, Nebraska

Gina Enk
William Fremd High School
Palatine, Illinois

Sara Hansen
La Costa Canyon High School
Carlsbad, California

Judy Johnston
Community College High School East
North Las Vegas, Nevada

Lynne Kelsey
Westlake High School
Westlake Village, California

Virginia Lefurgy
Carmel High School
Putnam Valley, New York

Julie Martinez
Southfield High School
Southfield, Michigan

Melanie Mayer
Port Aransas High School
Corpus Christi, Texas

Tanya Miller
Park Rapids High School
Park Rapids, Minnesota

Brigid Ovitt
Albuquerque Academy
Albuquerque, New Mexico

Denise Pivarnik-Nova
Breck School
Golden Valley, Minnesota

Karen Reisman
Henderson, Nevada

Rosemary Ruffenach
Prairie Center Alternative High School
Eden Prairie, Minnesota

Colleen Ruggieri
Boardman High School
Youngstown, Ohio

Henry Sampson
William Fremd High School
Palatine, Illinois

Nedra Segall
Stillwater High School
Stillwater, Oklahoma

Gail Setter
Southfield High School
Southfield, Michigan

Eileen Simmons
East Central High School
Tulsa, Oklahoma

Dwaine Spieker
Wayne High School
Wayne, Nebraska

Contents in Brief

Contents

Chapter 13   Thinking Like a Writer: Creative Nonfiction

Appendix A   Grammar, Usage, and Punctuation Handbook

Appendix B   Graphic Organizers

Appendix C   Writing for the ACT and SAT

Appendix D   Documentation Formats

Index

Acknowledgments

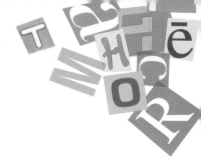

Foreword

What I love most about this book is its own frank and funny voice. There's a contagious spirit of empathic knowing here, which feels compelling and genuine. A book about writing should be written (if we are lucky) in an engaging, forthright style. And this one is—celebrate!

Expository Composition: Discovering Your Voice is smart, useful, and hopeful. It's deeply direct—no padding of text, that old problem that haunts so many student papers. A reader may quickly believe that Romano and Anderson *have been there*, in so many vivid classrooms, with real, live, idiosyncratic students, and good things have come of those relationships, on the page. They respect and value what their students know, suggesting they are rich in possibility and promise. This book offers myriad ways of tapping that richness.

The creation of an atmosphere in a classroom in which students might *want* to discover their writing voices and personal rich troves of material is much more critical than the specific set of strategies or principles suggested. But this volume offers both—ways to create a positive, vital mood in a room of writers, and ways to develop ideas on the page as well. The features, tips, quotations, and sample writings are punchy, exacting, and delicious.

Expository Composition: Discovering Your Voice is for writers of every age and for all instructors who *care*.

Naomi Shihab Nye

Introduction

Dear Student Writer,

Thank you in advance for the time you will spend reading and responding to this book. It is written specifically for you. With so many years of teaching experience behind us, we feel like we know some things about high school students: You are busy, passionate, idealistic, and curious about what your post-high school years will hold. We respect each of those traits, and we will honor them as we share with you what we know about writing. We will not waste your time or ask you to downplay your convictions or identity. On the contrary, we want to help you become wise, efficient, engaging writers capable of expressing yourself in any composition situation that you may encounter for the rest of your life.

Since the original edition of this book, we have seen students writing more than ever, especially online. With that in mind, we have included in this revised edition a new chapter devoted to helping you write effectively in online situations. We have also updated other sections of the book to reflect changes in how students interact with "new literacies," to use a little teacher terminology. We invite you to visit the *Expository Composition* Internet Resource Center at www.emcschool.net/expcomp and our *Discovering Your Voice* site at www.emcschool.net/expcompDYV.

We ask that you approach the reading, exercises, and assignments with an open mind and with a desire to improve yourself as a writer. If we have done our job well, and if you approach your part in good faith, don't be surprised if this time of concentrated writing instruction ends up being one of the most valuable academic experiences of your life as you discover your voice.

Tony Romano   Gary Anderson

Thinking About Writing

Imagine you have an eccentric uncle, Marty, who's excited about writing. Uncle Marty reads every writing book he can find from cover to cover, attends writing conferences and weekend seminars, and seeks advice from teachers and professional writers. Writing is his life, he decides.

Now imagine you have an aunt, Marilyn, who is also an aspiring writer. Aunt Marilyn spends about an hour each morning at her desk. She mostly stares out the window and jots down ideas that seem worth noting. After a while, one idea announces itself as more intriguing than another, so she writes about that for a few days. She spends a few more days revising and editing what she's written until she feels she's done; then she begins the entire process over again.

Uncle Marty is like a trapeze artist who reads about walking a tightrope but never climbs atop the rope. Aunt Marilyn may not be the most productive writer in the world, but she understands the obvious: writers write. They may also study writing, talk about writing, write about writing, attend conferences, and form writing groups; but most importantly, they write.

This book may be useful to you in many different ways, but ultimately, your responses to the lessons and exercises are primary. If a thousand students waded through this book, completed the chapter assignments, and took to heart the various writing tips, they would all gain different lessons. They would bring to the table their own judgments and talents, their own brands of humor, and their own voices. They would all discover their own truths. With this in mind, explore this text with curiosity and confidence. Believe you have something to say, and say it with authority.

Before we start sharing our own ideas on writing, we want you to briefly assess your own knowledge about it. Using your own sheet of paper, complete the following writing quiz. The answers begin on page 3, but please don't peek ahead until you've taken the quiz.

Writing Quiz

Short Answer

1. What's wrong with this introductory passage to a research paper?

   Peace: It's wonderful. I like it as much as the next man, and have no wish to be willfully gloomy at a moment when optimism about the future shape of the world abounds. Nevertheless, my thesis in this essay is that we are likely soon to regret the passing of the Cold War.

2. What's wrong with the second sentence in this passage?

   The AIDS virus is particularly insidious because it hides in the one place where antibodies cannot attack it: in the body's immune cells themselves. But [researchers] may have found a way to destroy HIV in its lair.

3. What's wrong with the second and third sentences?

   To carry enough propellant to get the Mars crew back to Earth, NASA's ship would have to be huge. And assembled in space. At a multibillion-dollar space station.

4. How many paragraphs should an ideal essay include?

True or False

5. The introductory paragraph of an essay should be nearly identical to the concluding paragraph.

6. An ideal paragraph should never have fewer than three sentences.

7. An ideal paragraph should have no more than seven sentences.

8. You should never use the term *you* in an essay.

9. Revision is a waste of time.

10. An essay that is grammatically correct and clear is about all any writer should strive for.

11. You should avoid the word *ain't* and other slang when writing essays.

Journal Topic

On your own sheet of paper, complete each sentence below. Why? From time to time you may feel you have nothing to write about. This five-minute exercise may help remind you what's important to you. Fill in the blanks, tuck your answers away, and peek at them one day when you're stuck. Also, your answers today may be different a week or two from now, so we encourage you to return anew to this exercise from time to time.

1. I am _____.
2. I want to know _____.
3. I admire _____.
4. I get upset when _____.
5. I'm glad I know _____.
6. I get confused when _____.
7. I wish I had more time to _____.
8. I enjoy learning _____.
9. One place I always remember is _____.
10. One person I'm glad I know is _____.
11. One story I like to tell is ____.
12. I like to read about _____.
13. I'd rather be _____.
14. I don't know _____.
15. People who really know me know _____.
16. Some people _____.
17. I get annoyed when _____.

Answers to Writing Quiz

Most students believe this is an easy quiz, yet most do poorly on it. Please don't read ahead unless you've already taken the quiz.

Short Answer

1. *What's wrong with this introductory passage to a research paper?*

> *Peace: It's wonderful. I like it as much as the next man, and have no wish to be willfully gloomy at a moment when optimism about the future shape of the world abounds. Nevertheless, my thesis in this essay is that we are likely soon to regret the passing of the Cold War.*

Most students argue that the writer should not use the first-person point of view. They don't believe *I* and *my* should be allowed in a research paper. Many of their former teachers, in fact, have insisted they not use these dreaded pronouns. Some students don't like the phrase *"my thesis in this essay is,"* either.

This passage is taken word for word from an essay that appeared in the *Atlantic*, a magazine that has been publishing articles on politics, science, social issues, music, and literature for more than 150 years. The magazine's editors apparently saw nothing wrong with the passage.

Why the discrepancy? Why do writers for a prestigious magazine like the *Atlantic* get away with using personal pronouns in what turns out to be a rather formal essay, while students have to wear straitjackets? Some teachers may feel bound by tradition, believing that when writing a research paper, the writer must remain objective and formal in tone. Otherwise, teachers fear, student writers will create a truckload of problems for themselves. There may be a grain of truth in this. Instead of offering hard evidence to support their opinions, students may resort to phrases such as, "Well, it's my opinion…I have a right to my opinion." This is often a sign that the writer can't support his or her point. Simply using *I* doesn't necessarily make an essay stronger. In fact, the first-person point of view may even be intrusive at times. On the other hand, it seems pointless to forbid the use of *I* in most essays. (By the way, the *Atlantic* essay was labeled a research paper because that's what it is; the rest of the essay is not the least bit personal.)

Now that you've been given permission to use *I*, and you can point that out to others—"Look, it says so right here; it's in print!"—you still need to be mindful of your **audience**, which consists of anyone who will read your paper. If your teacher forbids the use of *I* in essays, then you need to acknowledge that audience. You may also run across situations when the use of *I* would seem out of place, as it would in some technical writing.

A couple of final points: Look through some of your old papers (if you haven't saved them, start now), and sort out those that include personal pronouns from those that do not. The essays that include your *I*-voice are probably the most memorable and important to you. Even if this is not the case, your unique voice is much more likely to come through when you feel free to use personal pronouns.

When we began writing this text, we initially struggled with the urge to remain neutral. We briefly considered a more formal approach—after all, this is a textbook; textbooks should rise above plain language—but we quickly came to our senses and put aside the latent fears still residing in us from our grammar school days when prim, well-intentioned teachers instructed us on the fine art of diagramming sentences and following convention. In our final revision of this text, we did tally all instances of *we*, and cut back when the pronoun seemed unnecessary or intrusive.

What about the other objection to the passage, "my thesis in this essay is"? We're not thrilled with the phrase either, but it's a stylistic matter rather than an issue of right and wrong.

2. *What's wrong with the second sentence in this passage?*

> The AIDS virus is particularly insidious because it hides in the one place
> where antibodies cannot attack it: in the body's immune cells themselves.
> But [researchers] may have found a way to destroy HIV in its lair.

Students are eager to point out that writers shouldn't begin a sentence with *but*. Not long ago, beginning a sentence with *but* was poor form and even considered to be incorrect, but rules change with usage. And this rule seems to have gone the route of *ergo* and *ibid*, two terms that once were common but likely are unfamiliar to you. (Notice that we began the previous sentence with *and*, another old taboo.) This passage was taken from an article in the magazine *Discover*. You can find hundreds of examples like this by glancing through issues of *Newsweek*, *Time*, the *Atlantic*, and other popular magazines.

3. *What's wrong with the second and third sentences?*

> To carry enough propellant to get the Mars crew back to Earth,
> NASA's ship would have to be huge. And assembled in space. At a
> multibillion-dollar space station.

This is an easy one, right? Fragments, of course. Can't have them. Must avoid them. At all costs. But this passage about NASA appeared in *Newsweek*, and the editors surely identified the fragments. So why do teachers tell you to avoid fragments if national magazines use them? Teachers know that fragments sometimes create confusion for the reader. When this is the case, yes, avoid fragments. Once you can identify fragments and avoid the confusion they may cause, you can use them, sparingly, in your own writing. For effect!

Notice the effect of using fragments in the *Newsweek* passage. Carrying propellant and building a ship are gargantuan tasks. The sentence fragments slow our reading and highlight that. The fragments are there by design, and their use is clever.

We know what you're thinking. You're thinking, *Wait a second. I can break some rules now? How do I know which rules I can break and which will get me in trouble?* This is a tricky question. Before you use this textbook as a final source, consider your audience. Are you writing for peers, the general public, your teacher, a college admissions officer, or a scholarship committee? Will your audience be offended or put off if you veer from standard practice—or will they be delighted? In most cases, the answer lies somewhere in the middle, and you'll have to determine how far and why you want to veer.

Another important consideration that goes hand in hand with audience is what **tone** to adopt in a specific piece of writing. Tone refers to the writer's attitude toward his or her subject, and this attitude can range from light and humorous to serious and reverential. If your tone is serious, breaking or bending rules may draw undue attention and appear inconsistent with the tone you've established. (See Chapter 6 for more on tone.)

Here's our answer to your question: Once you master the rules, then, and only then, can you break them—sometimes. How's that for vagueness?

Let's try a major league baseball analogy to clarify. A ground ball is hit to the shortstop. The alert second baseman races to second base to field the throw from the shortstop, and then he wheels around and throws to first for a double play. To execute the double play, his foot needs to touch second base while the ball is in his mitt. If the runner is barreling down on second, however, most umpires will allow the baseman a little leeway for safety reasons. The baseman might get away with a "ghost tag," a brush behind the base. The umpire understands that the second baseman knows the rules, and so, if the second baseman's foot is close, he'll overlook the mistake. A Little League umpire, in contrast, needs to be more precise so that players learn the rules.

The same theory holds true for writing. Once you know and truly understand the rules, then you can bend or break them—provided you've considered your audience. It's probably a wise idea to let your teachers decide when you're ready for this.

Some of you will read this chapter, close the book, and remember the part about breaking the rules, but then conveniently forget the warning that accompanies this point, the warning about learning the rules first. Let us reiterate. Remember that second baseman who gets away with bending the rules? Imagine that same second baseman committing three errors early in the game. Is he going to get away with bending any rules? Not likely. If your writing is riddled with errors, the reader will have little patience for your fragments, even if they are purposeful.

Writers on Writing

1. *Keep your hand moving.* When you sit down to write, whether it's for ten minutes or an hour, once you begin, don't stop. If an atom bomb drops at your feet eight minutes after you have begun and you were going to write for ten minutes, don't budge. You'll go out writing....

2. *Lose control.* Say what you want to say. Don't worry if it's correct, polite, appropriate. Just let it rip....

3. *Be specific.* Not car, but Cadillac. Not fruit, but apple. Not bird, but wren. Not a codependent, neurotic man, but Harry, who runs to open the refrigerator for his wife, thinking she wants an apple, when she is headed for the gas stove to light her cigarette.

—*Natalie Goldberg*

4. *How many paragraphs should an ideal essay include?*

A great majority of students, when completing this quiz, say that five paragraphs constitute an ideal essay. They should point out instead, but rarely do, that this question is unfair. The question implies that an ideal length exists. In reality, essays should be as long as they need to be.

Why, then, has the five-paragraph essay become so prominent in student writing? The general format—introduction, body, conclusion—is a useful one. It forces the writer to develop a clear, detailed thesis. It helps the writer organize his or her body of the paper into three main chunks. And it provides a feeling of closure at the end. The five-paragraph format helps the reader, too. Most readers appreciate a brief preview of what they're going to read. They can easily digest three ideas. On the outside chance that readers start to daydream in the middle of the paper, the last paragraph neatly sums everything up for them. Readers won't miss a beat.

When teachers read a paper by a student who is obviously well-versed in the five-paragraph form, however, they usually have mixed feelings. They admire the organization and the clarity. They appreciate the writer's work ethic—in order to master this form, a student needs to follow directions well. But this is where problems often arise. The student follows directions so well that the writing seems polite, safe, formulaic, like a musician playing the notes of a song flawlessly but without any passion. What's missing is the writer's unique slant on his or her subject, the writer's voice, an element of risk.

Students, especially younger students, should learn the five-paragraph essay, but at some point, older students, whose organizational skills are more advanced, should try other methods of structuring an essay. Rather than obsessing about fitting everything into a five-paragraph format, you might try to focus on content first and then discover the best form for that content. This book will provide you with a variety of options for organizing an essay.

True or False

5. *The introductory paragraph of an essay should be nearly identical to the concluding paragraph.*

Given the discussion for Question 4, the answer here should be fairly obvious. Students who follow the five-paragraph format often tack on conclusions that mirror the introduction. At best, this seems like an insult to the reader, as it assumes that the reader will have forgotten the thesis in the first paragraph and needs to be reminded, point by point. Instead, even for five-paragraph essays, conclusions should seem fresh and insightful. Conclusions should resonate, not simply repeat. The seeds of an effective conclusion might be found in the introduction, but those seeds might bloom in a completely different way in the conclusion. In later chapters, we will more fully address how to write creative conclusions relevant to your purpose.

6. *An ideal paragraph should never have fewer than three sentences.*

We're confident that no such animal as an ideal paragraph exists. There may even be rare instances when a single word serves as an effective paragraph. On the other hand, if you've had teachers tell you that paragraphs must contain at least three sentences, they were probably urging you to develop your ideas. Their advice is sound.

7. *An ideal paragraph should have no more than seven sentences.*

See the discussion of Question 6.

8. *You should never use* you *in an essay.*

The second-person pronoun *you* can cause occasional problems with sentence construction. See if you can find the problem in the following passage.

> Nowadays when you go to a new doctor, the receptionist makes you fill out about twenty forms. Before you even meet the doctor, people have to wait thirty minutes.

The word *people* near the end of the sentence doesn't match the pronoun *you* earlier in the sentence. Changing *people* to *you* easily solves the problem, but this type of error is common when a writer casually uses *you*. For this reason, avoid *you* in such generic cases. On the other hand, if your audience is well defined, if you're speaking to someone specific, as we are throughout this text, using *you* is not problematic.

Another problem with *you* is that the writer runs into the danger of alienating some readers. Watch: "You've been invited to prom and need a dress in three weeks…" If you know your audience is strictly female, this might work, but otherwise the sentence borders on the ridiculous.

Obviously there's a place for *you*, as you can tell by skimming this first chapter. As long as *you* seems appropriate for your subject matter and for your audience, and as long as you're careful about its usage, there's no reason not to use it.

Notice how writer Judith Hooper in her essay on the spread of germs uses *you* to clarify what could be a difficult concept:

> Say you're a disease organism….Your best bet is to multiply inside your host as fast as you can. However, if you produce too many copies of yourself, you'll risk killing or immobilizing your host before you can spread. If you're the average airborne respiratory virus, it's best if your host is well enough to go to work and sneeze on people in the subway.

The sentence can be recast without *you*, of course, but the result would likely be less effective. The use of *you* demonstrates how pervasive—even sinister—germs are.

9. *Revision is a waste of time.*

False. Everyone gets this question right, but in practice, not everyone is eager to revise. Throughout this textbook, we'll provide numerous practical suggestions for revising your essays.

10. *An essay that is grammatically correct and clear is about all any writer should strive for.*

False. Clarity is critical, but if the writer doesn't have anything to say, the effort seems pointless, like a paint-by-number attempt instead of a bold splash on a new canvas.

11. *You should avoid* ain't *and other slang when writing essays.*

Avoiding slang will certainly help keep a writer out of trouble. On the other hand, some essays need a little trouble. (See Question 10.) As mentioned earlier, your audience must be clearly defined, which should help guide you in this regard.

What about the nonstandard usage of words and phrases, such as *alright*? As a writer, you ought to consult dictionaries and the most current usage guides, such as *Fowler's Modern English Usage* or *The Purdue Online Writing Lab* (OWL), since rules of usage do change. In this case, these guides will clearly explain that *alright* has never been standard English; instead, the phrase has always been two words: *all right*. Is it okay to break the rule here? We can't think of a single advantage or reason for doing so. Besides, a reader who knows the distinction will simply think the writer has erred.

In the long run, insisting on *all right* as two words may be a losing battle, since *alright*, though incorrect today, will probably one day become standard. This battle to change the language should be a struggle, though, and a prolonged one at that, which is why when we use e-mail and other forms of online communication, we doggedly resist relaxing standards of usage. Granted, the rules for written language change with common usage, but imagine today's typical online messages becoming the standard for written communication.

Why is this different from the rule-bending discussed earlier? In all those instances, the bending was calculated and purposeful. The use of nonstandard language and abbreviations in many online writing platforms, on the contrary, suggests a lack of precision, and in some cases, plain laziness. To their credit, however, people who write LOL, BRB,

Writers on Writing

A good device to remember is the fish-hook. It rises slowly and then hooks back, so it will dig in and stick. It is barbed. Its curve points back to its beginning, to remind itself and the reader where it came from.

Many professionals employ the Hook in their writing: They begin with a word, action, or symbol and at the end of their article or story come back to it. All that has intervened between the first and second mention makes its second appearance more exciting or significant than its first.

—*Ken Macrorie*

and OMG in e-mails possess a refined sense of audience. They wouldn't seriously write LOL in a college essay, would they? (See Chapter 12 for detailed guidance related to online writing.)

Journal Topic

Describe a piece of your writing that has meant a lot to you, such as an essay, a letter, a note, a poem. Briefly explain why the writing is important to you. Next, describe something you've read that has meant something to you. Again, explain why.

Defining Good Writing

One purpose of the writing quiz is to challenge some long-held beliefs you may have about writing, beliefs that tend to handcuff you when you sit down to write. If you "failed" the quiz, you may be more confused than ever about what qualifies as good writing.

Most writing teachers agree that the criteria outlined below describe good writing. Since this is a text on **expository writing**, or nonfiction writing that is informative or explains, we'll limit our remarks to nonfiction.

1. Good writing is worthwhile.

The reader enjoys the writing or learns something from it.

Every year we have students whose personalities seem at odds with their writing. The most striking are those students who like to clown around but write essays devoid of any humor. We call these "tie papers," essays so formal we feel we need to wear a tie to read them. These students have been well trained to objectively state a thesis and follow it with three or four main points and a conclusion. They believe that as long as they follow this formula, they'll earn decent grades—even if they have nothing to say. With some encouragement—"Where's your voice? Why don't you let *your* voice come through?"—many of these students begin to trust that they have something original to say.

As writing teacher and author Don Murray explained it, "Effective writing almost always creates the illusion of an individual writer speaking to an individual reader." How do you create this illusion? Choose topics that engage you. Write about people and places that move you. Take risks.

2. Good writing is developed.

The beginning of an essay creates a variety of expectations in the reader, and it's your job as a writer to address those expectations. If you're telling a story about the time your mother embarrassed you at the grocery store, the reader expects to hear all the relevant details. When details are scarce or vague, or if you rely on clichés or common images, the reader hungers for more. Or if you're comparing two colleges to show the advantage of one over the other, the reader will expect detailed information about both schools. The reader *needs* this information to understand your position.

"How long does the paper have to be?" students ask. The punch line: 8 1/2 by 11. Believe it or not, teachers would rather not prescribe a particular length. They usually do require a minimum, however, because they fear that students will not develop their ideas. Here are some simple guidelines:

a. Make your point.

b. Avoid repetition, wordiness, and vagueness.

c. Develop your ideas.

We'll provide numerous examples on how to achieve this.

3. Good writing is organized.

One sentence leads to another. One paragraph leads to the next. Each paragraph is focused and unified. The reader is able to discern some pattern or logic to the order of the paragraphs. In each of the subsequent chapters, we'll provide many tips on organization.

4. Good writing is clear and concise.

Communicating clearly, whether on paper or face to face, is a skill. Remember the red ink that your overzealous sixth-grade teacher smeared all over your composition? This is what she was trying to teach you: clarity! This is what your writing instructor is trying to teach you now. Pay attention.

5. Good writing is polished.

The writer has clearly made an effort to use proper grammar, syntax, and punctuation.

Some students become defensive about mechanics: "I'm just a poor speller; I never know when to put commas; I just don't get it." Any cognitive psychologist—these are psychologists who study thinking—will tell you that if you insist you don't get it, you won't. If teachers have told you year after year that your sentences run together and cause confusion, pay attention. Sometimes when you drop your defenses, the rules suddenly seem less complicated.

But most important, get some words down first. Finish a draft. Allow some time to pass so that you can view your writing from a fresh perspective. *Then* polish. You wouldn't polish your car and then wash it, would you? The same applies to writing. If you worry too much about cleaning up your mistakes *while you write*, you're more likely to become frustrated and stuck. The late poet William Stafford urged writers to lower their standards when they got stuck. Edit later.

When the time comes to polish, reread your paper several times. Most readers are understanding. They may overlook a mistake here and there. They have their own writing problems. But your effort should be genuine and thorough so that the reader can focus on content and not your mistakes.

One final practical suggestion: read your paper aloud. This can bring to the surface a surprising number of insights you hadn't previously considered.

Journal Topic

What is the toughest part of writing for you? What aspect of writing provides the greatest satisfaction?

Writing with a Purpose

If good writing is worthwhile, developed, organized, and clear, then how can writers best meet these criteria? The answer is fairly simple and one that you've probably heard before: write with a purpose in mind. When you have a purpose—somewhere you want to go—everything else falls into place. With purpose, you take your reader on a journey. The reader senses that you want to get somewhere and, if you do your job well, the reader becomes curious about how you're going to get there.

In general, your purpose while writing the essays outlined in this book will be to persuade your reader that your point of view or argument is a valid one. In this sense, all of the essays assigned throughout this text will be **persuasive essays**—which does not mean that your subjects need to be controversial. If you're writing a descriptive paper on a neighbor, for instance, make it clear why you're describing your neighbor. Make some point, such as: "Mrs. Carson helps hold the neighborhood together." Without a purpose, a descriptive paper on your neighbor will likely become a series of unfocused and unrelated anecdotes. If you're writing a narrative on a specific childhood experience, clarify why the event is important to you: "This experience taught me that lies don't really solve problems; lies only defuse problems for a while until they explode."

Does the purpose need to be as explicitly stated as in these examples? Probably not, especially in a narrative. In fact, the above sentence about lies might seem forced or corny or even tired. If the writer has done his or her work, the reader should be able to surmise the purpose. As long as the writer's purpose is clear throughout the essay, a specific statement of purpose can be implicit, which means that the purpose doesn't need to appear in the essay.

How do you determine what your purpose will be? One good way is to select a topic that interests you and write about it for fifteen or twenty minutes. Write quickly, without stopping. Put the writing aside for a day or so and when you return to it, write about the topic for a few more minutes. This exercise can seem unproductive at times, but more often, insights about your topic emerge from the very act of committing words to paper.

As insights emerge, narrow your possibilities, sharpen your focus and begin to decide on a purpose. At this point, it's a good idea to write down a possible **thesis statement**, a single sentence that clearly explains your purpose. You may never use this thesis statement in your essay—which would make it an **implicit thesis**—but it should serve to keep you focused. Writing down a thesis statement doesn't lock you in. In fact, your thesis will probably change slightly with each draft you write.

Your eyes may have glazed over a bit at the mention of the term *thesis statement*. And we don't blame you. You've been hearing about *the* thesis statement since third or fourth grade. At times you may have found a thesis statement to be quite useful; at other times you may have felt you were creating a thesis statement just for the teacher. If the latter has ever been true, here are two possible reasons.

Writing Tip

Reading your work aloud is probably the easiest and most efficient editing technique you can use. When you reread your work silently, your brain is more likely to skip over errors or fill in missing words, especially with a fresh draft. But when you involve the sensory experiences of saying words aloud and listening to them, you catch more errors. In addition to simply finding mistakes, you are also more likely to find ways to improve your language when you hear it read aloud. An awkward phrase or innocent-looking tongue-twister is more likely to surface when the printed words are converted into sounds.

This technique can be used at any point in the writing process. If you have finished a paragraph, especially if it didn't exactly flow effortlessly from your fingers, try reading it aloud. Don't be surprised if one or two ways to improve the paragraph come to mind. Reading aloud before creating a final draft can eliminate errors that might have sneaked in. Of course, reading your work aloud one more time before submitting it is the single best way to catch errors that eluded you in earlier editing sessions.

A useful variation of this technique is to ask someone else to read your work aloud to you. Then two people are involved in looking and listening for ways to improve the writing.

All too often, a writer creates the thesis statement much too early in the writing process—*before the writer knows what he or she wants to say.* Teachers, with worthy intentions (we know because we've done this ourselves), may assign a thesis statement days before any drafts have been written, before any discoveries have been made. The writer doesn't have a clue yet about purpose, and the resulting essay often seems artificial.

On the other hand, if you don't feel confined by writing down a thesis statement early in the writing process, and if this guides you, continue to use what works for you. For more experienced writers, a thesis is more like a compass providing direction. The actual wording of the statement is of less concern.

Another problem with many thesis statements is that they are too general. They typically include a main point and three supporting ideas that reveal more of a preview than a purpose. Here's an example: "During his many adventures, Huckleberry Finn matures spiritually, culturally, and socially." The writer here does offer some purpose—to argue that Huck matures—but the end result of such a thesis is painfully obvious. The writer will devote a paragraph to each of the ways in which Huck matures, followed by a summary of the main points. This sort of thesis might be valuable during an essay exam when time is a factor, but otherwise, the writer can create greater interest with a more original thesis. Here are three possibilities:

1. Huckleberry Finn is as selfish at the end of the novel as he is at the beginning.

2. Huckleberry Finn wrestles with his conscience throughout the novel, but in the end, his conscience loses.

3. Huckleberry Finn struggles with the same issues that teens face today, which is why the book should still be read.

Each thesis here deals with some universal theme that will potentially hold the attention of both the writer and the reader.

If reading about literature doesn't interest you, then even the revised thesis statements probably sound a little dry to you. Let's look at a more personal thesis statement: "My mother and father argue differently; they resolve conflicts differently; and they deal with discipline differently." This statement is certainly clear and includes a purpose. It promises lively examples. Yet the outcome, again, is fairly predictable. The writer will spend a paragraph or two on each of the areas mentioned and wrap up the essay with a safe conclusion. Unless the writer plans to develop this thesis into a lengthy paper, he or she won't have much time to elaborate on *any* of these areas. The writer can probably be more effective by focusing on one of these subtopics, by digging deeply into one specific area rather than dipping into all three.

How do you know if you have a good thesis statement? Try answering the following questions.

1. Can you state your thesis in a single sentence?

If not, maybe you're trying to tackle too much. Remember, this single sentence thesis statement doesn't have to appear in the essay. Whether the statement appears or not, every sentence in the essay should support the thesis.

2. Is your thesis statement specific?

Notice the difference between these two thesis statements.

> **General:** I'm going to tell you about my mom and dad and how they treat me differently.

> **Specific:** My mom and dad use different techniques for making me feel guilty.

The general thesis statement could lead the writer in a thousand different directions, which is almost a guarantee that the resulting essay will have *no* direction. Also, the writer announces the topic: "I'm going to tell you about…" This trumpet-blaring proclamation really says nothing; you are usually best off avoiding such statements.

3. Does your thesis have a limited focus?

If you're writing about the unfair policies at your school, your topic is relatively specific. However, if you attempt to describe each and every unfair policy, your focus will be scattered and your essay will lack direction.

> **Broad Focus:** North High School has too many outdated policies that cause more problems than they solve, and these policies are almost impossible to enforce.

> **Limited Focus:** North High School's attendance policy needs updating.

> OR

> North High School should update its athletic eligibility policy because it's impossible to enforce.

Likewise, a thesis that packs in too much information may create problems with direction.

Writing Tip

If an essay is due on Wednesday, do you wait until late Tuesday to finish it? Do yourself a favor: write down a few ideas well before the paper is due. Think about these ideas as you drive to school or eat lunch or walk from class to class. This process of mulling over ideas for a while is called **incubation**. You merely need to drop a few seeds here and there, and the result is often powerful. Even when you're not consciously thinking about these ideas, they're germinating beneath the surface.

Broad Focus: In a steady dating relationship, the guy and the girl need to set aside time for themselves and to make time for their own friends because friendships fall apart when taken for granted.

Limited Focus: In a steady dating relationship, each person needs to set aside time for him- or herself.

OR

Friendships fall apart when taken for granted.

4. Is your thesis simply a statement of fact?

North High School first opened its doors in 1965.

People must be 18 to vote.

Automobile A costs more than automobile B.

If these facts can be easily checked for accuracy, there's no need to write an essay about them.

5. Is your thesis merely a statement of your personal tastes?

I like rock-and-roll; you like country music. It's pointless for me to try to convince you that my tastes are better in any way. No amount of arguing or reasoning or logic will do any good. We should accept our differences.

We hope this chapter encourages you to use your confidence, maturity, wisdom, and individuality in your writing. With each piece you create, whether it's for a school assignment or some other purpose, you will discover more about your **writing voice**, a voice as unique as your personality. That voice, once it is developed, will enable you to communicate effectively in writing with any audience, for any purpose, to convey any message. Your clear thinking, persuasive reasoning, and impressive use of written language will become permanent personal assets.

On the next page you will find two charts showing common editing and teachers' marks. These will be useful when you get to the revision stage, on page 20 of this chapter.

COMMON EDITING MARKS

Note	What Note Means	Example	Correction
✐	Delete	the ~~very~~ big dog	the big dog
∧	Insert word	the∧big dog	the very big dog
≡	Capitalize	the big dog	The big dog
/	Change to lowercase	The big dog	the big dog
⌒	Close up space	the bi g dog	the big dog
⊙	Insert period	I want some⊙	I want some.
¶	Begin new paragraph	Right.¶ I want some.	Right. I want some.
ⓣⓡ	Transpose	"I quit."	"I quit."

COMMON TEACHERS' MARKS

Note	What Note Means	Example	Correction
SP	Misspelled word	exaggerrate	exaggerate
∿∿∿	Misspelled word	recieve	receive
RO	Run-on sentence	I like you you're nice.	I like you. You're nice.
Tense	Problem with shifts in verb tense	I sit. I watch TV. I turned it off.	I sit. I watch TV. I turn it off.
Awk	Awkward sentence	I like candy just like all of my friends.	My friends and I all like candy.
( )	Consider omitting	The day was sunny (and warm).	The day was sunny.

Practice

Before beginning the Chapter Assignment, try the following exercises to help you think about good writing.

1. Which of the following are good thesis statements?

   a. The first astronaut to set foot on the moon was Neil Armstrong.

   b. The language a parent uses to scold a child can affect the child's self-esteem.

   c. Football is a better game than basketball.

   d. An attentive fan can learn a great deal about physics by watching a baseball game.

   e. Michael Jordan is the best athlete who has ever lived.

   f. More than 10,000 Americans turn fifty each day.

   g. I'm going to tell you about drugs and how harmful they can be.

   h. High school students should not have part-time jobs.

   i. High school students learn life skills when they join a team sport.

   j. High school seniors should have more privileges than freshmen, and seniors shouldn't have to take final exams.

2. Revise each "poor" thesis from Question 1 into a good thesis. You may need to add information, as in the following example.

   Original: Nearly 3,000 students attend John Adams High School.

   Revision: Because the enrollment at John Adams High School is so high, the administrators run the school like a business.

3. Dig up a paper you've written in the past year. Refer to the section earlier in this chapter entitled Defining Good Writing (see pages 10–12) to evaluate your paper. Is it an example of good writing? Why or why not?

4. Find a paragraph of nonfiction that you believe exemplifies good writing. Explain why. (Fiction refers to novels and short stories; nonfiction includes everything else: essays, articles, biographies, history, and so on).

Chapter Assignment

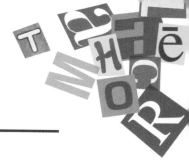

Prewriting

Your assignment in this chapter is to write an essay describing your writing. Use the following suggestion to help you choose a topic and clarify the purpose of your essay.

Draw two columns on a sheet of paper. On the left side, write all the positive attitudes you have toward writing. Include your strengths and ambitions. On the right side, write the negative attitudes you have toward writing. Include any obstacles you encounter when you write.

Writing Topic

The following list provides several questions you may want to address in your essay. Keep in mind that these questions are merely suggestions.

Don't simply scan the list and answer this or that question. Focus on two or three areas that you find most important, and present them in the order that makes the most sense to you.

1. How important or unimportant is your writing to you personally? Do you usually take pride in the writing you do for school or do you just write for a grade? How much writing do you do outside of school?

2. Have any people or books influenced your writing? For instance, did anyone read to you when you were a child? Did you have any teachers who provided encouragement?

3. What specific pieces have you written that are memorable to you? Why are they memorable? Has anyone else read these pieces?

4. What techniques help you think of writing ideas? Do you read, talk to friends, or ask teachers? Or do you just begin writing and discover ideas as you go along?

5. How has your writing changed over the last few years? Are there any areas in which you've noticed improvement? Are there areas in which you continue to struggle?

6. What are your notable writing habits? Do you have to use a certain pen or sit in a favorite chair? Do you compose your thoughts on paper first, or do you go directly to a keyboard? Do you listen to

music while you write, or do you prefer silence? Are there any writing habits you'd like to break?

7. Do you share your writing with anyone? Why or why not? Is an audience's reaction important to you?

8. How do you know when you're done with a piece of writing? Do you let it sit for a while and then reread it? Do you ask others for advice?

Revision

Revision refers to "re-vision," or seeing the paper in a fresh way, which is far different from editing. Editing refers to the corrections a writer makes: fixing spelling errors, fixing run-on sentences, fixing problems with verb tense, and so on. When teachers ask students to revise a paper, most students simply fix their mistakes. Editing should occur, of course. But a process of re-vision should also take place.

As you revise and edit your first draft, consider these questions.

1. How have you organized your essay? Is there a pattern? If not, how can you impose order?

2. Does your essay have a purpose? Does it make a point? What is your purpose?

3. Is your focus too broad? Do you try to cover too much material? If so, how can you correct this?

4. Read your paper aloud for clarity. Underline two or three sentences that could be clearer. (See the Writing Tip on page 13.)

5. What questions would you ask a peer reviewer?

Peer Review

Use these questions to help you evaluate another student's writing. Remember, specific suggestions and examples are most helpful.

1. What are the strengths of this essay?

2. What main point does the writer make?

3. What suggestions can you offer to make this essay stronger?

4. Which sections would you like to see developed?

5. What questions do you have for the writer?

You'll find sample essays at the end of each chapter in this book. The first several in each chapter are written by published writers. The last few are written by high school students.

So You Want to Be a Writer?

by Donald M. Murray

Meet the Writer

Don Murray was a beloved teacher and prolific writer whose influence is still far-reaching. He was a Pulitzer Prize-winning columnist for the *Boston Globe* and the author of many books, articles, and essays.

"You're a professional writer."

"Yes, I get paid. For some of it."

"Well, even if you don't get paid for all of it, don't you hate it when people retire and say they are going to write?"

"Or paint or dance or act or toot, now that they've finished with serious work?"

"Yes."

"No."

"Really? People don't retire and say they are going to become heart surgeons, marketing directors, trial lawyers, nuclear physicists. They know they can't do those jobs, but everyone thinks they can write."

"And they can. At least far more than believe they can."

"No resentment?"

"Well, a bit of a smile perhaps; they may discover it isn't quite as easy to write as it seems. But writing is more fun than anyone can imagine. Of course I want others to play at writing as I play art at drawing."

"Play?"

"Right. Writing—all the arts—are play."

"Do you have advice for a person who is going to retire and write?"

"I'm 69. I'm overflowing with advice. Much of it I give to myself. Just happens that in planning for 1994—the column, two new books, fifth edition of another, a couple of dozen poems—I've made myself a list...."

"Of New Year's resolutions?"

"No. Never. I've called them 'Cautions,' and they stand beside my computer IN LARGE PRINT."

"Can I see them? I've been thinking I might write something about my childhood on an alfalfa farm in..."

"Don't tell it, write it."

"The first piece of advice?"

"Yes. You can talk it and lose it."

"What are the 'Cautions'?"

—*Nulla dies sine linea* (never a day without lines). Writing breeds writing.

Good advice from Horace, Pliny and others. Habit is the parent of all art. There's no such thing as inspiration before writing; inspiration comes while writing.

—Feed the dragon the writing that no one wants or needs but you.

Don't market yourself. Editors and readers don't know what they want until they see it. Scratch what itches. Write what you need to write, feed the hunger for meaning in your life. Play at the serious questions of life and death.

—Cultivate the silence when writing speaks.

This is hard for those of us who have lived a busy life, loud with internal and external noise, but good writing rises out of silence—reflection, contemplation, reverie.

—Allow the page to lead.

The only instructor you need—and this comes from one who taught and publishes textbooks on writing—is the evolving draft. Write, then listen to what you have written and you will hear what needs to be written.

—Finish, then evaluate. Perfect is the enemy of good.

You have to lower your standards to write. We all establish premature standards that keep us from finishing, often from even starting. Practice what Minnie Mae tells me: "Get it down, then worry about making it better."

—Your strength is your strangeness.

Only recently I've come to realize that those qualities that made me weird at North Quincy High—and at home—were my strengths. That part of me that watched, that seemed anti-social and introverted, that saw and heard and thought what I was not supposed to, is the writer part of me.

—Write with ease. Enjoy the doing, not the done.

Write fast. Let language flow. Surprise yourself by what you say and do not worry about publication, awards, recognition. You are retired.

I spent far too many years supporting my family entirely or in part by writing. Publication was necessary. And yes, I lusted after recognition. Still, having sipped that wine, I know the most satisfying part of writing is the making of meaning when I am alone at my desk with language.

"That's it?"

"Pretty much. If you let the writing—or the line or tune or dance—flow, you will be carried where you never expected to go. Watch a grandchild at play."

"They do have such wonderful imaginations."

"And so did you. Write and you'll be young again."

"Guaranteed?"

"Money back. I say that and begin to feel an itch. Maybe I'll scratch it: 'The first time I asked for my money back I was only 11 or 10. My new red rubber ball didn't bounce, and I went back to the Five and Dime, stood outside until it started to get dark. I was scared to go in but...'"

Discussion Questions

1. Murray begins and ends his essay with a dialogue of sorts. Who are the two people talking? How would you characterize their relationship?

2. Murray could have written a more standard opening to introduce his "cautions." What does he gain by using dialogue instead?

3. Many of Murray's cautions could be applied not only to writing but also to everyday life. Provide one example of this.

4. "Feed the dragon the writing that no one wants or needs but you." What does this caution mean to you? What potential problems arise when writers don't follow this advice?

5. Explain how you will apply one of Murray's cautions to your own writing.

6. Why does Murray end with a story that he doesn't even finish?

7. Murray describes seven cautions. Add one of your own writing cautions to the list.

Write Anyplace

by Natalie Goldberg

Meet the Writer

Natalie Goldberg is the author of many books, including the bestselling writing text *Writing Down the Bones: Freeing the Writer Within*. She lives in Northern New Mexico, where she holds seminars on writing and painting.

Okay. Your kids are climbing into the cereal box. You have $1.25 left in your checking account. Your husband can't find his shoes, your car won't start, you know you have lived a life of unfulfilled dreams. There is the threat of a nuclear holocaust, there is apartheid in South Africa, it is twenty degrees below zero outside, your nose itches, and you don't have even three plates that match to serve dinner on. Your feet are swollen, you need to make a dentist appointment, the dog needs to be let out, you have to defrost the chicken and make a phone call to your cousin in Boston, you're worried about your mother's glaucoma, you forgot to put film in the camera, Safeway has a sale on solid white tuna, you are waiting for a job offer, you just bought a computer and you have to unpack it. You have to start eating sprouts and stop eating doughnuts, you lost your favorite pen, and the cat peed on your current notebook.

Take out another notebook, pick up another pen, and just write, just write, just write. In the middle of the world, make one positive step. In the center of chaos, make one definitive act. Just write. Say yes, stay alive, be awake. Just write. Just write. Just write.

Finally, there is no perfection. If you want to write, you have to cut through and write. There is no perfect atmosphere, notebook, pen, or desk, so train yourself to be flexible. Try writing under different circumstances and in different places. Try trains, buses, at kitchen tables, alone in the woods leaning against a tree, by a stream with your feet in the water, in the desert sitting on a rock, on the curb in front of your house, on a porch, a stoop, in the back seat of a car, in the library, at a lunch counter, in an alley, at the unemployment office, in the dentist's waiting room, at a bar in a wooden booth, at the airport, in Texas, Kansas, or Guatemala, while sipping a Coke…eating a bacon, lettuce, and tomato sandwich.

Recently, I was in New Orleans and went to visit a cemetery where the graves are above ground because of the water level. I brought my notebook, sat on the cement leaning against the thin shade of a tombstone in the thick heat of Louisiana, and wrote. An hour had passed when I looked up again. I thought to myself, "This is perfect." It wasn't the physical accommodations that were perfect, but when we are in the heart of writing it doesn't matter where we are: it is perfect. There is a great sense of autonomy and security to know we can write anyplace. If you want to write, finally you'll find a way no matter what.

Discussion Questions

1. Reread Goldberg's first paragraph and identify a pattern or two in her list of calamities.

2. Why does Goldberg repeat "Just write" in the second paragraph?

3. "Train yourself to be flexible," writes Goldberg. Describe one or two ways in which you could be more flexible in your writing.

4. Write your own version of the first paragraph, using details from your own life.

Introduction to

Escaping Into the Open

by *Elizabeth Berg*

Meet the Writer

Born in Minnesota and living now near Chicago, Elizabeth Berg is the author of numerous bestselling novels. She shares recipes, photos, and stories about her life on her website, which is easy to find.

All writing is communication; creative writing is communication through revelation—it is the Self escaping into the open.
—E. B. White

I am sitting in a coffeehouse, listening to the big band music they play here, to the explosive sounds of the espresso machines, to the subtler noise of cash registers and conversation. Across from me, a man of about sixty takes the hand of a woman about thirty and looks at her, sighing. Then he starts speaking in a low and urgent tone, in a language I can't understand. Two tables away from me, there is a serious-looking young man with a notebook before him, writing. He was here yesterday, too, doing the same thing. His handwriting is small and cramped, and he keeps one hand over what he's just put down. I'm dying to read it. I want to go up to him and say, "Can I see?" But I won't. Obviously, he's not ready to share. I watch him sipping his coffee, bending over the page to write a few lines, then staring into space, thinking.

It could be that the man is writing a term paper. Or a letter to his father, or to his girlfriend. But I don't think so. There is something about his face, about his manner. I think he's writing something more creative than that, answering an insistent call to transfer what's in him, out.

Last night, as we ate dinner, I told my partner about what I'd done that day. I said I had been to the pet store, where I watched the owner kiss a gray parrot that kissed him right back. I told him about the ragged V shape of the Canadian geese I saw fly across the sky, about the one goose in the rear that honked and honked, complaining about his seat assignment, no doubt. I described the waitress in the restaurant where I ate lunch, a stringy-haired blonde with cigarette breath who talked tough to all her customers, but who made one man finish his orange juice, because he had a cold. And then I told about a taxi driver I'd seen, a man who stood patiently waiting at the cab's open door while his fare walked toward it. She was an old woman, using a walker, and her progress was remarkably slow. But the cab driver did not look at his watch and curse his fate at having a customer who required so much extra care. Instead, he stood smiling, nodding, telling her to take her time, that she was doing just fine. It was a wonderful example of common kindness, the kind of thing that makes you think people are a pretty swell species after all. Everyone who saw that cab driver helping the old woman seemed to experience a certain elevation of spirit, as I did.

My partner listened quietly, as he always does when I tell him all the details of the things I've seen. He knows I have a need to tell stories. But whenever I say them out loud, there is something missing for me. To really tell a story, I need to write it. It's then that I understand what it is that I'm really trying to say. I find the deeper meaning—and the deeper satisfaction.

The same is true of many others. So many people have things they want to say, on paper. Some of these people write freely, and share what they write, even publish what they write. Others, who have wonderful stories inside them, don't tell them. Or if they tell them, they don't share them. If they don't *want* to share, that's fine. But I believe many people do want to share, do want to write, and are afraid to try. They need a gentle nudge to get going....

There are people who have never studied writing who are fully capable of being writers. I know this because I am an example. I was a part-time registered nurse, a wife, and a mother when I began publishing. I'd taken no classes, had no experience, no knowledge of the publishing world, no agent, no contacts. What I did have is the same kind of passion I see now in that young man sitting two tables from me. And what I want to say to that young man is what I want to say to anyone who wants to write: You feel the call. That's the most important thing. Now answer it as fully as you can. Take the risk to let all that is in you, out. Escape into the open.

Discussion Questions

1. Berg includes three sound images in the first sentence. What effect does this have upon you as a reader?

2. Consider the items in the third paragraph: the kissing parrot, the honking goose, the tough-talking waitress, and the patient cab driver. What is appealing about each of them? What do they have in common? Is a professional writer more likely to notice such things than other people? Why or why not?

3. Berg says that writing a story is more satisfying than merely telling it aloud. Do you agree or disagree? Why?

4. What are your fears or concerns about writing? How did they develop? What might help you overcome them?

Professional Model 1.4

We Had the Love, But I Long for the Letters
by William Shaw

Meet the Writer

William Shaw wrote this essay for *Newsweek*'s "My Turn," a column that welcomes essays from the famous to the everyday unknown writer who has something to say.

I don't believe I ever wrote my wife a letter. And I don't believe I ever received one from her. In the more than 46 wonderful years we spent together, I can't remember either of us sitting down and putting our thoughts on paper. That seems strange to me now that I have realized it, nearly two years after her death.

The other day I pounded out "Love Letters" on the piano. I still enjoy the song, which came out in 1945, and which I often played, among others, while my wife put the finishing touches on dinner.

Many times she whistled right along as I thumped my way through the old tune. It tells the story of a lonely person who is comforted by the words of a distant lover in a letter that came "straight from your heart."

I realized now that, during all our years together, from our first date on, we were never apart long enough to need a letter. Even though I was on the road for a number of years as a salesman for U.S. Steel, I was never away for more than five days except for two 12-day trips to the West Coast. On any of those brief separations, phone calls were enough to keep us in touch. I don't remember even contemplating writing to her and I don't imagine she ever thought about writing to me.

Certainly, there were notes to each other—thoughtful little greetings, even an occasional rhyme on cards that came on birthdays, Valentine's Day and with gifts. For some reason, early on I began to address any cards to her with her given name, Marion, in the middle and four pet names around it in a circle. That became a tradition with us and she signed cards to me in the same way: her name surrounded by "Mar," "Lucy," "Petunia," and "Marigold." One or two of those nicknames may have changed but most were constant all our lives.

What bothers me now is that I don't have anything tangible to look at. Yes, of course, I have pictures—photos, slides, even a couple of collections of slides on videocassettes. And, yes, it is heartwarming to see her and our family as it was and as it grew through all the stages of our lives. We were lucky enough to explore many fascinating parts of the world as a couple and with our two sons as they were growing up. The memories that pictures and souvenirs produce are marvelous, and I wouldn't part with them, but what I don't have, in black or blue on white, are her thoughts.

We had no secrets from each other, at least none that I know of or even suspect. We were close from that first date: a dinner during which she ate heartily but told me she "didn't like to eat," a remark that we laughed about all the rest of our days together; and a show, a musical, which I later discovered was her favorite form of entertainment and which I had stumbled upon by pure chance. I never so much as looked at anyone else as a soulmate after that. I never wanted to, or needed to, in all those years.

But what I don't have is a letter from her in her handwriting—on her stationery—from her heart to mine. I regret she never had one from me and I wonder if she ever wanted one, or ever missed having a little bit of the real me to hold on to. A letter can be that.

There is not much that is more personal than a letter, particularly a love letter. No card, no poem, no gift is as intimate as a letter. I'm sorry now that I never wrote to her, even if it would have been in my nearly indecipherable handwriting. I probably shouldn't feel this way—there never really was a need, and who thinks ahead to what might happen? I know that what I'm sorry about is that I don't have a letter from her, in her bold, beautiful script, to read and reread.

What I'm trying to say is that our lives have changed. That special something in a personal letter has disappeared with the advent of telephones, airplanes, and now e-mail—which is impersonal and limited by the lack of what I should call "personal ambience."

I've come across a few books in the last few years that have included the letters of many American presidents and statesmen—and in some cases even photographs of their handwriting. What a wonderful way to bring these men to life and humanize our country's history a bit.

That thought brings me back to my original realization: that no matter how close my wife and I were, no matter how much we loved each other, and no matter how many heartwarming memories I have of our togetherness, I don't have any tangible record of her heart speaking to mine. And how I wish I did.

Discussion Questions

1. The second sentence of this essay begins with *and*. The final sentence also begins with *and*. What is the effect of that usage?

2. Do you or your family have any treasured handwritten correspondence? Why is it important to you?

3. Notice Shaw's organizational pattern. He alternates descriptions of the richness of his relationship with his wife with discussions of what he wishes he had. Evaluate this organizational strategy. What are its advantages and disadvantages?

4. Find at least three examples of the various ways Shaw describes the nonexistent handwriting. How does Shaw's diction, or word choice, reveal what is important to him?

Scratching the Paper

by Tony Romano

I made a breakthrough this past summer. I can now compose *at* the computer! I've always been able to compose letters, class assignments, work for textbooks, even essays, at the computer, but that's because I've always considered this writing Nuts and Bolts writing. There's usually already some raw material I get to work with. I just need to fashion it, hammer out the chinks, and polish and polish—and polish again. But this summer I started writing fiction *at* the computer. Fiction is the stuff of dreams, lies, half-truths. You have to squeeze ideas from cold air, and that little hum from the computer screen had always been like a pesty fly to me, as if *IT* were reminding me to *come on* already. Sounds a little psychotic, I know, but I finally convinced myself to defy the computer's taunting and sit there and sit there until the stories spilled out.

So why did I abandon my 0.3mm rolling pen that softly scratches the paper as it glides along, a sound I've always found satisfying? I'm not really sure. I do know that when I sit at a desk writing fiction, the process is painstaking; ideas dribble out in quiet little spurts. On the other hand, when I write nonfiction—at the keyboard—my ideas flow fairly steadily. I don't worry as much about creating the perfect sentence. I write and write and know I can go back later and repair the clunkers. Some time last summer I thought, *Hmmm, maybe I could apply this fairly productive technique to my fiction-writing.* I could sit in front of a pulsating screen, and the story lies would break out in waves. That hasn't exactly happened, but I have been more productive. I don't censor myself as much during the first few drafts. I tap and tap and edit later.

Ah, but now I've created another monster. I'm tied to the computer. And since I'm committed to writing fiction in the morning—one habit I don't want to abandon just yet—I have to find a computer at the school where I work. And the computer needs to be in a room where I can be by myself without interruption for a good hour or two. Unless I decide to spend several hundred dollars on a laptop, which I don't want to do because my kids need new shoes, I have a problem, one which I haven't solved yet. This is only my third day back at school, so I'm not panicking yet, but I'm working on a novel and I have two characters sitting in a DeSoto, waiting for me to decide their fate. Whether they get out of that car through the scratching of the pen or the tapping of the keys is immaterial, I suppose. But they do need to get out. I feel them waiting.

Discussion Questions

1. Notice Romano's use of comparisons in the first two paragraphs. Which do you like best? Write your own comparisons to substitute for his.

2. What writing situations do you find most and least comfortable? What circumstances lead you to produce your best writing? Does being comfortable while writing make you more likely to produce good writing?

3. Romano does not explicitly state his writing purpose within the essay. State what you believe his purpose is.

4. What advice does Romano's essay offer to a struggling writer?

5. List several specific details from the essay that help you view the writing process from Romano's perspective. After each detail, clarify whether it appeals mainly to the sense of hearing, of sight, or of touch. (This technique of appealing to the senses will be discussed further in Chapter 2.)

Trying to Get Better

by James Kuo

Meet the Writer

James Kuo tries to read at least 25 books a year, a feat that he has accomplished only a few times so far. He actually cheated a few times, too. James is a semi-productive news editor for his school paper.

Many times when I take a seat to write, which is always in front of a keyboard and monitor, I have no idea what to write. What do I want to share, to tell, to say in my written words? For some reason, I lose all confidence when I actually sit down and am about to undertake the physical part of writing. Too often I find that I have nothing to say, nothing to contribute to a world that is already filled to a frothing top with writing, good and bad writing, excellent works and works as ugly as bearded women.

All of my ideas that I had bouncing around in my head suddenly calm down and stare blankly at me like little children waiting for instruction. Just hours ago I had a great idea for a great topic to write a great composition. I really did. It's just that several hours later, my idea has managed to elude me in a similar way that a helium-filled balloon drifts away toward the heavens or a 747. All too often, that idea does not return, and I am left gazing at a white electronic page and scratching my head for no apparent reason.

From experiencing that cold abandonment so many times, I now am somewhat apprehensive when I think of writing. The thought of writing leads immediately to the thought of failure. Nothing will happen. I wouldn't mind failure much if I actually produced something. Like many people I welcome failure, as it can open the learning barnyard doors to so much more than success can. But unfortunately, I am not gifted or talented enough to learn from a blank Word document. I find myself holding down the backspace key all too frequently, and sometimes that leads to having absolutely nothing.

As a high school student, I do about 99.8% of my writing for academic classes, so I have to have something. I write because my teacher/instructor told me I should, and he or she gave me guidelines of some sort to follow. Shamefully, the tighter the instructions, the easier it is for me to develop a paper or response or whatever it is I am supposed to create. So basically, if I cannot grasp a "good" idea, I just write anything I can because I have a deadline and other work to do. I don't want to stay up all night and deprive my eyes of rest just because I am a bad writer. I want to be a well-rested bad writer.

I remember reading somewhere Eric Clapton saying that the most important thing in learning to play the guitar is your set of ears. An important thing to do with the ears is to listen to recordings and what others have played. For blues and rock, listening to songs is just as important as actually touching the strings. Just as many musicians listen to other musicians, writers need to read other writers' work. This is by no means my original idea, but I am a strong believer in this, and I'm sure any decent writer will tell you the same. Probably the most I think about writing is when I'm reading someone else's work and thinking about how much better that writer is than me. When I read short stories by Edgar Allan Poe and Ernest Hemingway in English class, I was amazed that they could develop so much in such relatively little space. Back when my family subscribed to *Time*, I would admire the authors who managed to write such comprehensive feature articles. Even after an hour of reading my United States history book did I think to myself that the writer of that book knew what he was doing. These writers make me look like a bum who is the same status below another bum as that bum is from a king. In less confusing terms, they make me realize that I am pitiful and awful. But they also make me realize that I need to work much harder and still have a long way to go if I ever want to be an effective writer. Whenever I read something good, I always think about writing, even if it's just for a few seconds or unconsciously. Even bad writing can be helpful for improvement and offer valuable hints for the future.

For the most part, I find writing more enjoyable than thinking about writing. Usually when I am clicking and clacking away on my keyboard, I have some ideas that I happily toss onto the virtual page and everything flows in a way. I am satisfied that I actually have something. When I think about writing, I picture myself groping around for ideas. And then that picture becomes reality. And then I grab blindly and come up with nothing, like a fisherman who is using a net with a giant hole at the bottom.

Still, strangely enough, I like thinking about writing. At some point I even considered a possible career in writing, although I never thought about the details. I find that writing is something I enjoy, even if I have poor skills. After all, I think of writing as a great unique way of expression and communication that is relatively easy to do physically. Like the men and women who sing in the shower with terrible crimes-against-humanity voices, I continue writing even though I know the quality of my ability. The good thing is that writing ability is not static, so I can still work at improving my effectiveness. I think if I stopped thinking about writing, stopped looking at other writers and trying to gain useful things, stopped finding topics, stopped reaching around for ideas, I would become an even weaker writer, and that would be horrible. I don't know about you, but if I'm not trying to get better, I'm getting worse. Think about it.

Discussion Questions

1. Kuo experiences a range of emotions as he writes: apprehension, confusion, satisfaction, and enjoyment. What emotions do you associate with your writing process?

2. "Whenever I read something good, I always think about writing," says Kuo. What experiences inspire or deflate your attitude toward writing?

3. Do you agree with Kuo's statement about writing assignments, that "the tighter the instructions, the easier it is to develop a paper or response or whatever it is I am supposed to create"? What kinds of writing tasks do you prefer?

4. Kuo believes that thinking about writing and consciously trying to improve are critical factors in his growth as a writer. Do you agree, or do you believe that thinking about writing is detrimental to developing your writing skills?

Sustenance

by Amy Walter

Meet the Writer

Amy Walter learned the alphabet at age three in Seattle, wrote her first book at age nine in San Diego, and is the editor-in-chief of her high school newspaper. She lives with her parents, two younger sisters, and a hyperactive terrier named Daisy Potato.

Syllables slide over my tongue, more necessary than food. Like a conjurer I alter appearances, inhaling sensations and exhaling poetry. I'm convinced that the particles of quarks are actually breathing, moving commas and exclamation points; language is the most basic life-form. Writers attempt to trap cravings, eye-blinks, and games of hide-and-go-seek in precise, measured words. The trick is to cram the most meaning into the fewest letters.

When the muse calls, I snatch up a pen and become a spectator of the race between my hand and her. What will be left in the dust? Maybe fodder for a new piece. The primary task is to get everything down on paper. There will be time for revision later.

A Jamaican woman explains to me that she drinks a cup of water every night because she has no money for food, but still she praises God with her beautiful singing voice. Writers are scavengers; I think: "How can I use this person for that poem?" Or: "How can I use the emotions I see in her, and in my reaction to her?" I keep these images on index cards in my pocket for later inspiration. Just as often, though, I forget about them, and scraps of paper covered in runny ink resurface in the lint-catcher after a load of laundry.

I will never remember those exact lines, but by interpreting life as words I increase my awareness of the movement around. I write down every intelligible whim, understanding that some images dance on the page and others wither there.

Life is images, and images are words. These syllables—twisted, stretched, and allowed to flow freely—are the purest imitation of reality. Listen, and they will speak.

Discussion Questions

1. Essays sometimes resemble poetry in their rhythm, and Amy Walter clearly has a sense for this. Take one or two of her sentences, rewrite them word for word, but make the sentences look like a poem. Then read the "poem" aloud to your class and listen to the rhythm.

2. How can syllables be more necessary than food? In what way do syllables sustain this writer?

3. For Walter, words, syllables, and other elements of language seem to have a life of their own. What are some of the actions that these elements perform, particularly at the beginning and at the end of her essay?

4. Pick one vivid image from the essay and explain why it is effective, why it works for you. What does the image make you think or feel?

5. Walter says that writers are scavengers. What does she mean, and how can you possibly apply this to your own writing?

6. Describe one of your own writing dilemmas. You might address issues such as perfectionism, time constraints, deadlines, or writing habits.

Writing Everywhere

by Kori Zwald

Meet the Writer

Kori Zwald *lives* for writing. She *plans* to live in Arizona with her big sister Kasey—either doing some work with writing, or working in an OBGYN office. She is a junior in high school—currently living with her mom, little sister Kassidy, and her stepdad Dave.

Writing everywhere. On walls, paper, my agenda, in my school notebooks. Everywhere. The sky is the limit when it comes to my writings. I remember writing since I was a little girl. Not growing up with the best guidance and supervision. No one to look to and tell my secrets and problems to. Paper was my only way out. Writing is what keeps me sane. When I'm bored, alone—even if I'm surrounded by a sea of people, I still feel alone. So a pen and paper are always by my side.

If I could go back and collect everything that I've ever written since I was little, to the present, I would have series of books. It's hard to find something special that you admire and would die for in this lifetime. But I'm lucky because I don't have to search for that one special thing. Writing is it. Poems, lyrics, anywhere about anything. My writings are all nonfiction. All about life and personal things. It's real and things people can relate to. I like writing about my life. Things that happen daily. It may be hard to understand sometimes, but that's because my words are there but hidden at the same time. One of those where you want to keep reading, yet you're confused and have to figure it out.

I hoard my writings. I like to look back on them and compare them. I have a horrid memory, so my writings remind me. If I were to lose any of them, I would be lost. Since my words are all truth and my life story, it's like my path in life. So I would end up in a dead end if anything ever happened to them. Yes, it is very hard to keep them personal because they are everywhere you look. And yes there are some people that I open up to and let them read, but very few.

Life, songs, other people, all influence my writing. The weather. My mood. A show that I may be watching. I have some writing from 7th and 8th grade still, and sometimes when I have nothing to do, I will go get them and read them. It's unbelievable. Back then I thought I sounded so good, but looking at my present writing, then looking at those, it's a complete difference. The feeling I get when I write is fulfilling. I'm not done writing until my mind is clear. My words on a piece of paper mean more to me than my own life. I honestly feel gifted because I don't know what I would do if I didn't write.

Anyone can write. Writing is your soul. You don't have to rhyme. It doesn't even have to make sense. It can be about anything. Take pride. It's not hard. Just write. It's weird, because when a pen is in my hand, and paper of any kind is in front of my face, the world goes black, feelings become numb, everyone around me disappears. Whatever comes to my mind—is on paper the next second.

Discussion Questions

1. Zwald uses many short sentences and fragments. Describe the effect achieved through these short passages, using specific examples to support your answer.

2. Zwald's passion for writing seems at times exaggerated—yet sincere. What lines seem exaggerated? Which lines balance that exaggeration? What effect is achieved by this balance?

3. In both the first and last paragraphs, Zwald makes references to being alone. How does writing make her feel less alone?

4. If you were a peer editor for this essay, what suggestions would you offer? Be specific.

Free to Be Me

by Lin Wojciechowski

Meet the Writer

Lin Wojciechowski enjoys talking for great periods of time, which is one of the main reasons she is an active member of her school's speech team. Besides speech, she enjoys skating (both figure and hockey), acting, writing, and talking long distance to her many friends in other states.

A million thoughts penetrate my mind every day. A million observations enter through my senses. A million dreams and nightmares invade my soul every night. A million ideas, a million feelings, a million desires, a million words are in me, day in and day out, bouncing around, needing to do something, to be somewhere. I need to free some of them or I will be destroyed in an explosion of light, color, sound, and words.

That's where writing comes in.

Everything I just said may be just slightly overdramatic (all right, yes, it is overdramatic), but somewhere in all of that gooey wordiness lies an idea which is a basic truth for me, and, I suspect, for a lot of people. That truth is that I need to write to free up some cluttered space. Writing is something I've always enjoyed, and, though it often takes the "inspiration" of having an assignment to get me going, I always feel good after it's done.

How the piece turns out isn't the most important thing to me: it's the process of creating and manipulating worlds made by words which is the enjoyable part of writing. Creativity is key. The most annoying thing anyone has ever said to me is "Write what you know." I hate that expression. The most interesting things in life are the things which I don't know. I mean, I'm still young, I have so much to learn and will die having learned practically nothing in the scheme of things. I'd rather talk about what might be or what might not be, not what is.

The work which I am most proud of was one in which the teacher gave us an option of titles, from which we had to create a story. I chose "Graffiti Bridge." I thought this project was wonderful because I could be as free and creative as I wanted to be with the added challenge of making my vision fit the pre-set title. So, I sat down at the computer with one of the Beatles Anthologies blaring in my headphones (my favorite background music for writing: I can tell it's going to be a good piece if I'm typing furiously and suddenly notice I'm on song 22 on my cd) and started to type.

The story I was seeing unfold in front of me wasn't the story I had sat down to write. Within this new story I could still see the vague outline of my original plot, but the new focus took me a little by surprise. But that's the beauty of writing—so often it comes from somewhere inside of you that you don't even consciously know about. I've always been excited about how my audiences react to my work, but more importantly, I find myself reacting to my work and being able to see myself through it.

Everyone I know has some sort of qualm with writing, and mine is being restricted. I can't for the life of me understand why a teacher would want to read 50 papers on the same topic, all the same length and format, each spewing out the same views and facts as the last one. And yet teachers constantly demand papers to be about the same things. I remember being angry once about having no "choose your own topic" choice on a writing evaluation and, in defiance, made up the most gruesome, horrific story any fifth grader has ever put down on paper, claiming it fit into the "a dream I've had" category. Admittedly, it was not my best work. But I personally don't feel like I'm expressing myself by repeating why I like my dog or how boring it was driving to my grandmother's house. That isn't writing; it's spewing, and spewing has no place at my figurative table.

I don't know how much of this paper made sense. But, for my concluding paragraph, I'd like to share how I went about writing it. Parts of it I had written out earlier. Most of those parts aren't in existence anymore. But those prewritten parts led me to new thoughts which I hadn't explored, and so I just let the thoughts flow from my head to my fingers which danced over the keys in less-than-perfect form. I've just reread the whole thing and I'm wondering if my transitions are good enough. I'm wondering if this format is acceptable: this is the first time in a long time that I haven't written a paper with a clear thesis with three or more main points, sadly enough. Through all of this second guessing, though, I am feeling good about being able to finally write something which comes from me, and not from what feels like some lethargic text book writer. And now, just for the fun of it, I'm going to tack on a killer concluding sentence. Ready? And in conclusion, writing is a thrilling and cleansing experience, and I hope to be able to (freely) express myself through this medium throughout my life.

Discussion Questions

1. Lin Wojciechowski repeats the word *million* several times in the first paragraph. Careless repetition can make sentences seem sluggish, but that's not the case here. How does Wojciechowski use repetition to her advantage? What is the effect of this repetition?

2. What function does writing serve in Wojciechowski's life?

3. Wojciechowski becomes defiant when ordered to write on a specific topic. Can you identify with her or do you welcome assigned topics? Explain.

4. Wojciechowski suggests she discovers things while she writes. What kinds of discoveries does she make?

Description

Some things people ask us to do make sense: for example, to respect one another and keep ourselves and our belongings clean. Some requests only make sense within a certain context: "You hold on to this while I nail it down." Some requests seem designed to waste our time: "Count up these whatchamacallits and write down the number in all fourteen columns."

Unfortunately, being asked to describe something in writing can seem like it belongs in that final category. Why should we spend our time, talents, and mental energy putting into words an idea that can be more adequately conveyed through a photograph? When do we ever actually *need* to rely upon description to convey our needs or desires? And if we don't *need* to do it, why should we bother learning how to do it well?

Those are really good questions, and they deserve a good answer. First, photographs only convey a visual description, and then only from a certain angle or perspective. Second, developing excellent descriptive skills and approaches can provide our audience with more powerful, immediate, and rewarding information. This will fulfill any writing purpose better than simply writing what we have to say in more mundane language.

In fact, the tools of description can be applied to nearly all types of writing. For instance, if you want to argue that U.S. immigration laws need refining, you might supply examples of families who will be affected by your proposals; to make those examples effective, you'll probably want to *describe* the families. If your purpose is to explain the process one must endure to get ready for an interview, you'll probably want to describe the tension inherent in such a situation. In fact, it's difficult to think of an essay entirely devoid of description. Try comparing two presidents or two teachers without using description.

Let's break this down a bit. What descriptive tools should be in a writer's toolbox? These are the most important, and we'll explain each in detail in this chapter: knowing the difference between connotation and denotation; understanding how to employ imagery; using sensory appeal even when it seems out of place; appreciating the power of simile and metaphor; and choosing lively verbs—and knowing when to use each of these literary techniques.

Using Connotation and Denotation

Raise your hand if you read the dictionary for fun! If you actually raised your hand, then (1) you should recognize that you're taking this book way too seriously; or (2) you're a budding linguist, and you probably don't need much in the way of writing advice.

For the other 99.9 percent of you, the dictionary is a resource, a place to go for information, not a source of fun. Your pleasure reading comes from any of the many other possible sources. This leads us to the difference between denotation and connotation. **Denotation** is usually defined as the dictionary definition of a word. **Connotation** includes the various associations that go beyond the simple dictionary definition. Connotation is where our language comes to life.

For example, if we look up the words *street* and *road* in the dictionary, we will find definitions that have a lot of similarities, probably involving paths on which transportation and travel can take place.

Writing Tip

If you prefer to write with a pen rather than at the computer, consider skipping lines. When you begin to revise, all those blank lines are an invitation to add a detail here, an idea there. Give yourself some elbow room to work.

But those words have very different connotations. *Street* has a more urban, paved, hip feel to it, while *road* evokes a dustier, more rural, older feel. Would we ever be technically wrong if we used *road* in lieu of *street*, or vice versa? Probably not. But why not exploit the connotations of our chosen words to maximize their effects upon our readers? Why settle for the dryness of a technically correct denotation when we can draw upon the power of a word's connotations?

The message here is to choose words carefully. Choose the most powerful, evocative, perfect word you can come up with. Don't settle for "technically correct."

Of course, a thesaurus can provide us with virtually all of a word's synonyms so that we can make exactly the right choice. The wrong way to use a thesaurus is to choose long, ill-fitting words in the hope that your massive vocabulary will impress readers. This approach is doomed to failure. Choosing such words will not make your intellect seem more impressive any more than choosing an expensive, but ill-fitting pair of jeans will make your appearance seem more impressive.

A better way to use a thesaurus is to search for words whose connotations are helpful to your writing purpose. Some words listed will be archaic, some will be overly technical, some will be not quite right for other reasons, but one of them might just be perfect. Pick that one.

As long as we're in search of the perfect word, let's go one step further. Let's pick the word that *sounds* best. Yes, not only do words have connotations, but sounds have them, too. For example, words containing clusters of *t* and *k* sounds have a sharp or "techno" feel to them. Of course, "techno" has a *t* sound and a *k* (in the form of *ch*) sound clustered together. Other examples of this include *tatter, clutter, breakout, crank,* and *racket.*

Some sounds are warmer, friendlier, and fuzzier. These include the *m* sound and the *b* sound, as in *mumble, ramble, simple, moonbeam,* and *balm.* As you consider the perfect word, awareness of its connotative characteristics can do much to empower your message and enhance your purpose.

Journal Topic

Describe one of your most animated teachers. Bring to life what it's like to sit in this person's classroom.

Using Imagery

WGN radio announcer Pat Hughes understands imagery well. As a broadcaster for the Chicago Cubs, Hughes must paint precise and vivid pictures for his listening audience. This precision alone is difficult—try announcing a single inning—but to be compelling as well poses a daunting challenge. A typical Hughes broadcast includes a host of memorable lines: "The shortstop shovels the ball to second to retire the side"; "This guy here's a spray hitter"; "Last night the balls were flying out of the park like popcorn."

You've probably discussed imagery many times in your English classes, and you may already have a decent understanding of what imagery means and why writers rely on it. But you won't fully appreciate this fundamental tool until you make a concentrated effort to use imagery in your own writing. Imagery, simply put, refers to descriptions that appeal to the senses. If a shortstop *shovels* a ball to second, the listener can *see* that particular underhanded motion and perhaps *feel* the supple toss in his or her own arms. If a batter *sprays* hits, the listener can *envision* the varied directions the ball will fly, maybe *hear* the sound of spraying, though this latter may be a stretch since it is not a literal sound. If baseballs fly out like *popcorn*, the listener can clearly *see* the lively action of the ball and *hear* the crack of the bat. (Do listeners also *smell* popcorn when they hear this line? Maybe not.) In other words, imagery allows the listener, or reader, to fully participate in the description, to become immersed in the world created through the writing. Imagery invites the reader in.

Not only does imagery evoke rich sensations for the reader, but it also accomplishes this in an economical fashion. Imagine trying to literally describe *shoveling a ball*: "the shortstop cupped his hands and with palms up he…" Too many words, too much detail, and the writer loses the beauty of the simple action.

See if you can identify the imagery in the following passage from Michael Ondaatje's memoir *Running in the Family*:

> 2:15 in the afternoon. I sit in the huge living room of the old governor's home in Jaffna. The walls, painted in recent years a warm rose-red, stretch awesome distances away to my left to my right and towards the white ceiling. When the Dutch first built this house egg white was used to paint the walls. The doors are twenty feet high, as if awaiting the day when a family of acrobats will walk from room to room, sideways, without dismantling themselves from each other's shoulders.

As you probably found, identifying imagery in someone else's writing is a fairly simple task. In fact, the imagery seems effortless, which is usually far from the truth and explains why many students don't even begin to try.

Writing Tip

School schedules can be hectic, but writing thrives on habit. Try to set aside a particular time of day just for yourself and your writing. Those ten or thirty minutes are yours and not negotiable.

If your purpose is to describe something unusual, a subject not known intimately by the vast majority of people, your sensory task can be pretty easy. As you write about the subject, simply describe how it looks, sounds, feels, smells, and tastes (and add a healthy dose of the emotions or feelings associated with it). If you do that thoroughly and with an awareness of the connotations of your chosen words, you should be successful in transmitting to a reader your assessment of whatever it is you're discussing.

For example, if your writing purpose is to describe an orangutan, you might surmise that, although most people have a working knowledge of what your subject is—namely a large orange-ish primate—they don't know much more than that. But you know much more about orangutans than that perfunctory description, and so you set out to describe the animal for your less-informed reader. To begin, you might simply approach the subject in terms of the senses: What facial expressions does an orangutan make? What sounds does it make? How do its hands or fur feel to the touch? How does it smell? (Let's stop right there. You may have just crossed into the "too much information" zone.) If you do all of those steps thoroughly, with well-chosen words and phrases that reinforce your main impression of the orangutan, your reader should come away with a vivid understanding of how you perceive this subject.

If, on the other hand, your chosen subject is more familiar, your task is tougher in some ways. It's pointless for a reader to invest time and energy into reading something he or she already knows, unless the writer has provided a reason to do so. The best reason for a reader to stick with reading about something with which he is already familiar is because the writing is just so darn good that it's rewarding in a way that goes beyond mere information gathering. So, how do we make the writing "so darn good"?

If you combine the various strategies discussed in this chapter, you can do mighty things when it comes to description. For example, if you combine a simile (which we'll discuss in some detail in the next section) with a sensory appeal, you may provide your reader with a fresh way of understanding a familiar subject. Former U.S. poet laureate Ted Kooser, a master at this technique, explains:

> To say that a green delicious apple is like a Granny Smith apple is not likely to get anybody's attention, or to produce any kind of feeling of revelation, but to suggest that a fading light bulb is like a dissolving tablet is more of a leap—almost, I think, an epiphany.

The idea here is that if you can pair senses in unusual combinations, your readers can be surprised into understanding your subjects in new and powerful ways. For example, if you say that a fancy new sports car is bright red, that's wonderful, but it has only triggered one sense. If, on the other hand, you say that a fancy new sports car looks the way a sonic boom sounds, you have tapped into more than one sense, creating a more complex image for your reader.

When you attempt to create a memorable scene by appealing to the senses, you will, at first, feel self-conscious about your effort. It may seem as if you're trying too hard. This self-consciousness may be unavoidable, but the more skilled you become at using imagery, the more confident you'll feel.

Here's an advanced tip to move you in that direction, to help you feel less self-conscious: *put description in action.* Again, understanding this tip is much simpler than actually using the suggestion in your own writing. Let's say you want to describe your grandfather, a stately man with iron gray hair, leathery hands, and a broad chest, whose gravelly voice makes something in your own chest vibrate. You can simply offer a block of description using such details, which is adequate but runs the risk of drawing too much attention to craft. Or you can show your grandfather in motion, perhaps at supper reaching for a piece of bread. You might subtly insert a physical detail that the action reveals: "With his leathery hands, he reached for a piece of bread and tore it in two." Many instances will occur when the writing calls for a block of description, but pay attention to opportunities that allow you to try this more subtle method.

Journal Topic

Take a look around you right now and describe a person you see. If no one is around, describe the last person you saw. Describe not only the person's face but also how she or he moves, sits, and so on.

Using Figurative Language: Simile and Metaphor

Since about fifth grade, you have been learning that a **simile** is a comparison using *like* or *as*, and a **metaphor** is a comparison that does not use *like* or *as*. While those definitions are serviceable for literary analysis, particularly with the study of poetry, they don't begin to suggest the power of effectively using simile and metaphor.

Writers on Writing

Similes often startle us—even give us a good shiver once in a while. What accounts for this? First, just as 'story' happens when business-as-usual is interrupted by new events, comparison breaks up the status quo of ordinary description.

—*David Long*

Think of it this way. We each have our own bank of experiences, completely different from anyone else's. Each of our banks, however, contains some material that overlaps with that of other people. For example, everyone has the concept of *mouse* in his or her experience bank. Consequently, when we read the phrase *quiet as a mouse* we can draw upon that experience and make something meaningful from it. Of course, *quiet as a mouse* is a cliché, and as such, it should be avoided...like the plague.

Nevertheless, the connotative associations in virtually every word allow a writer to add a deft touch of emotion through the use of similes. We can achieve a very different emotional effect depending on whether we write *quiet as a burglar* or *quiet as a rose*. Adding shades of emotional content to an image enriches the overall mood of the description.

An important piece of advice on using similes and metaphors is to keep them simple, so that they do not overshadow the subject under primary consideration. If you're writing about a room in your home, for example, don't go so far as to say something such as, "My room is like a dungeon in a castle from the Middle Ages because it is dark, eerie, and has really scary posters." You're much better off writing, "My dungeonlike room…" and then delving into whatever you wanted to say about it. This approach will help you strike a balance between simplicity and liveliness.

Ted Kooser offers this advice on poetry, which holds true for any type of descriptive writing:

> When you want your poem to feel more casual and conversational, more like everyday speech, and you raise a comparison, a simile can sometimes be a better choice than a metaphor. But keep in mind that most similes lack the authority that metaphors convey. Metaphors almost always sound more forceful, more confident… A metaphor is emphatic: *a boat of cupped hands*…. Compared with a metaphor, a simile is always less sure of itself. It presents a different, less certain speaker: *cupped hands are like a boat*. You can imagine such a speaker saying something like, "Cupped hands are like…well, they're like…you know, they're sort of like…a boat."

One way to achieve balance between the mild simile and the bold metaphor is to use **submerged metaphors**, one of the most common and useful tools for description. Submerged metaphors are single words or short phrases that create the same rich associations as straight metaphors and similes, but they're more subtle, as the name implies. If you want to write about your parents and how they reconciled, you might say, "they *bridged* their differences." *Bridged*, in this case, is not literal, of course, but it conveys the idea that their differences were great, that they spanned great distances, that the effort required to unite your parents was tantamount to building a bridge. *Bridged* is a loaded word that conveys all this information in a beautifully economical manner.

Here are some other examples of submerged metaphors:

She *brushed* aside her fear.

The president made a *blanket* condemnation.

His indecent act *catapulted* him onto the front pages.

The coach *crushed* his fears.

Some of these submerged metaphors, especially the last one, probably remind you that we use figurative language frequently in conversation. In fact, we use figurative language so often in speaking that phrases sometimes become overused, or cliché, which, as suggested earlier, you should avoid when you write. Simply put, avoid writing phrases such as *strong as an ox, cold as ice, quick as a wink*. On the other hand, a slight twist on even tired phrases can be effective, especially if you submerge the key image: *He was ox-strong; her icy stare left me cold; the cat's pounce was wink-quick.*

Understanding Why Description Works

We've focused on several descriptive writing tools in this chapter, tools you should continue to experiment with as you work through the book. After a while you'll discover which tools best suit your voice and you'll begin to develop your own style. For instance, metaphors for you may arise sparingly but your ear might be finely attuned to rhythm and sound. Pay attention to these inclinations; pay particular attention to your strengths, and build on them.

Writers on Writing

I write because it gives me focus. There is a famous anecdote about an old lady's dying. She raises her head from the deathbed and says to her family, 'If I'd known it would go by so fast, I would have noticed more.' It seems to me that a writer's job is to notice, and to put his or her observations and conclusions down for others to share…. It is the role of the writer to create splendor from the world that surrounds us—even if it is Interstate 110. Literature should make us look freshly at our tired world. Writing is a way of seeing, not of saying, things.

I write because writing is renewal. Heraclitus said the sun is new every day—and so am I if I write something new. I write to find out who I am. But in order to find out who I am, I must first find out who I was. So I reflect on past experiences and examine them.

—*Robert Phillips*

But why are these techniques so fundamental? Why do they make such a profound difference in your writing? The answer is rooted in the physiology of the brain. The brain seeks order, yet it craves stimulation and change. If you hold a rattle in front of an infant, you'll witness both of these tendencies. The infant grips the rattle and turns it, seeking understanding, and soon begins to shake the toy in amusement, satisfying an elementary need for stimulation. The rattle shaking may last several minutes until restlessness sets in, and then a new toy, which might be nothing more than two measuring cups the infant can bang together, will need to be introduced. A similar process occurs in a reader who picks up an essay and "turns" it for a glimpse of understanding or insight. The reader may be patient enough to get through a few pages, but if he or she finds the writing formulaic and devoid of any surprises, the reading will become a chore.

Psychologists in the 1950s conducted experiments to find out how humans would react when deprived of sensory stimulation. Participants in the study wore goggles that allowed nothing in but diffused light; headphones blocked out sounds; and loose gloves dulled their sense of touch. Subjects rested on cots and moved about only for meals and toilet breaks. Those involved in the experiment did not suffer any long-term consequences, but during the experiment subjects did begin to hallucinate, a phenomenon to which any weary, late-night highway driver will attest. Straight lines began to waver, flat walls took on three dimensions, numbers on office walls looked as if they were momentarily peeling away, and one subject even reported seeing squirrels marching with sacks over their shoulders. As these examples demonstrate, so constant is the brain's need for stimulation that the brain creates its own when the world does not provide any. This may also explain, in part, why we dream, and why, as nutritionists are finding, we always have room for dessert: it's different!

When we suggest that you appeal to the senses in your writing, we're really saying, stimulate the reader's brain—and not just the part that processes language. Scientists once believed that memories were stored in neat compartments. The memory of your third-grade teacher yelling was stored in one filing cabinet, and the memory of your field trip to the zoo was stored in another. It turns out that memories are not really stored anywhere but created anew each time by tracing, or re-creating, familiar pathways in the brain. For instance, your third-grade teacher's voice once stimulated your temporal lobe, which processes auditory information; her face stimulated your occipital lobe, which processes visual information, and so on. When you recall your third-grade teacher, these areas are stimulated again, and another part in the center of your brain, the hippocampus, assembles this separate information into a seamless, or not-so-seamless, memory. This complex process of recollection brings the teacher to life momentarily in a compelling illusion. Appealing to the senses triggers a similar process in the brain, bringing your subjects to life for the reader in much the same way as a memory from the past.

Journal Topic

Describe a group to which you belong from the point of view of someone outside that group. For example, you might describe your family members from the point of view of someone who has just met them.

Using Effective Verbs

Some young writers believe they need to pile on adjectives and adverbs to describe well. While adjectives and adverbs are indispensable, you should rely mostly on strong nouns and verbs, which convey meaning more precisely. Instead of rambling on about a "sleek, low-riding, souped-up speedy car," you might simply write "sports car," or "Ford Mustang." Instead of "old, gray, stooped and crippled man," try "old man"—a single adjective and noun. If you still want to convey "stooped and crippled," you can achieve this with a simple action verb: "The old man *limped* toward me."

But before we offer tips on verb usage, here's a brief refresher on verbs. In general, verbs can be divided into three groups:

1. State-of-being verbs, which include all forms of *to be*.

is, was, were, are, am, be, being, have been

2. Helping verbs, which help the main verb in a phrase to tell about an action.

must	is	do	should	have	will
may	was	does	could	has	can
might	were	did	would	had	shall
	are				
	am				
	be				
	being				
	been				

3. Action verbs, which include thousands of words, such as *throw*, *catch*, *run*, and *sit*.

The state-of-being and helping verbs are central to English, but writers sometimes become lazy and forget about the mother lode of action verbs available to them. For example, notice the difference in these two sentences:

A. The time *is* right for Congress to *be* looking for ways to improve health care in this country because so many poor people *are* suffering, and they *don't have* a way out.

B. Since so many people in this country cannot *escape* the cycle of poverty, Congress should *seek* to improve health care.

The first sentence is cluttered because it relies so heavily on state-of-being and helping verbs. The second sentence eliminates most of these instances and adds the more effective action verbs *escape* and *seek*.

What about these sentences?

A. Lincoln *is* regarded today as a great president, but he *was* depressed during most of his presidency.

B. Though *regarded* today as a great president, Lincoln *suffered* from depression during most of his presidency.

Although the second sentence eliminates the state-of-being verbs, it doesn't seem to be much of an improvement over the first. Why? The first sentence is clear and precise and doesn't include the clutter from the previous example. Why would you use one sentence over another in an essay? If you read both sentences aloud, you may notice a slight difference in rhythm. As a result, one sentence may fit a particular paragraph better than another. For instance, if a paragraph includes one compound sentence after another, like the first sentence in this example, then you may want to use the second sentence instead for the sake of variety.

Nearly five hundred years after Shakespeare asked, "To be, or not to be?", the question remains significant for writers. If you worry about this question early in the writing process, though, you're bound to become frustrated. Our language relies on the different forms of *to be*, and you cannot entirely avoid using them, nor should you try. A more realistic option is to finish a first draft, then underline all the state-of-being and helping verbs in your paper. If a single sentence contains numerous instances, the likelihood of clutter is high. When you revise and edit, you don't need to eliminate every instance; in fact, as Shakespeare knew so well, *to be* can be quite powerful. But replacing some instances of *is*, *was*, *has*, and so on, with submerged metaphors and other rich alternatives will eliminate clutter.

Writers on Writing

When we have spent enough years on earth and gained knowledge of the longings that exist within us and in the hearts of others, we may finally understand that if there is anything truer than truth, it is the legend with which we frail mortals embellish that truth.

—*Harry Mark Petrakis*

Here are some specific verb techniques you can try while editing, followed by examples of student sentences.

1. Omit state-of-being and helping verbs.

> **Original:** Her voice *is* as soft as a summer's eve, and the way it bends *is* like grasses in the rain.

While the sentence makes good use of imagery, it falls a little flat to our ears. Listen to how the rhythm changes in the revision, when the clutter is removed.

> **Revision:** Her voice, soft as a summer's eve, *bends* like a pine tree in a storm.

2. Replace state-of-being and helping verbs with more active verbs.

> **Original:** My uncle only *has* a high school diploma.

> **Revision:** My uncle only *earned* a high school diploma.

3. Replace state-of-being and helping verbs with active verbs rich in imagery.

> **Original:** This one time he *was* making sandwiches and needed lettuce.

> **Revision:** One time, while *slapping* sandwiches together…

4. Avoid the passive voice.

> **Passive voice:** The ball *was thrown by* Luis.

> **Active voice:** Luis *threw* the ball.

With the passive voice, the subject is acted upon. While this construction may be necessary at times, the active voice is usually clearer and more powerful. Note that using active voice also eliminates a helping verb.

The ability to effectively choose and combine words to achieve your purpose is the most important ability of a skilled writer. In this chapter, you learned specific devices to enhance your writing: connotations, imagery, figurative language, and effective verbs. As you practice using these strategies, you will find that your writing grows stronger, appeals more to your audience, and becomes a clearer expression of your unique voice.

Practice

Before beginning the chapter assignment, warm up and hone your descriptive tools with these fun exercises.

1. Follow these steps to learn more about denotation and connotation.

   a. On a separate sheet of paper, reproduce the following chart:

	Positive	Neutral	Negative
1.			
2.			
3.			
4.			
5.			
6.			
7.			
8.			
9.			
10.			
11.			
12.			

   b. Place each of the following words into the column that best matches that word's connotation. If you think the first word, *cheap*, has positive connotations, place the word in the first column, and so on. There are no right or wrong answers; trying to reach consensus with a partner or two can make this exercise even more interesting.

   1. cheap   **5.** quiet   **9.** jealous

   2. talkative   **6.** thin   **10.** arrogant

   3. forgetful   **7.** intelligent   **11.** picky

   4. elderly   **8.** tough   **12.** cautious

c. Now that you've assigned each word to an appropriate column, think of two synonyms for each word that carry different connotations.

Positive	Neutral	Negative
unique	different	weird

Discuss your answers with a friend or your classmates to see if your awareness of connotation matches theirs.

2. With a partner, think of new names for each of the fifteen haircuts on the following page. Consider imagery and connotation.

3. Make a list of five emotions. Next to each, write down what the emotion feels like, sounds like, tastes like, looks like, and smells like. You may not be able to complete all five senses for each emotion, but try to think of at least three.

Here are some sample student responses:

Depression looks like week-old road apples.

Depression looks like gray mist on an oceanfront.

Anger sounds like dragsters lining up for the quarter mile.

Confusion smells like a cologne counter.

Confusion tastes like a glass of orange juice after brushing your teeth.

Hatred tastes like a freezer's frost.

4. Try Exercise 3 again, but this time preface each line with a situation instead of an emotion:

Breaking up smells like getting a perm.

Breaking up sounds like an alarm clock in the morning.

Breaking up tastes like liver.

5. Finding the right simile is often an act of play. To put you in this playful mode, try answering the following questions:

a. What does the taste of hot peppers sound like?

b. What does the taste of mashed potatoes sound like?

c. What does the sound of a violin look like?

d. What does the loud crack of a baseball bat feel like?

e. What do bright clouds taste like?

f. What do smelly socks feel like?

The Flattop with Fenders   The Professional   The Crew

The Businessman's   The Teddy Boy   The Bowl Cut

The Short Layered   The Hockey Cut   The Caesar

The Slick-Back   The Graduation   The Flattop

The Falcon   The Pompadour   The Forward Brush

g. What does a rainy day smell like?

h. What does the taste of pepperoni look like?

6. Try writing a poem in the style of Michael Ondaatje's list poem "Sweet Like a Crow." The entire poem is prefaced with "Your voice sounds like…"

Here are some of his lines:

> Your voice sounds like a scorpion being pushed
>
> through a glass tube
>
> like someone has just trod on a peacock
>
> like wind howling in a coconut…
>
> [like] a frog singing at Carnegie Hall
>
> Like a crow swimming in milk.

Here are some of our endings:

> Your voice sounds like a garbage disposal
>
> mashing tuna fish cans
>
> like someone tortured by a mad woodpecker
>
> like the clatter of perfume bottles on an upended tray
>
> like the vacuum bag that needs changing
>
> like the catch before the hiccup.

Think of five or six of your own endings. The voice you describe can be more endearing if you'd like.

7. Take these ordinary sentences and infuse them with vigor by replacing the tame words with submerged metaphors.

a. Rachel *threw* her purse to the ground.

b. Hector *walked* into his boss's office.

c. Fran *started* a new company.

d. Will *worked* his way up to the top of his field.

e. Kim *ran* from the room in a fury.

8. Write three bad similes.

> Her lips were as shiny as glazed doughnuts.

9. Using your own paper, revise these sentences by using more effective verbs.

   a. I think my brother's supportive words have always been an encouragement to me.

   b. A few months later, I was looking for a bow that was a good match with my violin.

   c. My brother is a senior this year, and soon, on June 2, he is going to graduate.

   d. In sports, no matter where or what the game was, he was always there.

   e. Helen Keller became the person she was due to the influence of Annie Sullivan.

   f. My father was a pilot in the Air Force when he was seventeen.

   g. To be a famous architect was a dream of my grandfather's when he was young.

   h. This was the time when I would avoid my mother because she was in a bad mood.

   i. It was the first day of school, and everyone was moving in a thousand different directions, and I didn't know whom to follow.

   j. I was going to the orthodontist for the first time and was nervous because I knew what he was going to say.

Chapter Assignment

Prewriting

Your assignment in this chapter is to write a descriptive essay. First, decide what you want to describe—you may want to choose from the following topics—and then set aside about ten minutes to brainstorm ideas or images that might appear in your description. Write quickly, trying not to pause.

Writing Topics

Select one of the following suggestions to develop into an essay. Feel free to tailor these topics to suit your needs.

1. Describe your first day of high school. Your first impulse may be to organize your response chronologically, which could work, but consider other possibilities. For instance, your essay could focus on expectations and how the first day met or defied those expectations.

2. Describe a person you know well. You will certainly include a physical description of this person and his or her mannerisms, but don't forget to describe non-visual characteristics, such as the sound of the person's voice or the person's exact words on some issue or another.

3. Describe a typical day at a job you've had or still have. Make it clear to the reader why you continue to work there or why you quit—or got fired. Think about audience. You might pretend that the reader is a prospective employee to whom you are offering advice.

4. Describe a first date. Again, establish an audience for your description. For instance, imagine the reader is the person you went on the date with, or all inexperienced daters, or everyone from the opposite or same sex. Remember to *show* more than *tell*. For instance, if you want to convey how nervous you both were while you waited for the food, don't say "we were nervous." Instead, consider showing that emotion through the dialogue or other aspects of the description.

5. Describe your neighborhood or another place that holds great significance to you, such as a secret hideaway or old house. What particular details about this place still make you feel some visceral reaction? (If you don't know what *visceral* means, look it up. It's

okay to use challenging vocabulary, as long as you're not doing so just to impress. We think the word fits.)

6. Describe a physical ailment or disability with which you are familiar, such as a migraine headache or a broken leg. How has your experience with this ailment or disability affected the way you view the world?

7. Using words that appeal to the senses, describe an object that means a great deal to you. You might choose an old toy, a family heirloom, a treasured souvenir, a gift, a collection, an old diary, a musical instrument, or a trophy. What memories does this object elicit? Why does the object still mean so much to you?

Revision

Write down your thesis, or main point. Although it need not appear in your essay, establishing a thesis may help sharpen your focus during revision. Then answer these questions:

1. Does every sentence in the essay support your thesis in some way?

2. Do you use effective verbs?

3. Do you incorporate figurative language?

4. Is your imagery original and suitable to your topic?

5. What questions do you have for a peer reviewer?

Peer Review

Use these questions to help you evaluate another student's writing. Remember, specific suggestions and examples are most helpful.

1. What main point does the writer convey?

2. List several examples of effective imagery, words, or phrases that appeal to the senses.

3. Could any phrases be more original? Please explain.

4. If the writer were to work on a second draft of this essay, what suggestions would you offer? What would you like to see developed?

5. What questions would you ask the writer?

A Country Road Song

by Andre Dubus

Meet the Writer

Andre Dubus II was known mainly for his short stories and essay collections, as well as for his generosity and generosity. His stories have been adapted for film, including *We Don't Live Here Anymore*. Dubus lost the use of legs in a car accident in 1986.

On a country road in Bradford, Massachusetts, there is a hill without trees in a meadow. It is two miles from an apartment where I lived alone, and, after writing in the morning, I ran on the asphalt road, went through a wooden gate, ran on grass to the hill, then slowly ran up it. It is a deceptive hill, and a friend who sometimes ran with me named it Agony Hill. I ran to a crest and looked up at another, and ran to that one and looked up at another; at the top, I stood, sweating and breathing fast and deeply, and looked across the field at a long, curving stretch of the Merrimack River, and a line of trees at its bank. I ran up this hill in all seasons, unless there was snow on the earth.

Sometimes I drove to Lake Kenoza in Haverhill, and ran on a dirt trail in woods. The trail followed the lake and turned up a long hill, and I ran up it and looked down between trees at the water and ran down, and back along the trail, and came out of the woods, and, before going to the water fountain and my car, I ran up a short, steep hill, a very good sledding hill when snow covers it. I named this Marine Green Hill, after a friend running up it behind me yelled: "Up that hill, Marine; up that hill," and suddenly I was eighteen years old again, running up a hill at Quantico, Virginia, and a Marine sergeant was yelling, giving my legs, my lungs, my will the push they needed.

One very cold and windy and sunlit day, I ran on a country road, then on a neighborhood street toward home, and saw ahead of me a woman I knew. She was walking toward me. She was in her sixties then, and I knew that every Sunday she walked at Rye Beach, and often I thought of her walking in snow at the edge of the sea. She worked at Bradford College, where I taught; she worked at the switchboard, and one day in my first spring in New England, I ran into the building, out of cold rain, and said to her: "When is spring coming?" and she said: "This is spring." Now in the cold wind, we approached each other; she wore an overcoat and gloves and a scarf around her head and ears. Her cheeks were red. She waved, and called into the wind: "Where is everyone? Why are you and I the only ones out here, on this beautiful day?"

It was a beautiful day, and I believe she and I were outdoors not because of pride or discipline, but love. For fifteen years in New England, I ran in all seasons to exercise my body, because exercising my body cleared my brain, and gave me joy. Then for five years, I walked fast but without lengthening my stride, inhaling for three steps, holding my breath for three, exhaling for three; it was peaceful, and I loved it more than running. On a warm spring day, on a road between Bradford and Boxford, I was walking past a line of trees and I heard above me the low sound of something hard, in motion, striking something soft at rest, and a squeal of terror that I felt in my body, and I looked up, to see a hawk flying up from a branch, with a sparrow in its talons, climbing in the blue sky. Sometimes, walking among meadows and trees, I sang. Once in summer, while singing "I Get a Kick Out of You," I passed a farmhouse and a woman opened the front door and called: "Far out."

I was. When I ran, when I walked, there was no time: there was only my body, my breath, the trees and hills and sky, the birds and chipmunks and squirrels, the cold or hot or cool air, the rain on my hat and face, the white and silent motion of snow. The rhythm of running and walking and deep breathing soothed my soul, and the landscapes and weather thrilled it. I always felt grateful, but I did not know it was gratitude, and so I never thanked God, or the leaves, or air, or my legs. Eight years ago, on a starlit night in July, a car hit me, and I was in a hospital for seven weeks, and in September the surgeon cut off my left leg, at the middle of the knee, and I went home with my right leg in a full cast that would not come off till June. The femur and tibia of my right leg had been shattered, the nerves were damaged, the muscles atrophied and tightened with scar tissue, and my knee would not bend. It still does not. I worked with physical therapists for three years, exercising my leg, walking with an artificial leg and crutches, trying to strengthen muscles and bend my knee. Walking with my right leg and an artificial one was harder than anything I had ever done with my body. Finally, I knew it was time to stop going for three hours three times a week to physical therapy; time to expect my leg to be no more than an often-painful limb that I am glad I have, for it keeps me five feet and nine inches long, and it is mine; time to accept life in a wheelchair. In summer, I swim; some days in fall and spring, I push myself around the church parking lot, singing. In all seasons, I play Sinatra on compact discs, and in my chair I sing with him, and shadowbox and dance.

It is time now to sing of my gratitude: for legs and hills and trees and seasons. Spring here comes at its own pace, and without consistence. It comes as rain, snow, sunlight, days of gray sky, and buds are on tree branches, and the grass is green. I ran and walked in sweatpants and sweatshirt till I no longer needed them; then I wore shorts and a T-shirt and a folded bandanna tied around my head to keep sweat from my eyes. Then it was summer and I wore only the shorts and bandanna, the shoes and socks, and loved the feel of sweat coming out of my body, dripping on my skin, and I felt that these long sunlit days would keep coming, one after another after another after another. I ran or walked five miles and went into my house, my socks damp, my shorts wet, and I wrung sweat from the bandanna, and ate tomatoes grown in this earth that months ago was frozen. In fall, the sweat dried more quickly on my skin, and dead leaves gathered on the ground, and the taste and smell of the air were the taste and smell of change. The sun moved toward the tops of distant trees sooner than in summer, poised at their crowns, lightning in the sky with red and orange and gold, and the leaves were red and yellow, moving like benevolent flames in the air.

In November, if I ran or walked to the west in late afternoon, the low sun shone straight into my eyes, and in December, late afternoon was dark. For me, it is not the cold air that makes winter long and sometimes sorrowful, but the darkness: the early twilight and dusk, and the nights that seem longer than night should ever be. I wore thermal underwear, a T-shirt, sweatpants and sweatshirt, a light parka that shielded me from the wind, mittens and a ski cap, and if the wind was strong and very cold, I spread Vaseline on my face, from my beard to my eyes. And I sweated, running or walking on gray asphalt, up and down hills with brown grass and bare trees and evergreens, and past brown fields. I ran or walked in snow gently floating down, or falling fast as rain, or swirling in the wind: I smelled it and tasted it and sometimes it froze on my beard, and my sweat did too, and they formed tiny icicles. Then there was sunlight for days and I passed meadows of glaring snow, and woods where snow was shaded by pines and bright under trees without leaves. In spring, water ran down hills to the roads, and down them to ditches and lowlands and the river, where melting ice floated to the sea, and I did not wear the parka and mittens and cap, and finally I did not wear the sweatpants and sweatshirt; I ran or walked in shorts and T-shirt, with the bandanna around my head, under a blue sky that in a few days or weeks would host a sun so warm that, save for shorts and socks and shoes, I could run or walk naked on the green earth.

I mourn this, and I sing in gratitude for loving this, and in gratitude for all the roads I ran on and walked on, for the hills I climbed and descended, for trees and grass and sky, and for being spared losing running and walking sooner than I did: ten years sooner, or eight seasons, or three; or one day.

Discussion Questions

1. Note the small episodes that Dubus imbeds in his descriptions, such as his Marines memory, meeting a woman he knows while running, and the hawk and sparrow. How does each affect your understanding of Dubus's purpose?

2. Look at the fifth paragraph, the one beginning with "I was." Dubus could have easily divided that paragraph into two or three shorter paragraphs. What effect does he achieve with this paragraph construction?

3. In the final paragraph, Dubus states his purpose rather explicitly. What effect does this have on you as a reader?

In Bed

by Joan Didion

Meet the Writer

Joan Didion is an American writer best known for her nonfiction pieces examining how societal influences affect individual well-being. She won the National Book Award in 2005 for *The Year of Magical Thinking*, a memoir about the sudden death of her husband, writer John Gregory Dunne. She lives in New York.

Three, four, sometimes five times a month, I spend the day in bed with a migraine headache, insensible to the world around me. Almost every day of every month, between these attacks, I feel the sudden irrational irritation and the flush of blood into the cerebral arteries which tell me that migraine is on its way, and I take certain drugs to avert its arrival. If I did not take the drugs, I would be able to function perhaps one day in four. The physiological error called migraine is, in brief, central to the given of my life. When I was 15, 16, even 25, I used to think that I could rid myself of this error by simply denying it, character over chemistry. "Do you have headaches *sometimes? frequently? never?*" the application forms would demand. "Check one." Wary of the trap, wanting whatever it was that the successful circumnavigation of that particular form could bring (a job, a scholarship, the respect of mankind and the grace of God), I would check one. "*Sometimes*," I would lie. That in fact I spent one or two days a week almost unconscious with pain seemed a shameful secret, evidence not merely of some chemical inferiority but of all my bad attitudes, unpleasant tempers, wrongthink.

For I had no brain tumor, no eyestrain, no high blood pressure, nothing wrong with me at all: I simply had migraine headaches, and migraine headaches were, as everyone who did not have them knew, imaginary. I fought migraine then, ignored the warnings it sent, went to school and later to work in spite of it, sat through lectures in Middle English and presentations to advisers with involuntary tears running down the right side of my face, threw up in washrooms, stumbled home by instinct, emptied ice trays onto my bed and tried to freeze the pain in my right temple, wished only for a neurosurgeon who would do a lobotomy on house call, and cursed my imagination.

It was a long time before I began thinking mechanistically enough to accept migraine for what it was: something with which I would be living, the way some people live with diabetes. Migraine is something more than the fancy of a neurotic imagination. It is an essentially hereditary complex of symptoms, the most frequently noted but by no means the most unpleasant of which is a vascular headache of blinding severity, suffered by a surprising number of women, a fair number of men (Thomas Jefferson had migraine, and so did Ulysses S. Grant, the day he accepted Lee's surrender), and by some unfortunate children as young as two years old. (I had my first when I was eight. It came on during a fire drill at the Columbia School in Colorado Springs, Colorado. I was taken first home and then to the infirmary at Peterson Field, where my father was stationed. The Air Corps doctor prescribed an enema.) Almost anything can trigger a specific attack of migraine: stress, allergy, fatigue, an abrupt change in barometric pressure, a contretemps over a parking ticket. A flashing light. A fire drill. One inherits, of course, only the predisposition. In other words I spent yesterday in bed with a headache not merely because of my bad attitudes, unpleasant tempers and wrongthink, but because both my grandmothers had migraine, my father has migraine, and my mother has migraine.

No one knows precisely what it is that is inherited. The chemistry of migraine, however, seems to have some connection with the nerve hormone named serotonin, which is naturally present in the brain. The amount of serotonin in the blood falls sharply at the onset of migraine, and one migraine drug, methysergide, or Sansert, seems to have some effect on serotonin. Methysergide is a derivative of lysergic acid (in fact Sandoz Pharmaceuticals first synthesized LSD-23 while looking for a migraine cure), and its use is hemmed about with so many contraindications and side effects that most doctors prescribe it only in the most incapacitating cases. Methysergide, when it is prescribed, is taken daily, as a preventive; another preventive which works for some people is old-fashioned ergotamine tartrate, which helps to constrict the swelling blood vessels during the "aura," the period which in most cases precedes the actual headache.

Once an attack is under way, however, no drug touches it. Migraine gives some people mild hallucinations, temporarily blinds others, shows up not only as a headache but as a gastrointestinal disturbance, a painful sensitivity to all sensory stimuli, and abrupt overpowering fatigue, a strokelike aphasia, and a crippling inability to make even the most routine connections. When I am in a migraine aura (for some people the aura lasts fifteen minutes, for others several hours), I will drive through red lights, lose the house keys, spill whatever I am holding, lose the ability to focus my eyes or frame coherent sentences, and generally give the appearance of being on drugs, or drunk. The actual headache, when it comes, brings with it chills, sweating, nausea, a debility that seems to stretch the very limits of endurance. That no one dies of migraine seems, to someone deep into an attack, an ambiguous blessing.

My husband also has migraine, which is unfortunate for him but fortunate for me; perhaps nothing so tends to prolong an attack as the accusing eye of someone who has never had a headache. "Why not take a couple of aspirin," the unafflicted will say from the doorway, or "I'd have a headache, too, spending a beautiful day like this inside with all the shades drawn." All of us who have migraine suffer not only from the attacks themselves but from this common conviction that we are perversely refusing to cure ourselves by taking a couple of aspirin, that we are making ourselves sick, that we "bring it on ourselves." And in the most immediate sense, the sense of why we have a headache this Tuesday and not last Thursday, of course we often do. There certainly is what doctors call a "migraine personality," and that personality tends to be ambitious, inward, intolerant of error, rather rigidly organized, perfectionist. "You don't look like a migraine personality," a doctor once said to me. "Your hair's messy. But I suppose you're a compulsive housekeeper." Actually my house is kept even more negligently than my hair, but the doctor was right nonetheless: perfectionism can also take the form of spending most of a week writing and rewriting and not writing a single paragraph.

But not all perfectionists have migraine, and not all migrainous people have migraine personalities. We do not escape heredity. I have tried in most of the available ways to escape my own migrainous heredity (at one point I learned to give myself two daily injections of histamine with a hypodermic needle, even though the needle so frightened me that I had to close my eyes when I did it), but I still have migraine. And I have learned now to live with it, learned when to expect it, how to outwit it, even how to regard it, when it does come, as more friend than lodger. We have reached a certain understanding, my migraine and I. It never comes when I am in real trouble. Tell me that my house is burned down, my husband has left me, that there is gunfighting in the streets and panic in the banks, and I will not respond by getting a headache. It comes instead when I am fighting not an open but a guerrilla war with my own life, during weeks of small household confusions, lost laundry, unhappy help, canceled appointments, on days when the telephone rings too much and I get no work done and the wind is coming up. On days like that my friend comes uninvited.

And once it comes, now that I am wise in its ways, I no longer fight it. I lie down and let it happen. At first every small apprehension is magnified, every anxiety a pounding terror. Then the pain comes, and I concentrate only on that. Right there is the usefulness of migraine, there in the imposed yoga, the concentration on the pain. For when the pain recedes, ten or twelve hours later, everything goes with it, all the hidden resentments, all the vain anxieties. The migraine has acted as a circuit breaker, and the fuses have emerged intact. There is a pleasant convalescent euphoria. I open the windows and feel the air, eat gratefully, sleep well. I notice the particular nature of a flower in a glass on the stair landing. I count my blessings.

Discussion Questions

1. Pain is an extremely difficult concept to describe. Find examples of how Didion shows the effects of her pain without actually describing the pain itself.

2. Examine the beginnings of Didion's paragraphs. In each case, how has she provided a transition from the previous paragraph?

3. Describe Didion's tone, her attitude toward the subject. What phrases or sentences most clearly convey this tone? What other tones could a writer choose for discussing the subject of migraine headaches?

4. The fourth paragraph, which begins, "No one knows…" includes scientific information. How does this paragraph help Didion achieve her purpose?

from
One Writer's Beginnings
by Eudora Welty

Meet the Writer

Eudora Welty was an award-winning American fiction writer, essayist, and photographer. Her novel *The Optimist's Daughter* won The Pulitzer Prize in 1973. Welty received the Presidential Medal of Freedom in 1980 from President Jimmy Carter. Her home in Jackson, Mississippi is a National Historic Landmark and receives thousands of visitors each year. The following reading is an excerpt from Welty's autobiography, *One Writer's Beginnings*.

When I was young enough to still spend a long time buttoning my shoes in the morning, I'd listen toward the hall: Daddy upstairs was shaving in the bathroom and Mother downstairs was frying the bacon. They would begin whistling back and forth to each other up and down the stairwell. My father would whistle his phrase, my mother would try to whistle, then hum hers back. It was their duet. I drew my buttonhook in and out and listened to it—I knew it was "The Merry Widow." The difference was, their song almost floated with laughter: how different from the record, which growled from the beginning, as if the Victrola were only slowly being wound up. They kept it running between them, up and down the stairs where I was now just about ready to run clattering down and show them my shoes.

In our house on North Congress Street in Jackson, Mississippi, where I was born, the oldest of three children, in 1909, we grew up to the striking of clocks. There was a mission-style oak grandfather clock standing in the hall, which sent its gong-like strokes through the living room, dining room, kitchen, and pantry, and up the sounding board of the stairwell. Through the night, it could find its way into our ears; sometimes, even on the sleeping porch, midnight could wake us up. My parents' bedroom had a smaller striking clock that answered it.

Though the kitchen clock did nothing but show the time, the dining room clock was a cuckoo clock with weights on long chains, on one of which my baby brother, after climbing on a chair to the top of the china closet, once succeeded in suspending the cat for a moment. I don't know whether or not my father's Ohio family, in having been Swiss back in the 1700s before the first three Welty brothers came to America, had anything to do with this; but we all of us have been time-minded all our lives. This was good at least for a future fiction writer, being able to learn so penetratingly, and almost first of all, about chronology. It was one of a good many things I learned almost without knowing it; it would be there when I needed it.

My father loved all instruments that would instruct and fascinate. His place to keep things was the drawer in the "library table" where lying on top of his folded maps was a telescope with brass extensions, to find the moon and the Big Dipper after supper in our front yard, and to keep appointments with eclipses. There was a folding Kodak that was brought out for Christmas, birthdays, and trips. In the back of the drawer you could find a magnifying glass, a kaleidoscope, and a gyroscope kept in a black buckram box, which he would set dancing for us on a string pulled tight. He had also supplied himself with an assortment of puzzles composed of metal rings and intersecting links and keys chained together, impossible for the rest of us, however patiently shown, to take apart; he had an almost childlike love of the ingenious.

In time, a barometer was added to our dining room wall; but we didn't really need it. My father had the country boy's accurate knowledge of the weather and its skies. He went out and stood on our front steps first thing in the morning and took a look at it and a sniff. He was a pretty good weather prophet.

"Well, I'm *not*," my mother would say with enormous self-satisfaction.

He told us children what to do if we were lost in a strange country. "Look for where the sky is brightest along the horizon," he said. "That reflects the nearest river. Strike out for a river and you will find habitation." Eventualities were much on his mind. In his care for us children he cautioned us to take measures against such things as being struck by lightning. He drew us all away from the windows during the severe electrical storms that are common where we live. My mother stood apart, scoffing at a caution as a character failing.

"Why, I always loved a storm! High winds never bothered me in West Virginia! Just listen at that! I wasn't a bit afraid of a little lightning and thunder! I'd go out on the mountain and spread my arms wide and *run* in a good big storm!"

So I developed a strong meteorological sensibility. In years ahead when I wrote stories, atmosphere took its influential role from the start. Commotion in the weather and the inner feelings aroused by such a hovering disturbance emerged connected in dramatic form. (I tried a tornado first, in a story called "The Winds.")

From our earliest Christmas times, Santa Claus brought us toys that instruct boys and girls (separately) how to build things—stone blocks cut to the castle-building style, Tinker Toys, and Erector sets. Daddy made for us himself elaborate kites that needed to be taken miles out of town to a pasture long enough (and my father was not afraid of horses and cows watching) for him to run with and get up on a long cord to which my mother held the spindle, and then we children were given it to hold, tugging like something alive at our hands. They were beautiful, sound, shapely box kites, smelling delicately of office glue for their entire short lives. And of course, as soon as the boys attained anywhere near the right age, there was an electric train, the engine with its pea-sized working headlight, its line of cars, tracks equipped with switches, semaphores, its station, its bridges, and its tunnel, which blocked off all other traffic in the upstairs hall. Even from downstairs, and through the cries of excited children, the elegant rush and click of the train could be heard through the ceiling, running around and around its figure eight.

All of this, but especially the train, represents my father's fondest beliefs—in progress, in the future. With these gifts, he was preparing his children.

And so was my mother with her different gifts.

I learned from the age of two or three that any room in our house, at any time of day, was there to read in, or to be read to. My mother read to me. She'd read to me in the big bedroom in the mornings, when we were in her rocker together, which ticked in rhythm as we rocked, as though we had a cricket accompanying the story. She'd read to me in the dining room on winter afternoons in front of the coal fire, with our cuckoo clock ending the story with "Cuckoo," and at night when I'd got in my own bed. I must have given her no peace. Sometimes she read to me in the kitchen while she sat churning, and the churning sobbed along with *any* story. It was my ambition to have her read to me while *I* churned; once she granted my wish, but she read off my story before I brought her butter. She was an expressive reader. When she was reading "Puss in Boots," for instance, it was impossible not to know that she distrusted *all* cats.

It had been startling and disappointing to me to find out that story books had been written by *people*, that books were not natural wonders, coming up of themselves like grass. Yet regardless of where they came from, I cannot remember a time when I was not in love with them—with the books themselves, cover and binding and the paper they were printed on, with their smell and their weight and with their possession in my arms, captured and carried off to myself. Still illiterate, I was ready for them, committed to all the reading I could give them.

Neither of my parents had come from homes that could afford to buy many books, but though it must have been something of a strain on his salary, as the youngest officer in a young insurance company, my father was all the while carefully selecting and ordering away for what he and Mother thought we children should grow up with. They bought first for the future.

Discussion Questions

1. This excerpt from Eudora Welty's memoir, *One Writer's Beginnings*, is rich in description. Each detail, sentence, and paragraph supports a specific thesis. State what you believe is Welty's thesis. How do you know?

2. List sensory images in the passage that appeal to sight, sound, smell, and touch. Find two examples of each sense.

3. Welty includes brief bits of dialogue between her mother and father. How does Welty construct these passages so that they reveal each individual personality?

Is This Heaven? No, It's Wrigley Field

by Gary Anderson

"Welcome to heaven," a grey-haired, angelic-looking gentleman whispered as we took our seats. On this, only our second visit to Wrigley Field, my wife and I had seats way back in the upper deck, as close to heaven as you can get and still be in Wrigley Field, but we were already starting to expect magical things to happen on our visits to the revered baseball palace.

On our first trip to Wrigley Field on Mother's Day, 1989, we found our way there with only the vaguest of directions. We stepped up to the ticket window, and I asked for the two best seats available. The ticket vendor said, "Two club boxes behind the Cubs dugout OK?" I couldn't believe it. We had two of the best seats in the park, and we had purchased them only fifteen minutes before the game started. Something truly extraordinary was going on here. The usher was a benevolent senior citizen who wiped off our seats and said to be sure to let her know if we need anything.

Back in those days, we had only lived in the Chicago area for a short time, and our experiences with baseball parks up to that point were somewhat less pleasant than what we would come to expect from the Friendly Confines. The only ballpark near where we lived in Iowa was the venerable Sec Taylor Stadium in Des Moines, home of the Iowa Cubs. It was fine for what it was: a minor league park in a minor league city. The seats were hard bleachers, and the quality of the games was not much of a thrill. After Iowa, we lived in Texas and endured the horrors of Arlington Stadium, the home of the Texas Rangers. If you can imagine baseball played inside a tin can, you pretty much have the idea of Arlington Stadium. The best part of a game there was the way the announcer said, "Oddibe McDowell!" every time the hapless right fielder came up to bat.

Needless to say, it didn't take long for us to begin to appreciate the beauty and tradition of Wrigley Field. After dozens of trips to Wrigley Field under all sorts of conditions, I no longer expect quasi-mystical experiences whenever I step through the gates, but I can honestly say I have had a blast every time I've gone to a Cubs game.

Sometimes they are subtle blasts, if that makes any sense. At least once a year, I go to a Cubs game by myself. I usually do this on a weekday, and I try to arrive at 1060 West Addison by 9:00 a.m. I like to watch the park wake up. The workers arrive. Vendors set up their booths. The players arrive and usually don't mind signing autographs or exchanging small talk with fans who are insane enough to be at the park four-and-a-half hours before game time.

When the game starts, I get completely into it when I'm by myself. George F. Will said that baseball rewards you for paying attention. With this in mind, I try to focus on one of the nine defensive players for each of the nine innings; I watch every little movement he makes, and try to pick up nuances of his position. Usually, I keep score on one of the souvenir scorecards hawked by guys who have been at it for decades. Midway through the seventh, I stretch along with Harry Caray and everybody else, but while the game is in progress, I have a pure baseball experience, watching the game and trying to learn new aspects of the old game.

A completely different kind of experience happens when I go to games with my wife and/or some friends. We still watch the game, and we still pay attention, but not quite as much. When I'm with other people, I tend to get more into the emotional aspects of the game, cheering and jeering, and generally turning up the rowdiness a notch.

One of my best memories of this kind of game experience was the time a friend and I were at a night game seated by the visitor's bullpen. It was a pretty close game against the Pittsburgh Pirates when the Pirates pitcher started to tire, so Bill Landrum went to work in the Pirates bullpen. Unfortunately, Mr. Landrum had drooled some tobacco on his pristine uniform, so we rode him about it throughout his warm-up pitches: "Don't worry Billy. That **** looks good on you!" "Need a bib?" "Couldn't they fix you up with a *clean* uniform?" He ignored us, and I can't blame him. But when Bill Landrum went into the game, he couldn't get a pitch remotely close to the plate, and he was pulled after facing two batters. My buddy and I took complete credit for the two walks that ended up winning the game for the Cubs, and—obviously—I still like to tell the story.

I'll admit that my perception of baseball was dramatically affected by the movie *Field of Dreams*. For me, baseball is not just a game. It's almost a philosophy, almost a religion, a way of looking at the world. Maybe someday I'll grow up and only see baseball as a business or as a way to spend time when I don't have anything better to do. Until then, I can't think of anything better to do than go to a game, and I can't think of a better place to watch a game than at Wrigley Field, baseball's heaven.

Discussion Questions

1. Anderson quotes several lines of dialogue in this piece. What effect is created by these direct quotes?

2. Find the shortest sentences. What effect do these short sentences create?

3. Notice Anderson's use of transitions at the beginnings of paragraphs. Which are the smoothest ones? Which ones—if any—are clunky?

4. What advice do you have for Anderson about how he might improve this essay? Write it briefly but politely.

5. What memories of yours can be developed in writing?

6. Pay attention to the choices Anderson makes regarding organization. For example, notice how the last paragraph echoes the first, effectively *framing* the essay. Discuss how Anderson achieves this framing—in other words, which bits of text echo others? Point out other patterns in this essay that help to achieve order.

I Can't Be Him All the Time

by Jonathan Congdon

Meet the Writer

Jonathan Congdon began reading voraciously as a small child, when he had to hurry to finish his older brother's books before his brother went back to school with them. His lifelong love of LEGO blocks has inspired him to pursue an engineering career, and he enjoys building robots and Rube Goldberg machines.

I cannot speak. That is to say, I cannot speak to people. I become flustered, I mumble, I seem to ignore them. This is the way I have always been. But I can speak *at* people. I can control a crowd with the skill of a maestro, balancing the many various facets of public speech—tone, rate, word choice, gestures, and expressions. A good speech has little in common with a good piece of writing, for a speech must flow over the tongue, not through the mind. The audience cannot go back to what has already been said and review it, and thus speeches must avoid excessive complexity, yet not be patronizing. All of this I mastered, but no matter how many times I go up in front of a group of people, the fear never goes away. Always, there is that wretched pull in my stomach, that trembling of my arms and legs, that feeling of warmth across my face. All that has changed is my reaction.

The first time I gave a speech as part of speech class, it was an unqualified disaster. My words ran together, the thoughts, which had seemed so simple in my head (I was only introducing a classmate) becoming a poorly put together morass when I spoke. But I tried. It was painful, and I was exhausted when I finished. I knew that it hadn't been a very good speech, and I was ashamed of this. Like most conversations I have, it ended indecisively, trailing off aimlessly instead of ending definitively. The first speech didn't have the knowledge of my previous failure to precede it, however, and this knowledge all but doomed me.

That second time I stepped up to the podium, I could feel my pulse quicken. I could hear the blood rushing, reddening my ears, and making my vision pulse most unpleasantly. I felt as though I had run a marathon in record heat, and I hadn't even started yet. As waves of nausea made my stomach clench and unclench, I desperately wanted to scream at the teacher. I wanted to explain my anguish, I wanted to shout, "I tried! I tried to do my best but I failed and now I'm ready to quit this class. I just can't do this. I can't. Just let me leave, please, just let me leave."

I fumble my note cards. They are better written than those from my first speech, which means that they contain nothing more than garbled phrases that should, in theory, prevent me from merely reading off of them, forcing me to make eye contact with my audience. But now, those notations that I had so carefully agonized over in the safety of my house seem worthless, as useless as if they had been written by someone else for a totally different speech. I can't remember my opening sentence; I don't remember what I had planned to say to draw my audience in. Said audience is sitting right in front of me, waiting expectantly. I can almost hear their collective breathing; I can almost see some of them roll their eyes, expecting to have to sit through another botched speech. They have the digital clock behind me to watch, one that doesn't betray the seconds. I, however, have an analog one, its second hand smoothly sweeping, an undisturbed orbit no different from the thousands of other such rotations it has made.

By its measure, less than ten seconds have passed since I placed myself behind the podium, and I still have the excuse of organizing my note cards to prevent the teacher from taking any action, to prevent him from asking me if I plan on going. I don't even know if I plan on going, so quickly do my emotions vacillate. Drilled into my head, though, is a message from years and years ago, perhaps from second or third grade. That message is a paltry scrap to hold onto, but what remains of my rational thoughts desperately grabs it, deciding that there is logic enough in it, and even the blind panic I feel recedes a little. "If you try and fail, you'll probably get more credit than if you just give up without trying at all."

Even now, feeling as though my legs might collapse at any moment, there is still someone who cares about his grade inside my head, and this amuses me greatly for some reason, this logical thought in the midst of an emotional maelstrom. So I take a deep, shuddering breath, filling my lungs, breathing in through my mouth. I realize that my face has remained a stoic mask since I left my seat—by some miracle, I have not betrayed an iota of what I feel. I try to stay in this logical, stoical mode, and I manage to ask, actually speaking aloud, "May I begin?"

The teacher nods an affirmative, and I start to speak. I have practiced this speech four times in front of the mirror, and with a lurch I realize that something isn't right. My voice doesn't sound the way it did while I practiced, a voice that was merely my own, albeit louder and slower. The voice that is exiting my mouth is indeed louder and slower. But it is sonorous, filling the room with my words. I have never spoken in a voice like this, and suddenly I find myself totally detached from what is going on. I'm still speaking, but I am filled with calm rationality. My fear has vanished, and I am everything I have always wanted to be—smooth, confident, and in control. The audience doesn't exist anymore, and I am speaking fluidly, garbling not a single word. When I make a mistake, my relaxed mind corrects it automatically, giving my sentences the same meaning in different words, allowing me to shuffle the order of my points without having to stop and think. The audience laughs in all the right places, but their laughter is all I hear, besides the beautiful voice that isn't mine.

That voice wraps the speech up, and there is a wondrous moment when the person who isn't quite me is the one listening to the applause. The moment lasts perhaps half a second, and then it is gone, and it is just myself standing behind that podium. I stand there, feeling tired and worn out, but fiercely happy. I have succeeded, and I can retake my seat, walking those few paces on legs that tremble. I sit down, and still I am undeniably proud, a glow that won't fade as the day progresses.

But at the same time, my success is a tragedy. The person who gave the speech shows up only behind the podium, when he can deal with people not as individuals, but as a group. His feet are immobile, holding him erect but not permitting movement; separating him from those he speaks to. Behind the podium, he springs to life, this persona of mine.

He has the ability to say things in a deadpan manner I only wish I could imitate. He could tell the funniest joke known to man without so much as a laugh in his voice or the tiniest upturn of his lips, and the joke would be indescribably hilarious because of it. He is a part of me, but I cannot be him all the time. But I can be him any time I give a speech, and I suppose that is more than I deserve.

Discussion Questions

1. Find places where Congdon describes his physical actions and reactions. What do they reveal about his frame of mind?

2. Which mode of communication do you prefer, writing or speaking? Why?

3. Congdon describes how his audience—other students and his teacher—affects his performance as a speaker. When you write, how do you take your audience into consideration?

4. Congdon describes his persona as a public speaker as a sonorous, beautiful voice that is smoother and more confident than his normal one. Describe the voice you want to project as a writer.

5. List several examples of imagery. What is the effect of each?

6. Think about your own experiences with delivering speeches. List two examples you would add if this were your essay.

7. Imagine that the essay began like this: "I cannot speak to people because I become flustered and I mumble." Compare this flat revision to the more effective actual opening. What does Congdon achieve with the first sentences of his essay? What is lost in the flat revision?

Day One

by Hannah Wolfe

Meet the Writer

Hannah Wolfe is a 16-year-old, self-proclaimed pineapple addict and professional Facebook creep. She enjoys competing in pageants, harassing her friends, and frolicking around her living room in mix-matched Christmas socks to Justin Bieber and Taylor Swift. She hopes to one day become Miss America or to take over the world with Ellen DeGeneres.

I was going to puke. I was absolutely, positively, going to vomit all over Emily West's two year old, meticulously kept, slate gray, Chevy Cobalt. I could feel my stomach doing flips Shawn Johnson style. The breakfast I didn't eat, because I was way too nervous, was coming back up and I was going to puke.

I didn't puke. I wasn't even close. My fear of starting high school was evident in my shortness of breath and deer-in-headlights facial expression. I was terrified of getting lost. I was even more scared of what I would do if I did get lost. I had no idea what to expect of high school except for the unrealistic circumstances portrayed by bad sitcoms. That day was the beginning, and my biggest fear was screwing up the story.

Luckily for me, I had the calming lyrics of Taylor Swift to hum around in my head all day. I did everything Taylor told me to do. I took a deep breath as I walked through the doors; I just forgot to breathe out. I was on the verge of a Mel Gibson-style freak out, but thanks to Taylor, I didn't feel so alone in what I was going through. There were eighty-seven other freshmen facing the impending doom I was expecting. And, Taylor Swift had survived it too. Yet knowing that still didn't keep away the butterflies.

I gave myself a panic attack about every detail of that day, especially my outfit. I spent days considering what I should wear to make the best first impression possible, and hours actually putting an outfit together. My mind was in too big of a mess to acknowledge the fact that I already knew everyone at my rinky-dink, small town high school; it was a little late for a good first impression. At first, I was proud of the olive-green tank with the white short-sleeve cardigan over the top. What I didn't consider was how wearing a color called "olive" would make me feel that I looked like an olive. Once arriving at school, contemplating how I looked like an appetizer, I was humiliated to see all of my friends wearing T-shirts. Since when do people dress down on the first day?! I was over-dressed and I looked like that freshman that is way too eager to have yet another school year starting.

I can't ever remember being as shoot-me-now nervous as I was that first day of high school. But, like most things I have ever been nervous about, once it is all said and done, I instantly regretted all of the time and energy that I spent worrying. I realized within a matter of minutes that you literally have to try-- hard-- to get lost in a high school with exactly two hallways. I was thankful that I had Taylor Swift singing in my head all day, but I did not need her interpretation of high school; I had to make my own. I realized that high school is exactly what you make it. If I wanted high school to be great, I would have to do the great things that would make it great for myself. I have learned to live my life in high school like it will be the most fun I will ever have, but I also know that if four short years define my life, I am doing something terribly wrong.

Discussion Questions

1. In your own words, describe Wolfe's thesis.

2. List three sensory details Wolfe uses. What is the effect of each?

3. Wolfe makes many pop culture references. How do these references help her to achieve her purpose?

4. Wolfe laughs at herself and at her predicament. Offer one example of this, and describe the effect of this strategy.

My Sanctuary

by Emily Bruflat

Meet the Writer

During high school, Emily Bruflat was active in band, choir, speech, and musicals, among many other church and music activities in her community. Since then she has been working toward a major in instrumental music education and a minor in English at Nebraska Wesleyan University.

Miranda sat across the table from me, glancing at our "unsuspecting" teacher and then at me for the umpteenth time. I timidly raised my hand to ask if I could get a drink. Permission granted, I slipped out and up the stairs to wait for Miranda. She came, laughing nervously, and we then proceeded to the old sanctuary. Fifth and sixth grade Sunday school was boring, and as ten- or eleven-year-olds, we did not possess the attention span to actually sit and listen for an hour. We should have been in trouble more often than we were, given our adventurous natures; nevertheless, we used the same escape tactics week after week. In all of Wayne, Nebraska and out of every nook and cranny in Our Savior Lutheran Church, our favorite place was the Old Sanctuary. Permanently etched into my mind are its appearance, my explorations with Miranda, and its profound emptiness.

Up a dimly lit staircase, then a break around a landing to a smaller one, and finally to the right and into one of three plain wooden doors was the sanctuary. What little light flickered through the stained glass in the windows cast shadows on the bare floor. The sun's rays came only from the north side; the new changes and additions to the church blocked the other windows, making them look almost broken. All about the ceiling hung the most peculiar light fixtures. They were long hexagons of black bars, heavy-looking like wrought iron, with cream colored glass forming diamonds and other geometric shapes up their tall sides. These lights, as well as the intricate architecture around them, fascinated me. From the heart of the church, I could trace these crossing beams to the balcony and all its darkness. The rail across the top could barely be seen, and nailed in the gap beneath that was a picture of the Last Supper.

Just below was the entry, and one strong push would lead me to the outside doors. I never dared to go that far when by myself. Each door had a portrait-sized window set slightly toward the middle seam, and just below were long, brass rectangles opposite the handles on the exterior. Consequently, light pouring through these windows turned them into eyes and the rectangles into an open mouth. I could see reflections of the cross on cloudy days.

The altar rested below that cross. It looked rather humble; it was smaller, stained a pale color similar to yellow. This piece of furniture served as a perfect hiding place, as did the areas under the pulpit and lectern. Further into the room, where the pews used to be, a linoleum tile floor shone in the light, pale and speckled like sand. Red carpet ran in a path from the entrance doors and covered the three wide steps, which led to this sacred area. From the top stair, everything was symmetrical. The cross and altar were in the middle, flanked by white candles. Communion rails with red velvet cushions on the floor next to them protruded from either side; the larger center rail was stored away. This is the Old Sanctuary as I remember it best.

The sanctuary was not just my hideaway. There was not a corner of that room that I didn't know, but Miranda was often with me. We repeatedly skipped Sunday school and burrowed in various places. Many times, our giggling would reveal our hideouts to our teachers, but occasionally we would go unnoticed. It was in our exploring for shelters that we found the key closet. Right next to Pastor Jack's old office sat this little room, which was just large enough to squeeze in a secretary and a few files. For Miranda and me, reaching the cabinets that lined the room was a difficult task. One in particular stood out. When we knocked on it, we heard jingling on the other side. Using a chair or each other to aid in our height, we managed to break open a secret. The inside of the cupboard door was home to rows and columns of hooks; each had at least one key, and all were labeled to the doors they belonged to.

One key intrigued us. We would remove it from its hook, tiptoe through the dark sanctuary, and push our way into the old narthex. When we were together, the eyes of the windows were not as frightening, but their presence caused us accordingly to quicken our pace. We hurried to the left where a simple wooden door blocked our way. It was the one and only passage to the balcony. In slid the key into its familiar keyhole, and the door creaked open. Running up the split flight of stairs, we would meet another door. Try as we might, no key would ever let us in. Eventually, the first door did not open either. We never made it to the balcony, and to this day, it remains a mystery.

I preferred to be alone in the vacant sanctuary. The escape acts with Miranda added excitement to the space, but it was almost more alive as it stood bare. In my isolation, I could feel the room age; now and then the foundation would settle, or a draft from an unidentified source would gently nudge one of the lanterns above. I could see dust floating in the patches of light, its swirling motions creating a blizzard-like haze. I watched the dust with as much fascination as other children watched TV. This forlorn enchantment made me remember the time when the sanctuary was not such a desolate place. Pews lined either side of the aisle, and the room illuminated with light and with happiness. The sturdy little pipe organ could be heard sounding hymn number 448; I would sing "Amazing Grace" so loudly that the people in front of me would glance over their shoulders. The baby grand piano in the front added to the regal aura of the sanctuary. Everything—the organ, the pews, the joy—was gone. It was forever missing as I sat there willing it to reappear; I hated the changes which had deserted the once lively church. The sanctuary was no longer a hiding place when it truly felt empty.

Therefore, this sanctuary provides me with good memories of its looks and the fun I had with Miranda, as well as more depressing thoughts of change. Since those early Sunday school years, the Old Sanctuary has become the "Upper Room." The scarlet path and hard floors are covered in brown carpet. Dividers box off areas for Sunday school classes. The area around the altar has become a storeroom cluttered with junk. Even with the lights turned on and little children smiling and singing their hearts out, it seems dull and lifeless. As I stand there now, I think only one thing: it was my sanctuary.

Discussion Questions

1. Describe Bruflat's tone in this essay. Which details or sentences convey the tone? What tones could other writers adopt for similar subject matter?

2. Make a list of Bruflat's best verb choices. Think of a synonym for each.

3. **Concrete words** are nouns that refer to things that you can hear, see, smell, taste, and touch. List three concrete words that work well in Bruflat's essay. What effect do these words convey?

4. The word *sanctuary* has at least two meanings. How does each meaning apply to this piece?

5. Describe the mood of this piece in one word. Find specific words that help to achieve this mood.

6. Bruflat uses imagery that appeals primarily to the senses of sight and sound. Where might you suggest she use sensory imagery that appeals to smell, taste, and touch?

7. What ideas for your own writing do you derive from this essay?

The Scarf

by Elizabeth Johnson

Meet the Writer

Elizabeth Johnson is positive-minded and somewhat of a romantic. Her passion for artistic pursuits such as singing, acting, and painting often exceeds her interest in math and science. She is especially ardent about the culture of the '20s and '30s and is the founder of her high school's Ballroom Dancing Club.

My grandmother was a very spunky lady who loved fancy clothing and gaudy jewelry. Everything she wore shouted, "Look at me!" Her favorite bright red lipstick was applied immediately before and after she lunged at each family member's cheek, leaving a perfect imprint of her puckered lips. She then stated afterward, "Now you're a part of my tribe." It was never any use to try to wipe off the brand; it only smeared into one red cheek. It was easier to just be one with the tribe. Her hair coordinated with her lipstick, as she dyed her hair a ruby red, which was a nice complement to her naturally olive-colored skin. She liked to refer to herself as a "red hot mama," although we called her Mema.

Mema's wardrobe consisted of many flashy accessories, including a scarf she wore quite often. Today, the scarf remains on a shelf in the depths of my parents' closet, but when I see it I remember her. The scarf is made of black nylon but appears to have a metallic luster because of the shiny gold thread embedded through the fabric. The pattern of the scarf resembles that of a delicate lace tablecloth. She wore it everywhere from Braum's and McDonald's to Joseppi's and the Stillwater Bay; from winter to summer it was ever-present around her neck. With no amount of coaxing could she be convinced to remove it. Recently, I have tried it on and found that I too am drawn to its shiny gold thread. I sensed an overwhelming urge to leave it on. At that moment, I knew I must be her granddaughter because I experienced the same pride and exhilaration that she did when she wore it.

Now looking back I know it was a trademark of her exquisite taste and personality. When I see the scarf, I picture her wearing it, smiling and telling a few inappropriate jokes that I have never understood. This image makes me smile. My grandmother has passed away; I wish she was here to wear it and never take it off.

Discussion Questions

1. Johnson includes her grandmother's actual words. What does she achieve by doing this?

2. Johnson states that her grandmother was spunky. What evidence does the writer supply to prove this?

3. If you were to write about a family member of yours, whom would you write about? What object would you associate with this person? To answer this question, write the opening paragraph of such an essay.

4. Describe a possession that you feel reveals a great deal about you. To explain why it reveals so much, recount a brief story about the possession and/or yourself.

Narration

Try a little experiment. Approach a friend and say something like, "Do I have a story for you!" Then observe closely. Pay attention to how your friend's eyes widen, how he or she leans toward you, ready to take in each detail. And when the friend realizes you have no choice story to unleash, watch the frustration unfold.

One student found great satisfaction through a similar experiment of his own. At a party he'd sit next to someone he didn't know and mutter, "Tell me a story." He claimed that most people, while initially surprised, didn't require much prompting and were glad for the invitation. Even the more reluctant ones, when pressed, always dug around for some small tale.

This craving to hear and tell stories seems quaint at first, a brief diversion from the hard business of life—studying and working and paying bills—yet imagine life without it. Imagine a world without stories. No cave paintings, no Homer or Virgil, no Shakespeare, and as a result, since those artists most certainly fed and nourished our need for stories today, no movies or television or even many video games. You can probably think of exceptions, movies and TV shows that rely less on story than on other techniques, but they'd be just that, exceptions. Even newscasts begin with "Our top story today…." Perhaps stories provide us with a way to shape and make sense of the world.

This chapter focuses on the techniques of effective storytelling. For clarity, we will use the term *narrative* instead of *story*. A **narrative** is a written account of something that happened, usually told in chronological order. Narratives may be fiction or nonfiction, but in this book, we will deal with nonfiction narrative.

Choosing a Topic

We usually wait until the end of each chapter to ask you to choose a writing topic, but in this chapter, we want to offer a few immediate suggestions. You've already written one or more narratives over the years, and you probably have some notions about this process, some of which may be helpful. In fact, you might be thinking that an entire chapter on narration is unnecessary, that all you need to do is pick some event in your life and write about it.

Although your ideas about narration may be fairly accurate, don't just hone in on bold-faced, capital letter events in your life and forget about the quieter moments. You can certainly write about a big event—the accident, the gold ribbon race you won, the time you met the president, the overseas vacation, the rockin' concert—but these essays run the risk of sounding like objective newspaper reports devoid of insight or purpose: *this happened, that happened, she said this, he said that.* A good narrative should answer questions such as, What did the event *mean* to you? How did it change you? Why write about it? While a big event may elicit worthwhile answers to these questions, more often, the answers can be reduced to, "Well, it was, uh, memorable. And amazing." This might not be enough.

If you insist on writing about a marquee event, that's fine, but be sure to read carefully the next section on purpose. At the very least, consider some of the more poignant moments in your life, moments that helped define who you are or urged you to solidify or question your beliefs. Maybe your beliefs on friendship began that day you ran out of lemonade at your corner stand and you blamed your best friend, which ended the friendship. Or maybe you learned about conviction when you hid that low test grade at the back of your folder so your parents wouldn't find out. Maybe that discussion you had with your uncle dying of lung cancer is worth writing about. You can write about the big event, of course, the day of his dying, but maybe this discussion, weeks before his death, holds more power.

Writers on Writing

If you tell me you saw a 'bird,' you haven't said much; I may even have reason to distrust you. *Bird* is an idea, a category. Maybe you were lazy, maybe you didn't think I was worthy of the details, maybe, in fact, you *weren't* there. But say 'Late morning a pair of juncos landed on the feeder by the north window,' and you've let me see something. Even if I can't remember precisely what a junco looks like, it already sounds sort of finchlike, and—here's the thing—I can place you at the window observing it. I grant you the right to tell me what's what; I'm easy, unless you hold back. I want to feel I'm in the presence of someone who knows more than I do, who has an agile and interesting mind, or life experiences different from my own....

What do concrete, naming words do for a prose artifact? They roughen up its surface, making it less easy to skim; they give more complex information; they offer pleasure over and above the conveying of information. Such words are also a way to avoid the dull cast of the overfamiliar.

—*David Long*

As always, before you latch on to a topic, mull over several options. Take your time. Jot down ideas. Pay attention to events in your life that have a particular emotional draw for you or that involve conflict. At this point you don't need to know that your essay will make some point about friendship or conviction or anything else. In fact, you'll probably discover the purpose of your narrative as you write. You'll begin to view a familiar scene in a new light, like opening a drawer full of socks and finding a forgotten item hidden at the back.

Journal Topic

Write about an activity, chore, or job that you initially dreaded but came to enjoy or appreciate. If you dreaded it, why did you begin? Why did your feelings change?

Writing with Purpose

Suppose you decide to write a narrative about a favorite childhood game you once played. You're not sure why you want to write about this game, but the memory resonates, and you want to spend time sharpening that memory, reliving those days. At this point, it's too early, in most cases, to be thinking consciously about thesis and purpose. Instead, brainstorm for ten minutes. Jot down as much as you can remember: images, sounds, smells, and so on. Don't forget dialogue—what you said, what you heard. Try to recreate the exact wording, which seems like an impossibility unless you walked around with a video camera back then. But capture the essence of the words: the halting speech of your rival; the soothing cadence of your best friend; the quick retort from the kid who annoyed everyone.

Next, ask yourself the typical reporter questions. What were the rules of the game? Who played? Where and when did you play? Then ask the tougher questions as well. Why did you play? Who was your biggest ally or foe in the game? Was winning important to you? Why does the memory of the game stick with you after all these years? What would your life have been like if you had never played this game? Do you recognize a kernel of your present self in the way you played back then? Why was the game so much darn fun—or not so fun?

You can certainly think of better questions, tailored to your particular memory, and you can opt to answer some of the tougher questions *after* writing a first draft. As you can already surmise, answering these questions will help lead to a discovery of your purpose.

When you're ready, write a fast first draft, allowing your memory to flow freely, stifling all impulses that threaten to slow you down, even the ridiculous ones: *This story is so lame; I have to help with the dishes; calculus is calling my name; I really need to watch that* Full House *marathon.*

Put the completed draft aside for a while, overnight if possible, and reflect on what you've written. This reflection may be the most important part of the process. Most likely you're happy with your topic: at least a few of the passages in your first draft contain some element of drama or humor or whimsy to hold your reader's attention; some of your descriptions are vivid and clear. But what does the piece mean as a whole? What do all the descriptions add up to? What's the point? What is your purpose?

Even if you never articulate responses to these questions, your answers are critical and they should be clear—to you. Here are several possible thesis statements related to the preceding questions: (1) We need childhood games; (2) Childhood games make an imprint on our futures; (3) Childhood games teach us values and skills.

When stated so bluntly, such thesis statements, at least in a narrative essay, tend to sound hollow and preachy, which is why we're going to urge what may seem contradictory: develop a clear thesis statement that guides you in writing this essay, but never state this thesis directly. Instead, craft a compelling story and let your story suggest the meaning.

If this confuses you, consider the difference between showing and telling. You can *tell* someone you're scared of heights and explain which situations evoke the greatest anxiety, all with stark clarity, but if you never *show* your fear, primarily with sensory details, the reader may remain detached and perhaps even uninterested in your predicament. Showing invites readers in, holds their attention, and actually creates a memory for your audience.

The great film director Alfred Hitchcock mastered this elegant technique of showing rather than telling, which is both economical and powerful. When Jimmy Stewart's eyes widen at a critical moment near the end of *Vertigo*, the audience sees his suspicion. When the couple at the beginning of *Psycho* move toward, then away from each other, the audience *feels* their desperation. Some telling is necessary, of course—the characters do speak to each other—yet the underlying, suggested meanings shout louder than the words. Imagine if the characters explained everything—or worse, if the director came onscreen to interpret for the audience.

For this essay, the reader should come away with a clear sense of what you're trying to say without directly being told. For instance, if you write an essay about your father scolding you, and your purpose is to convey that a certain type of discipline is more effective than another, simply recount the story, relying on specific details, and allow the reader to provide the point. Be sure to make use of the tools presented in Chapter 2, especially imagery and figurative language.

Journal Topic

After all these years in school, you probably have a few good classroom stories. Pick one that includes conflict and write about it.

Writing Beginnings

Say you want to write about the weekend you spent in a remote cabin with your grandparents, a trip that promised hiking and canoeing and fishing. This was a trip you anticipated for months, a trip you had earned because of your improved grades at school.

Where do you begin? Do you start with the poor grades that prompted your parents to broker such a deal for you? Do you reach back further into the past and explain why you earned such poor grades in the first place? Or do you start by describing your relationship with your grandparents, explaining how this trip would mean as much to them as to you? Or how about starting with the day your grandparents proposed this plan to your parents, adding rich details about the excitement on their faces? Perhaps you don't want to retreat so far into the past. Do you begin then with the night before, outlining the steps you took to pack and prepare? Do you begin with the early morning alarm clock blaring? Or how about the light tap of the horn outside as your grandparents pulled up to your house? All these choices seem quite logical, don't they?

Writers on Writing

I make a conscious effort to have quiet in my life. Sometimes I don't listen to music when I drive or to the stereo in my office, and I resist the notion that I'm missing something if the television isn't on. This past summer I freed myself from responsibility for an entire week and checked into a bed and breakfast with the express intent of doing nothing, perhaps to write, but mostly just to sit…. I am convinced that mental trips abroad will never make me crazy, but keep me sane. For me, it is the quiet, leisure spaces between activities that feed my writing, and it is the writing in turn that keeps me fed. Now, when I'm feeling crazy, I know it's not that I need to be more in control, but that I need to let go and wander.

—Sara Holbrook

There is not a precise right or wrong place to start a narrative. You can make any of the perceding suggestions work, provided you don't begin with *"Ring, ring"* or *"Toot toot."* You should have left these simple sound effects behind with your pencil cases and cartoon lunchboxes (though these, for some reason, sometimes become cool again at the end of high school). While any starting place can work for you, try this: start in the middle. "Grandpa handed me the oar." "Grandma took Grandpa's hand." "At first I didn't think my grandparents would make it up the hill, but I soon realized I should have worried more about my own sorry body."

Admit it. You want to know what happens next, don't you? These kinds of sentences create anticipation in the reader, which is much more effective than the writer explaining his or her own anticipation of the trip. Why do so many student writers fall into the trap of beginning at the beginning?

1. The sequence of beginning, middle, end makes sense, even though memory doesn't work that neatly.

2. Students think that the reader requires setup and background information to fully understand the story, which may be true, but all this necessary information can be subtly inserted along the way, perhaps in brief flashbacks.

3. Students hear teachers say that details are important, so they supply plenty of details, but they fail to realize that not all details are created equal. In the previous example, most of the details about getting there can be omitted. The reader doesn't need to know that the car ride took two hours, which included a gas stop where the writer bought snacks two for a dollar, and so on.

How will you know which details are relevant? At first, you may not, at least until you discover your purpose. That's why the section in this chapter on Writing with Purpose (see pages 91–93) is so critical and why you may want to consult that section again as you work on your narrative. Once your purpose is clear, you may be able to cut whole sections of your first draft that add little to your thesis.

Writing Endings

Once you have a solid draft filled with relevant details that support your thesis—an exciting prospect because this means your narrative is streamlined and your pace is brisk—you need to think about an effective ending. Endings may not come easily to you, because they're not easy to write. Think about something you've read recently that was deeply satisfying. What happened to the pace of your reading, which had been consistently breakneck, when you neared the end? Did you slow down? You might have wanted to languish, to take in the end's full import. Perhaps you wanted to be fully immersed in the process of everything falling into place. Or maybe for you reading is not quite so dramatic. In any event, you owe the reader some satisfaction after she or he has read several pages of your words.

As with beginnings, there are no surefire techniques to deliver a satisfying ending; anything can work. Rather than following some formula, you need to rely on your own reserves of creative intuition. If this idea seems daunting to you, we do have a few concrete suggestions.

Writers on Writing

The positive reason for ending well is not just to avoid ending badly, but because a good last sentence—or paragraph—is a joy in itself. It has its own virtues, which give the reader a lift and which linger when the article is over. The perfect ending should take the reader slightly by surprise and yet seem exactly right to him.

—*William Zinsser*

1. Consider the philosopher Aristotle's maxim on effective storytelling: he implored writers to remain keenly aware of the unity of time and place. In other words, maintain the discipline to write about one time and one place. If you're writing a narrative about the first time you were left alone without a babysitter, try to limit your essay to that single span of three or four hours. At the end, don't leap ahead to the present to describe your maturity today. You can certainly suggest this—in fact, it could be your main point—but at the end, don't remove yourself from the scene. Instead, think about a gesture or comment someone made or a thought you had at the time that would clearly suggest maturity. Maybe your mom's usual routine of announcing your bedtime was shelved that night. Or maybe on your way to bed you had thoughts about your newfound independence and wondered what you would do with that freedom the next day. (Thoughts of the next day might seem to defy Aristotle's maxim, but these are still thoughts you had that night.) Or maybe you can simply describe your parents, the way they looked at you anew, proud but awkward and tentative.

If you prefer to compose at the computer, you sometimes need a place to store all the fleeting thoughts that occur to you while writing. You don't, however, want to interrupt the work flow. Simply press Return a few times, quickly type in the random thoughts at the end of the document, then scroll up and continue where you left off. You'll be surprised at how many of these notes find their way into your essays.

Or let's say you're trying to decide on which word to include (or use? employ? keep?). Don't omit any of them—at least not right away. Place parentheses around the extra choices. Decide later during editing.

2. Pay attention to key images, phrases, and ideas you used earlier in the narrative. At the end, echoing some of these key words or lines can often provide a poignant sense of closure. For example, if in your opening you're walking through the halls on the first day of

high school, returning to the halls at the end can frame the essay, highlighting the changes that took place in between.

3. Endings require a degree of restraint, as we've suggested, but they also require a dose of risk. You have to risk baring your emotions, coming clean with stark honesty, undressing your flaws: *this is who I am, this is what happened, and this is how I felt about it.* All of this runs the different risk of telling rather than showing, which means that endings are nothing less than great balancing acts. For instance, if you're writing about your role in the painful breakup of a friendship, you can end the essay by explaining your feelings of regret, but it might be more effective to simply describe how you turned away from your friend when she most needed you. Study the sample essays at the end of the chapter. Notice how each writer creeps toward disclosure, risking sentimentality while avoiding the pitfall of sappiness. Note also how each writer's thesis is implied or subtly interwoven rather than stated bluntly, as in "The moral of the story is...."

Journal Topic

Write about a time when your expectations or perceptions clouded your judgment. Maybe you sent away for something big in the mail but received only a tiny package. Maybe you spent months avoiding someone who turned out to be one of your best friends. Maybe you were the only one to dress in a costume at the seventh grade Halloween party.

Selecting Verb Tense and Point of View

At some point in the process of writing a narrative essay, you'll have to make two decisions.

1. Should you use present or past tense?

   Present Tense: My father hands the instructions to me. (The action is happening now.)

   Past Tense: My father handed the instructions to me. (The action happened in the past.)

Present tense creates immediacy, which can be quite effective, but it also creates potential problems. Whenever we read a student essay that begins in the present tense, red flags fly. Almost invariably, the student will drift into the past tense after several paragraphs, which creates inconsistency and confusion about what happened when. For that reason we recommend that you stick with past tense, unless you have a specific reason to do otherwise.

2. From whose point of view should you write your narrative?

Your logical choice will be the first-person point of view: "I threw the javelin that soared too far and hit my coach." This is the safest, surest, and most recommended choice, but you do have other options.

You can stick to a more objective third-person point of view, especially if your role in the story is not that significant. Maybe someone else threw the javelin, for instance, and you want to write a narrative that highlights the coach's reactions.

Or you can use a more personal third-person point of view, in which the *he* or *she* in the essay is really you: "She visited her old neighborhood for the last time." If you're really talking about yourself, why wouldn't you just use *I*? If, for example, you wanted to highlight your detachment, this unusual choice might serve you well.

In Chapter 1 we urged you to avoid the casual use of the second-person *you*, but consistent use of this point of view for a narrative could work, despite its risk: "You walk into the hospital and spot a streak of red on the linoleum…." As with the personal third-person point of view, the *you* could actually be you, the writer, a thinly disguised first-person narrator. If you like the idea of using the second-person point of view but lack the confidence to try, consider this idea: write your first draft from the point of view that makes you feel most comfortable, probably the first-person point of view, then convert a paragraph or two to a different point of view to determine which version you prefer. Here's an example.

> **A.** Walking across that field, I knew I couldn't patch up our friendship.

> **B.** Walking across that field, you knew you couldn't patch up your friendship.

Version B, inserted here without context, sounds awkward, perhaps even accusatory, but if you have consistently used the second-person point of view in the entire essay, this could be an effective option that highlights the regret or the resignation you may have felt.

Telling or writing stories is a basic human impulse. Reading and hearing those stories is one of the most satisfying, compelling human experiences. In this chapter, you have learned ways to make your narratives memorable and appealing for your audience. Practicing these techniques will improve your ability to relate a narrative that fulfills your purpose and engages your audience.

Practice

Before beginning the Chapter Assignment, try the following exercises to practice writing narratives.

1. How would you begin a narrative about your first day of high school? Based on your answer, write an opening paragraph for that narrative. Now think of a different starting point and write a new opening paragraph.

2. **a.** Dialogue in a narrative is usually interrupted by brief descriptions and details, but sometimes it's more productive in a first draft to write only the dialogue and then insert the details later. Think of an interesting conversation you've had or heard recently, and write out the dialogue. Leave out "he said" and "she said" and anything else other than dialogue.

   b. After you record the dialogue, place parentheses around phrases and sentences that now seem unnecessary—that is, phrases that don't add much to the story or that slow down the pace.

3. In a paragraph or two, describe a time when you felt betrayed. Put aside the paragraphs for a while. When you return to them, write down a possible thesis that might emerge from your description. Thinking of a thesis after only a few paragraphs may seem forced, but this is good practice in finding the meaning in stories.

4. Find an old family photograph and explore the narrative possibilities it presents. Who is shown in the photo? What is happening? Who took the picture? What is intriguing about the photo that might inspire you to write about it? What's the angle, the narrative hook?

Chapter Assignment

Prewriting

Your assignment in this chapter is a narrative essay. Use the following suggestions to help you choose a topic and clarify the purpose of your essay.

Select one of the following topics, then spend at least ten minutes responding to it, generating ideas for your essay. This brainstorming could take several forms: (1) you can create a rough outline of your essay to see the relationship between ideas; (2) you can draw some sort of graphic organizer, if that best matches the way you think (see Appendix B for examples); or (3) you can regard the selected topic as a journal entry and write a brisk response.

If you'd rather choose your own topic, make a list of stories in your life that seem worth writing about. At this point, do not second-guess yourself; include everything that comes to mind. To jog your memory, you may want to write this list in the format of a time line.

If you responded to one of the journal topics in the chapter and want to develop that response instead of choosing one of the following topics, you can regard that journal entry as your prewriting and begin writing your essay.

Writing Topics

Select one of the following suggestions to develop into an essay. Feel free to tailor these topics to suit your needs.

1. Write about one of your earliest childhood memories. As you write, think about why the memory still lingers, why it still affects your thoughts or beliefs today.

2. Write a narrative about one of the key moments in your life that marked your independence. Did you welcome or dread the independence?

3. Write about an event that shaped your view of the world. This could be an event in which you did not directly participate.

4. Write about an event that evokes a particular emotion for you, such as grief, joy, disappointment, or surprise.

5. Write about a significant family event. This might range from being forced to exchange rooms with a sibling to grieving over a grandparent's death.

6. Write a narrative about an event that helped define your attitude on friendship.

7. Write about something that you saw or heard but weren't meant to see or hear. How did this change you?

Revision

As you revise and edit your first draft, consider these suggestions.

Put your essay aside for a while. When you return, ask yourself the following questions. Do *not* simply answer yes or no; explain your answers. If possible, ask a friend to read your narrative and to address the same questions.

1. Does the essay begin at the right moment? Is there a better point at which to begin?

2. Does the essay end at the right moment?

3. Do you write about one place and one time?

4. Do you show more than tell? In which passages can you show more?

5. What is your thesis? Is this thesis implied or stated directly?

6. Do any sentences fall flat because of weak nouns or verbs?

7. Can any sentences be improved through the use of imagery or figurative language?

Based on your answers to these questions, along with reactions from others, write a second draft of your narrative.

Peer Review

Use these questions to help you evaluate another student's writing. Remember, specific suggestions and examples are most helpful.

1. In your own words, what is the writer's purpose?

2. How does the writer make the chronology clear? If the time shifts, are the shifts handled smoothly?

3. What scenes or images work particularly well? Which ones could be developed more?

4. Is the opening engaging? What is a different way to begin? Does the ending resonate? Suggest a different ending.

5. Suppose the writer wants to use more dialogue. Where would be a good place to insert it?

6. What questions do you have for the writer?

Education by the Numbers

by Daniel Ferri

Meet the Writer

Daniel Ferri is a teacher, writer, and radio commentator living in Australia. He was one of the originators of the poetry slam movement in America.

Several Marches ago, I, like thousands of other sixth grade teachers across the state of Illinois, stood in front of my classroom and tore the plastic from a stack of papers. On those papers were printed the topic my sixth graders, and dozens of thousands of other Illinois sixth graders, would spend the next 40 minutes writing about. We are all graded on the results, the students, teachers, and the schools.

We took the Illinois Goal Assessment test, the IGAPs. It was a state law, so all across the state students wrote about the same topic, took the same test, at the same time, followed the same rules, so that everyone, everything, would be the same.

It was a law because the easiest way for politicians to pretend they care about education is to stand up and declare that students are not learning because teachers can't teach and the schools are rotten, and we are gonna fix it by…taking a test. Not that those politicians had any idea what we would test for, or how we would test for that if we knew, but that does not matter, it sounds good on TV. So the Illinois State Legislature told our state bureaucrats to design tests in reading, writing, math, science, and social studies, and make everyone take them. And so, for two weeks in March, we all took the IGAPs; that way everyone, everything, would be the same, almost.

So by law, Illinois students learned to write by the numbers. The first paragraph of a paper must do this this this this and this, the three main body paragraphs must do that that that that and that, and the conclusion paragraph must begin with two thises, followed by three thats, and end with an exciting this. Now I am not making this up…or that…it's that bad. And those were just the rules for a persuasive type paper. This is not how people write. This is how they fill out tax forms. We learned different rules for writing expository and narrative papers. Then we have the reading test, then the math test, then the multiple choice science test, then God help us.

Measuring the richness of learning by taking standardized tests is like judging chili by counting the beans.

The kids hate it. The best writers especially hate it. "Mr. Ferri, if I want to tell my story a different way, why can't I?"

I explained that our state legislature has determined that we must have standards of instruction. The children looked at me like I needed to blow my nose. I told them about basics of form that once mastered can be improvised on. They kept looking at me. I tried to convince them that these are efficient formulas for clear writing. They snickered.

Finally I said, "Look, neither of us have any choice here, you have to take these tests, I have to give them, and some poor soul in North Carolina has to read and grade 500 of them a day. They have a list of the rules you learned for writing each kind of essay. If you don't follow a rule they take points from your score. They don't care what you write. They only care about the rules. If you don't follow the rules, you get a bad score. The scores are published in the paper. If our scores aren't good, then people won't think our schools are good and they won't want to move here, which will make the real estate people mad, and they will yell at the school board, who will yell at the superintendent, who will yell at the principal, who will yell at me. This is not about writing, this is about not getting yelled at." This, they understood.

Each student received an IGAP test booklet. Its front page is for student information. Students must record their name, grade, student ID#, date of birth, ethnicity, and God knows what else on it.

Each letter or number goes in a box, then under the box, in #2 pencil, the student must fill in a circle that corresponds to that letter or number or ethnicity. The page looks like if a loan application and an optical illusion had a baby. If the boxes and circles aren't filled out right, or the marks aren't dark enough, the machines can't read them, and we get yelled at.

We filled out the information pages on the day before we began the tests. Some of them came back a mess with random marks everywhere. So my teaching partner and I stuck Post-it notes on the worst of them saying, "Print your name more clearly," "Fill in circles under date of birth," or "Darken circles."

The morning of the first writing test my students sat expectant and resigned like Pickett's Virginians waiting for the charge. I handed out the packet of prompt pages with the writing topic printed on them. Then we handed out the students' test packets, some sporting Post-it reminders to "Print your name more clearly" or to "Darken circles." Then I stood in front of the class and read from my booklet, which by law, were the exact same words thousands of other sixth grade teachers would also read these mornings. "This is the test I told you about. You will have 40 minutes to…blah blah blah…" ending with, "Turn over the prompt page, read what the topic is, and begin writing. Good luck."

I wasn't bound by state law to say good luck, but I thought it might be OK to wing it there. The topic was, "Should students be required to wear uniforms to school?" The children picked up their pencils, took a breath, and wrote. The only sound was the turning of pages, the scratching, and the sharpening of pencils.

As required by law, I announced when 20 minutes were left, then five, then when time was up. We collected the prompt pages because they must be counted and sent back to the state. We collected the test packets and I set them on my desk while the students stretched and talked quietly. Then I heard Duane ask Becky, "What did you write about?"

"Well, I wrote about uniforms, we all did, it said so on the paper."

"Mine didn't say that. Mine said to write about dancin' circles."

Becky and I both said, "What? What did you write about?"

"I wrote about dancin' circles. Here, I'll show you."

I reached for the pile of prompt pages, but Duane was already rummaging through the stack of test booklets; he said, "No it's not on that page, it's on these."

Becky said, "Those didn't say what to write about!"

"Mine did." Duane pulled his test booklet out of the stack and pointed to the Post-it stuck to the front page.

On that Post-it I had written, "Darken circles."

"See, right here, it says 'Dancin' circles,' so that's what I wrote about."

That morning, thousands of sixth graders across the state of Illinois sat at their desks, they curled themselves around their pencils, stuck their tongues between their teeth, and wrote five paragraph essays about wearing uniforms. All, except one. His essay began, "Well, I never thought much about dancin' circles before today, but if that's what you want to know about, well here goes."

And somewhere in North Carolina some poor soul would reach into the stack of 500 essays she would read that day. Four hundred and ninety-nine of them would be about wearing uniforms, and one would not. I would have loved to watch her face when she read it.

There may still be hope.

Discussion Questions

1. Ferri uses an effective and humorous analogy in the fifth paragraph, comparing the measuring of learning to the judging of chili. Think of your own ending: "Measuring the richness of learning by taking standardized tests is like _____."

2. List Ferri's main criticisms of the IGAP tests. What kinds of assessments do you think Ferri uses in his own class?

3. Why do the "best writers" especially hate the IGAP writing tests?

4. Ferri writes Post-it notes to several students, giving them instructions on how to better fill in their test blanks. Why is this ironic, considering Ferri's feelings about the test?

5. What is Ferri's thesis? Does he state his thesis explicitly or is it implied?

6. List an example of imagery; that is, a place where Ferri shows rather than tells.

Aria

by Richard Rodriguez

Meet the Writer

Richard Rodriguez is an American writer, journalist, and educator living in California. The following essay is taken from his 1982 autobiography *Hunger of Memory: The Education of Richard Rodriguez*, which highlighted the complexities of bilingual education.

Supporters of bilingual education today imply that students like me miss a great deal by not being taught in their family's language. What they seem not to recognize is that, as a socially disadvantaged child, I considered Spanish to be a private language. What I needed to learn in school was that I had the right—and the obligation—to speak the public language of *los gringos*. The odd truth is that my first-grade classmates could have become bilingual, in the conventional sense of that word, more easily than I. Had they been taught (as upper-middle-class children are often taught early) a second language like Spanish or French, they could have regarded it simply as that: another public language. In my case such bilingualism could not have been so quickly achieved. What I did not believe was that I could speak a single public language.

Without question, it would have pleased me to hear my teachers address me in Spanish when I entered the classroom. I would have felt much less afraid. I would have trusted them and responded with ease. But I would have delayed—for how long postponed?—having to learn the language of public society. I would have evaded—and for how long could I have afforded to delay?—learning the great lesson of school, that I had a public identity.

Fortunately, my teachers were unsentimental about their responsibility. What they understood was that I needed to speak a public language. So their voices would search me out, asking me questions. Each time I'd hear them, I'd look up in surprise to see a nun's face frowning at me. I'd mumble, not really meaning to answer. The nun would persist, 'Richard, stand up. Don't look at the floor. Speak up. Speak to the entire class, not just to me!' But I couldn't believe that the English language was mine to use. (In part, I did not want to believe it.) I continued to mumble. I resisted the teacher's demands. (Did I somehow suspect that once I learned public language my pleasing family life would be changed?) Silent, waiting for the bell to sound, I remained dazed, diffident, afraid.

Because I wrongly imagined that English was intrinsically a public language and Spanish an intrinsically private one, I easily noted the difference between classroom language and the language of home. At school, words were directed to a general audience of listeners. ('Boys and girls.') Words were meaningfully ordered. And the point was not self-expression alone but to make oneself understood by many others. The teacher quizzed: 'Boys and girls, why do we use that word in this sentence? Could we think of a better word to use there? Would the sentence change its meaning if the words were differently arranged? And wasn't there a better way of saying much the same thing?' (I couldn't say. I wouldn't try to say.)

Three months. Five. Half a year passed. Unsmiling, ever watchful, my teachers noted my silence. They began to connect my behavior with the difficult progress my older sister and brother were making. Until one Saturday morning three nuns arrived at the house to talk to our parents. Stiffly, they sat on the blue living room sofa. From the doorway of another room, spying the visitors, I noted the incongruity—the clash of two worlds, the faces and voices of school intruding upon the familiar setting of home. I overheard one voice gently wondering, 'Do your children speak only Spanish at home, Mrs. Rodriguez?' While another voice added, 'That Richard especially seems so timid and shy.'

That Rich-heard!

With great tact the visitors continued, 'Is it possible for you and your husband to encourage your children to practice their English when they are home?' Of course, my parents complied. What would they not do for their children's well-being? And how could they have questioned the Church's authority which those women represented? In an instant, they agreed to give up the language (the sounds) that had revealed and accentuated our family's closeness. The moment after the visitors left, the change was observed. 'Ahora, speak to us *en inglés*,' my father and mother united to tell us.

At first, it seemed a kind of game. After dinner each night, the family gathered to practice 'our' English. (It was still then *inglés*, a language foreign to us, so we felt drawn as strangers to it.) Laughing, we would try to define words we could not pronounce. We played with strange English sounds, often overanglicizing our pronunciations. And we filled the smiling gaps of our sentences with familiar Spanish sounds. But that was cheating, somebody shouted. Everyone laughed. In school, meanwhile, like my brother and sister, I was required to attend a daily tutoring session. I needed a full year of special attention. I also needed my teachers to keep my attention from straying in class by calling out, *Rich-heard*—their English voices slowly prying loose my ties to my other name, its three notes, *Ri-car-do*. Most of all I needed to hear my mother and father speak to me in a moment of seriousness in broken—suddenly heartbreaking—English. The scene was inevitable: One Saturday morning I entered the kitchen where my parents were talking in Spanish. I did not realize that they were talking in Spanish however until, at the moment they saw me, I heard their voices change to speak English. Those *gringo* sounds they uttered startled me. Pushed me away. In that moment of trivial misunderstanding and profound insight, I felt my throat twisted by unsounded grief. I turned quickly and left the room. But I had no place to escape to with Spanish. (The spell was broken.) My brother and sisters were speaking English in another part of the house.

Again and again in the days following, increasingly angry, I was obliged to hear my mother and father: 'Speak to us *en inglés*.' (*Speak*.) Only then did I determine to learn classroom English. Weeks after, it happened: One day in school I raised my hand to volunteer an answer. I spoke out in a loud voice. And I did not think it remarkable when the entire class understood. That day, I moved very far from the disadvantaged child I had been only days earlier. The belief, the calming assurance that I belonged in public, had at last taken hold.

Shortly after, I stopped hearing the high and loud sounds of *los gringos*. A more and more confident speaker of English, I didn't trouble to listen to *how* strangers sounded, speaking to me. And there simply were too many English-speaking people in my day for me to hear American accents anymore. Conversations quickened. Listening to persons who sounded eccentrically pitched voices, I usually noted their sounds for an initial few seconds before I concentrated on *what* they were saying. Conversations became content-full. Transparent. Hearing someone's *tone* of voice—angry or questioning or sarcastic or happy or sad—I didn't distinguish it from the words it expressed. Sound and word were thus tightly wedded. At the end of a day, I was often bemused, always relieved, to realize how 'silent,' though crowded with words, my day in public had been. (This public silence measured and quickened the change in my life.)

At last, seven years old, I came to believe what had been technically true since my birth: I was an American citizen.

But the special feeling of closeness at home was diminished by then. Gone was the desperate, urgent, intense feeling of being at home; rare was the experience of feeling myself individualized by family intimates. We remained a loving family, but one greatly changed. No longer so close; no longer bound tight by the pleasing and troubling knowledge of our public separateness. Neither my older brother nor sister rushed home after school anymore. Nor did I. When I arrived home there would often be neighborhood kids in the house. Or the house would be empty of sounds.

Following the dramatic Americanization of their children, even my parents grew more publicly confident. Especially my mother. She learned the names of all the people on our block. And she decided we needed to have a telephone installed in the house. My father continued to use the word *gringo*. But it was no longer charged with the old bitterness or distrust. (Stripped of any emotional content, the word simply became a name for those Americans not of Hispanic descent.) Hearing him, sometimes, I wasn't sure if he was pronouncing the Spanish word *gringo* or saying gringo in English.

Matching the silence I started hearing in public was a new quiet at home. The family's quiet was partly due to the fact that, as we children learned more and more English, we shared fewer and fewer words with our parents. Sentences needed to be spoken slowly when a child addressed his mother or father. (Often the parent wouldn't understand.) The child would need to repeat himself. (Still the parent misunderstood.) The young voice, frustrated, would end up saying, 'Never mind'—the subject was closed. Dinners would be noisy with the clinking of knives and forks against dishes. My mother would smile softly between her remarks; my father at the other end of the table would chew and chew at his food, while he stared over the heads of his children.

My *mother!* My *father!* After English became my primary language, I no longer knew what words to use in addressing my parents. The old Spanish words (those tender accents of sound) I had used earlier—*mamá* and *papá*—I couldn't use anymore. They would have been too painful reminders of how much had changed in my life. On the other hand, the words I heard neighborhood kids call their parents seemed equally unsatisfactory. *Mother* and *Father; Ma, Papa, Pa, Dad, Pop* (how I hated the all-American sound of that last word especially)—all these terms I felt were unsuitable, not really terms of address for my parents. As a result, I never used them at home. Whenever I'd speak to my parents, I would try to get their attention with eye contact alone. In public conversations, I'd refer to 'my parents' or 'my mother and father.'

My mother and father, for their part, responded differently, as their children spoke to them less. She grew restless, seemed troubled and anxious at the scarcity of words exchanged in the house. It was she who would question me about my day when I came home from school. She smiled at small talk. She pried at the edges of my sentences to get me to say something more. (What?) She'd join conversations she overheard, but her intrusions often stopped her children's talking. By contrast, my father seemed reconciled to the new quiet. Though his English improved somewhat, he retired into silence. At dinner he spoke very little. One night his children and even his wife helplessly giggled at his garbled English pronunciation of the Catholic Grace before Meals. Thereafter he made his wife recite the prayer at the start of each meal, even on formal occasions, when there were guests in the house. Hers became the public voice of the family. On official business, it was she, not my father, one would usually hear on the phone or in stores, talking to strangers. His children grew so accustomed to his silence that, years later, they would speak routinely of his shyness. (My mother would often try to explain: Both his parents died when he was eight. He was raised by an uncle who treated him like little more than a menial servant. He was never encouraged to speak. He grew up alone. A man of few words.) But my father was not shy, I realized, when I'd watch him speaking Spanish with relatives. Using Spanish, he was quickly effusive.

Especially when talking with other men, his voice would spark, flicker, flare alive with sounds. In Spanish, he expressed ideas and feelings he rarely revealed in English. With firm Spanish sounds, he conveyed the confidence and authority English would never allow him.

The silence at home, however, was finally more than a literal silence. Fewer words passed between parent and child, but more profound was the silence that resulted from my inattention to sounds. At about the time I no longer bothered to listen with care to the sounds of English in public, I grew careless about listening to the sounds family members made when they spoke. Most of the time I heard someone speaking at home and didn't distinguish his sounds from the words people uttered in public. I didn't even pay much attention to my parents' accented and ungrammatical speech. At least not at home. Only when I was with them in public would I grow alert to their accents. Though, even then, their sounds caused me less and less concern. For I was increasingly confident of my own public identity.

I would have been happier about my public success had I not sometimes recalled what it had been like earlier, when my family had conveyed its intimacy through a set of conveniently private sounds. Sometimes in public, hearing a stranger, I'd hark back to my past. A Mexican farmworker approached me downtown to ask directions to somewhere. '¿Hijito...?' he said. And his voice summoned deep longing. Another time, standing beside my mother in the visiting room of a Carmelite convent, before the dense screen which rendered the nuns shadowy figures, I heard several Spanish-speaking nuns—their busy, singsong overlapping voices—assure us that yes, yes, we were remembered, all our family was remembered in their prayers. (Their voices echoed faraway family sounds.) Another day, a dark-faced old woman—her hand light on my shoulder—steadied herself against me as she boarded a bus. Her Spanish voice came near, like the face of a never-before-seen relative in the instant before I was kissed. Her voice, like so many of the Spanish voices I'd hear in public, recalled the golden age of my youth. Hearing Spanish then, I continued to be a careful, if sad, listener to sounds. Hearing a Spanish-speaking family walking behind me, I turned to look. I smiled for an instant, before my glance found the Hispanic-looking faces of strangers in the crowd going by.

Discussion Questions

1. An *aria* is a dramatic vocal solo, usually within an opera. Why is "Aria" an appropriate title for this essay?

2. What is Rodriguez's thesis? Is it explicitly stated or implied? Is it reinforced throughout the essay, or is it emphasized in only one or two places?

3. Which moments in the narrative reveal the most about Richard? The anecdote about him with the nuns at school? The exchanges with his mother and father?

   Explain.

4. Look at the places where Rodriguez uses quotations of the exact words spoken by various individuals. What is the effect of each of these passages?

3.3 **Professional Model**

My Mother Never Worked

by Bonnie Smith-Yackel

Meet the Writer

Bonnie Smith-Yackel is a writer and holistic health care worker living in St. Paul, Minnesota.

"Social Security Office." (The voice answering the telephone sounds very self-assured.)

"I'm calling about...I...my mother just died...I was told to call you and see about a...death-benefit check, I think they call it..."

"I see. Was your mother on Social Security? How old was she?"

"Yes...she was seventy-eight..."

"Do you know her number?"

"No...I, ah...don't you have a record?"

"Certainly. I'll look it up. Her name?"

"Smith. Martha Smith. Or maybe she used Martha Ruth Smith...
Sometimes she used her maiden name...Martha Jerabek Smith."

"If you'd care to hold on, I'll check our records—it'll be a few
minutes."

"Yes..."

Her love letters—to and from Daddy—were in an old box, tied
with ribbons and stiff, rigid-with-age leather thongs: 1918 through
1920; hers written on stationery from the general store she had
worked in full-time and managed, single-handed, after her graduation from high school in 1913; and his, at first, on YMCA or Soldiers
and Sailors Club stationery dispensed to the fighting men of World
War I. He wooed her thoroughly and persistently by mail, and though
she reciprocated all his feeling for her, she dreaded marriage...

"It's so hard for me to decide when to have my wedding day—
that's all I've thought about these last two days. I have told you dozens of times that I won't be afraid of married life, but when it comes
down to setting the date and then picturing myself a married woman
with half a dozen or more kids to look after, it just makes me sick...I
am weeping right now—I hope that some day I can look back and
say how foolish I was to dread it all."

They married in February, 1921, and began farming. Their first
baby, a daughter, was born in January, 1922, when my mother was
26 years old. The second baby, a son, was born in March, 1923. They
were renting farms; my father, besides working his own fields, also
was a hired man for two other farmers. They had no capital initially,
and had to gain it slowly, working from dawn until midnight every
day. My town-bred mother learned to set hens and raise chickens,
feed pigs, milk cows, plant and harvest a garden, and can every fruit
and vegetable she could scrounge. She carried water nearly a quarter of a mile from the well to fill her wash boilers in order to do her
laundry on a scrub board. She learned to shuck grain, feed threshers,
shock and husk corn, feed corn pickers. In September, 1925, the third
baby came, and in June, 1927, the fourth child—both daughters. In
1930, my parents had enough money to buy their own farm, and that
March they moved all their livestock and belongings themselves, 55
miles over rutted, muddy roads.

In the summer of 1930 my mother and her two eldest children
reclaimed a 40-acre field from Canadian thistles, by chopping them
all out with a hoe. In the other fields, when the oats and flax began

to head out, the green and blue of the crops were hidden by the bright yellow of wild mustard. My mother walked the fields day after day, pulling each mustard plant. She raised a new flock of baby chicks—500—and she spaded up, planted, hoed, and harvested a half-acre garden.

During the next spring their hogs caught cholera and died. No cash that fall.

And in the next year the drought hit. My mother and father trudged from the well to the chickens, the well to the calf pasture, the well to the barn, and from the well to the garden. The sun came out hot and bright, endlessly, day after day. The crops shriveled and died. They harvested half the corn, and ground the other half, stalks and all, and fed it to the cattle as fodder. With the price at four cents a bushel for the harvested crop, they couldn't afford to haul it into town. They burned it in the furnace for fuel that winter.

In 1934, in February, when the dust was still so thick in the Minnesota air that my parents couldn't always see from the house to the barn, their fifth child—a fourth daughter—was born. My father hunted rabbits daily, and my mother stewed them, fried them, canned them, and wished out loud that she could taste hamburger once more. In the fall the shotgun brought prairie chickens, ducks, pheasant, and grouse. My mother plucked each bird, carefully reserving the breast feathers for pillows.

In the winter she sewed night after night, endlessly, begging cast-off clothing from relatives, ripping apart coats, dresses, blouses, and trousers to remake them to fit her four daughters and son. Every morning and every evening she milked cows, fed pigs and calves, cared for chickens, picked eggs, cooked meals, washed dishes, scrubbed floors, and tended and loved her children. In the spring she planted a garden once more, dragging pails of water to nourish and sustain the vegetables for the family. In 1936 she lost a baby in her sixth month.

In 1937 her fifth daughter was born. She was 42 years old. In 1939 a second son, and in 1941 her eighth child—and third son.

But the war had come, and prosperity of a sort. The herd of cattle had grown to 30 head; she still milked morning and evening. Her garden was more than a half acre—the rains had come, and by now the Rural Electricity Administration and indoor plumbing. Still she sewed—dresses and jackets for the children, housedresses and aprons for herself, weekly patching of jeans, overalls, and denim shirts. She still made pillows, using the feathers she had plucked, and quilts every year—intricate patterns as well as patchwork, stitched as well as tied—all necessary bedding for her family. Every scrap of cloth too small to be used in quilts was carefully saved and painstakingly sewed together in strips to make rugs. She still went out in the fields to help with the haying whenever there was a threat of rain.

In 1959 my mother's last child graduated from high school. A year later the cows were sold. She still raised chickens and ducks, plucked feathers, made pillows, baked her own bread, and every year made a new quilt—now for a married child or for a grandchild. And her garden, that huge, undying symbol of sustenance, was as large and cared for as in all the years before. The canning, and now freezing, continued.

In 1969, on a June afternoon, mother and father started out for town so that she could buy sugar to make rhubarb jam for a daughter who lived in Texas. The car crashed into a ditch. She was paralyzed from the waist down.

In 1970 her husband, my father, died. My mother struggled to regain some competence and dignity and order in her life. At the rehabilitation institute, where they gave her physical therapy and trained her to live usefully in a wheelchair, the therapist told me: "She did fifteen pushups today—fifteen! She's almost seventy-five years old! I've never known a woman so strong!"

From her wheelchair she canned pickles, baked bread, ironed clothes, wrote dozens of letters weekly to her friends and her "half dozen or more kids," and made three patchwork housecoats and one quilt. She made balls and balls of carpet rags—enough for five rugs. And kept all her love letters.

"I think I've found your mother's records—Martha Ruth Smith; married to Ben F. Smith?

"Yes, that's right."

"Well, I see that she was getting a widow's pension..."

"Yes, that's right."

"Well, your mother isn't entitled to our $225 death benefit."

"Not entitled! But why?"

The voice on the telephone explained patiently:

"Well, you see—your mother never worked."

Discussion Questions

1. The story of Martha Smith's adult life is sandwiched between dialogue by the author and a Social Security employee. What are the advantages and disadvantages of this organizational strategy?

2. What is Smith-Yackel's thesis? Is it explicitly stated or implied? Is it reinforced throughout the essay, or is it emphasized in only one or two places?

3. Reread the quote from Martha's letter near the beginning of the essay. What effect does this paragraph have upon you as a reader?

4. What is Smith-Yackel's tone, her attitude toward the subject? What phrases, sentences, or sections convey this tone? What other tones might a writer use with this subject?

In the Shoes of a True Ethiopian

by Noah Begashaw

Meet the Writer

Noah Begashaw is a typical high school junior who enjoys sports such as soccer, basketball, tennis, and skateboarding, as well as music and other generically angsty activities. As a child of Ethiopian immigrants who came to the U.S. in the 1980s for political asylum and a better life, he also has many unique traits, such as perseverance and diligence in academics, an awareness of international affairs, and a rich cultural heritage and pride in his country of origin. Most of all, he has a desire to make his parents proud and to make them feel that coming to this land of opportunity was for good reason.

Bright lights shining in the midnight sky, happy folk walking the streets entering restaurants and other public places, even men with mules carrying grain going to the local market. I couldn't believe these were the sights I had been lamenting. That is what I saw after landing in Addis Ababa, Ethiopia, in the summer of 2007. Being twelve, there were many other things I'd rather have been doing that did not include going to some poor country in east Africa, or so I thought. Before the trip was planned, I was looking forward to hanging out outside with my friends the whole summer playing sports, riding bikes, skateboarding, and anticipating eighth grade; little did I know by accepting to go on this trip I was in for a life-changing experience.

We arranged to go to my Uncle Abebe's house after landing in Addis Ababa, which was going to be where we stayed for the two week duration of the trip. We arrived at my uncle's house at about 3 A.M., so my family and I unpacked and went to sleep. The next day I woke up to a beautiful ethnic breakfast and the smell of the fresh

Ethiopian air that entered the house through the open doors and windows. Then I encountered my uncle whom I hadn't seen since I was about two years old. He was a short old man with glasses, and he wore traditional Ethiopian clothes. I didn't really know him, but he gave me such a welcoming smile that I felt right at home.

Everything about his features were pleasant and caring, and then in the warmest voice he said, "In demen ale?"

My dad then said to me, "Respond to your uncle's greeting, Noah."

I then responded in Amharic, "Dena nehn." There are certain phrases in Amharic that every parent teaches their child, and this one happened to be one of them.

At breakfast we were joined by many kids whom I thought were my uncle's sons. But they turned out to be children who were formerly homeless that he cared for. I couldn't believe they were formerly homeless, because they were wearing all the hippest clothes from America and looked so well kempt. They wore the newest Adidas and Nike high top shoes; they also had skinny jeans and cool shirts to match. After breakfast the kids took me out sightseeing in the city. I couldn't speak Amharic as well as they could, so I tended to nod and shake my head so that I wouldn't embarrass myself. What they didn't know was that I could understand the language fully so I heard all the things they called me like American spoiled brat, and rich boy, but I tried to make it seem as if I didn't know. I didn't really want to cause a conflict, but rather I wanted to enjoy the sights. After seeing all the attractions like the local tea house, which was where all the cool kids hung out, and the arcade, we returned back home.

Over the next few days my family and I visited many culturally rich historic sites in Ethiopia. One site we saw was the Ancient Church of Lalibela. There I saw monks and priests with huge crosses and traditional garments chanting and praying. I felt as if time stood still in this holy area. My dad told me all the ancient stories that went along with the church, like there were thirteen of these churches connected underground all carved from the same boulder, and that the arc of the covenant was being guarded in one of those churches. I was awed by this ancient Ethiopian history that I never knew. The trip to the holy churches was a really cool experience.

Later that day we took a trip to the countryside of a little town called Gore where my great-grandfather's farm used to be. My dad told me that technically the estate was still our land but it was taken away by an oppressive military government in the 1980s. I was angry, it was our land! I told my dad I was going to take our property back, but he just laughed and patted me on the head. We met some of our distant relatives in the countryside. One kid I will always remember was a 10-year-old boy named Mekonen. He had delightfully curly hair and an innocent face that showed he had no care in the world. I later found out from my mother that behind his innocent face was a boy who was deprived of his mother and father at an early age, and was therefore orphaned. He invited me to play soccer with him and some of the neighborhood kids, so I did. We walked to an open dirt field where one of the kids had a dirty deflated soccer ball. Few of the kids had shoes, and their feet looked terribly beat up.

After a long game of soccer, in which I was the worst player, Mekonen and I sat down and talked. I practiced my Amharic while he practiced his English. My parents then called me over to let me know it was time to go, and then Mekonen said something I will never forget.

In the sweetest most sincere voice, he said, "I go America. I go America with you."

I realized that I could have been Mekkonen. If my parents had never moved to the U.S. I could have been in the same place he was. At that instant I lost all sense of taking things for granted, and appreciated everything I'd ever had. I stared at him for a little while, knowing I couldn't bring him back home. I then gave him a hug out of emotion, and gave him my shoes and socks. After realizing he only had one beat-up torn shirt I took the shirt off my back and handed the clothing to him.

Excitedly, Mekkonen threw on his new clothes faster than I could blink. He profusely thanked me, gave me one last hug and ran home in his new shoes. When I told my mom what I did, she started crying and hugging me; at the time I was a little confused.

But now I know they weren't tears of sorrow, but tears of pride and joy that I had, as she said, "*ante dembenia yagersew neh,*" which meant, "became a true Ethiopian."

Discussion Questions

1. What details help put you in Begashaw's shoes?

2. How does the use of foreign phrases such as *dena nehn* and *ante dembenia yagersew neh* affect your reading of this piece? How do they help Begashaw achieve his purpose?

3. Begashaw's essay describes a transformation in his attitude. Identify the points where his attitude shifts, however subtly.

4. What parts of Begashaw's experience are relevant to you personally and could serve as inspiration for your own narrative? Explain.

3.2 Student Model

My Slide
by Angela Zade

Meet the Writer

Angela Zade aspires to become the world's first paid day-dreamer. She enjoys reading, writing and dancing. Miss Zade also has a bossy sweet tooth.

Stomping my small, purple boots through the elegant gown of white snow, I yanked my plastic, red sled with every eager step. Once I spotted the highest hill in sight, I turned around to tell my younger sister where I was headed.

My sister, Dee, had little, first-grade legs and couldn't tread the thick ground to keep up. I squinted closely at her face from my distance. She looked like a cherry! Her cheeks were all flushed and her nose poked out like a tiny radish.

"Come on, Dee," I called to hurry her.

"You aw wunning too fast!" she shouted back.

I stood in my fluffy, purple snowpants and adjusted my fat hat. I was so anxious to go sledding that once I saw Dee safely skipping behind in her small, pink suit, I rushed off into the white horizon.

My heart twirled like a tornado as I pushed my path up the hill. As a child, I surely thought the slope was like a mountain in size. I became so excited that my heavy breathing let some high-pitch shrieks out. Some snowflakes landed on my brown eyelashes as I blinked at the short distance left until I was on top of the world. I forgot about waiting for Dee and I didn't care where she was because I was busy planning exaggerations to tell my girlfriends in my third-grade class.

Like a stumpy balloon of purple padding, I looked down at the treacherous slant. I positioned the red sled on the edge of heaven. I saddled up and gripped the two black plastic hand strips. I sat there for a few minutes just staring into the deadly field. There were no trees in my way to worry about. I couldn't find Dee anywhere in her pink snowsuit down on Earth. I didn't care; I was ready to go! My heart felt like it was popping out of my jacket with every beat, so on one quick breath, I jerked my icy rear end forward and started to slide!

At first I began whining my girlish pout. The winter air punched my face and clogged my lungs. My mouth hung open from shock. The speed of my sled had picked up so fast that I stopped pouting. My eyes teared up because the force of the wind tore at their sensitivity. I tried to inhale bits of winter freshness through my numb nostrils, but that was tough, too. I flexed all my mini arm muscles to remain steady on the sled and I held the black strips tightly.

Still sliding, I closed my eyes because the intensity was just too scary. I felt the planet flying away beneath me! I soared over the ground. I could hear the sound of my plastic sled skimming the snowy surface of the hill. Then I began hearing other people scream from around the distance.

"What are they yelling at?" I thought, "I must look so cool going so fast."

I opened my wet eyes to see the people praise my slide and… SMACK!

Lying on my back with my arms and legs sprawled out like a spider, I sat up. I knew I wasn't on my sled anymore because water was seeping in through the seams of my padding so I quickly shuffled my boots to the ground and stood. My body ached from the collision. I felt like one big bruise.

I noticed a red dot about ten feet over which I assumed was my sled. I sighed and put my mittens on my hips, scanning for the enemy that I had hit. I also noticed a pink bundle hunched over crying. I found Dee.

I pranced as fast as my purple, tree-stump legs would move. I plopped into the snowy cushion beside her and asked if she was okay.

"My butt huwts. You hit me hawd," she cried.

"Sorry," I mumbled.

"I wanna go home," Dee said when she got up. She was so little, barely reaching three feet but her face was certainly powerful. Still kneeling, I looked up at her angry expression.

Despite my craving to sled all day, I didn't bother opposing the little authoritarian. Instead I moseyed over to my sled, grabbed the pull string and began the sad trek home. This time I stomped behind Dee.

Discussion Questions

1. Notice how Zade uses dialogue. Is it effective? How does it help her achieve her purpose?

2. What is Zade's tone, her attitude toward the subject? Which phrases and sentences most effectively convey that tone?

3. Which details and descriptions show more than tell? List three examples. Next to each, write down what the detail shows.

4. Zade clearly follows Aristotle's advice to focus on one time and one place. As a reader, were you satisfied? Do you want or need more background or information about what happened later?

5. Good writing tends to evoke envy in writers: "I like the phrasing of that sentence. I wish I'd written that." What surprises does Zade present in her essay that might evoke this sort of response?

6. What do you believe is the thesis of this essay? Is the thesis explicitly or implicitly presented?

Her Time to Go

by Laura Flynn

Meet the Writer

Laura Flynn graduated as valedictorian of her class and plans to major in psychology at the University of Minnesota. Her interests include reading, writing, singing, and playing volleyball.

High-pitched giggles and laughter flood the warm, moist air as my cousins and I chase one another around the pool. Water slips beneath my toes, and I welcome the sting of chlorine on my face and in my eyes. I am caught up in the excitement of the moment, and let out squeals of delight. I lift my skinny legs to my chest, and cannon-ball back into the cool water.

C'mon Inn. It's quite a clever name for a hotel, actually. It is inviting, and makes one feel at home. Yet ironically, at this very place where all are welcome, I will learn that sooner or later, we all wear out our welcome. Sooner or later, it is time to go.

"Laura Ann, come here please," my mother shouts from across the hotel pool area. Fearing that I may be in trouble, I pretend not to hear. She shouts again, and I turn my head to look at her. She and my dad are seated in the bubbling hot tub across from my aunt and uncle. Their wet skin glistens in the light like the morning dew on grass. My mom's long, chestnut hair hangs down her back. She is about to yell again when she sees my leg curl over the edge of the pool. I hoist myself up and walk briskly past the rows of white, plastic tables and chairs holding scattered towels, tee shirts, and pool toys to see what she wants.

To my relief, I am only supposed to check on my younger sister. Slightly annoyed that I was torn away from the fun, I feel the urge to whine and protest, but decide to appease my parents instead. I make my way toward the poolside room as quickly as I can without running, all the while trying to pretend that I can't hear my cousins and siblings playing in the pool behind me. Their shrieks and laughter echo throughout the pool area, and amplify in my ears. The open space rings with excitement and liveliness.

As I enter the bedroom though, I feel something change. The air seems heavy and stale, leaving a bitter taste in my mouth. I peer over at my delicate sister lying on the deep green bedspread. Her head rests upon the fluffy pillows, and her long, chestnut hair hangs in a braid beside her porcelain face. She looks beautiful, yet somehow different. I lean in to look at her more closely. This is when I realize that she is not breathing.

I quickly spin around to yell for help, as my aunt is walking in. From this point on, I feel like I am on a disturbing ride at the fair. Everything is spinning. I can't focus. The white walls in the room are like the hope I can't find. I am being pushed from every direction. Rough hands shove me down the narrow hallway towards the bathroom to change out of my wet bathing suit.

As I step onto the smooth, white tile, hot tears well up in my eyes. I look at myself in the mirror, and think of how much I love my sister. I can't imagine losing her. I tug at my wet bathing suit, and eye the tiny bathroom. Neat stacks of white bath towels, hand towels, and washcloths rest on a rack above the gleaming, white toilet. The tidy cleanliness of it all contradicts what is going on. My world feels as though it is falling apart, yet everything is in its proper place. Even the little bottles of shampoo and lotion sit in orderly rows by the sink. The bright light is a bully on the playground staring down at me. I feel small and insignificant. Suddenly I am angry at this bathroom. I am furious at it for mocking how I feel, for laughing at my adversity.

I yank on my clothes, and open the dark, wood door. Immediately I am thrown back into reality. No longer is everything white and clean. Hope evaporates as I watch my parents rush around the room. My father scoops my limp sister off the bed, and rushes her out the door. My mom follows closely behind.

All of this is too much to take in. I sit down on the bed opposite the one my sister was just lying on. It feels stiff and unforgiving. I look down at the hunter green bedspread that stretches over it awkwardly. It is adorned with beautiful, bright flowers that seem much too cheerful to be appropriate. I run my small hand over the wrinkles that form beside my leg as if trying to smooth away my fears.

The faint smell of chlorine and damp clothes lingers in the air. I push my fingers through my stringy, wet hair as I sit and wait anxiously. My aunt speaks in a low, soothing voice to my brother and sister, offering reassuring words. An undertone of uncertainty creeps into her speech. I listen as she fights to suppress it, but only ends up sounding overly optimistic. Her words are forced, fake. She is filling them with false hope. Even as an eight-year-old, I can detect that.

My thoughts are interrupted by the shrill sound of the hotel phone ringing. It is an obnoxious siren screaming in my ear. I watch as my aunt slowly reaches for the white receiver. She puts it to her ear and smiles. That smile quickly vanishes, though, and is replaced with a look of sheer horror.

My heart drops, and my worst fear is realized.

My sister is dead. My ears begin to ring, and I am hurried out of the room. I cannot believe that this is really happening. My aunt grabs my hand, and leads me through the busy pool area. I watch my brother's and sister's long legs stride in front of me. They push through the heavy glass door, and I follow closely behind. The bitter cold bites at my face as I step outside. The wind whistles through the night air, and blows the snow across the black parking lot. I look up, searching for answers, but see only the stark contrast of the glowing C'mon Inn sign against the midnight sky.

Discussion Questions

1. Now that you know the outcome of the essay, reread the second paragraph. What did the paragraph mean to you on the first reading? What does it mean to you now?

2. Flynn shows the torment she feels by describing the order she sees in the world. Identify three examples of this order.

3. Identify three sensory details Flynn uses to help the reader understand her pain. Explain the effect of each example.

Backwards Tumble

by Michele Nimetz

Meet the Writer

Michelle Nimetz is a senior in high school and a young athlete. She is the middle child in a family of six, striving to keep up with the antics of her older sister. She intends to major in psychology in college.

When I entered freshman year, I was nervous to meet new people. I joined the radio club, the gymnastics team and Students Against Drunk Driving because my older sister was in all three, and I knew she would help me out. I was shy in radio and SADD, but we had done gymnastics for years, so that was the place I came alive. One of my friends joined as well, so we always had fun. The team was combined of two schools: Plainview-Old Bethpage High School and Bethpage High School, so we knew we didn't have to worry about competing, because there were many girls much better we were. Although I have been involved in gymnastics for so long, I had never competed before.

The first meet of the season my coach came up to me and said, "There is one spot left on the balance beam and I want you to take that place." With a smile I said I would do it, but on the inside I was filled with nerves. I felt my nerves driving inside of me. Like a rollercoaster. Riding through my body, speeding, sometimes making loops, putting knots inside my stomach. Once they reached my heart, I realized that was all I had to give. All or nothing. Beam is the last event to be judged, so for the first three events I was tense watching my teammates, as well as anxious to get it over with.

Finally it was my turn. All the girls competing get a five minute warm-up before going, and I remember taking that time to complain to my sister, Lauren. "Is there any way to get anyone else to go for me? I don't think I can do it!" I said to Lauren in a panic. I glimpsed at the beam, waiting for the judge to call me. "Please, Lauren! You do it!" I said, feeling like I was about to cry. That's when Lauren told me, "Coach Rut believes in you, and so do I, which is why you have to go. Prove it to yourself and the judge that you believe in yourself and your capabilities too."

The five minutes seemed to pass in what felt like seconds, and it was my turn. The judge called my name and saluted, and I stood next to the beam and saluted back with a nervous smile. Shaking, I jumped on the beam and swung one leg around, twisting to a seated position, smiling at the judge. *It is time, lift one hand and then the other and pose, you'll be fine.* Laughter. I looked at the team, and at Coach Rut who was now walking towards me. I was currently on my back...on the floor. I sat up; I could not believe I had fallen off the beam doing nothing but sitting. I had sat on the beam about a thousand times. "You will be fine, get up and go. You got this," Coach Rut said as she helped me up and walked away again. I looked at my sister who mouthed, "Prove it," and I got back up. As I went on to do my full turn, jump series, cartwheel and other requirements, I started to feel better. Landing my dismount and saluting to the judge, I almost forgot about my fall earlier. The team, on the other hand, would not let me forget, and for the rest of the year they called out whenever I was on the beam, "Stick it on your butt."

Although I was upset when it happened, I look back to it now, four years later, and laugh. A whole-hearted and genuine laugh. I was going way too fast and my nerves were chasing me, causing my head to spin (if only my body could do that while on the beam, to impress the judge!).

I am glad my mom caught the whole thing on tape because whenever I doubt myself, or need a good laugh, I re-watch it to see what I can accomplish if I set my mind to it, even if it doesn't work out in the beginning.

Four years since that event, our team has split from Bethpage, and I am captain. I compete in every meet, two events, and while I still get nervous I handle it a lot better. Before every meet I give a pep talk to the girls to get them motivated, and at the start of every season my coach and I tell the story, to let the girls know it is okay to fail, as long as you get up and try again. The varsity gymnastics team is undefeated this year, as it has been for the past three years on our own.

Discussion Questions

1. How does Nimetz create suspense in her narrative? Offer specific examples.

2. List one example of figurative language used in the essay. What is the effect achieved by this figurative language?

3. Comment on the dialogue used in this essay. What is the purpose of the dialogue? What does the dialogue add to the essay?

Example

Your friend turns to you and announces, "I've worked at the same job for more than two years, but I'm going to quit because my boss is a jerk." What do you expect to hear next, aside from a little bellyaching and whining? Plenty of examples, right? "One time my boss did this; another time my boss did that." Without examples, your friend's pronouncement rings hollow and leaves you wondering: *Has my pal been slacking off at work lately? Is this just one of those rebellion deals? Does he resent all authority figures? Does he just want to borrow a few dollars?*

If, on the other hand, your friend tells you about the time he was five minutes late and his boss docked him half a day's pay, or about the time the boss offered popsicles to everyone *except* your friend, then you listen, then you understand his point of view. You may not end up agreeing with him, but at least you've walked in his shoes for a while.

You've probably written scores of papers in which you used examples to support your main point. In fact, you've been trained your entire life to offer examples. You may recall conversations that went something like this:

> CHILD: I hate school.
> PARENT: You hate school? Why?
> CHILD: Because I do.
> PARENT: That's not a reason, honey.
> CHILD: Yes it is. I hate it.
> PARENT: OK, give me one reason.
> CHILD: School is stupid.
> PARENT: Oh, so school's stupid now. Why is school stupid?
> CHILD: Because I hate it.

Your parents gave up after five minutes and immediately found a babysitter for you. But next time they persevered and demanded specific reasons for your unrest. They, along with teachers, friends, and just about everyone else with whom you spoke, trained you to supply examples. They wanted to know more. They wanted to understand.

Even the most ordinary exchanges often require examples. Let's say you want a friend to join you at a party this weekend. The friend is reluctant, so you claim that this guy has the greatest parties. You can prod and insist and repeat your plea, but if you don't provide specific examples about some of these great parties—the streamers, the balloons, and, get this, the karaoke machine—your friend will probably be content to sit home and watch reruns of *Saved by the Bell*. (A note on *tone*, or the writer's attitude toward his subject: the reference to balloons and streamers is meant to be ridiculous. If you thought this was a serious example, you missed the light tone.)

The purpose of this chapter is to remind you of the power of supplying examples and to show you how to incorporate effective examples into your paper to support your thesis. One of the biggest problems with most student writing is the lack of development, which means that the writer hasn't provided enough support to make a convincing argument. It's as if the writer has constructed a three-story building, but the stairs are so rickety, no one is willing to climb them. Using examples is one important way to build the necessary support, to reinforce those stairs.

Journal Topic

Write about one of the following statements for five minutes, providing as many examples as you can think of:

1. Everyone is creative.
2. Everyone is intelligent.
3. Everyone is [provide your own adjective].

Writing with Purpose

In Chapter 2, your writing purpose was to describe a person, place, or thing, a task that required close and careful observation. In Chapter 3, you discovered meaning in some of the stories in your life. In both cases, you shaped your observations and memories into a cohesive whole for your reader. Much of the material for those essays was already located

Example   129

just outside your window or in the storehouse of your brain; you had more than enough subject matter to write about. And in the process of describing or narrating, you discovered meaning. The formation of a thesis probably occurred relatively late in this process.

This time your task is a bit different. Description and narration will still serve as essential tools, but they will become secondary to your main goal, which is to state a thesis and develop that thesis using several solid examples. To accomplish this, you'll need to decide on a thesis fairly early in the process. You will still make discoveries, revising your thesis along the way, but changes to your thesis will be relatively subtle.

How will you generate a thesis? First, keep in mind that a good thesis is an opinion and not simply a statement of fact. It's not enough to write about all the clubs your school has to offer. You must adopt a position and make some point about these clubs, about their worth perhaps. Second, avoid thesis statements that are merely a reflection of your tastes. You can argue that chess club is more beneficial to one's future than ping-pong club, but it would be useless to argue that one activity is more satisfying to you than another.

Perhaps the easiest way to decide on a thesis is to create a list of opinion statements—about human nature, school, work, culture, and so on. Some of the items can be nonpersonal:

> Parents nowadays are too lenient with their young children.
> Children learn how to respect others by watching their parents.
> Parents who try too hard to be friends with their teens invite rebellion.
> Sometimes teens need to rebel against their parents.

Some can be personal:

> My parents treat me like a child.
> My parents say they trust me but they don't act that way.
> My parents wisely treat each of their children differently.
> My father understands my needs better than my mother does.

Notice that all of these statements beg for examples. Not one is a statement of fact, such as "My parents have been married for fifteen years," and none appeals to personal tastes, as in "I like my mom more than my dad."

You might want to pore through a newspaper or magazine to help you select a thesis, searching for stories that hold interest for you. You may find, for example, a column about people helping in the aftermath of a major hurricane. The column causes you to wonder why people are willing to help strangers, and you begin to formulate a thesis about human nature. In this case, you have discovered one of your examples before deciding on a thesis statement. Comedians like Jerry Seinfeld and Jon Stewart are masters of this technique. They share a recent news item, draw a conclusion, and then spend fifteen minutes supporting that conclusion—that thesis—with numerous other examples. The examples may be outlandish, but they achieve their purpose.

One final suggestion, which may prove to be more fruitful in the long term, is to take note of your immediate world. Notice the way students communicate without words in class, or the way drivers become automatons behind the wheel. Notice how adults in department stores treat teenagers, and how teenagers react to this treatment. Detach yourself for a while. Consider yourself an anthropologist or psychologist. Search for patterns and angles that no one has ever considered. This is a habit that will serve you well as a writer.

Writing Tip

If you often find yourself staring at a blank page because of writer's block, you might also keep telling yourself, "I need to be inspired to write." Nonsense. While inspiration plays its part, discipline is much more important. If at all possible, develop a routine. Sit down to write in the same place at the same time every day. From this routine will spring inspiration because after a while, as you go about the rest of your day, you will pay closer attention to your surroundings, seeking ideas for the next day's writing session.

Determining How Many Examples

Each essay you write creates a unique burden of proof. Sometimes three examples are enough, and sometimes thirty are needed. In general, follow this common sense guideline: use precisely enough examples to make your point. Yes, trust your instincts, but also check with several friendly readers for a more objective assessment. This will be a fairly simple task for them. Ask them to mark various sections of your paper with one of three notations: (+++) too many examples; (---) not enough examples; or (OK) just right. You can devise your own system of notations, of course. Your readers' responses won't always be consistent, but when a pattern emerges—say, if all of them mark "underdeveloped" in the same spot—this can be most helpful.

Writers on Writing

Clutter is the disease of American writing. We are a society strangling in unnecessary words, circular constructions, pompous frills and meaningless jargon.

—*William Zinsser*

Example   **131**

How can you have too many examples? Don't play the numbers game, padding your papers with fluff just to reach a certain minimum length. When you do that, examples dominate the paper and overshadow the thesis. Usually, the examples are similar in nature, and they block any chance for an original thought to surface. Under the pressure of a deadline, we've all felt this temptation to pad. Do your utmost to avoid this temptation—in other words, don't wait until midnight to write your papers. Perhaps you've been rewarded in the past with a good grade for all your "hard work"—for the sheer bulk of pages you've handed in. Keep in mind, however, that your ideas are primary, and examples are not just filler; examples provide the specifics to support your ideas.

This focus on the number of examples may strike you as artificial. If a teacher asks you to write a three-page essay using examples to support your thesis, you probably think, *Well, I'm going to throw in as many examples as I can.* Length, however, should have less sway on your decision than subject matter. In such a short essay, two or three well-developed examples can suffice, each example adding something slightly different from the previous one, one example building on another. As a general rule, a few well-developed examples are more effective than many insufficiently developed ones. An insufficiently developed example offers few details and adds little to the writer's overall purpose. If you're writing about the broad issue of poverty, for instance, and you want to show the extent of the problem, offering statistics about a single geographical area would be insufficient. Instead, perhaps in the opening paragraph, you can offer several brief examples to show how poverty grips populations in many diverse areas.

Using Different Types of Examples

Say you decide to write a paper on how beliefs influence behavior. You notice the way people staunchly defend their beliefs, even in the face of contrary evidence. Rarely does someone say, "You know what? I was wrong." After a while, an idea for a thesis begins to dawn on you: People wage war over their stubbornly held beliefs. After further deliberation you devise a thought-provoking thesis: people often fight just to preserve and protect their beliefs, just to be right.

Imagine writing an entire essay on this topic without using a single example. The thesis, though intriguing, will remain a generality, a thing to be politely admired, generic. But assign

Writers on Writing

There may be some writers who contemplate a day's work without dread, but I don't know them. Beckett had, tacked to the wall beside his desk, a card on which were written the words: 'Fail. Fail again. Fail better.

—*Mary Gordon*

this thesis to a hundred students, each intent on supplying specific examples, and each will carve a different path.

Some will support the thesis with **personal examples**, in which they share something from their own lives:

> My mother and I fight constantly over my curfew. She knows she can trust me, but she believes that teens today are too wild. If she allows me to stay out late, she feels she's letting me out into that wildness, which causes her great stress. Instead of admitting that not all teens are wild, she'd rather blindly believe what she has always believed. In fact, she seems to find comfort in her stubbornness, which is ironic. I would think, since her daughter is a teen, she'd find more comfort in believing that not all teens are wild.

Others may offer a **hypothetical example**, in which they imagine a situation that illustrates their point:

> Consider grief. Imagine a man setting a place at the table for his dead wife, months after she has passed away. He knows she is dead, but he can't let go entirely, not yet. An irrational part of him believes she will return. When his children confront him, he argues, not to convince them, but to preserve that small, wishful belief tucked in his heart.

Others may include statistical and other **factual examples**, providing hard evidence to support their thesis:

> Nearly 3,000 innocent people died on September 11, 2001, because a group of men obsessed for years over their belief that the United States was their enemy. They drove planes into buildings, killing everyone aboard, including themselves, to preserve their belief. Rather than entertain the notion that maybe they were wrong, they chose suicide.

You can use these various types of examples in combination, of course, depending on your purpose, one example reinforcing another. Regardless of the types of examples you use, be certain that each one clearly and directly supports your thesis. It's tempting to use examples that are only vaguely related, but your ideas deserve strong examples.

One other important consideration: are your examples fair and representative? If you make the claim that students at your school are helpful and generous, use a broad brush. Don't show only seniors acting generously, or your argument will seem to lack authenticity. If you can't think of enough examples to cover your thesis, you may need to modify the thesis.

Example   **133**

Journal Topic

Fill in one of these blanks:

1. School is _____.

2. Work is _____.

3. My family is _____.

Think of several examples to support your answer. Rather than merely listing the examples, use sentences to describe them.

Organizing Examples

If you have a bias against outlines, put that bias aside for the moment. If you think creating an outline is useless busywork involving precise indentation and proper subheadings, it's time to challenge that belief. There may be instances when a detailed outline is necessary, as with a long research project, but in general, outlines don't have to be formal. And they can be extremely helpful, even *after* you've written a first draft, providing a wider view of your paper that you may have overlooked.

Let's say you're writing about what it's like to be the youngest child in the family, arguing that last-borns must endure greater hardships than older siblings. After writing a quick first draft, you're satisfied with your examples, but the paper as a whole doesn't seem unified. You decide to map out what you've written:

Opening example to create interest, to show unfairness

Thesis: Last-borns endure greater hardships than older sibs

Strict curfew

Hand-me-downs

Fewer photos of me

Everyone still thinks of me as "the baby"

Always have to call home to say where I am

More chores but less independence

Even a bare outline such as this one allows you to view your ideas in a different light. Perhaps some ideas can be grouped together or rearranged. For instance, it might make sense to discuss *curfew* and *independence* back to back. The outline may also cause you to consider the order in which you present your ideas. Should you begin with relatively minor issues such as the lightweight photo albums and build up to more critical concerns, or do the opposite? Should you begin with amusing ideas and gradually turn more serious? Should you follow a chronological approach to show how the problem has grown worse with the passing of years? What pattern can you impose upon your ideas? Without a pattern, your essay runs the risk of seeming like a list of examples rather than a cogent, dynamic argument.

Along with aiding you in finding a pattern, an outline can also help you refine your thesis. Perhaps you notice in the preceding list that your ideas fall more or less into two broad categories: (1) last-born children are not as spoiled and fussed over as first-borns; (2) parents are over-protective of last-borns. You originally intended to argue that last-borns have to endure hardships. This refined insight doesn't contradict that thesis, but it does add a layer of specificity that might help to unify your essay. In fact, the idea that last-borns get both too little and too much attention from their parents is an interesting paradox that might help to communicate the frustration of being the youngest. Yet you probably wouldn't have reached this conclusion without an outline.

Using Transitions

A clear thesis supported by specific examples, arranged in some log-ical order, may bring your reader to the table, eager to feast. However, without one other key element, the use of smooth transitions, your reader will remain dissatisfied.

Simply put, **transitions** link one sentence or paragraph to another. They guide and clarify, nudging the reader to the next idea. In some cases, transitions are announced with key words or phrases such as *consequently*, *on the other hand*, and *therefore*. We'll call these "obvi-ous" transitions. In other cases, transitions are subtle: "Throughout his career George Washington faced all his duties with utmost seriousness. *As an infantryman* he toiled night and day...." Notice how the second sentence builds on the expectation created in the first sentence.

We could simply paste here a list of obvious transitions, a list you've seen before. In fact, teachers can easily spot the use of such a handy list in student essays. The essays are littered with transitions such as *never-theless*, *subsequently*, *moreover*, and many others, but their use is more or less random. Purposeful transitions, on the other hand, link sentences by clarifying the relationship between one sentence and another. In other words, the links should make sense. The following guide will help you use transitions more precisely.

Example   135

Types of Transitions

You're probably already aware of the value of using different types of transitions, or at least you should be. This awareness, this conscious selection of using this transition and not that one, helps you clarify your thinking, not only for the reader but also for yourself. It forces you to ask yourself, *Is this what I really mean?*

You probably also use the more subtle types of transitions but are less conscious of this. Subtle transitions serve the same function: to clarify thinking and to help one sentence build on the previous one. Maxine Hairston, in her classic text *A Contemporary Rhetoric*, explains how to accomplish this: "Each sentence or paragraph...should leave a little residue, a little trace, out of which the next sentence or paragraph develops. It can be an expectation, a hint, a repeated word, or a pattern, but there should be something." To better understand what she means, take note of the key words and phrases used to link the sentences in this paragraph from Malcolm Gladwell's fascinating book *Blink*:

> On West Harrison Street in Chicago, two miles west of the city's downtown, there is an ornate, block-long building designed and built in the early part of the last century. For the better part of one hundred years, this was the home of Cook County Hospital. It was here that the world's first blood bank opened, where cobalt-beam therapy was pioneered, where surgeons once reattached four severed fingers and where the trauma center was so famous—and so busy treating the gunshot wounds and injuries of the surrounding gangs—that it inspired the television series *ER*.

The paragraph doesn't include obvious transitions, but the sentences are united by many subtle transitions. "For the better part of one hundred years" echoes back to "century." "This," also from sentence two, refers back to "building." The parallel repetition of "where" creates rhythm and connects to "It was here." Readers don't need to study the paragraph to make these connections; they do so nearly effortlessly—provided that the writer has made the effort to craft these connections.

To become more proficient at providing such links in your writing, study other writers. Observe how they maneuver from one sentence to the next. Underline key words and passages. Do this until tedium sets in; then go see a movie and watch how good directors glue one scene to another in much the same way.

As discussed throughout this chapter, examples act as the key building blocks of paragraphs. Examples clarify and help develop your thesis. As you finish a draft, ask yourself these questions: *Have I been specific enough? Do I need more examples to make my point? Would fewer examples be better?*

Table Transitions

Purpose of Transition	Words Used	Example
Links similar ideas	*likewise, similarly, also, in addition to, just as*	A child feels threatened when a younger sibling is born and is lavished with attention. *Likewise,* employees feel threatened by rewards bestowed upon newer workers.
Links opposing ideas	*but, yet, although, in spite of, nevertheless, on the other hand*	The students were scolded. *Nevertheless,* they continued to cause problems.
Shows a shift in direction	*either, or*	We can continue to throw money at the problem, *or* we can try a different solution.
Builds on the previous point	*in addition, for instance, moreover*	Some so-called "advanced" classes emphasize rote memorization; *moreover,* they discourage critical thinking skills.
Shows consequences	*therefore, thus, so, as a result, consequently*	Child labor laws are not strictly enforced; *as a result,* young teens work longer hours and lose critical sleep.
Shows cause and effect	*for, because, since*	*Because* the directions were not clearly explained, many students failed the assignment.
Shows sequence or order of importance	*first, second, next, finally, the*	Write a quick first draft. *Next,* read the draft aloud.

Example   137

Achieving Gender Balance in Pronoun Use

Just before touching down on the moon, astronaut Neil Armstrong paused, seemed to catch his breath, and proclaimed, "That's one small step for man, one giant leap for mankind." Armstrong's use of "man" still resonates because it echoes "mankind." But had Armstrong taken his small step today, he may have had second thoughts.

One of the most common dilemmas in writing has to do with the gender-specific pronouns *he* and *she*, as well as their possessive forms, *his* and *hers*. There are many times when we do not wish to specify a person's gender, but without a gender-neutral pronoun available in English, we can find no elegant way to do this.

For instance, imagine that someone knocks on your door and leaves a package behind? Not knowing whether the package-deliverer was male or female, what do you say? Many writers resort to the plural: "Someone knocked on my door, but *they* took off before I answered. And look—*they* left a package." However, this is not a great solution. Because *someone* is singular, and *they* is plural, the words do not agree in number, and that's a grammatical error.

"*He or she* left a package." Technically and grammatically, this is acceptable, but stylistically it feels awkwardly self-conscious, especially if *he or she* is used repeatedly. The best advice is to simply avoid those kinds of sentence construc-

tions by leaving out the pronouns altogether: "I found a package left behind."

Another example arises when discussing hypothetical situations where the person involved can be either male or female: "When describing your college plans to a guidance counselor, your responsibility is to make sure _____ understands you."

Because a guidance counselor can be either male or female, how do you fill in this blank? You can use *he or she,* as well as *she or he,* although both of those choices seem too wordy. Another possibility is to recast the sentence: "When describing your college plans to a guidance counselor, your responsibility is to make sure you are understood."

A commonly accepted approach to this dilemma is the one used in this book. Simply balance the gender references between male and female in the course of your writing. For example, it's perfectly fine to write this sentence: "When describing your college plans to a guidance counselor, your responsibility is to make sure she understands you." It's just as fine to write this sentence: "When describing your college plans to a guidance counselor, your responsibility is to make sure he understands you."

However, the next time the same issue arises, and when it doesn't compromise clarity, use the other gender to achieve balance. For example, later in the same piece, you may write this sentence: "When a college admissions officer meets with you during a campus visit, _____ will answer all of your questions about the school."

Since the college admissions officer is clearly not the same individual as the guidance counselor discussed previously, this is a good opportunity to balance the gender references. If you used *she* the first time, use *he* this time. It's probably wise, however, not to switch pronouns too often or you will draw undue attention; if you begin a paragraph with a particular gender pronoun, stick with that pronoun until the end of the paragraph or section. This approach is grammatically correct, stylistically satisfying, and demographically enlightened.

Practice

Before beginning the Chapter Assignment, try the following exercises to practice supporting your thesis with examples.

1. You need a job. To prepare for the interview, you need to think of several personal examples that demonstrate your responsibility and your work ethic. Write down two such examples.

2. You want to visit a college for the weekend. Write a hypothetical example to convince your parents to let you go.

3. You believe your teachers assign too much busywork. Write several factual examples to support this view.

4. Rewrite the following sentences, inserting transitions to better unify the paragraph. Right now, the sentences will seem stiff and odd because they are nearly devoid of transitions. You may need to combine some sentences.

> Parents need to be consistent with their discipline. Their children will receive mixed messages. Their children will never learn to behave. If a child gets punished one day for throwing toys and rewarded the next, the child never learns right from wrong. The parent has created a gambler. Teachers need to send consistent messages. Students will never know when to settle down. Someone walking into such a classroom might assume the students are unruly. The teacher created the disorder.

5. Find a paragraph that you think represents good writing. Underline the key transitional words and phrases that unite the paragraph.

Example   **139**

Chapter Assignment

Prewriting

Your assignment in this chapter is to write an example essay. Try using the following process to help you come up with examples to use in your essay.

Once you select a topic, write that topic at the top of a sheet of paper, and beneath it create three columns with these headings: (1) personal examples; (2) hypothetical examples; and (3) factual examples. Spend about ten minutes filling in as much of this chart as possible. If one column is more complete than another, that's fine.

Writing Topics

Select one of the following suggested topics to develop into an essay. Feel free to tailor these topics to suit your needs.

1. Think about the people who have had a great influence on you. *Why* were these people so inspiring? Write an essay in which you answer this question, using personal examples as support.

2. Write an essay supporting or denouncing the amount of homework assigned by your teachers. Develop your essay with examples.

3. Write an essay on apathy in your school or community, providing numerous factual examples. Or refute this stance and write about the high level of student involvement in your school or community.

4. Write an essay in which you assert that your school offers activities that will satisfy nearly any interest. Or write an essay on activities you think your school *should* offer. Develop your essay with examples. Your school newspaper might be interested in publishing your final draft.

5. Write about technology. You might focus on devices that are designed to save time but rarely do. Or you could focus on devices that are sleek but not functional, or vice versa. Notice how both of these ideas call for the use of many examples to support your argument.

6. Write about relationships: friendships, rivalries, romantic love, or breakups. State a thesis and support it with plenty of examples.

7. Write an essay in which you highlight some aspect of human nature by offering examples from history.

8. Create your own idea.

Revision

As you revise and edit your first draft, consider the following questions.

1. Is your thesis clear? Does every example support your thesis?

2. Are your examples presented in a logical order? Can you use a more effective pattern?

3. Think of a few more examples to support your thesis. You may feel that you've already done this before writing the paper, but keep an open mind and see what you discover. Are any of these new examples better than any that appear in your draft?

4. Did you make use of both obvious and more subtle transitions to unify sentences and paragraphs? Can you do more with this?

5. What questions would you ask a peer reviewer?

Peer Review

Use these questions to help you evaluate another student's writing. Remember, specific suggestions and examples are most helpful.

1. What did you like best about this essay?

2. The writer develops this essay using examples. Which examples are most effective?

3. Are any examples unclear? Could any be more effective? Explain.

4. List one or two instances of effective transitions. Are any transitions awkward or ineffective? Explain.

5. Are the examples presented in a logical order? Present an idea for a different order.

6. What questions do you have for the writer?

Example   141

So Much to Hate, and So Little Time

by Mike Royko

Meet the Writer

Longtime Chicago newspaper columnist Mike Royko was best known for his irreverence toward politicians, his deadpan humor, and his support for the underdog. His columns were syndicated nationwide in more than 600 newspapers. For more than 30 years, readers on buses and train platforms, in kitchens and around water coolers, enjoyed a dose of Royko's simultaneously serious and madcap point of view. This column was written in 1990 as the U.S. prepared to fight its first war against Iraq, known as Operation Desert Storm or the Gulf War.

Although the shooting hasn't begun yet, I've been trying to work up a healthy hatred for Iraq. It seems like the patriotic thing to do. And I've always believed that if people go through the bother of killing each other, they shouldn't be impersonal about it. After all, it is a very intimate act.

Although I haven't reached the point of gnashing my teeth at the thought of an Iraqi, I'm sure it will come, because I've had so much experience at this sort of thing.

The first time I developed a patriotic hatred was in 1939, when newsboys came through the neighborhood at night, waving special editions and shouting: "Extra, extra, Germany invades Poland!"

Although I was just a kid, within a couple of years I dutifully hated Germans, Japanese, and Italians. (I didn't hate Italians very long, though, because they surrendered as soon as it was convenient.)

At the same time, I loved and admired the brave Russians and Chinese because they had joined us in hating the evil Germans, Japanese, and Italians.

But as soon as World War II ended, and I could stop hating the evil Germans and Japanese because they weren't evil anymore, I had to start hating the brave Russians and Chinese, because they weren't brave anymore, but had become evil.

While I was adjusting to that, along came the North Koreans. Even though I didn't know a North Korean from a South Korean, or any Korean from a chipmunk, I went along and hated them. The North Koreans.

Not long after that, I discovered that I could still hate some Germans. Not West Germans, because they had become good and even gave us some of their ex-Nazi scientists to help us build rockets. But East Germans had become evil commies and were to be hated.

However, this created some confusion, since Poland, Czechoslovakia, Yugoslavia, and other countries had become commie, too, so I felt a responsibility to hate them. But I was told that they didn't really want to be commies: The Russians made them do it. So I didn't have to hate them as much as I hated the Russians and Chinese.

Then came Cuba. I had never paid much attention to Cuba because I didn't smoke cigars. But when a heroic Fidel Castro overthrew an evil, corrupt regime, I was urged to admire the heroic Castro, which I did, although he looked like he needed a bath. Then, almost overnight, Castro became an evil commie and I had to start hating Cuba. My hatred reached the boiling point when we had the Cuban Missile Crisis. But in recent years, it's been reduced to a simmer.

Naturally, I joined in really hating North Vietnam. And some Cambodians, although I'm still not certain which Cambodians I was supposed to hate. It's possible that in the confusion I was hating Cambodians that I should have been liking, in which case I apologize.

The 1960s may have been one of my hate-peaks, second only to the 1940s. I found myself hating the Russians, Chinese, North Vietnam, and Cuba, while still nursing an intense dislike for North Korea and not thinking highly of Albania. There were a few other countries that I occasionally cursed, but their names slip my mind.

Shortly thereafter, though, President Nixon said I didn't have to hate the Chinese anymore, although I wasn't expected to hug them. And I haven't hated them since, except for that recent month or two when I could again hate them because of the way they kicked around

Example   143

their students. But that seems to have calmed down and President Bush says it's OK not to hate them, so I don't.

In fact, I don't have to hate the Russians, or hardly anyone in Europe, because we've become pals and they're all eager to eat Quarter Pounders with Cheese like decent folk do.

And it couldn't have happened at a better time, because of the need to hate Iraq. I can be vicious, but I have only so much hatred to spread around.

Actually, it isn't that hard to hate Iraq. It's simply a matter of shifting my hatred a few miles. Until recently, I hated Iran and kind of liked Iraq because it was fighting with Iran. But now that it's time to hate Iraq, it's not necessary to hate Iran. Unless Iran cuts a friendly deal with Iraq, in which case I'll have to hate it again. Iran, I mean.

Fortunately, there is less pressure to hate some of the other Arab nations, which I formerly hated because they went in for terrorism. But now they say they hate Iraq, too, which means that I can like them. At least for the time being. Things can change quickly, and I might have to start hating them once more, so I'm not going to like them a lot just in case.

I wonder if there will come a time when there isn't anyone I have to hate. Nah. Not as long as there are New York Mets.

Discussion Questions

1. Mike Royko was beloved by his readers for his clever use of irony and sarcasm. While Royko seemingly promotes hate in this essay, how do you know his tone is not serious—that he in fact means the opposite?

2. What is Royko's thesis? How does he support this thesis?

3. Most of the paragraphs in this essay are relatively short. What effect does this have on readers? Take note of several places where paragraphs might be combined. What effect is achieved through this combining?

4. This essay was written in 1990. In what ways does it seem both dated and current?

5. Why does Royko end his article by bringing up a different type of hatred? How is this hatred different from the other examples he gives in the piece?

Involuntary Conversions, Preemptive Counterattacks, and Incomplete Successes: The World of Doublespeak

by William Lutz

Meet the Writer

Author William Lutz is an expert on clear and concise language. For 14 years he was the editor of the *Quarterly Review of Doublespeak*, and he is the author or co-author of seventeen books, including *Doublespeak Defined* and *The New Doublespeak: Why No One Knows What Anyone's Saying Anymore*. Lutz is Professor of English at Rutgers University in Camden, New Jersey.

There are no potholes in the streets of Tucson, Arizona, just "pavement deficiencies." The Reagan Administration didn't propose any new taxes, just "revenue enhancement" through new "user's fees." Those aren't bums on the street, just "nongoal oriented members of society." There are no more poor people, just "fiscal underachievers." There was no robbery of an automatic teller machine, just an "unauthorized withdrawal." The patient didn't die because of medical malpractice, it was just a "diagnostic misadventure of a high magnitude." The U.S. Army doesn't kill the enemy anymore, it just "services the target." And the doublespeak goes on.

Doublespeak is language that pretends to communicate but really doesn't. It is language that makes the bad seem good, the negative appear positive, the unpleasant appear attractive or at least tolerable. Doublespeak is language that avoids or shifts responsibility, language that is at variance with its real or purported meaning. It is language that conceals or prevents thought; rather than extending thought, doublespeak limits it.

Example   145

Doublespeak is not a matter of subjects and verbs agreeing; it is a matter of words and facts agreeing. Basic to doublespeak is incongruity, the incongruity between what is said or left unsaid, and what really is. It is the incongruity between the word and the referent, between seem and be, between the essential function of language—communication—and what doublespeak does—mislead, distort, deceive, inflate, circumvent, obfuscate.

How to Spot Doublespeak

How can you spot doublespeak? Most of the time you will recognize doublespeak when you see or hear it. But, if you have any doubts, you can identify doublespeak just by answering these questions: Who is saying what to whom, under what conditions and circumstances, with what intent, and with what results? Answering these questions will usually help you identify as doublespeak language that appears to be legitimate or that at first glance doesn't even appear to be doublespeak.

First Kind of Doublespeak

There are at least four kinds of doublespeak. The first is the euphemism, an inoffensive or positive word or phrase used to avoid a harsh, unpleasant or distasteful reality. But a euphemism can also be a tactful word or phrase which avoids directly mentioning a painful reality, or it can be an expression used out of concern for the feelings of someone else, or to avoid directly discussing a topic subject to a social or cultural taboo.

When you use a euphemism because of your sensitivity for someone's feelings or out of concern for a recognized social or cultural taboo, it is not doublespeak. For example, you express your condolences that someone has "passed away" because you do not want to say to a grieving person, "I'm sorry your father is dead." When you use the euphemism "passed away," no one is misled. Moreover, the euphemism functions here not just to protect the feelings of another person, but to communicate also your concern for that person's feelings during a period of mourning. When you excuse yourself to go to the "rest room," or you mention that someone is "sleeping with" or "involved with" someone else, you do not mislead anyone about your meaning, but you do respect the social taboos about discussing bodily functions and sex in direct terms. You also indicate your sensitivity to the feelings of your audience, which is usually considered a mark of courtesy and good manners.

However, when a euphemism is used to mislead or deceive, it becomes doublespeak. For example, in 1984 the U.S. State Department announced that it would no longer use the world "killing" in its annual report on the status of human rights in countries around the world. Instead, it would use the phrase "unlawful or arbitrary deprivation of life," which the department claimed was more accurate. Its real purpose for using this phrase was simply to avoid discussing the embarrassing situation of government-sanctioned killings in countries that are supported by the United States and have been certified by the United States as respecting the human rights of their citizens. This use of a euphemism constitutes doublespeak, since it is designed to mislead, to cover up the unpleasant. Its real intent is at variance with its apparent intent. It is language designed to alter our perception of reality.

The Pentagon, too, avoids discussing unpleasant realities when it refers to bombs and artillery shells that fall on civilian targets as "incontinent ordnance." And in 1977 the Pentagon tried to slip funding for the neutron bomb unnoticed into an appropriations bill by calling it a "radiation enhancement device."

Second Kind of Doublespeak

A second kind of doublespeak is jargon, the specialized language of a trade, profession, or similar group, such as that used by doctors, lawyers, engineers, educators, or car mechanics. Jargon can serve an important and useful function. Within a group, jargon functions as a kind of verbal shorthand that allows members of the group to communicate with each other clearly, efficiently, and quickly. Indeed, it is a mark of membership in the group to be able to use and understand the group's jargon.

But jargon, like the euphemism, can also be doublespeak. It can be—and often is—pretentious, obscure, and esoteric terminology used to give an air of profundity, authority, and prestige to speakers and their subject matter. Jargon as doublespeak often makes the simple appear complex, the ordinary profound, the obvious insightful. In this sense it is used not to express but impress. With such doublespeak, the act of smelling something becomes "organoleptic analysis," glass becomes "fused silicate," a crack in a metal support beam becomes a "discontinuity," conservative economic policies become "distributionally conservative notions."

Example   147

Lawyers, for example, speak of an "involuntary conversion" of property when discussing the loss or destruction of property through theft, accident, or condemnation. If your house burns down or if your car is stolen, you have suffered an involuntary conversion of your property. When used by lawyers in a legal situation, such jargon is a legitimate use of language, since lawyers can be expected to understand the term.

However, when a member of a specialized group uses its jargon to communicate with a person outside the group, and uses it knowing that the nonmember does not understand such language, then there is doublespeak. For example, on May 9, 1978, a National Airlines 727 airplane crashed while attempting to land at the Pensacola, Florida airport. Three of the fifty-two passengers aboard the airplane were killed. As a result of the crash, National made an after-tax insurance benefit of $1.7 million, or an extra 18 cents a share dividend for its stockholders. Now National Airlines had two problems: It did not want to talk about one of its airplanes crashing, and it had to account for the $1.7 million when it issued its annual report to its stockholders. National solved the problem by inserting a footnote in its annual report which explained that the $1.7 million income was due to "the involuntary conversion of a 727." National thus acknowledged the crash of its airplane and the subsequent profit it made from the crash, without once mentioning the accident or the deaths. However, because airline officials knew that most stockholders in the company, and indeed most of the general public, were not familiar with legal jargon, the use of such jargon constituted doublespeak.

Third Kind of Doublespeak

A third kind of doublespeak is gobbledygook or bureaucratese. Basically, such doublespeak is simply a matter of piling on words, of overwhelming the audience with words, the bigger the words and the longer the sentences the better. Alan Greenspan, then chair of President Nixon's Council of Economic Advisors, was quoted in *The Philadelphia Inquirer* in 1974 as having testified before a Senate committee that "It is a tricky problem to find the particular calibration in timing that would be appropriate to stem the acceleration in risk premiums created by falling incomes without prematurely aborting the decline in the inflation-generated risk premiums."

Nor has Mr. Greenspan's language changed since then. Speaking to the meeting of the Economic Club of New York in 1988, Mr. Greenspan, now Federal Reserve chair, said, "I guess I should warn you, if I turn out to be particularly clear, you've probably misunderstood what I've said." Mr. Greenspan's doublespeak doesn't seem to have held back his career.

Sometimes gobbledygook may sound impressive, but when the quote is later examined in print it doesn't even make sense. During the 1988 presidential campaign, vice-presidential candidate Senator Dan Quayle explained the need for a strategic-defense initiative by saying, "Why wouldn't an enhanced deterrent, a more stable peace, a better prospect to denying the ones who enter conflict in the first place to have a reduction of offensive systems and an introduction to defensive capability? I believe this is the route the country will eventually go."

The investigation into the Challenger disaster in 1986 revealed the doublespeak of gobbledygook and bureaucratese used by too many involved in the shuttle program. When Jesse Moore, NASA's associate administrator, was asked if the performance of the shuttle program had improved with each launch or if it had remained the same, he answered, "I think our performance in terms of the liftoff performance and in terms of the orbital performance, we knew more about the envelope we were operating under, and we have been pretty accurately staying in that. And so I would say the performance has not by design drastically improved. I think we have been able to characterize the performance more as a function of our launch experience as opposed to it improving as a function of time." While this language may appear to be jargon, a close look will reveal that it is really just gobbledygook laced with jargon. But you really have to wonder if Mr. Moore had any idea what he was saying.

Fourth Kind of Doublespeak

The fourth kind of doublespeak is inflated language that is designed to make the ordinary seem extraordinary; to make everyday things seem impressive; to give an air of importance to people, situations, or things that would not normally be considered important; to make the simple seem complex. Often this kind of doublespeak isn't hard to spot, and it is usually pretty funny. While car mechanics may be called "automotive internists," elevator operators members of the "vertical transportation corps," used cars "pre-owned" or "experienced cars," and black-and-white television sets described as having "non-multicolor capability," you really aren't misled all that much by such language.

Example   149

However, you may have trouble figuring out that, when Chrysler "initiates a career alternative enhancement program," it is really laying off five thousand workers; or that "negative patient care outcome" means the patient died; or that "rapid oxidation" means a fire in a nuclear power plant.

The doublespeak of inflated language can have serious consequences. In Pentagon doublespeak, "pre-emptive counterattack" means that American forces attacked first; "engaged the enemy on all sides" means American troops were ambushed; "backloading of augmentation personnel" means a retreat by American troops. In the doublespeak of the military, the 1983 invasion of Grenada was conducted not by the U.S Army, Navy, Air Force, and Marines, but by the "Caribbean Peace Keeping Forces." But then, according to the Pentagon, it wasn't an invasion, it was a "predawn vertical insertion."

Doublespeak Throughout History

Doublespeak is not a new use of language peculiar to the politics or economics of the twentieth century. In the fifth century B.C., the Greek historian Thucydides wrote in *The Peloponnesian War* that

revolution thus ran its course from city to city…. Words had to change their ordinary meanings and to take those which were now given them. Reckless audacity came to be considered the courage of a loyal ally; prudent hesitation, specious cowardice; moderation was held to be a cloak for unmanliness; ability to see all sides of a question, inaptness to act on any. Frantic violence became the attribute of manliness; cautious plotting, a justifiable means of self-defense. The advocate of extreme measures was always trustworthy; his opponent, a man to be suspected.

Julius Caesar, in his account of the Gallic Wars, described his brutal and bloody conquest and subjugation of Gaul as "pacifying" Gaul. "Where they make a desert, they call it peace," said an English nobleman quoted by the Roman historian Tacitus. When traitors were put to death in Rome, the announcement of their execution was made in the form of saying "they have lived." "Taking notice of man in the ancestral manner" meant capital punishment; "the prisoner was then led away" meant he was executed.

In his memoirs, *V-2*, Walter Dornberger, commanding officer of the Peenemünde Rocket Research Institute in Germany during World War II, describes how he and his staff used language to get what they needed from the Bureau of Budget for their rocket experiments. A pencil sharpener was an "Appliance for milling wooden dowels up to 10 millimeters in diameter," and a typewriter was an "Instrument for recording test data with rotating roller." But it was the Nazis who were the masters of doublespeak, and they used it not just to achieve and maintain power but to perpetrate some of the most heinous crimes in the history of the human race.

In the world of Nazi Germany, nonprofessional prostitutes were called "persons with varied sexual relationships"; "protective custody" was the very opposite of protective; "Winter Relief" was a compulsory tax presented as a voluntary charity; and a "straightening of the front" was a retreat, while serious difficulties became "bottlenecks." Minister of Information (the very title is doublespeak) Josef Goebbels spoke in all seriousness of "simple pomp" and "the liberalization of the freedom of the press."

Nazi doublespeak reached its peak when dealing with the "Final Solution," a phrase that is itself the ultimate in doublespeak. The notice, "The Jew X.Y. lived here," posted on a door, meant the occupant had been "deported," that is, killed. When mail was returned stamped "Addressee has moved away," it meant the person had been "deported." "Resettlement" also meant deportation, while "work camp" meant concentration camp or incinerator, "action" meant massacre, "Special Action Groups" were army units that conducted mass murder, "selection" meant gassing, and "shot while trying to escape" meant deliberately killed in a concentration camp.

George Orwell and Language

In his famous and now-classic essay, "Politics and the English Language," which was published in 1946, George Orwell wrote that the "great enemy of clear language is insincerity. When there is a gap between one's real and one's declared aims, one turns as it were instinctively to long words and exhausted idioms, like a cuttlefish squirting out ink." For Orwell, language was an instrument for "expressing and not for concealing or preventing thought." In his most biting comment, he observed that, "in our time, political speech and writing are largely the defense of the indefensible…. [P]olitical language has to consist largely of euphemism, question-begging and sheer cloudy vaguenes…. Political language…is designed to make lies sound truthful and murder respectable, and to give an appearance of solidity to pure wind."

Example   151

Orwell understood well the power of language as both a tool and a weapon. In the nightmare world of his novel, *1984*, Orwell depicted a society where language was one of the most important tools of the totalitarian state. Newspeak, the official state language in the world of *1984*, was designed not to extend but to *diminish* the range of human thought, to make only "correct" thought possible and all other modes of thought impossible. It was, in short, a language designed to create a reality that the state wanted.

Newspeak had another important function in Orwell's world of *1984*. It provided the means of expression for doublethink, the mental process that allows you to hold two opposing ideas in your mind at the same time and believe in both of them. The classic example in Orwell's novel is the slogan, "War Is Peace." Lest you think doublethink is confined only to Orwell's novel, you need only recall the words of Secretary of State Alexander Haig when he testified before a congressional committee in 1982 that a continued weapons build-up by the United States is "absolutely essential to our hopes for meaningful arms reduction." Or remember what Senator Orrin Hatch said in 1988: "Capital punishment is our society's recognition of the sanctity of human life."

At its worst, doublespeak, like newspeak, is language designed to limit, if not eliminate, thought. Like doublethink, doublespeak enables speaker and listener, writer and reader, to hold two opposing ideas in their minds at the same time and believe in both of them. At its least offensive, doublespeak is inflated language that tries to give importance to the insignificant.

Discussion Questions

1. Using your own phrasing, briefly define the four types of doublespeak: (a) euphemism; (b) jargon; (c) gobbledygook; and (d) inflated language. Next to each definition, supply an original example.

2. Lutz explains that euphemisms and jargon are not always examples of doublespeak. What does he mean?

3. Lutz presents the four types of doublespeak in a certain order. What effect is achieved with this order? Explain.

4. What do you think is the thesis of this essay?

5. How would you describe Lutz's tone? Is it effective in helping him achieve his purpose? Explain.

6. Lutz develops his essay with numerous examples, listed one after another. What is the effect of all these examples?

7. Schools are often ripe ground for doublespeak. Describe a recent example you've heard that might constitute doublespeak.

The Nature of Things
by Ruth Cherry

Meet the Writer

Ruth Cherry is a clinical psychologist living in California. Her essay was published in the March 3, 1997, issue of *Newsweek* magazine.

Just like the people I have worked with as a psychologist, my things have personalities and likes and dislikes. As I've lived with them I've learned what to expect from my possessions, most of them anyway, and I know what they expect from me. As in any group, there is cooperation, adjustment and competition, but we are always in relationship.

I question the stability of papers. I know that they aren't necessarily where I put them. They may slink away under cover of darkness or transform into vapor and waft out the door. Where I left them is not usually where I find them.

This logically brings into question the nature of objects. Is their nature static and relentlessly predictable or does it vary depending upon their moods or their reactions to me? For instance, if the objects in my kitchen were happier, would they keep themselves cleaner? Are those dirty pots a sign that my kitchen is conflicted and uncommitted to neatness? When I walk into the kitchen in the morning I'm shocked by the disarray. I couldn't possibly have left it this messy.

Another force must be operating here, and I need to understand what it is. I have to work out my relationships with all these things in my life. Unlike rubber bands, which are always in their home in the

Example   153

plastic cup in the corner of the bottom shelf to the left of the stove, safety pins seem to float around. I can't usually keep track of their whereabouts. When I need one, several appear—on the locker-room floor, in the console of my car, on the sidewalk. Safety pins are always there for me when I call. The safety-pin god smiles on me.

In contrast, my answering machine is highly temperamental. For a while it wasn't recording messages at all, so that when I returned home it delivered only a series of beeps. Because of that I missed some appointments, after which the machine and I had a talk. It doesn't respond to anger, so I know better than to scold it. I asked it gently and patiently, giving it my full attention, what is the concern? Is something not OK? Have I taken it for granted?

I can't be condescending. My answering machine picks that up right away and then won't work at all. But if I acknowledge its boundaries and needs, it responds by recording my messages. A very equal relationship. Mutually respectful.

Not like my lamps. I have two halogen lamps (one in my office and one in my living room), a floor lamp in my bedroom and a desk lamp in the den. What are the chances that they are all working at the same time? Slim. Add in the fluorescent lights in my dressing area and kitchen and that estimate plummets to nil.

I currently have two lamps in my garage, waiting for me to figure out how to remove their glass covers to replace the tiny little bulbs. And another that takes a five-inch fluorescent bulb but has burned out three in the past month. I refuse to fight with these appliances any longer. They have won. I am defeated.

I am not ashamed, however, of being outsmarted by a lamp (or several lamps). I suspect that they communicate about me in lampspeak when I am gone. They share their secrets to frustrate me. I don't know why they hate me, but I know that they do. I can accept that, and I don't pressure them to change. Some machines you just never get along with.

Not all of my appliances have an emotional reaction to me. My Cuisinart is stoic. I turn it on, it does its job, I turn it off. It is always difficult to clean. It never changes. Cut and dried, so to speak.

My toaster, on the other hand, is out to get me. I know it is. I don't use it much because I fear that it is waiting for the day I forget to unplug it. As soon as I turn my key in the door and walk away, it will burn my condo down. What else can I expect from something whose job it is to turn good food black?

The animistic force is benevolent when it comes to my car. I know my car and I are one. I drive an '87 Toyota Celica I bought the first week they were out, in September 1986. I love my car. Before I started working out of my home, it carried me 50 miles a day to work and back, and during that time we bonded.

After I got up from the flu that laid me low for three days in January, the car battery was dead. That's accurate empathy. I so appreciate its telling me that it knows just how I feel.

Recently I locked the keys in the car and left it for four hours. I had cheerfully walked away, anticipating the play I was attending. I realized only at the end of the evening when I searched my purse in front of the theater that the keys were gone. They were not lying on the front seat of the car, but were still in the ignition with the motor running, car doors locked. But no problem. No one had broken in, and no damage had been done. AAA opened the door, and my car drove away just as though I had done nothing out of the ordinary. Not a peep of disapproval.

After that episode, I decided it would be prudent to keep an extra key in my wallet, thus allaying any anxiety about being separated with my key chain. Within two weeks I had left my purse with my wallet and extra key in my car with the door open in an underground residential parking lot while I delivered packages. Returning 30 minutes later, key chain firmly in hand, I discovered that I had provided anyone with a nefarious motive complete access to my car and my identity. But, of course, nothing was missing. My car protects me.

The other day, my toaster joined my lamps in the garage, under protest. Now I think the group of them is plotting something horrible. My only safety is in knowing that my car is in there most of the time. It won't let things get out of hand. It is bigger than they are and will subdue any uprising on their part.

Just as I know that my car loves me, I know that my lamps hate me, my papers are flighty, my answering machine demanding. Safety pins are pleasing and toasters are malevolent. That's just how it is. In my world, anyway.

Discussion Questions

1. In your own words, what is Cherry's thesis? In what ways is the thesis merely light and comical? In what ways is the thesis serious?

Example   155

2. Identify the main categories to which the objects belong. Next, identify the conflicts Cherry presents between one category of objects and another. What effect does she achieve by contrasting one set of objects with the other?

3. Note several transitions. What do many of the transitions have in common?

4. Add your own paragraph to the essay, highlighting the personality of objects in your world.

The Joy of the Wild

by Theodore Roosevelt

Meet the Writer

Theodore Roosevelt was the 26th President of the United States. He championed many causes, including the building of the Panama Canal and the preservation of national parks and forests. In 1906, he was awarded the Nobel Peace Prize.

The man should have youth and strength who seeks adventure in the wide, waste spaces of the earth, in the marshes, and among the vast mountain masses, in the northern forests, amid the steaming jungles of the tropics, or on the deserts of sand or of snow. He must long greatly for the lonely winds that blow across the wilderness, and for sunrise and sunset over the rim of the empty world. His heart must thrill for the saddle and not for the hearthstone. He must be helmsman and chief, the cragsman, the rifleman, the boat steerer. He must be the wielder of axe and of paddle, the rider of fiery horses, the master of the craft that leaps through white water. His eye must be true and quick, his hand steady and strong. His heart must never fail nor his head grow bewildered, whether he face brute and human foes, or the frowning strength of hostile nature, or the awful fear that grips those who are lost in trackless lands. Wearing toil and hardship shall be his; thirst and famine he shall face, and burning fever. Death shall come to greet him with poison-fang or poison-arrow, in shape of charging beast or of scaly things that lurk in lake and river; it shall lie in wait for him among untrodden forests, in the swirl of wild waters, and in the blast of snow blizzard or thunder-shattered hurricane.

Not many men can with wisdom make such a life their permanent and serious occupation. Those whose tasks lie along other lines can lead it for but a few years. For them it must normally come in the hardy vigor of their youth, before the beat of the blood has grown sluggish in their veins.

Nevertheless, older men also can find joy in such a life, although in their case it must be led only on the outskirts of adventure, and although the part they play therein must be that of the onlooker rather than that of the doer. The feats of prowess are for others. It is for other men to face the peril of unknown lands, to master unbroken horses, and to hold their own among their fellows with bodies of supple strength. But much, very much, remains for the man who has "warmed both hands before the fire of life," and who, although he loves the great cities, loves even more the fenceless grassland, and the forest-clad hills.

The grandest scenery of the world is his to look at if he chooses; and he can witness the strange ways of tribes who have survived into an alien age from an immemorial past, tribes whose priests dance in honor of the serpent and worship the spirits of the wolf and the bear. Far and wide, all the continents are open to him as they never were to any of his forefathers; the Nile and the Paraguay are easy of access, and the borderland between savagery and civilization; and the veil of the past has been lifted so that he can dimly see how, in time immeasurably remote, his ancestors—no less remote—led furtive lives among uncouth and terrible beasts, whose kind has perished utterly from the face of the earth. He will take books with him as he journeys; for the keenest enjoyment of the wilderness is reserved for him who enjoys also the garnered wisdom of the present and the past. He will take pleasure in the companionship of the men of the open; in South America, the daring and reckless horsemen who guard the herds of the grazing country, and the dark-skinned paddlers who guide their clumsy dugouts down the dangerous equatorial rivers; the white and red and half-breed hunters of the Rockies,

Example   157

and of the Canadian woodland; and in Africa the faithful black gun-bearers who have stood steadily at his elbow when the lion came on with coughing grunts, or when the huge mass of the charging elephant burst asunder the vine-tangled branches.

The beauty and charm of the wilderness are his for the asking, for the edges of the wilderness lie close beside the beaten roads of present travel. He can see the red splendor of desert sunsets, and the unearthly glory of the afterglow on the battlements of desolate mountains. In sapphire gulfs of ocean he can visit islets, above which the wings of myriads of sea-fowl make a kind of shifting cuneiform script in the air. He can ride along the brink of the stupendous cliff-walled canyon, where eagles soar below him, and cougars make their lairs on the ledges and harry the big-horned sheep. He can journey through the northern forests, the home of the giant moose, the forests of fragrant and murmuring life in summer, the iron-bound and melancholy forests of winter.

The joy of living is his who has the heart to demand it.

Discussion Questions

1. Politicians sometimes claim to believe in causes when they're really interested in votes. What details sway you to believe or disbelieve that President Roosevelt had great respect for nature?

2. How does Roosevelt create rhythm in the first paragraph? What is the effect of this rhythm?

3. Roosevelt titles his essay "The Joy of the Wild." Provide two examples from the essay to show that joy is derived from an appreciation of nature. Find two examples that show joy is derived from within one's self.

4. Identify several direct and subtle transitions used in this essay. Discuss the effectiveness of each.

5. What is Roosevelt's main message? Is the message still valuable today? Explain.

6. Describe Roosevelt's tone. What phrases, sentences, or paragraphs effectively convey this tone? What other possible tones could a writer adopt when writing about this subject?

7. In the fourth paragraph, Roosevelt writes, "The grandest scenery in the world is his to look at if he chooses." How could you apply this lesson to your own life, in your own immediate world? Be specific.

Laugh Out Loud Good English

by Katherine Lee

Meet the Writer

Katherine Lee enjoys playing the alto saxophone and trying to work Yiddish and movie references into everyday conversation. She would like to thank her elementary and middle school English teachers for correcting her grammar all those years, as well as speech coach Jim Wyman for his encouragement and help in writing this piece.

As I wander through this world, utilizing my field of vision and literary ability, I sense the coming of an ominous black cloud that shall rain down a plague of darkness. I fear this imminent evil shall forever block out the golden rays—of good language. The premonitions have already begun gouging my eyes with blatant misspellings and poor, lost commas wandering the page while my ears ring with enough "likes" to kill a small animal. And if that's not enough, just as I check my e-mail, a blinding light of Internet lingo radiates from the computer screen.

But believe it or not, I am not the only one haunted by these linguistic omens. Author Lynne Truss agrees in her book *Eats, Shoots and Leaves: the Zero Tolerance Approach to Punctuation* saying, "We [grammar geeks] are like the little boy in the movie *The Sixth Sense* who can see dead people, except that we [grammar geeks] can see dead punctuation," that is, forgotten grammar rules. Proper grammar is only one factor in the problem of teetering linguistics. Online lingo creates a new slang of empty shorthand in our typing while an increasing number of informalities appear in both formal writing and speech. I'm even sometimes left wondering if people greet their bosses with, "Yo man! Whassup?" We all face poor language use every day, even from ourselves. English seems to be in a decline

Example   159

towards becoming communication lacking depth and the display of intelligent thought.

In order to let these linguistic rays shine through for a sunny day, we must first examine how modern society and technology are catching us in showers of poor language practices; then, we can open an umbrella and delve into how this problem of fading English skills can be solved. Technology may to be blame for a new shorthand now in place for typing. While the Internet has sparked remarkable progress in communication, the Web has its own language faults. According to a 2003 Reuters survey regarding Internet use, teenagers spend approximately seventeen hours a week online, not including the time they spend writing e-mails. A significant portion of this time is spent using the AOL Instant Messenger which allows users to hold typed conversations with others online, often communicating via as few keystrokes as humanly possible. According to Neil Randall, an English professor at the University of Waterloo in Ontario, "This [online shorthand] is really an extension of what teenagers have always done: recreate the language. But this new lingo combines writing and speaking to a degree that we've never seen before."

And then, there are the online acronyms. What begins with an innocent little T-T-Y-L for *talk to you later* soon spirals out of control into the most dreaded and emotionally draining acronym of all *evil laugh* L-O-L, for laugh out loud. It may seem like all fun and games until someone actually finds him or herself chuckling or possibly even howling and then chooses to limit self-expression to L-O-L. However, this has become the "proper" online way of expressing hilarity.

Also, in order to compensate for personality lost in monotone online rhetoric, people create typing styles which can include cute spellings and brutally sporadic capitalization. Call me old-fashioned, but I don't think anything is cool if it's spelled with a k-E-W-l, with the two middle letters capitalized for no real reason.

In online writing, it seems that putting down information rather than sounding intelligent is what matters. This in turn diminishes the eloquence and potential depth of the English language. Berkeley Linguistics professor John McWhorter describes in his book *Doing Your Own Thing* that we are comfortable writing e-mails in this terse and somewhat shallow way because it is a symptom of how our oral English has changed into a more casual and brief form. "We write e-mails like we talk," says McWhorter. Thanks to this correlation, the conciseness of online lingo is not limited to the computer monitor and is affecting other forms of communications.

Even after logging off the Web, English becomes increasingly informal through fading grammar and word usage. In Truss's *Eats, Shoots and Leaves*, she notes punctuation errors in store signs and even in newspaper headlines. An English teacher in my high school confided that simple grammatical errors such as, "Me and Jim went to the store" often appear in speech and formal writing. As my peers and I have been reading and writing for ten to twelve years, simple errors such as "me and Jim" should not be acceptable. Students may also over-rely on computer grammar and spelling checks. Words with similar sounds but different meanings can be easily mixed up while typing. But a computer does not catch the difference between "desert" and "dessert." "Me and Jim" goes unnoticed while other recommendations that are not even correct, like those accusing my complete sentences of being fragments, blaze forth underlined on the screen. Thank you Microsoft Word, but I can type poorly on my own.

What was like once associated with only, like, the California Valley Girl has, like, spread to the edge of, like, teenage rhetoric. Cornell University English professor Dan McCall worries about his students, saying, "What breaks my heart is their talk. It's all, 'Like, like, you know.'" In a lighter view, Eils Lotozo describes in his *Chicago Tribune* article "Like Is, Like, a Likeable Word" that the word "like" has come to serve a conversational purpose in filling in pauses for thought or hesitance. It is this uncertainty that leads to the connection of "like" to an image of unintelligence.

In order to help solve these linguistic mishaps, the education system needs to promote the teaching of a full curriculum in English and literature that develops and encourages the language arts. The importance of proper language in the professional world must be emphasized to students, particularly those planning to attend college. However, the most pragmatic solutions begin with you and me. Embrace the inner grammar geek and try to type with correct punctuation and spelling. I'm not asking that you to go out and join the Apostrophe Protection Society. Just make an effort. It's okay if you don't know your pronouns from your participles. Go out and buy a grammar book. If anyone sees you, just say it's for a friend. What's important is that we have the resources and will to check for ourselves.

Example   161

It is time for us to unsheathe our mighty swords of language and wield them against this impending doom. We must help these poor, lost commas end their identity crisis, fight back those hesitant likes, and spread the word that typing "G2G" has "got to go" in more ways than one. The ways we write, type, read, and speak are all intertwined. Without its rules, language lacks an intelligible flow. Without thorough expression, our intelligence is severely diminished. We must part those black clouds and let those dazzling linguistic rays shine through in order to truly laugh out loud.

Discussion Questions

1. Lee offers numerous examples to support her thesis. Which examples are most effective? Think of an original example that would fit well in this essay.

2. Would you join the Apostrophe Protection Society? Why or why not? Be specific.

3. In what ways has technology contributed to the "downfall" of language? What else contributes to this downfall?

4. Examine the first paragraph of "Laugh Out Loud Good English." What tone is immediately established? Which words contribute to that tone? What if the essay had begun with a more somber phrase, such as "I fear the downfall of good language"? This revision is clear, direct, and viable, but what is lost?

Beauty Is in the Eye of the Beholder

by Colleen Veit

Meet the Writer

Colleen Veit taught herself to read in preschool. She loves to make her own clothes and shops at least every other week. She lives with her parents, two sisters, and her King Charles spaniel, Bailey.

This past Halloween, I semi-permanently dyed my hair black as part of my costume. While the resulting hue was more of a dark purple, I thought I would enjoy the comments my new hair color would gather during school the next day. However, I found that some of my friends were so shocked by my locks that they insulted them before even greeting me. I noticed that some people went so far as to alter their paths to avoid me and my apparently socially unacceptable hair.

Of course, some of my friends complimented my hair, and I did receive some of the expected responses. However, by the end of the day, I was ready to go home and wash as much of the color out as I could. I was dismayed to learn that my appearance matters more to some of my friends than my personality.

In society, what should be viewed as more important: someone's exterior or their interior? Unfortunately, appearances are the trait most people judge others upon. Beautiful people have advantages over others in many situations. When presenting people with pictures of faces and asking them what attributes these people might have, for his book *The Day You Discard Your Body*, Marshall Brian discovered, "The more attractive the presented faces were, the more successful, content, friendly, intelligent, sociable, accessible, exciting, creative and busy the persons were estimated. The opposite applies to unattractive faces: The more unattractive the faces were the more negative characteristics were attributed to the person." This is a

Example **163**

huge attribute for the attractive, and a huge deficit for the unattractive. Because of this, the less beautiful people of society are often disregarded and even treated with contempt. Furthermore, better jobs and opportunities are often rewarded to beautiful people because of their appearances, not because of their skill and focus.

However, I do understand that most attractive people try not to take advantage of their looks in most situations to achieve their desires. But when chosen for a job position over their more qualified, yet less attractive competition, how many beautiful people could honestly say they would turn the job down? And if someone attractive happened to be in a hurry at a store, and they were helped before a less beautiful person who had been waiting longer, how many could say they would refuse the help and risk being late? I am not blaming this discrepancy on the attractive people themselves, and I realize their looks were not their decision. However, in society today, beauty is a prejudice that nearly all of us share. In order to combat this, we must first look at the important points surrounding this issue.

Most of society's idea of beauty is roughly confined to the same stereotype. Also, people who do not find themselves attractive often look down upon others to lift their self-esteem. Many people compare themselves to false images of beauty they see in today's celebrities. In reality, many photos of stars and models are heavily retouched in order to enhance the picture. Furthermore, these very same people whom we idolize for their appearances usually possess low self-esteem and often become prey to anorexia, bulimia, and plastic surgeries to maintain the outer façade they believe to be acceptable.

On the whole, society today has fallen into a vicious and relentless cycle of judging others based on their looks. On a recent episode of *Dr. Phil*, his son, Jay McGraw, a man viewed as handsome, visited the same mall twice in one day to test society's tolerance of certain appearances. For his first visit, Jay dressed up in a fat suit and donned a fake nose, large glasses, and makeup to make him appear tired and less attractive. The second time, he went as himself. At the mall, Jay participated in average activities, such as asking passersby for directions and requesting a job application at various stores. The responses he received at each visit were so drastically different, it is almost difficult to believe the scenarios involved the same person. When he visited the mall as himself, asking for directions prompted conversations, and store owners encouraged him to return completed applications. However, when Jay visited the mall dressed less attractively, passersby would not stop to give him directions, and store owners conveniently "misplaced" job applications, even when "Help Wanted" signs were posted in the window.

On the other end of the spectrum, the conception of beauty can often be a hardship for those who are found attractive to society. Most people expect more attractive persons to be highly cooperative and kind. In comparison to these expectations, the exalted persons often appear more selfish and impolite, when in reality, they are no or more less personable then those we view as unattractive.

Beauty has rapidly become a main factor in the way we judge people in society today. Often, this prejudice causes extreme stress in young people to fit a certain mold they are told is pretty. In older people, more options of permanently altering the body are available that should maybe not be. The elderly are told they are universally unattractive, which damages their self-worth and brings ageism to a whole new level. Of course, one way to fight the stereotypes of appearance is to take away everyone's vision. While that could completely eliminate the problem, it hardly seems realistic.

Instead, we must focus on looking beyond someone's exterior and evaluating her as a person, not as a mannequin. Everyone possesses flaws, both in personality and appearance. By allowing exterior blemishes to be disregarded, we can allow a person to prove her inner worth. Furthermore, would it be so hard for society to expand the mold of an "attractive" stereotype? For so long, the idea of an attractive female has been slender and blond; for a male, tan and muscular. There are so many different body types in this world, who are we to say what's beautiful? Moreover, in professional situations, appearances should be observed as a first impression, not as qualification criteria. Should thirty extra pounds cost a friendly and talented job applicant a position she was vying for? And is it fair to make someone wait in line longer than needed just because of a crooked nose?

At this point, society needs to determine for itself which is more important: The soul and mind of a person, or the body that encases it?

Discussion Questions

1. Which examples are most effective, and why? Think of your own original example that would support Veit's thesis.

Example   165

2. Describe one encounter you've experienced that confirms or negates Veit's main point—that we place too much emphasis on appearance.

3. Assume Veit wanted to adopt a more humorous tone. Pick a short passage from the essay and rewrite it, incorporating humor.

4. Writers sometimes frame an essay by making the conclusion echo the opening. If Veit had chosen to use this technique, describe how she might have done so.

Student Model 4.3

The Caroline Chronicles
by Caroline VanAcker

Meet the Writer

While she admits to being a nerd, Caroline VanAcker also participates in varsity soccer and volleyball, National Honor Society, peer mentoring, and occasionally the school newspaper. In college, she hopes to double major in architecture and engineering.

"I've got another diary. It's got a lock! It has dates so I have to write in it every day." Yet another collection of blank pages waited to receive an eight-year-old's microcosm of Palatine, Illinois. I spared no detail of anything remotely interesting to the juvenile brain. An ever-infamous character in that world was "MTV," the older brother who violated the privacy of the diary's passages. Eight years removed from those certainly traumatizing experiences, I question now if time has changed me so that I myself am an intruder.

Systems of written communication have advanced throughout millennia and been traced diligently by historians. The extremely sophisticated method known as "cursive" only recently continued on its evolutionary path after finding me in first grade. The recognizable printed alphabet was only able to supersede my prehistory of indiscernible scribbling after I labored for countless hours over writing tablets and was reminded innumerable times to slant my letters. By first grade, the ideology of a calligrapher had been drilled into me, though I was soon to be enlightened to the cursive way of writing. I was empowered by continued slaving over manuscripts to finally inscribe in my diary with a flourish, "In school we are learning cursive. May 26, 1996." In later years, I rebelled, dabbling in radical experimentation with acceptable shapes and challenging the traditional forms of lettering. I remembered to dot my i's, but the dot swelled to the size of a small donut. I soon reverted to the comfortable and classic original type, suppressing my revolutionary nature. My evolutionary pedigree still compels me to turn my paper forty-five degrees before I write with my "elementary-school teacher" script.

I had discovered the written word, but, unfortunately, there was not a direct correlation between that and spelling. The confines of Noah Webster failed to constrain me as I composed my first short story "A gret Srprise" on January 23, 1996. Double-spaced, and lasting a remarkable two and one-half pages, it is the harrowing story of my favorite stuffed animal Snow Flake's birth, recounting her canine liberation from "a loup-sided box" by my scissor-wielding father. I also perceived the living souls of my stuffed animals and frequently wrote to or about them. Numerous diary entries explored my fledgling world, with an over-emphasis on underlining and interjections by the author. One-sentence entries were common, and the occasional doodle spiced up monotonous text. When I was informed in 1997 that I needed glasses, I composed a letter to my mother. My epistle informed her of my absolute rejection of being bespectacled and the consequence of permanent emotional torment. I included a helpful visual of glasses broken over a fire, with the promise that "Ice cream won't help."

I encountered a new ally in my quest to master language when I was nine. Its standard rectangular shape hid a vast trove of literary gems between the covers. My assignment was to create a dragon story, and I concocted the exoticism from not only my imagination but also from the most spectacular word provided by the thesaurus. My whopping five-page story full of extravagant wording was a source of immense pride. I recently found the fifth-grade masterpiece on my family's old computer. I see this now, although ridiculous, as

Example   167

a beginning for my maturation as a writer. Granted, I unabashedly overused the thesaurus, but I had started the process of developing and revising drafts to achieve a perfected and polished final form. That same year the *Young Poet's Anthology* published my work, and I submitted another poem to *Chicken Soup for the Soul*. I learned the utility of sophisticated expressions and the well-worded phrase; even with my synonym misadventures, I had discovered the beauty of description and the nature of conveyed emotion.

Subsequent years provided similar opportunities for growth. In sixth grade "The Presidential Postman" was born—twenty pages of illustration, rhyming stanzas, and letters in the form of "The Jolly Postman." The rhyming was slightly off in some places, but I was able to juxtapose my artistic and linguistic abilities, creating a written marvel. I discovered *Harry Potter* and later *The Lord of the Rings*. Deciding that Middle Earth was too remarkable to remain a Muggle, I interposed my own character and scenes into the creations of Rowling and Tolkein. My English skills continued to improve in junior high due to quarterly in-class essays, frequent grammar lessons, and the discovery of the formal outline. I had previously snubbed any type of organizational device prior to writing, but in the outline, I was able to capture trains of thought and manage all of my ideas. I wrote persuasive, expository, and narrative essays, analyzing and synthesizing information into a cohesive script. Freshman year reintroduced me to the plethora of poetry structures, and I continued to electronically word-process to my heart's—and my teacher's—content.

I have progressed far from my one-line diary entries, first-grade days of cursive, fifth-grade dragon stories, and junior high essays. Through constant work with written compositions, I have found English not only a high school course but also a hobby. Bookstores and my creative writings apart from school have spawned a love of literacy and language, which I satiate with the *Logue* sports beat and journaling. My style and voice have developed tremendously from my original diary, and even with so many more experiences and resources now, I am still the young author of those pages.

Discussion Questions

1. VanAcker presents her examples in chronological order. What do you think she hopes to achieve through this?

2. Which examples are most effective? Why?

3. VanAcker shows her maturity through changes in her writing. If you wrote a similar essay on the theme of maturity, what subject would you focus on?

4. VanAcker begins her essay with, "I've got another diary. It's got a lock!" She ends it with the words, "I am still the young author of these pages." In what way does the last line reinforce the first one?

Example   169

Comparison and Contrast

What if all the people in the world looked essentially the same to you? What if all the houses in your neighborhood were identical, as far as you could tell? What would it be like if you couldn't discern any meaningful difference between classical music and rap, or between Chinese food and Italian? And what if you didn't really have any likes or dislikes, preferences or passions, and everything in your world was just "pretty much okay"? Such inability to distinguish would make our lives much less meaningful and certainly less interesting.

One of the fundamental ways that we make sense of the world is by recognizing the similarities and differences that make up our perceptions. When your writing purpose is to convey the similarities or differences between two or more ideas or subjects, certain principles come into play that make your work both efficiently organized and appealing to a reader.

A common tendency for students writing comparison essays is to write in an overly analytical tone. (Tone, you may recall from earlier chapters, is the writer's attitude toward his subject.) This type of essay usually calls for a dissection of the subjects under consideration and an examination of their parts. Unfortunately, this process lends itself to overly formal language. For comparison writing, your *thinking* needs to be formal and precise, but your *writing* can still be friendly and engaging. The formal way that you examine and align your points of comparison is important, but—as always—your writing voice should appeal to your audience.

Before getting too technical, let's agree on the meanings of some frequently used terms. You already know that the *thesis* is the primary message or assertion of your paper. This thesis will be your *topic*, which refers to the overall content matter of your paper, including the subjects under comparison as well as the thesis. *Subject* will refer to an item under comparison, and a *point* will be one of the aspects of comparison between those subjects.

For example, you may be writing about the *topic* of using an online social network instead of e-mail to stay in touch with distant friends. Your *thesis* is that a social network is preferable to e-mail. The *subjects* here are social networks and e-mail. The *points* used to develop this might include: (1) the capability of social networks to communicate with many people at the same time; and (2) one's ability to include video and photos on social networks. For easy reference, here's a chart.

As you work through this textbook and complete the assignments, you'll notice a subtle transformation in the way you think. You will begin to think like a writer, always searching for ideas about which to write. If you're going to think like a writer, you might as well behave like one, too. Carry around an index card or two and jot down ideas as they occur to you. Flip through magazines and newspapers or listen to the news, writing down items that spark your interest. You'll be surprised by how many of these random notes make their way into your essays.

thesis	the primary message or assertion of your paper
topic	the overall content matter of your paper, including the subjects under comparison as well as the thesis
subject	an item under comparison
point	one aspect of comparison between two or more subjects

When writing a comparison essay, students often wonder whether or not it's okay to discuss both similarities and differences. The answer is an emphatic yes. If your focus is primarily the similarities between your subjects, you will have a lot of *comparison*. If your focus deals mainly with differences, that's fine, too. In that case, your discussion will have a lot of *contrast*. Contrast is simply a kind of comparison that highlights dissimilarity. Your topic and purpose will determine how much comparison and how much contrast is appropriate, and whether or not they should be balanced.

Think of one of your favorite activities. Compare that activity to going to a circus or carnival.

Choosing a Topic

In the "real" writing world, an author chooses to write in a comparative mode because that approach best serves the theme or purpose he is writing to achieve. In other words, the comparison exists only because an author decides it's the best way to develop his thesis. Ideally, that is how it will work for you, too.

Frequently in academic writing, however, that relationship between comparison and thesis is reversed: You may be assigned to write a comparison essay, and it needs to have a thesis. That's not necessarily a bad approach. After all, you are a student, and you're supposed to be learning. In this case, you are learning to develop a thesis through the use of comparison so that when a similar purpose arrives on your writing doorstep later in life, you will know what to do.

As always, your purpose as a writer will direct the way you choose a topic. When your assignment is to write a comparison piece, your purpose is to engagingly illuminate a thesis by describing the similarities and differences between phenomena. With enough creativity, virtually anything can be compared to anything else. As the late comedian George Carlin once said, "They keep saying you can't compare apples and oranges. I can. An apple is red and distinctly non-spherical; an orange is orange and nearly spherical. So, what's the problem?"

Sure, a writer can compare fancy dining and fast-food dining. But why not compare fast-food dining with shopping at a mall? Instead of comparing the processes of applying to a college and applying for a job, why not compare applying to college to running for elective office? Almost anyone could write a serviceable comparison between action movies and romance movies; a more interesting comparison might be between an action movie and a rock concert. The more dissimilar the subjects under comparison, the more interesting your writing is likely to be.

For example, poet and mother Beth Ann Fennelly found common ground between her two roles:

A thing I love about mothering is a thing I love about poetry: both make you a child again. Pound said famously about poetry: "Make it new." Toddlers at play make the same demand. Both disallow dead metaphors and clichés, the fossils of our language. Everything is alive with mystery and "Why is the meantime mean?" and "I have a big apple tight" and "I wear make up then make down." We are dipped in turpentine, the film is wiped from our eyeballs, we really see what we are looking at (Why do we so rarely see?). Both poetry and motherhood are humbling, they do not care whether you appear civilized to your neighbors, they are greedy, they demand you eat with your fingers, they lie in wait for the moment you announce you've got it nailed (fool!), and then it is all tantrums, or all silence. Both cost you more than you think you can bear, repay you more than you deserve. How to get the right last line, or how to get the child to eat asparagus—both are problems that repel logic, oh ridiculous limited logic. The kryptonite of creativity alone can solve them. Why should Claire eat her asparagus? Because it's the lion tamer's whip, and she doesn't want to be tamed. Naturally. "Why?" both poetry and motherhood ask, and when they receive the answer, ask "Why?" again. Both terrify us because we can't control them. "Why," they ask, "Why," they answer, "Why?"

When you begin to tackle a comparison essay, first choose a subject you are comfortable writing about. The tricky part is choosing the other subject, the one you then will compare to the "comfortable" subject. For example, maybe you know a lot about assembling computer or video systems, or babysitting, or military airplanes, or shoes. Choose a subject that makes you feel like you're on solid ground.

Someone who knows about assembling video systems could compare that process with another assembly process, such as assembling a sandwich. But our suggestion is to stretch a little further and choose something less obvious, perhaps comparing assembling a video system with forming a new club at your school.

An expert babysitter could easily compare her important work to having a job at a clothing store. But why not stretch a bit more and compare babysitting to growing a flower garden? An expert on shoes might be tempted to compare various kinds of shoes based on style, but wouldn't it be more interesting to compare types of shoes with types of friends?

If the points of comparison on these "stretched" topic suggestions are not immediately apparent to you, that's fine. The main idea here is that you should choose items or ideas to compare that are personally relevant to you and also unique from those your classmates will likely choose.

Another approach to selecting a topic is to find those areas of your life and experiences that involve choices. When you are faced with the

Effectively used, good similes can light up a paragraph as a smile lights up a face; the image comes alive. The first rule is that similes must be accurate. The things compared or equated have to be genuinely alike.

—*James J. Kilpatrick*

opportunity of doing two fun things that cannot be accomplished simultaneously, how do you choose? That can be the basis of a creative comparison essay. Do you have certain friends or relatives on whom you can rely for different needs? That dynamic can also form the basis of an interesting comparison piece.

Here are a few examples:

> Some students do not take enough care when choosing a college. We can see this by comparing the college selection process with the act of choosing a movie to see on the weekend.

> Driving an energy-efficient vehicle is an important patriotic act. This can be made clear by understanding the similarities and differences between driving such a vehicle and protesting against a war.

> Keeping a secret from a friend is a bad idea. We can understand this by comparing keeping a secret to having a cold.

> Applying to college is like weeding a lawn.

The most appealing comparison topics and essays will be those that show readers new ways of thinking about something familiar, or those that reveal something new about readers' own circumstances. As you ponder the topics available to you, consider choosing a topic that will allow you to write from your own experiences.

Keep in mind that you are doing this comparison to illuminate a thesis and fulfill a purpose. Your paper needs to say more than "Look here! These can be compared!" What exactly do you want to say? How does the comparison help you to say it? What new insights have you discovered by comparing these two subjects? The comparison should lead a reader to some new awareness. You will know you have a solid topic and approach when you can fill in these blanks:

> My thesis is _____ , and it will be clear to anyone who understands the similarities and differences between _____ and _____ .

Organizing a Comparison Essay

Organizing a comparison essay requires a writer to have several points of comparison between two or more subjects. Your teacher may suggest or require a certain number of comparison points. Three is usually the minimum number, but the more discussion points you have, the more likely your essay will be convincing and satisfying. For now, it's fine if you only have the most basic idea of your comparison points. Later in this chapter, we'll discuss ways to enrich and enhance these points. To some extent, the way you develop your comparison points will be determined by your organizational pattern.

You can organize a comparison essay by following one of two patterns: point-by-point or block-by-block.

Point-by-Point

In point-by-point organization, your first task is to choose one point of comparison between the subjects and write about that point, first covering subject A, then applying the point to subject B. (Of course, if you have more subjects than two, you will go deeper into the alphabet.) Then you will choose a second point of comparison and write about its relevance to each subject, proceeding like this until you have covered each point.

For example, you may be writing about this topic: how females and males differ in emotional intelligence. The *subjects* here are females and males. The arguable *thesis* might be the assertion that females are more emotionally intelligent than males. The *points* used to prove this thesis might include a discussion of females' and males' (1) emotional self-awareness, (2) awareness of others' emotions, (3) willingness to express emotions, and (4) willingness to discuss others' emotions.

A point-by-point organizational outline of this topic would look like this:

I. Self-Awareness of Emotions

    A. Females are more aware of their emotions.

    B. Males are not as aware of their emotions.

II. Awareness of Others' Emotions

    A. Females are more aware of others' emotions.

    B. Males are less aware of others' emotions.

III. Willingness to Express Emotions

    A. Females are more willing to express their emotions.

    B. Males try to hide their emotions.

Writers on Writing

Almost all good writing begins with terrible first efforts. You need to start somewhere. Start by getting something—anything—down on paper. A friend of mine says the first draft is the down draft—you just get it down. The second draft is the up draft—you fix it up. You try to say what you have to say more accurately. And the third draft is the dental draft, where you check every tooth, to see if it's loose or cramped or decayed, or even, God help us, healthy.

—*Anne Lamott*

IV. Willingness to Discuss Others' Emotions

    A. Females are more willing to discuss others' emotions.

    B. Males are less willing to discuss others' emotions.

Block-by-Block

In block-by-block organization, you will first write a block, or section, about one of your subjects, covering each comparison point with regard only to that subject. In that first block, you will not fully reference the other subject. Then you will write a block about the other subject, covering each of the comparison points discussed previously in relation to the other subject, probably in the same order. In this block, you will focus only on the second subject. (If you are comparing more than two subjects, more blocks will be necessary.)

A block-by-block organizational plan for the same topic discussed in the point-by-point section would look like this:

  I. Females

    A. More aware of their emotions.

    B. More aware of others' emotions.

    C. More willing to express their emotions.

    D. More willing to discuss others' emotions.

  II. Males

    A. Not as aware of their emotions.

    B. Less aware of others' emotions.

    C. Try to hide their emotions.

    D. Less willing to discuss others' emotions.

Articulating Your Thesis

Whichever organizational method you choose, you need to convey your thesis. Although each sentence in the essay should somehow support or relate to your overall message, a comparison essay provides you with numerous choices for articulating your thesis. You might choose a traditional format, in which the thesis is stated near the beginning, reinforced throughout the essay, and restated near the end.

A more sophisticated approach available in a comparison format is to allow the thesis to gradually emerge as you develop the points of comparison, and then state the thesis in more direct language near the end. Readers tend to like this method because it makes them feel smart as they make the connections and discover your message before you tell them in overt language. When an essay makes a reader feel smart, the reader usually rates the writer pretty highly.

Developing Your Comparison

The good news about developing your points is that you already know how to do it! Earlier in this book, you learned how to effectively employ description, narration, and examples. Each point in your comparison essay can be developed using these methods. Feel free to mix and match them, but always keep your purpose in mind. If you think of an anecdote regarding one of your points, and it illuminates your thesis, use it, even if you do not have anecdotes for your other points. The other points may be developed through effective description and rich examples.

Writers on Writing

If you want to improve your spelling, let yourself become attracted to the faces of words, as if they're the faces of people. Abandon yourself shamelessly to words. Stare rudely at them. When you sit before the television screen, gape at the words projected there. On the way to class, let yourself become hypnotized by the words you pass—on store windows, posters... or billboards... Study the words on the spines of books... Break them down into recognizable or familiar parts. Look for patterns.

—Ken Macrorie

For example, if your thesis is that fathers and mothers treat their children differently, you might support that thesis by giving examples of differences in how they assign chores, give allowances, and enforce house rules. You may employ narration if you have good stories about how chores have been assigned by your parents or your friends' parents. If you have examples of how household rules are used by various parents you know, you might use those examples to make your point. The descriptive techniques from Chapter 2 can and should be used regardless of how you choose to develop your points.

Transitions are always important in expository writing, but they are especially critical in comparison essays. Comparison involves a certain amount of going back and forth between subjects and points. Attempting to do that without transitions has the ugly effect of making your audience feel as though they are being slammed back and forth with no cushioning, or accelerating unpredictably through a roller-coaster ride. Smooth transitions between points and subjects will lead your readers gently through your writing, and they'll arrive at exactly the realization that you intend.

Readers are not the only people who will benefit from your comparison essay. The experience of developing a thesis through the use of comparison will sharpen your own intellectual ability to recognize and articulate similarities and differences. Recognizing differences is how we make sense of our world, and making meaningful comparisons is a valuable skill in a complex society.

The legendary architect Frank Lloyd Wright created coherence and beauty through the repetition of horizontal lines. Writers achieve similar coherence and beauty when they build phrases that mirror each other, sometimes quite directly through purposeful repetition, and sometimes more subtly through a concept called **parallelism**.

Notice how Martin Luther King uses repetition in his famous "I Have a Dream" speech (see Chapter 8, pages 299–303, for the entire speech):

> I have a dream that one day this nation will rise up and live out the true meaning of its creed: "We hold these truths to be self-evident: that all men are created equal." I have a dream that one day on the red hills of Georgia the sons of former slaves and the sons of former slaveowners will be able to sit down together at the table of brotherhood. I have a dream that the state of Mississippi, a desert state sweltering with the heat of injustice and oppression, will be transformed into an oasis of freedom and justice. I have a dream that my four little children will one day live in a nation where they will not be judged by the color of their skin but by the content of their character.

If you read the passage aloud, your body may even begin to sway to the beat, as one phrase creates an expectation of the next. Also, each repetition adds layers that deepen meaning. The composite effect is nothing short of eloquent.

With parallelism, the grammatical structure of a phrase is repeated, which may strike you as boring, but this repetition is often necessary to be grammatically correct, and the effect can be quite pleasing. Here's a simple example:

> To earn high grades, students must listen, study, and review.

Listen, *study*, and *review* are all active verbs that help hold the sentence together.

But note the disorder when a slight break occurs in the pattern:

To earn high grades, students must listen, study, and review is important, too.

To indicate such problems with parallelism, teachers will usually draw parallel lines (//) or write an abbreviation of "parallelism" in the margins of papers.

Here's another example of a problematic passage, along with a revision:

> Teachers should write assignments on the board, remind students when assignments are due, and need to give extensions sometimes.

The helping verb *should* applies to all three clauses, which makes the last clause grammatically incorrect. The sentence should read:

> Teachers should write assignments on the board, remind students when assignments are due, and sometimes give extensions.

Whether used dramatically or subtly, purposeful repetition and parallelism can help you write sentences that resonate with sound and meaning.

Journal Topic

Think about how much you've changed in the past few years. Compare how you are now with how you were then. To organize your thoughts, you might create a chart like the following one.

Similarities	Differences
1. _____	1. _____
2. _____	2. _____
3. _____	3. _____

Practice

Before beginning the Chapter Assignment, try the following exercises to practice writing compare and contrast essays.

1. Use a Venn diagram graphic organizer (see Appendix B) to compare two or more people, days of the week, months of the year, courses you are taking right now, or any other subjects. After filling in the diagram with as many ideas as possible, write one conclusive sentence about the information you generated.

2. Practice seeing unique points of comparison between unlikely subjects: Look around the room. Choose an inanimate object. Now choose another inanimate object elsewhere in the room. List as many similarities between these objects as possible. If you are doing this exercise in class, partners can each choose an object and then work together to generate similarities.

3. Make a list of five adjectives that describe something you like to do. Then write as many synonyms and antonyms as possible for each of those adjectives.

4. Create two columns on a sheet of paper. On the left side, list some of the jobs you've done or would like to do. On the right side, list several bad habits. Take any item from the left column and compare it to any item on the right. For example, you might compare working at a fast-food restaurant with procrastination. Come up with at least three similarities and three differences between your subjects.

Chapter Assignment

Prewriting

Use the following suggestions to help you choose a topic and clarify the purpose of your essay.

Choose one of the following questions—or come up with one of your own—and write about it for one minute without stopping. Then repeat this task with two more questions. If you suddenly realize one of your responses might form the seed of a workable comparison essay, quickly jot down the points of comparison you might write about.

1. What was a choice you recently made?

2. Who has changed more since junior high, you or your friend(s)?

3. Who are your favorite and least favorite relatives?

4. What is a choice you need to make in the near future?

5. Who are some adults you admire or despise?

6. How is your current life different from your ideal life?

Writing Topics

Select one of the following topics to develop into a comparison essay. Feel free to tailor these topics to suit your needs.

1. Compare two people or groups: family members, friends, celebrities, freshmen, or seniors. Or compare a product with someone you know well.

2. Describe your relationship with your parents and how it differs from your friends' relationships with their parents. Or compare one of your parents with a well-known character on television.

3. Compare two sports you play. Or compare a sport you play with a common childhood game.

4. Compare two jobs you've held. Or compare a disease with a job you've held.

5. Compare yourself now to how you were when you started high school. Or compare the process of growing up with the growth of a garden.

6. Compare female and male approaches to solving relationship problems. Or compare problems in a relationship with working at a drive-in restaurant.

7. Compare the roles of player and coach, or performer and director. Or compare your coach, teacher, or other authority figure in your life with a well-known historical figure.

8. Compare your view of your future with your parents' view of your future. Or compare how people plan for the future with how they deal with illness.

9. Compare high school today to what it was like when your parents went to high school. Or compare the mixture of students in a high school to the components in a chemical reaction.

Revision

As you revise and edit your first draft, consider the following checklist.

1. Is your topic unique and unlikely to be written about by anyone else in your class?

2. Is your voice inviting and accessible?

3. Is your organizational plan clearly either point-by-point or block-by-block?

4. Is each point fully and interestingly developed for each subject?

5. Do you have smooth transitions between each point and paragraph?

6. By the end of the essay, is your thesis illuminated and easy to identify?

7. After reading this essay, will your reader have at least one new realization?

Peer Review

Use these questions to help you evaluate another student's writing. Remember, specific suggestions and examples are most helpful.

1. How do you feel about the title?

2. Is the voice authoritative but not overly formal? If not, what are some words or phrases that the author might reconsider?

3. Does the organizational plan follow the block-by-block or point-by-point method?

4. Which points are the most interesting to you? How has the author generated that interest?

5. Look at the transitions between points and between paragraphs. Do they smoothly connect the ideas? Are they subtle or do some of them seem too obvious? Which are the best transitions?

6. What is the author's thesis? Is it clearly identifiable?

7. What ideas from this essay led you to new realizations or fresh perspectives?

8. What questions do you have for the writer?

from

Life on the Mississippi

by Mark Twain

Meet the Writer

Mark Twain is perhaps the best-known and most beloved American author and humorist. The posthumous publication of his autobiography in 2010 returned Twain to the best-seller lists a century after his death. Before making a name for himself as a writer, Twain was a riverboat pilot on the Mississippi.

Now when I had mastered the language of this water, and had come to know every trifling feature that bordered the great river as familiarly as I knew the letters of the alphabet, I had made a valuable acquisition. But I had lost something, too. I had lost something which could never be restored to me while I lived. All the grace, the beauty, the poetry, had gone out of the majestic river! I still keep in mind a certain wonderful sunset which I witnessed when steamboating was new to me. A broad expanse of the river was turned to blood; in the middle distance the red hue brightened into gold, through which a solitary log came floating black and conspicuous; in one place a long, slanting mark lay sparkling upon the water; in another the surface was broken by boiling, tumbling rings that were as many-tinted as an opal; where the ruddy flush was faintest, was a smooth spot that was covered with graceful circles and radiating lines, ever so delicately traced; the shore on our left was densely wooded, and the somber shadow that fell from this forest was broken in once place by a long, ruffled trail that shone like silver; and high above the forest wall a clean-stemmed dead tree waved a single leafy bough that glowed like a flame in the unobstructed splendor that was flowing from the sun. There were graceful curves, reflected images, woody heights, soft distances; and over the whole scene, far and near, the dissolving lights drifted steadily, enriching it every passing moment with new marvels of coloring.

I stood like one bewitched. I drank it in, in a speechless rapture. The world was new to me, and I had never seen anything like this at home. But as I have said, a day came when I began to cease from noting the glories and the charms which the moon and the sun and the twilight wrought upon the river's face; another day came when I ceased altogether to note them. Then, if that sunset scene had been repeated, I should have looked upon it without rapture, and should have commented upon it, inwardly, after this fashion: "This sun means that we are going to have wind to-morrow; that floating log means that the river is rising, small thanks to it; that slanting mark on the water refers to a bluff reef which is going to kill somebody's steamboat one of these nights, if it keeps on stretching out like that; those tumbling 'boils' show a dissolving bar and a changing channel there; the lines and circles in the slick water over yonder are a warning that that troublesome place is shoaling up dangerously; that silver streak in the shadow of the forest is the 'break' from a new snag, and he has located himself in the very best place he could have found to fish for steamboats; that tall dead tree, with a single living branch, is not going to last long, and then how is a body ever going to get through this blind place at night without the friendly old landmark?"

No, the romance and beauty were all gone from the river. All the value any feature of it had for me now was the amount of usefulness it could furnish toward compassing the safe piloting of a steamboat. Since those days, I have pitied doctors from my heart. What does the lovely flush in a beauty's cheek mean to a doctor but a "break" that ripples above some deadly disease? Are not all her visible charms sown thick with what are to him the signs and symbols of hidden decay? Does he ever see her beauty at all, or doesn't he simply view her professionally, and comment upon her unwholesome condition all to himself? And doesn't he sometimes wonder whether he has gained most or lost most by learning his trade?

Discussion Questions

1. Examine the language Twain uses to explain each way of looking at the river. Which key words and phrases convey each perspective?

2. What is Twain's thesis? Is it implied or explicitly stated? What is Twain's strategy for proving his thesis?

3. Does Twain use block-by-block or point-by-point comparison? What are the advantages and disadvantages of his strategy?

4. How can you adapt the approach used in this essay to an essay about your own experiences? For example, can you think of a time when your attitude toward something changed after you became more familiar with it?

Once Unique, Soon a Place Like Any Other

by Abe Whaley

Meet the Writer

Abe Whaley lives in Knoxville, Tennessee. In this essay, Whaley compares and contrasts the pristine countryside of his boyhood home in Tennessee to the exploited and overdeveloped landscape of the present.

I grew up in the mountains of East Tennessee, on a modest farm where we raised a lot of what we ate, watched sunsets on the porch and had supper together every night. For nine generations, mine included, both sides of my family have lived and died in the shadows of the surrounding peaks.

My formative years were spent listening to Papaw (my grandfather) saw away on an old fiddle and Dad flat-pick his six-string guitar as they taught me the songs of Southern Appalachia and handed down a centuries-old musical tradition. A great-great-great-greatgreat grandfather of mine was baptized into the Forks of the Pigeon River Baptist Church in 1796, which he later pastored for 31 years—we are still faithful members, though the name has changed. No one ever really moves away from here and no one ever used to move in. Lately, though, they've been coming in droves.

The Great Smoky Mountains National Park, where my family lived before 1933, and Dollywood, Dolly Parton's theme park, draw year-round crowds. New home construction has been climbing steadily for years, and the rental housing market, mostly overnight log-cabin outfits, has exploded. It seems that no ridge is too steep, no mountaintop too high, no creek too pristine to bulldoze and build on.

I haven't been home much since I graduated from high school six years ago. College, a "real" job, extended international travel, the Tennessee Air National Guard, and work on a master's degree have kept me pretty busy. As much as I love visiting, I hate the trip back. Every time I drive the road into town I see more ridges in the distance that have fallen to construction.

Do not misunderstand me, it is not the simple single-family homes that are so irritating; I have framed up quite a few of those over my summer breaks from school. What bothers me is the way developers feel the need to put up a subdivision on the most beautiful piece of mountain farmland they can find. Of course, the farmers cannot be blamed much—a million-dollar buyout sounds a lot better than trying to make ends meet for another 20 harvests and then losing it all to the bank during their retirement years. But the land magnates, most of whom are from out of town, have no excuse. They wreak wholesale destruction on the surrounding mountaintops and ridgelines as they build their rental cabins and condominiums. They ruin the views that make our piece of Southern Appalachia so enviable in the first place.

I traveled extensively in New Zealand last year and I was amazed by the environmental ethos that seems to be shared by its government and citizens. I rarely saw mass development that went higher than halfway up the mountains that surrounded any given town. The locals I talked to told me that most places had laws that limited construction. What a novel idea—to zone in such a way as to minimize the environmental havoc that developers can impose. Our planners and decision makers could use a lesson in that kind of logic. But so often government officials seem more interested in privately investing in land deals than publicly regulating them.

Those of us seeking to preserve the countryside in Tennessee were dealt another blow by the Supreme Court's recent decision in *Kelo v. City of New London*. The court upheld the government's power of eminent domain, which allows it to take private land for public purpose. Unfortunately, the court ruled that public purpose can be interpreted as economic growth. The chairman of the

Tennessee Valley Authority, which acquired most of its waterfront property through eminent domain years ago, has already stated that the fate of 181,000 acres of wild land set aside for natural-resource conservation is negotiable. This has developers licking their lips in anticipation as they dream of building houses on top of hiking trails. It is obvious that nothing is sacred. It scares me. It scares me a lot.

Though native Appalachians like me are gradually being outnumbered by newcomers, we remain tied to the land in a way outsiders will never understand. It provides for us physically, socially, spiritually and emotionally. Without it, we lose our cultural identity and, ultimately, ourselves. This is not a new fight; it has raged in these mountains for generations as our land has been exploited again and again. For too long, we have suffered the effects of clear-cutting, strip mining and unscrupulous land grabs by timber companies, coal companies and even the federal government. Developers are simply the latest to try their hand at making a buck.

My home is fast becoming a place like many others in this country, homogenized and prepackaged. My roots are neither of those things, and the land I grew up on deserves something better than the reckless development now disgracing its rugged beauty.

Discussion Questions

1. What is Whaley comparing in this essay? Does he use point-by-point or block-by-block comparison? What are the advantages and disadvantages of that strategy?

2. What is Whaley's thesis? Is it implied or explicitly stated? In your opinion, does he prove his thesis? Why or why not?

3. How does Whaley establish his credibility on this topic?

4. Who is Whaley's intended audience? How is his diction, or word choice, tailored to this audience? What other audiences could Whaley target? How might those choices affect his diction?

5. Compare the first paragraph to the last paragraph. What does Whaley achieve by beginning and ending in this fashion? Which particular details convey Whaley's message?

Male-Female Conversation
Is Cross-Cultural
Communication

by Deborah Tannen

Meet the Writer

Deborah Tannen is a professor of linguistics and author of popular books that explore the effect of everyday language on relationships and behavior. This essay compares and contrasts the development of communication skills in men and women.

If women speak and hear a language of connection and intimacy; while men speak and hear a language of status and independence, then communication between men and women can be like cross-cultural communication, prey to a clash of conversational styles. Instead of different dialects, it has been said they speak different genderlects.

The claim that men and women grow up in different worlds may at first seem patently absurd. Brothers and sisters grow up in the same families, children to parents of both genders. Where, then, do women and men learn different ways of speaking and hearing?

It Begins at the Beginning

Even if they grow up in the same neighborhood, on the same block, or in the same house, girls and boys grow up in different worlds of words. Others talk to them differently and expect and accept different ways of talking from them. Most important, children learn how to talk, how to have conversations, not only from their parents but from their peers. After all, if their parents have a foreign or regional accent, children do not emulate it; they learn to speak with the pronunciation of the region where they grow up. Anthropologists Daniel Maltz and Ruth Borker summarize research showing that boys and girls have very different ways of talking to their friends. Although they often play together, boys and girls spend most of their time playing in same-sex groups. And, although some of the activities they play at are similar, their favorite games are different, and their ways of using language in their games are separated by a world of difference.

Boys tend to play outside, in large groups that are hierarchically structured. Their groups have a leader who tells others what to do and how to do it, and resists doing what other boys propose. It is by giving orders and making them stick that high status is negotiated. Another way boys achieve status is to take center stage by telling stories and jokes, and by sidetracking or challenging the stories and jokes of others. Boys' games have winners and losers and elaborate systems of rules that are frequently the subjects of arguments. Finally, boys are frequently heard to boast of their skill and argue about who is best at what.

Girls, on the other hand, play in small groups or in pairs; the center of a girl's social life is a best friend. Within the group, intimacy is key: Differentiation is measured by relative closeness. In their most frequent games, such as jump rope and hopscotch, everyone gets a turn. Many of their activities (such as playing house) do not have winners or losers. Though some girls are certainly more skilled than others, girls are expected not to boast about it, or show that they think they are better than the others. Girls don't give orders; they express their preferences as suggestions, and suggestions are likely to be accepted. Whereas boys say, "Gimme that!" and "Get outta here!" girls say, "Let's do this," and "How about doing that?" Anything else is put down as "bossy." They don't grab center stage—they don't want it—so they don't challenge each other directly. And much of the time, they simply sit together and talk. Girls are not accustomed to jockeying for status in an obvious way; they are more concerned that they be liked.

Gender differences in ways of talking have been described by researchers observing children as young as three. Amy Sheldon videotaped three- to four-year-old boys and girls playing in threesomes at a day-care center. She compared two groups of three—one of boys, one of girls—that got into fights about the same play item: a plastic pickle. Though both groups fought over the same thing, the dynamics by which they negotiated their conflicts were different. In addition to illustrating some of the patterns I have just described, Sheldon's study also demonstrates the complexity of these dynamics.

While playing in the kitchen area of the day-care center, a little girl named Sue wanted the pickle that Mary had, so she argued that

Mary should give it up because Lisa, the third girl, wanted it. This led to a conflict about how to satisfy Lisa's (invented) need. Mary proposed a compromise, but Sue protested:

MARY: I cut it in half. One for Lisa, one for me, one for me.

SUE: But, Lisa wants a *whole* pickle!

Mary comes up with another creative compromise, which Sue also rejects:

MARY: Well, it's a whole half pickle.

SUE: No, it isn't.

MARY: Yes, it is, a whole half pickle.

SUE: I'll give her a whole half. I'll give her a *whole whole*, I gave her a whole one.

At this point, Lisa withdraws from the alliance with Sue, who satisfies herself by saying, "I'm pretending I gave you one."

On another occasion, Sheldon videotaped three boys playing in the same kitchen play area, and they too got into a fight about the plastic pickle. When Nick saw that Kevin had the pickle, he demanded it for himself:

NICK: [Screams] Kevin, but the, oh, I *have* to cut! I want to cut it! It's mine!

Like Sue, Nick involved the third child in his effort to get the pickle:

NICK: [Whining to Joe] Kevin is not letting me cut the pickle.

JOE: Oh, I know! I can pull it away from him and give it back to you. That's an idea!

The boys' conflict, which lasted two and a half times longer than the girls', then proceeded as a struggle between Nick and Joe on the one hand and Kevin on the other.

In comparing the boys' and the girls' pickle fights, Sheldon points out that, for the most part, the girls mitigated the conflict and preserved harmony by compromise and evasion. Conflict was more prolonged among the boys, who used more insistence, appeals to rules, and threats of physical violence. However, to say that these little girls and boys used *more* of one strategy or another is not to say that they didn't use the other strategies at all. For example, the boys did attempt compromise, and the girls did attempt physical force. The girls, like the boys, were struggling for control of their play. When Sue says by mistake, "*I'll* give her a whole half," then quickly corrects herself to say, "I'll give her a *whole whole*," she reveals that it is not really the size of the portion that is important to her, but who gets to serve it.

While reading Sheldon's study, I noticed that whereas both Nick and Sue tried to get what they wanted by involving a third child, the alignments they created with the third child, and the dynamics they set in motion, were fundamentally different. Sue appealed to Mary to fulfill someone else's desire; rather than saying that *she* wanted the pickle, she claimed that Lisa wanted it. Nick asserted his own desire for the pickle, and when he couldn't get it on his own, he appealed to Joe to get it for him. Joe then tried to get the pickle by force. In both these scenarios, the children were enacting complex lines of affiliation.

Joe's strong-arm tactics were undertaken not on his own behalf but, chivalrously, on behalf of Nick. By making an appeal in a whining voice, Nick positioned himself as one-down in a hierarchical structure, framing himself as someone in need of protection. When Sue appealed to Mary to relinquish her pickle, she wanted to take the one-up position of serving food. She was fighting not for the right to have the pickle, but for the right to *serve* it. (This reminded me of the women who said they'd become professors in order to teach.) But to accomplish her goal, Sue was depending on Mary's desire to fulfill others' needs.

This study suggests that boys and girls both want to get their way, but they tend to do so differently. Though social norms encourage boys to be openly competitive and girls to be openly cooperative, different situations and activities can result in different ways of behaving. Marjorie Harness Goodwin compared boys and girls engaged in two task-oriented activities: The boys were making slingshots in preparation for a fight, and the girls were making rings. She found that the boys' group was hierarchical: The leader told the others what to do and how to do it. The girls' group was egalitarian: Everyone made suggestions and tended to accept the suggestions of others. But observing the girls in a different activity—playing house—Goodwin found that they too adopted hierarchical structures: The girls who played mothers issued orders to the girls playing children, who in turn sought permission from their play-mothers. Moreover, a girl who was a play-mother was also a kind of manager of the game. This study shows that girls know how to issue orders and operate in a hierarchical structure, but they don't find that mode of behavior appropriate when they engage in task activities with their peers. They do find it appropriate in parent-child relationships, which they enjoy practicing in the form of play.

These worlds of play shed light on the world views of women and men in relationships. The boys' play illuminates why men would be on the lookout for signs they are being put down or told what to do. The chief commodity that is bartered in the boys' hierarchical world is status, and the way to achieve and maintain status is to give orders and get others to follow them. A boy in a low-status position finds himself being pushed around. So boys monitor their relations for subtle shifts in status by keeping track of who's giving orders and who's taking them.

These dynamics are not the ones that drive girls' play. The chief commodity that is bartered in the girls' community is intimacy. Girls monitor their friendships for subtle shifts in alliance, and they seek to be friends with popular girls. Popularity is a kind of status, but it is founded on connection. It also places popular girls in a bind. By doing field work in a junior high school, Donna Eder found that popular girls were paradoxically—and inevitably—disliked. Many girls want to befriend popular girls, but girls' friendships must necessarily be limited, since they entail intimacy rather than large group activities. So a popular girl must reject the overtures of most of the girls who seek her out—with the result that she is branded "stuck up."

Discussion Questions

1. What is Tannen's thesis? Is it implied or stated explicitly? What is Tannen's strategy for proving her thesis? In your opinion, is she successful?

2. Describe Tannen's tone. What phrases, sentences, or paragraphs most effectively convey this tone? What other possible tones could a writer adopt for this subject matter?

3. Examine the beginnings of Tannen's paragraphs. What transition words and phrases does she use to connect each paragraph to the preceding one?

4. What strategy does Tannen rely on to organize her essay, block-by-block or point-by-point comparison? Provide evidence for your answer.

5. Provide two original examples that would either support or refute Tannen's conclusions. These examples can be hypothetical or real.

Meet Me at Half-Time

by Karen Werling

Meet the Writer

Karen Werling started dancing at age four and has continued to take lessons ever since. She has never once joined a sports team. Her first poem was published when she was in second grade and her love for writing grew from there. She is currently planning to attend Northwestern University, where she will study English and journalism.

I can recite the official names of the positions on a volleyball court, I know how to calculate a player's batting average and I understand soccer's "offsides" rule, but I have never played on a sports team in my life. Growing up in a very athletic family, I was introduced to the terms and concepts of sports at a young age. I spent hours at my sisters' tournaments, baking in the summer sun as I learned how Donna was dipping her shoulder on her swing, or how Kristine was using too much toe on her goal shot. In the car on the way home, I listened to my dad lecture my sisters about aggression and attack while I sat quietly in the backseat, pulling my hair into a tight bun and trying to remember my ballet combinations.

At the age of four, I asked to start taking dance lessons after watching a few minutes of a class through the window of the studio that was next door to the Chinese restaurant where we always ordered our take-out. I never showed the slightest interest in joining an athletic team—no softball, no soccer, no volleyball, not even tennis or track. At first my family was confused with even the basic terminology of dance; they asked me when I had "practices," who was my "coach," what color was my "uniform," and what "position" I held on the "roster." In actuality, my *director* gave me my pink *costume* at my *rehearsal* because, on the *cast list*, I had been assigned the *role* of a flower.

While my sisters jumped from sport to sport, quickly learning and excelling in every one, I continued to work at my dancing. One summer, my older sister decided to take a dance class; it became the one "sport" she could not conquer. She discovered that dancing requires more than just the knowledge of rules and regulations, more than just the ability to turn natural movements into strategies and skills. You cannot be a good dancer without being a good performer—a talent that cannot be taught; you are either born with it, or you're not. Dancing also involves very unnatural movements. One must become accustomed to and comfortable with these movements in order to be considered a good dancer. Athletes cannot just become dancers; it takes years to become at ease with the movements, and even more time to look beautiful while dancing them. In this way, you cannot simply teach someone to dance; there are no written rules or regulations to define the art.

Therein lies the defining difference between athletics and dancing; one is a sport, one is an art. Sports were created simply for the sake of competition, while dance was created for beauty and entertainment. While watching my sisters play, I witnessed players skin their knees or tackle each other, all in the fervor of competition. The spectators encouraged these injuries. In dancing, however, I have witnessed people land a jump incorrectly and break their ankles—something the audience does not want to see. In sports, the bruises and scars can be worn like medals, displaying the athletes' toughness. But in dance the pain is hidden; the dancer with the broken ankle must finish the dance without showing any pain, without making the audience uncomfortable in any way. The pain of dance lies in the fact that pain cannot be shown; one must look beautiful while dancing, making the movements appear easy and painless.

Sitting at a baseball game, a basketball tournament, or practically any other sporting event, you can hear music played to rally the crowd—to create an exciting atmosphere. With dance, the music is much more than that; it is essential to the story and directs the movements. At sporting events, the athletes do not generally participate in the excitement and camaraderie created by the music, and it is not at all unusual or frowned upon for one of the players to take a lead, stepping out ahead of his teammates to become the "star." But in a dance performance, if the dancers were to ignore the music and move too quickly, too slowly, off-count, or not at all, the audience would become uneasy and dissatisfied. If one dancer were to step out of line and broadcast himself as the star, he would be looked down upon for drawing attention away from the storyline and for altering the planned actions.

Over the years, I have continued to introduce a new world of ideas and interpretations to my family through dancing. They have developed an appreciation for the art and the hard work that it requires, and I have not lost my appreciation for their sports. I still find joy in a local team's win or an unlikely comeback, while my family has learned to recognize a good dancer and to admire the effort required to create a successful performance. Just as I sat through their games as a young girl, my sisters willingly watch my every performance—although I forgive them if they ask to meet me at "half-time."

Discussion Questions

1. Which organizational plan does Werling use to organize her essay? What are the advantages and disadvantages of using that pattern in this essay?

2. Describe Werling's tone. Which phrases, sentences, or paragraphs most clearly convey this tone? What other tones might a writer adopt for this subject?

3. What is Werling's thesis? Is it stated explicitly in the essay or is it implied? In your opinion, has she proven her thesis? Which of her points are most interesting or compelling?

4. Choose one of Werling's paragraphs and examine how she provides transitions between sentences. What words or phrases does she use to connect each sentence with the preceding sentence?

Writing Road:

An intellectual journey through the progression of a student's writing

by *Joe Pacilio*

Meet the Writer

Some have called him their hero…some their anti-drug… but most just call him Joe Pacilio. Joe hopes to become a mechanical engineer and plans to continue inspiring the masses with his breathtaking collections of words.

"Bobby Hull was a hockey playr. He playd sentrman. I got Bobby Hull's adagraf." That's an excerpt from a piece of my first grade writing. I obviously despised vowels and tried to rebel against the dictionary. Boy, those were the days. I still remember being in early elementary school and absolutely despising writing. I hated everything about writing, right down to the frail, dirty colored paper with the HUGE blue and red lines.

I remember one time in first grade, Mrs. Curtis (my first grade teacher), assigned us to write a mile-long story about whatever we wanted. (Well, it seemed "mile-long" at the time.) That day I was just blown away. I didn't want to write anything, much less a lengthy, imaginative story. I remember thinking, "When did I enter college?" I was completely lost, so what did I do? Did I ask the teacher for help? Nope. Did I ask my parents for a little guidance? Nope. I just decided to fill up the majority of my pages with gigantic illustrations! (Wow, I was such a bright kid back then). Unfortunately, I ended up getting a below-average grade on that paper.

In fourth grade, while sulking down Writing Road,* I came upon a house.** The house was the home of my new friend, Expository Composition. Yes, that's right, my fourth-grade teacher introduced me to expository writing and I fell in love.

I can still recall Mrs. Gunderson's analogy of a good expository five-paragraph paper. She compared it to a hamburger! There was the top bun as the introductory paragraph. The lettuce represented the first body paragraph, while the tomatoes stood for the second body paragraph. (I think you can see where this is going, but I'll finish making the sandwich for those of you who don't know where this is going) The actual meat patty corresponded to the best and meatiest paragraph, the third body paragraph. The papers would end with a conclusion paragraph, also known as the bottom bun. Mrs. Gunderson had a little diagram depicting this relationship up on the front bulletin board. This "sandwich" approach to writing was awesome for me.

Back in elementary school I excelled at math, science, history, and those more factual disciplines. Writing had always been too "creative" for me…until I learned about expository writing. Once I had the "hamburger plan" to follow and a topic in hand, I became a robotic writing machine. That year I finally found my writing niche.

Factual, structured writing defined me through the rest of my elementary school career and into the beginning of my junior high days. It wasn't until halfway through seventh grade that I finally became a creative writer. Mr. Hanson, my awesome English teacher, forced me to be creative and express my thoughts, and I hated him for it at the beginning of the year. I had done just fine so far in my life with expository writing. Why did I need to break away from my previous successes? Well, part of that answer may lie in the fact that I never really wrote what I thought. I just put some words on paper and organized them in five orderly paragraphs. However, my seventh-grade teacher gave me a reason to write from my heart. We read the kind of books, like *The Giver* and *Animal Farm*, that make you take a second look at society. Those books helped me think about real life and really develop some strong opinions. It was the first time in my life I'd ever felt obligated to be heard, and the more I expressed my opinions, the more positive feedback I received. I came to crave that praise.

---

*   There actually is no "Writing Road." It stands only as a metaphor for the progression of my writing.
** Likewise, there is no house on Writing Road, as Writing Road doesn't actually exist.

Then, Mr. Hanson assigned us to create an adventure story. There were no guidelines except that it had to have a climax and at least one twist in the plot. Normally I would've cringed at the thought of so much brainstorming and idea developing, but not anymore. Now I wanted to show everyone what I had in me...I was finally going to use my writing voice! (Before reading on, you must know that I was a *Lord of the Rings* freak during seventh grade and those books, as you will see, greatly influenced my "creativity.") I ended up writing a five-and-a-half page story (a personal record at the time) about a little man named Bobo Balou. When I went to turn it in, I remember the giant smile plastered to my face. It was the first time I had ever created a character from scratch and developed a story for five and a half pages. That paper marked the end of an era. There was no more essay writing in my future. I became a "creative writing man"!

My trip down Writing Road*** has been a long, winding one. I've gone from a little boy who hated putting pen to paper to a struc-tured- writing robot to a creative writing fanatic. (Ok, maybe fanatic was a little over the top, but honestly, I enjoy writing now.) As much as I've loved walking down Writing Road with you, I'm going to have to let you off here because although the road seems long and straight, I'm sure a fork is on its way and when it comes I need to be ready.

Discussion Questions

1. How many subjects does Pacilio compare in this essay? Identify his primary point about each subject.

2. What is Pacilio's thesis? Is it implied or stated explicitly? In your opinion, does Pacilio prove his thesis? Why or why not?

3. What method does Pacilio use to develop this essay: block-by-block or point-by-point? What are the advantages and disadvantages of this approach?

4. Describe Pacilio's tone. What phrases or sentences most effectively convey this tone?

*** There still is no "Writing Road." It still stands only as a metaphor for the pro-gression of my writing.

Grandmother's House
by Anastasia Kotsakis

Meet the Writer

Anastasia Kotsakis swims and plays water polo. She lives with her parents, her younger brother and sister, and her dog, Chloe.

After a month of anticipation, the winding six-hour drive began. We passed the rolling fields of cows and the forests of pine trees only to end at the 20 foot "iron man" dressed in his yellow mining gear and finest mustache. The mild climate of Iron Mountain, Michigan, hit me as I hopped out of the car past the ivy stained chimney up to the porch of my grandparents' house. As the door opened, excitement crept over me. After the traditional sloppy kisses and bear hug I immediately ran upstairs and claimed my bedroom. The cozy yellow room with the antique armoire and plush little bed was perfect for a little girl of the age of six. As I wandered around to familiarize myself with the house, I stumbled upon a secret kept by the house. It was one of those secrets that makes a girl jump with anticipation; it was a secret passageway. It led from behind the bathroom next to my bedroom all the way down a narrow stairway to the pantry. The darkness overtook me as I quietly made my way past the magnified window against the wall and down the stairs. It was the perfect way to play a joke on anybody reaching for the cereal. However, little girls have very little patience, so after a few minutes it was time to discover another wonder within the house.

Through the kitchen and to the left was the living room, the most terrifying of all rooms. A chill would creep up my spine as I stared into the abyss. The room was blanketed with darkness, with only the silhouettes of pictures visible against the walls and tables. The room screamed "DO NOT ENTER" to anyone who got within an arm's length of the entrance. However, if you moved your head only 180 degrees to the right, the darkness would be replaced by the fireworks of colors outside. Curiosity overcame me and I sneaked outside to investigate the source of this brightness. Above me, accented against the bright white fence, was a garden of lilies, daisies, and petunias. As in a fairytale, I would swing next to the bed of flowers, admiring their beauty. The most fascinating part of the yard, though, was the little wooden shed in the corner of the property. As I approached the shed, the four foot tall forest green door stood out against the white siding. The inside was painted an off-white, like the color of sand from the ocean. The little house was complete with a picture of monarch butterflies fluttering their way across a field, an oval mirror just as big as my head, and a bench lined with cushions. Opposite the tiny door was a thick four-panel window overlooking the garden. With so much to entertain me in Iron Mountain, I had no reason to go home. I was intrigued by my grandparents' house and all the mysteries it held within.

However, as I grew in age, my interests changed from wanting adventure and mystery to not wanting to get out of bed in the mornings. Now, for a month, I dread the long walk into the family van for a six-hour drive that is barely tolerable, even with a new sleek 1-pound DVD player in front of me. I dread how boring the next week will be staying in my grandmother's ancient house. After many torturous hours of watching reruns of *Friends* and feeling sick (probably from watching the DVD screen) we finally pass the rusted image of a man holding a mining tool of some sort. I get out of the car and breathe the chilly air. I straggle up the steps to the house and after a loving a kiss from my grandmother, I bolt to the television like an Olympic sprinter runs to the finish line. The day passes surely but slowly and after what seems like a year it is time to go to bed. I leave a dent on the couch as I slowly make my way up the stairs to the yellowish bedroom and settle myself in the tiny bed with moth-eaten sheets. I wake up too early and clamber out of bed with my neck and back aching from the old, stiff mattress on the bed. I open the pantry door, reach in, and grab the Honey Nut Cheerios before someone else steals them, not concerned by the secret that lies just beyond them. After wasting away many more hours, the family gathers in the living room for the annual "so what have you been up to?" questions. A room that can be lit up by simply lifting the curtains up no longer intimidates me. I look around and I stare blankly at the pictures of my ancestors, falling in and out of daydreams, not caring about anything but being able to go home in six days, four hours, 34 minutes, and 15 seconds.

Outside, I finally see an opportunity to get something done in this monotonous place. As I walk outside in my bathing suit the door creaks from the pressure of having the weight of a house pressing down on it for over a hundred years. I settle myself in a lawn chair facing the sun and my iPod ear buds in my ears. I see only the glare of the sun and ignore the colors that entertained me through most of my childhood. Straight in front of me, the little shack still stands, cracked and chipped from years of extreme winters. The four-paneled window is full of dust and cobwebs and spiders occupy the inside of the shed. The butterflies on the wall are faded and the mirror is barely visible through the air, which is thick with years of dirt and dust. All I can think about is that this is not how I remember it looking when I was a child. I don't understand how it is all different, yet little has changed about my grandmother's house. All I know is I will forever miss the time spent in the little white shed, swinging with no purpose, and exploring the unknown.

Discussion Questions

1. Compare Kotsakis's word choices in the first half of the essay with her word choices in the second half. Offer three examples and explain what is achieved with each choice.

2. What seems to be Kotsakis's ultimate message about adventure and mystery?

3. Describe a situation in which your viewpoint changed over time.

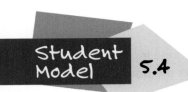

It Doesn't Take a Genius to Notice...

by Dipika Chaudhuri

Meet the Writer

Dipika Chaudhuri is 17 years old and has enjoyed writing since she was a child. She is the managing editor of her school newspaper and enjoys dancing in her free time. She lives with her parents and younger sister.

As I walk into my 5th period AP Government class, I cower with fear. The walls are plastered with covers of old *Time* magazines displaying politicians wearing phony smiles and waving to believing audiences. There are complicated charts with snaking arrows trying to explain the responsibilities of our government. Print-outs of human evolution and a detailed description and analysis decorate the top of one bulletin board. The bottom is covered in various news articles and current events. I look around the room at the other students. They are sitting up straight, awaiting the bell to ring, baby birds waiting for their mothers to feed them. They have their notes out, their hands itching to begin writing, their brains impatient to start processing information. I'm surprised that these students' heads aren't bigger, because the intelligence in their brains is massive.

These are the all-knowing AP Kids. They travel in tight packs and take pride in their academic achievement. They can recite all the elements of the periodic table in alphabetical order and conjugate the verb "oír" (which is known to be a tricky one) in all fourteen tenses in less than four minutes. They can draw the unit circle in their sleep and list all the U.S. presidents and their major achievements forwards and backwards. No physics problem is too complicated and no English paper is too long. What these AP Kids can't do is still unknown to mankind.

The powder-white piece of chalk comes in contact with the board, and the lesson begins. I take a look at everyone's organized notebooks. There are no stray doodles of undersea life, cascading waterfalls and breezy palm trees, only perfectly legible handwriting marching across the page, as highlighted words scream "look at me!" and gain a little more attention from my wandering eye. Brightly colored Post-it notes peek out from other pages, hoping to get a second glance from the AP student. Some words are deemed especially important and are underlined with thick, heavy black ink, while other words fight for room on the side of the page.

As our teacher lectures, students' hands race across the page to jot everything down. Our teacher's voice is like a fan humming in the background, mostly the same with a few ups and downs sprinkled in randomly. Students have stacks of books under their desks that boast the names of the classes they're enrolled in. The AP Kids who are precise and accurate carry calculus books, those who enjoy literature carry English or history books, and of course all of us have our government books. As we open up our books we can smell the scent of those who used our books in the past. There were students who enjoyed the sea of words and the insight it gave them about our government. There were also the students who preferred to use the book as a pillow, perfect for those midday naps.

After my government class and five minutes in the vicious, oxygen-scarce jungle of the hallways, I enter my Social Studies class. My IQ seems to increase by 20 points instantaneously, as this class does not come with an "AP," "honors" or "accelerated" label.

In contrast with the room décor of my government class, this room is decorated in cute, baby pink fur. Advertisements for mascara and tennis shoes don the side wall, while the back wall is covered with colorful art projects from a freshman class.

Students saunter in casually and instead of heading to their seats to prepare for class, they begin drawing on the white board. Beautiful designs of pretty pink petunias blending with a lush green grass under a bright and exuberant sun. Students sign their flashy autographs on the board, as if they are superstars. After spending five more minutes showing off their artistic abilities, the students take their seats.

The room definitely lacks the AP vibe; I can tell because no one is discussing college. The biggest worry seems to be where to go for lunch: will it be a greasy, oil-caked pizza or a fresh and crisp Subway sandwich? Meanwhile back in the AP realm, students discuss who will apply early decision to MIT or NYU.

Homework is another issue that is treated differently in this room. AP Kids would be delighted with their good fortune if their teachers were so kind as to only assign an hour and a half of homework. However in this class, one and a half hours of homework is the equivalent of falling out of a moving bus, being run over by gaggle of wild hissing geese, and having to eat liver for dinner.

And where do I fit in? Somewhere in between the two extremes. It's the best of both worlds.

Discussion Questions

1. Chaudhuri sometimes exaggerates to make her point. Offer two examples and describe the effect in each instance.

2. Chaudhuri writes that she exists "somewhere in between the two extremes." List several details to show that she admires students from both extremes.

3. In comparing AP and regular level students, Chaudhuri focuses on several points of comparison: the décor and atmosphere in the two classrooms, attitudes toward homework, and classroom behavior. On what other points could she have focused?

Writing About a Process

ucky you! You just won grand prize in the contest! You're the proud owner of a new home entertainment system: big-screen plasma television, state-of-the-art sound system, the newest video game program and components, and even a telephone/intercom that interfaces with the other components.

On the day your prize arrives in about twenty-five boxes of different sizes, you're excited. The room is ready. You already know which movie you're going to watch first (with the volume on full blast), and you've invited over some friends to play the latest video games on this megascreen. All you have to do now is assemble the system.

One of the boxes is labeled "Open This Box First." You open it first. After all, you know the importance of following instructions during an assembly process like this. You find the packet of directions in a plastic bag on top of the box's other contents. You turn to the first page. Uh, oh. As you begin to read, you realize that the instructions are overly technical. They assume that you are an expert who sets up a system like this every day. Also, the descriptions of the components do not match what you see in front of you. The ultimate insult is that the instructions do not tell you how to begin; instead, they direct you to do several things, seemingly all at the same time. Your original enthusiasm is quickly dampened by the daunting task of following a process that is explained poorly.

We have all had a similarly frustrating experience of attempting to assemble a system, toy, or product with poorly written instructions. The steps in the instruction booklet are delivered in unclear language, or the pictures bear no resemblance to the actual parts or processes you have in hand.

If you get stuck, write at the top of a blank document or blank piece of paper: "What am I trying to say?" Try to capture in a few simple words the primary essence of your writing purpose. Another way to think of this is to follow the advice of Ernest Hemingway, a fellow who knew a thing or two about writing in a distinctive and compelling voice: "All you have to do is write one true sentence. Write the truest sentence you know."

If you're stuck, be aware that you might be victimizing yourself with panicky self-talk: "I'm never going to finish this! I'm such a bad writer! Why does this always happen to me?" If your linguistic mechanism is busy shouting at you, it will have trouble doing the work you want it to do. Tell it to shut up, and then focus on the question, "What am I trying to say?" This should be enough to get you back on track.

Recipes provide another example of the importance of carefully written directions. If a recipe is created without attention to steps, order, and ingredients, the result can be disappointing for both the cook and those obligated to sample the finished product.

Perhaps you have had a similar experience with someone giving you directions: "You go down that one road for a ways and at the stoplight—either the second or third one—you turn left. When you see the Starbucks, you're almost there." Sometimes those kinds of directions lead us successfully to our destinations, but because they are so sketchy, we still make the trip with some anxiety.

If those scenarios sound familiar, then the importance of this chapter's focus—writing about a process—is already clear to you. When your purpose involves describing or discussing a process, several tasks are critical: managing the "chunks" or steps, putting them in the proper order, and connecting the steps with helpful transitions.

Process assignments can vary in levels of complexity. If your assignment is to describe the process of making or assembling something concrete or doing something physical, your task is relatively straightforward but not necessarily simple. If the assignment, or your chosen way of fulfilling the assignment, is more abstract—for example, a discussion of how to achieve perfect happiness or of the best way to build consensus among disagreeing parties—your process discussion will be more complex.

Choosing a Topic

Let's consider some basic learning theory. After all, this business of writing about a process actually involves you acting as a teacher, while your reader is cast in the role of student. This is important to understand as you choose your topic. Consider these phases of acquiring knowledge or a skill as described by learning theorists:

1. **Unconscious Incompetence:** I don't know it, and I don't even know I don't know it.

2. **Conscious Incompetence:** I don't know it, but I'm aware that I don't know it.

3. Conscious Competence: I know it, but I have to consciously think about it.

4. Unconscious Competence: I know it, and I don't even have to think about it.

If your topic involves a process that you don't know at all—something from those unconscious incompetence or conscious incompetence zones—you will have the challenge of writing about a topic with which you're not comfortable and which you have perhaps never considered or expressed in language.

If your topic involves a process that you know quite well—something in that unconscious competence zone—that is both good news and potentially bad news. The good news is that the confidence you have in your expertise will enable you to approach writing about the process without undue anxiety. However, if you know your topic and its inherent processes so well that you can do them relatively unconsciously—that is, without thinking about them—you face the challenge of putting them into words, perhaps for the first time in quite a while.

Writers on Writing

First, begin at the beginning, but be prepared to discover fairly quickly that it's not the beginning at all. This is the "Get Anything Down" philosophy, and works on the principle that nothing is more paralysing than searching for that combination of vowels and consonants which will comprise the Perfect First Sentence. School teachers are eager advocates of this approach: "Write your opening paragraph, then cross it out," they used to tell us over and over again… "Write the first page, then throw it away."

—*Susan Sellers*

For example, if you are a skilled equestrian, then you have followed the steps in outfitting a horse countless times, and you can probably do it without your full attention. You can probably saddle a horse and put on its halter and bridle while thinking about your spring break, your lunch plans, or your life's ultimate goals. The point is that when the time comes to explain that process to someone else, your writing challenge is to convey in language something that you do without language.

If you have a choice regarding your topic, the best one will probably come from the skills you have in the conscious competence zone. Those areas of expertise are comfortable for you to write about, but because you still have to talk to yourself a little bit as you do them, the language will come more easily for you as you write.

Here are three points to remember when writing about a process, regardless of the level of complexity or abstraction:

1. Divide the process into manageable steps.

2. Discuss the steps in order.

3. Provide very clear transitions between steps.

In the following sections we'll look at each of these points in more detail. Having a potential topic in mind will help you apply each of the steps that follow. If you decide to change topics after considering the following steps, that's fine.

Journal Topic

Describe the steps one would need to take to become just like _____ _____. (Fill in the blank with the name of a cherished family member, relative, friend, or famous person—or insert your own name.) Consider adopting a light and humorous tone.

Dividing the Process into Manageable Steps

This phase of writing about a process is similar to assembling the ingredients for a recipe. You first make sure that everything you need is on hand. Then you lay it out on the counter before beginning. For a writing project involving a process, the difference is that you must first "write the ingredients" before combining them.

Regardless of your level of expertise with the process, identifying and delineating its steps early in your planning is crucial.

Sometimes we may be so familiar with a process that the steps seem to flow together in ways that make it difficult to separate them. (This is especially true when we are operating in the unconscious competence zone.) When you write about such a process, it is especially important that you consider the process from your audience's perspective, not your own. A process over which you have some level of mastery may look very different to a reader unfamiliar with the process. After all, your purpose in writing this paper is to communicate to your audience an understanding of the process. (If you are simply writing to yourself so that *you* don't forget the process, much less formality is necessary.)

Writers on Writing

Writing permits us to understand not only the world but also the self. We discover who we are by the writing.

—*Erika Lindemann*

For example, consider the way a basketball team's best player might describe how she shoots free throws so successfully. The language she uses with her teammates will be very different from how she explains the process to non-athletes. With her teammates, she is more likely to employ technical terminology understood by athletes or maybe even codes or slang that her team uses for specific moves or maneuvers. With a more general audience, she must use vocabulary that is suitable to her listeners' level of knowledge or there is no point in even having the discussion.

As you work to shift from your own perspective to that of a reader, here are some useful questions about your chosen process topic:

1. Why is this process important or interesting? (The answer to this question may provide the seed of your introduction and conclusion.)

2. What tools or preparation do I need before beginning the process?

3. What do I do first? How do I know when that first action is complete or needs an additional component?

4. What do I do next, and how do I know when that next step is finished? And after that, and after that?

5. What is the final step, after which no other actions are needed or possible?

Answering these questions will identify for you the manageable chunks that will serve as the rough material for the first draft of your process paper. Take a few moments now to scratch out some notes in response to these questions.

As you answer these questions, you will eventually come up with a list of steps, a few ideas about each of those steps, and the beginning of a thesis about why someone would even bother with this process.

Writing About a Single Step

Now it's time to write about the steps. Go ahead. Choose a step. Any step. (Most people will choose the first step, and that's fine.) Eventually, you will need to put the steps in order, but you don't have to write them that way the first time through, unless that seems like the most natural approach to you. It might seem more natural for you to write about the second step, or the one right before the last step, or maybe you want to write about the last step first.

Review your notes about the step you chose. Then take a moment to visualize the step. If your topic involves a physical process, imagine how this step feels in your fingers or other body parts. Think about any emotional associations involved. For example, if the step is near the beginning, you might be aware of excitement, enthusiasm, or anxiety about what's ahead. If you are writing

Writers on Writing

The quality of one's writing should be a concern not only of those whose profession is to write. Businessmen, lawyers, ministers, accountants, and fund-raisers ought also to be concerned. A man is known, so the proverb goes, by the company he keeps. At certain levels of correspondence, a man may be judged by the letters he writes.

—*James J. Kilpatrick*

about diving into a pool, concentrate on how you would precisely align your body as you prepare for the dive, as well as any feelings you might experience before the dive, such as apprehension or confidence. If this step is near the end, an appropriate emotional response might be relief that the end is just ahead, or perhaps some measure of sorrow that a beloved process is winding down. For example, if you are describing the process of giving your friend a haircut, exactly how does it feel when you step back to assess your final product and await your friend's reaction?

Write. Write everything you can think of about this step. What exactly do you do, in minute detail? How does it look, sound, smell, taste, and feel (both physically and emotionally)? How is this process similar to other processes the reader may know? Look for opportunities to use figurative, descriptive language to enhance your reader's understanding of this step and its role in the overall process. After writing thoroughly about this step, take a little break, enough to clear from your mind most of the thoughts you had involving that step.

Then choose another step. It may be the one immediately before or after the one you just covered, or it may be from elsewhere in the process. It doesn't matter at this point. Work your way like this through each of the steps. Don't worry yet about the order of the steps, especially if it's not obvious. Also, don't worry yet about how to connect the steps. Order and connections are important, but they come later.

Journal Topic

Describe the steps a friend or family member should take to ensure he or she buys you a good gift.

Discussing the Steps in Order

Now that you have these carefully described steps, it's time to put them in order. This might be easy. If each step has a clear beginning and ending point, and the process can only be accomplished one way, then your ordering decisions will be obvious.

If, on the other hand, your process is more complex or abstract, the order might not be as clear to you. For example, if you are writing about the relatively abstract process of discovering personal fulfillment, the steps may not be immediately obvious. What if your process topic involves simultaneous steps? What if, under some circumstances, an early step needs to be repeated later? What if the order of some of the steps simply doesn't matter?

For each of these special circumstances, you have decisions to make. You are the author, as in *authority*. Because you have some expertise in this area, you are more qualified than your audience to determine the best order. A definite order provides a sense of security for your audience, and it enhances your authorial credibility more than a wishy-washy approach.

For those situations in which the order of some of the steps is unimportant or they must be accomplished simultaneously, ask yourself if something else can help you determine the order in which you present the steps. Does one step involve more or less equipment? Does it require more or less time? Is one step more fun than another? Consider moving from more intricate steps to simpler ones, or from simpler steps to more intricate. For example, if you are writing about how to pack for a vacation, the order of items to include in your suitcase or backpack might be relatively unimportant. However, if you pack your gear in a certain order, you probably have a reason for that order. Including your reasons as you write the steps makes a more solid impression on your reader than simply saying that the order doesn't matter.

Later on, when you add transitions between steps, you may explain the special circumstances surrounding some of the steps, but for now it is critical that you choose the order.

To complete this stage of writing about a process, it's time for you to make decisions and arrange the steps that you wrote about earlier. If you wrote those steps on a computer, be sure to save your writing, and then use the cut-and-paste commands to arrange the steps in order. A good idea is to create a new word-processing document for this step. A name for this new document might be "Steps in Order." If you are writing longhand, consider actually using scissors and tape to arrange in order these versions of your steps.

Now let's take stock of where you are in this process. Assuming that you have some choice about your topic, you have surveyed your areas of expertise and chosen just the right process to discuss. You have thought carefully about what steps are involved, and you have written about each step in fresh, vivid language. You have arranged those steps in the best possible order as determined by obvious means or by your own expertise. Now it's time to connect those ordered steps so that your reader can easily follow the process you have so carefully arranged.

Journal Topic

Describe the steps in making a peanut butter and jelly sandwich.

Providing Transitions Between Steps

Since elementary school, you have probably heard that smoothness, or flow, is a desirable quality in writing. (For the most part, that is true. Depending on a writer's purpose, sometimes roughness can be desirable too, if it's used strategically for a certain effect.) When writing about a process, smoothness or connectedness is highly desirable. You want your reader to see how each step leads to the next to arrive at a completed product or goal. This sense of smoothness or connectedness is achieved by the use of transitions, those little words and phrases that connect sentences or paragraphs to one another. You learned about transitions in more detail in Chapter 4, but here are a few important ideas to remember:

1. Use transitions at the beginnings of paragraphs and, when possible, within paragraphs, too.

2. Weak transitions are better than none, but good transitions work best.

3. Ideally, readers won't notice your transitions, but they will appreciate them anyway.

The guiding principle for using transitions is to write a word or phrase at the beginning of each paragraph that subtly signals your reader about the direction you are going to take next. If the next step involves continuing in the same direction, appropriate transitions for that might include *along the same line, similarly,* or *in much the same way.* Your goal may be to completely reverse direction, so you might write *on the other hand, on the contrary,* or even a simple *however.* If your intention is to move on to another step in a process, possible transitions include *when this is complete, next,* or *afterward.*

These examples should be enough to give you the idea of how to write transitions. The best transitions emerge naturally from your own vocabulary and the circumstances of the writing. Weak transitions are self-conscious, formulaic, and obvious. The most obvious transitions for process writing are *first, second, third,* and *in conclusion.* But, as we noted earlier, weak transitions are better than none. If these are the only transitions you can think of, use them. Also feel free to use them in early drafts. You can always change them later. The important thing to remember is that the purpose of transitions is to subtly signal to your reader the direction of the next paragraph.

When you edit your paper, examine your transitions between paragraphs. Look at each one. Does it do its job in a natural, effective way? In places where the steps were ordered by something other than sequence—intricacy, time involved, or level of fun—do transitions help the reader follow your method of organization?

If you use effective transitions, readers won't notice them, but they *will* notice that your process description is particularly smooth and easy to follow. For more ideas on transitions, see pages 135–137.

Considering Your Tone

Awareness of audience and purpose is important when writing about a process, and this awareness has implications for the tone you adopt. If, for example, you are writing to an audience of underclassmen with the purpose of explaining how to successfully survive the social dynamics of your school's cafeteria, you can choose to convey your expertise in a serious tone, concentrating on the importance of various cliques and traditions, or you can poke fun at the whole business, focusing on the ridiculous lengths some students go to eat mediocre food surrounded by people who dress the same way they do. You might include the same process steps in either approach, but your **diction**, or choice of words, will change depending on the tone you adopt.

Similarly, if you are writing to an audience of your peers with the purpose of providing advice about how to talk to parents, you will most likely include some insider tips on persuasive arguments to use with parents. If you choose to write with professional diction, using terms from psychology, your writing will have a scholarly tone that may impress your audience and convince them of your competence and credibility on the subject. On the other hand, if you choose to adopt a friendlier tone, using more everyday language, your readers may perceive you as being more "real" or more in touch with how people your age really think.

Using this chapter as a guide, you can now approach the discussion of any process with a plan. When you have a choice of process topics, you know how to determine which topics will work best for you. You also know what questions to ask to identify and delineate the steps involved in the process. After these steps are delineated, you have strategies for putting them in the best order, and you have advice for smoothly and subtly connecting your steps. Finally, you know how to consider your audience and your purpose when deciding upon a tone for your writing.

Beyond the rhetorical uses of these guidelines, the ability to effectively discuss and describe a process can be useful in other areas of your life too. The principles behind these steps will help you to be more organized, more efficient, and a more effective learner or teacher.

Practice

Before beginning the Chapter Assignment, try the following exercises to practice writing about a process.

1. One of the challenges of writing about a process is recognizing how you can break the process down into separate steps. Jot down the steps involved in two or three of these activities:

   • Brushing your teeth

   • Traveling from your home to your school

   • Opening your locker

   • Writing an online status update

   • Choosing the clothes you wore today

   • Finding a part-time job

   • Turning on a computer and finding a particular file

2. Choose *one* of the preceding topics and write down several steps involved in that topic. Assuming that each step is a paragraph, create a transition for the beginning of each paragraph. Make each transition different from the others.

Chapter Assignment

Prewriting

Your assignment for this chapter is to write an essay describing a process. Use the following suggestions to help you choose a topic and clarify the purpose of your essay.

Begin with an inventory of your skills and knowledge, those areas of expertise that might form the basis of a process discussion. Jot down a few thoughts about each of the following questions.

1. What are your favorite activities—things to do outside of school, in school, or in extracurricular areas?

2. What activities do you perform almost every day or at least several times a week?

3. What things do you do with some regularity that probably no one else in your class would choose to write about?

4. What are some activities you are particularly skilled at?

5. What are some things you have learned to do most recently?

Writing Topics

Select one of the topics either from Prewriting or from the following list to develop into an essay about a process. Feel free to tailor these topics to suit your needs.

Go back through the list from the Prewriting section and label the items CI (conscious incompetence), CC (conscious competence), or UC (unconscious competence). This may help you to identify the topics that will work best for your assignment. As discussed earlier in this chapter, the best topics to write about are usually those in the conscious competence category, because the conscious thinking you do while accomplishing those processes will help provide you with the language you need to do this writing.

If the "Prewriting" exercise yields no useful topics, here are several others to consider. You may need to narrow your focus for many of these.

1. How to succeed in school (in class, in the hallways, in the cafeteria, on the field)

2. How to convince your parents to say *yes*

3. How to convince your employer to give you a raise

4. How to be optimistic in the face of adversity, or how to be happy when life isn't going so well

5. How to make the most of attending a concert

6. How to organize a busy day

7. How to plan a vacation

8. How to eat a healthy diet

9. How to recover from the breakup of a relationship, or how to maintain a long-term relationship

Revision

As you revise and edit your first draft, consider these questions.

1. Have you provided an introduction that suggests why this process is important, satisfying, or interesting?

2. Have you divided this process into steps that your reader will understand? Have you used terminology that those who are not experts will understand?

3. Have you provided an order that will make sense to a nonexpert reader?

4. Do your transitions at the beginning of each paragraph signal to a reader the direction of the paragraph?

5. Do the transitions clarify the order of the steps?

6. Does your conclusion leave your reader with a satisfying final thought or realization regarding the process you wrote about?

7. Do you understand everything you have written? If not, where do you need to simplify or clarify?

Peer Review

Use these questions to help you evaluate another student's writing. Remember, specific suggestions and examples are most helpful.

1. How do you feel about the title?

2. In what ways does the introduction let you know why this process is important, satisfying, or interesting?

3. Look at the beginning of each paragraph. How has the author provided a smooth transition from the previous paragraph?

4. How do the transitions help you understand the relationship between steps in the process?

5. What satisfying final thought or realization about the process does the conclusion provide?

6. Is there a step in the process that needs to be expanded or broken down into smaller steps? Is there a step that might be cut out or reduced? Explain.

7. Could you successfully follow these steps? Why or why not?

8. What questions do you have for the writer?

That's What I Call Funny

by Dave Chappelle

Meet the Writer

Dave Chappelle is an American comedian, writer, and actor. His successful sketch comedy show, *Chappelle's Show,* ran from 2003–2006 on the cable television network *Comedy Central.*

Laughter is mysterious. Laughter is such an involuntary response, it's unpredictable. You just don't know what will make you laugh until it makes you laugh. Talking about laughter is tough, and I should warn everyone who reads this that I don't really know what I'm talking about. I'm 31 years old, and I've been doing stand-up since I was 14, and I'm still trying to figure it all out.

Stand-up has unequivocally been the most consistently fun thing I've done in my life. It's what makes me happy. I like doing my show, but stand-up has the most freedom in it artistically. It's direct—there are no intermediaries between you and the audience. I don't have to go to Standards and Practices [the broadcast industry's self-censoring panel] to clear my material. I don't have to worry about advertisers and what they'll say. I just tell people jokes off the top of my head.

The evolution of my jokes happens very organically. If there's something I see on the news or something I'm thinking about, I might go down to the club and just talk it out, almost conversationally, and funny things will arise. I don't sit at a desk and think, "I want to tackle the issue of AIDS" or "I want to tackle the issue of racism." I don't look at things that way. Sometimes I'll think up things just because I know they're inappropriate, which is kind of the fun of comedy. It's liberating.

Some things are so painful that they seem as if they're not funny, but it's not like people will never laugh at them. A lot of times the humor doesn't come from pain exactly; it comes from things that make you anxious or afraid. It just helps you put them in perspective if you laugh at them. When the war first started, I was doing war material, but as the news changed, the response to the material changed. Something is funny one day, but the next day someone would get decapitated, and it might not be as funny. Whether people will laugh just depends on what's going on at the time. One of the reasons people go to see comedy is that there's always an element of escapism to any kind of entertainment. But I've had other experiences where you'd think people wouldn't want to talk about a subject, and it turned out that they loved talking about it. I remember there were some Marines who had just been in Iraq who came to a show I was giving in a club, and when the subject of the war first came up, they might have been a little tense about it. But as the show went on, they were laughing about it. They would scream stuff out, and I could see that for them it was kind of a relief—or a release—to just get it off their chests.

There are some comics who are really well-adjusted, and there are some of these guys who walk around kind of wounded. I think I fall somewhere in between. There's something powerful about being able to translate unhappiness into something positive. It's a kind of alchemy that artists perform. I think that's sort of the God-like part in man—the part of people that can transcend their personal problems and make something beautiful out of them. Maybe that's why people respond to pain-riddled artists, whether it's Tupac or Kurt Cobain or Billie Holiday.

There are some things you don't want to do to get a laugh. Every once in a while, you'll have what my writing partner Neal Brennan calls "buyer's remorse" where I'll say something, and it'll get a laugh, and after that I'll regret it and think, "Oh, I shouldn't have said that." Sometimes it's obvious to you, and you've got to call foul on yourself. Generally, I like the jokes to be empowering or enlightening on some level. But then again, part of being a comic is saying things that people haven't said before—so you're gonna say inappropriate things from time to time. The trick is not to pay too much attention to the boundaries. When your humor becomes too self aware you might be less effective.

The happiness that humor brings doesn't have to be temporary. You take a guy like Chris Rock—people quote him all the time. People quote Mark Twain or Will Rogers to this day. And I'm sure my kids will learn about Richard Pryor. So there are guys who are like that, whose comedy kind of endures. If it's a good point and it's eloquently said, then people will remember it.

Discussion Questions

1. Based on what Chappelle says about himself in the first paragraph, how might he classify his level of expertise on stand-up comedy: unconscious incompetence, conscious incompetence, conscious competence, or unconscious competence? Why?

2. Chappelle's process discussion is woven in with other commentary. What are his actual steps in developing comedy? State these steps in the fewest possible words. Do any of these steps need to be followed in a particular order?

3. Describe Chappelle's purpose in this essay. What phrases, sentences, or paragraphs effectively convey this purpose?

4. Describe Chappelle's tone. What phrases, sentences, or paragraphs do you think exemplify this tone? What other tones could a writer adopt for this subject?

6.2 **Professional Model**

Home to the Hills
by Chris Offutt

Meet the Writer

Writer Chris Offutt grew up in a Kentucky mining community located in the foothills of the Appalachian mountains. His works include novels, short stories, essays, and comics.

No matter how you leave the hills—army, prison, marriage, job, college—when you move back after 20 years the whole county is watching carefully. They want to see the changes that the outside world put on you. They are curious to know if you've become bitter and lost your laughter as a victim of the land beyond the hills. They are worried that perhaps you've gotten above your raisings.

Put their mind at ease. Dress down except when you have to dress up; then wear your Sunday-go-to-meeting clothes. Make sure and drive a rusty pickup that runs like a sewing machine. Hang dice from the mirror and a gun rack in the back window. A rifle isn't necessary, but something needs to be there: a pool cue, a carpenter's level, an ax handle. Where the front plate should be, screw one on that says, "American by birth, Kentuckian by the grace of God."

Be polite to everybody. Even if you are certain you have never seen this lady in your life, ask how her family is. No matter that this man once tore you up in the worst skull-dragging in county history, let bygones be bygones. Smile and nod, smile and nod. When any conversation ends, always say, "See you in church."

Tell them it's a big world out there. The desert is hotter than Satan's Hades. The Rocky Mountains are higher than a cat's back. The ocean is polluted, cities smell bad and a working man never gets ahead. Don't talk about the beautiful people in stylish clothes. Never mention museums, opera, theater or ethnic restaurants. Forget the time you visited a movie star in his home, drank a thousand-dollar bottle of wine or rode all over Chicago in a limo. That sunset walk across the Brooklyn Bridge doesn't hold a candle to crossing Lower Lick Fork creek on a one-man swaying bridge. Fine dining will make you fat, but fresh butter on corn bread will make you cry.

Take as many books as you can back to read. Every bookstore at home for 100 miles around is heavy on cookbooks, mysteries and romance but is a little short on poetry. Remember, poetry there emerges from the palms of babies and old folks. Poetry in the hills is found, not written. It lies in the handles of tools passed down through families, an ax sharpened so many times the blade is the size of a pocketknife.

Bring palpable evidence of where you've been. Bring back objects to hold and smell—no photographs. Take back your turquoise-encrusted steer skull, subway tokens, a hockey puck, petrified rock, a porcupine quill, sea shells, a buffalo hide. Be prepared at all times to say it's better here. You spent 20 years trying to leave this land and 20 more trying to get back.

Before you leave the city, don't forget to borrow CD's from your friends and make 100 cassettes of music no radio station plays and no store sells. Jazz in the hills is a verb, and pop is what you drink. Motown sound is a sweet rumble made by muscle cars. Soul is the province of the preacher, and the blues is what going to town will fix. Remember, you won't ever get tired of sitting on the back porch facing the woods with a group of men and women playing banjo, guitar, mandolin and fiddle. They will make music through dusk and into the night. That sound is so sweet songbirds lie down and die.

Now that you've got a houseful of what you can't get, think about what you don't need anymore. Best left behind is the tuxedo. You'll never wear it here. May as well trade your foreign car for American if you want to get it worked on. You'll not need burglar alarms, bike locks or removable car stereo systems, either. The only gated community is a pasture. The most important things you can get rid of are the habits of the outside world. Nobody here lies except the known liars, and they're great to listen to. Here, you won't get judged by your jeans and boots, your poor schooling or your country accent. Never again will you worry that you're using the wrong fork, saying the wrong thing or expecting people to keep their word.

No more will you need to prove your intelligence to bigots. You can go ahead and forget all your preplanned responses to comments about wearing shoes, the movie "Deliverance," indoor plumbing and incest. You don't have to work four times as hard because the boss expects so little. You don't have to worry about lying in wait to intellectually ambush some nitwit who thinks you're stupid because of where you're from.

You won't hear these words spoken anymore: redneck, hillbilly, cracker, stump-jumper, weed-sucker, ridge runner. You are no longer from somewhere. Here is where you're from. This is home. This dirt is yours.

Discussion Questions

1. What process is Offutt describing? Notice how he provides one step of the process in each paragraph. What are the advantages and disadvantages of ordering the steps in this way?

2. What is Offutt's tone? Which specific words or sentences convey this tone? What other tones might a writer use for this subject?

3. Who is Offutt's intended audience? Point out examples of diction that are tailored to this audience.

4. Examine the last paragraph. How does each sentence refer back to and/or build upon the preceding sentence?

When You Camp Out,
Do it Right

by Ernest Hemingway

Meet the Writer

In the following essay, Hemingway uses the pattern of process analysis to order his materials on the art of camping. He wrote the following piece for the *Toronto Star* in the early 1920s, before he gained worldwide recognition as a writer. The piece reveals Hemingway's lifelong interest in the outdoors as well as his perfectionism—his desire to do all things well.

Journal Topic

As you prepare to read this essay, take a minute or two to think about your own experiences in nature or any unknown place you once visited. If you have ever camped out or attended summer camp, how did you prepare for, enter into, and survive the experience? Which problems did you encounter, and how did you cope with them?

Thousands of people will go into the bush this summer to cut the high cost of living. A man who gets his two weeks' salary while he is on vacation should be able to put those two weeks in fishing and camping and be able to save one week's salary clear. He ought to be able to sleep comfortably every night, to eat well every day, and to return to the city rested and in good condition.

But if he goes into the woods with a frying pan, an ignorance of black flies and mosquitoes, and a great and abiding lack of knowledge about cookery, the chances are that his return will be very different. He will come back with enough mosquito bites to make the back of his neck look like a relief map of the Caucasus. His digestion will be wrecked after a valiant battle to assimilate half-cooked or charred grub. And he won't have had a decent night's sleep while he has been gone.

He will solemnly raise his right hand and inform you that he has joined the grand army of never-agains. The call of the wild may be all right, but it's a dog's life. He's heard the call of the tame with both ears. Waiter, bring him an order of milk toast.

In the first place, he overlooked the insects. Black flies, no-see-ums, deer flies, gnats, and mosquitoes were instituted by the devil to force people to live in cities where he could get at them better. If it weren't for them, everybody would live in the bush, and he would be out of work. It was a rather successful invention.

But there are lots of dopes that will counteract the pests. The simplest perhaps is oil of citronella. Two bits' worth of this oil purchased at any pharmacist's will be enough to last for two weeks in the worst fly and mosquito-ridden country. Rub a little on the back of your neck, your forehead, and your wrists before you start fishing, and the blacks and skeeters will shun you. The odor of citronella is not offensive to people. It smells like gun oil. But the bugs do hate it.

Oil of pennyroyal and eucalyptol are also much hated by mosquitoes, and with citronella they form the basis for many proprietary preparations. But it is cheaper and better to buy the straight citronella. Put a little on the mosquito netting that covers the front of your pup tent or canoe tent at night, and you won't be bothered.

To be really rested and get any benefit out of a vacation, a man must get a good night's sleep every night. The first requisite for this is to have plenty of cover. It is twice as cold as you expect it will be in the bush four nights out of five, and a good plan is to take just double the bedding that you think you will need. An old quilt that you can wrap up in is as warm as two blankets.

Nearly all outdoor writers rhapsodize over the browse bed. It is all right for the man who knows how to make one and has plenty of time. But in a succession of one-night camps on a canoe trip, all you need is level ground for your tent floor, and you will sleep all right if you have plenty of covers under you. Take twice as much cover as you think that you will need, and then put two-thirds of it under you. You will sleep warm and get your rest.

When it is clear weather, you don't need to pitch your tent if you are only stopping for the night. Drive four stakes at the head of your made-up bed, and drape your mosquito bar over that; then you can sleep like a log and laugh at the mosquitoes.

Outside of insects and bum sleeping, the rock that wrecks most camping trips is cooking. The average tyro's idea of cooking is to fry everything and fry it good and plenty. Now, a frying pan is a most necessary thing to any trip, but you also need the old stew kettle and the folding reflector baker.

A pan of fried trout can't be bettered, and they don't cost any more than ever. But there is a good and a bad way of frying them. The beginner puts his trout and his bacon in and over a brightly burning fire; the bacon curls up and dries into a dry tasteless cinder, and the trout is burned outside while it is still raw inside. He eats them, and it is all right if he is only out for the day and going home to a good meal at night. But if he is going to face more trout and bacon the next morning and other equally well-cooked dishes for the remainder of two weeks, he is on the pathway to nervous dyspepsia.

The proper way to cook is over coals. Have several cans of Crisco or Cotosuet or one of the vegetable shortenings along that are as good as lard and excellent for all kinds of shortening. Put the bacon in and when it is about half-cooked, lay the trout in the hot grease, dipping them in cornmeal first. Then put the bacon on top of the trout, and it will baste the fish as they slowly cook.

The coffee can be boiling at the same time, and in a smaller skillet, pancakes being made that are satisfying the other campers while they are waiting for the trout. With the prepared pancake flours, you take a cupful of pancake flour and add a cup of water. Mix the water and flour, and as soon as the lumps are out, the batter is ready for cooking. Have the skillet hot, and keep it well greased. Drop the batter in, and as soon as it is done on one side, loosen it in the skillet and flip it over. Apple butter, syrup, or cinnamon and sugar go well with the cakes.

While the crowd has taken the edge from its appetite with flapjacks, the trout have been cooked, and they and the bacon are ready to serve. The trout are crisp outside and firm and pink inside, and the bacon is well done—but not too done. If there is anything better than that combination, the writer has yet to taste it in a lifetime devoted largely and studiously to eating.

The stew kettle will cook you dried apricots when they have resumed their pre-dried plumpness after a night of soaking; it will serve to concoct a mulligan in, and it will cook macaroni. When you are not using it, it should be boiling water for the dishes.

In the baker, mere man comes into his own, for he can make a pie that to his bush appetite will have it all over the product that Mother used to make. Men have always believed that there was something mysterious and difficult about making a pie. Here is a great secret. There is nothing to it. We've been kidded for years. Any man of average office intelligence can make at least as good a pie as his wife can.

All there is to a pie is a cup and a half of flour, one-half teaspoonful of salt, one-half cup of lard, and cold water. That combination will make pie crust that will bring tears of joy into your camping partners' eyes. Mix the salt with the flour; work the lard into the flour, and make it up into a good workmanlike dough with cold water. Spread some flour on the back of a box or something flat, and pat the dough around a while. Then roll it out with whatever kind of round bottle you prefer. Put a little more lard on the surface of the sheet of dough, and then slosh a little flour and roll it up. Then roll it out again with the bottle.

Cut out a piece of the rolled out dough big enough to line a pie tin. I like the kind with holes in the bottom. Then put in your dried apples that have soaked all night and been sweetened, or your apricots, or your blueberries, and then take another sheet of the dough, and drape it gracefully over the top, soldering it down at the edges with your fingers. Cut a couple of slits in the top dough sheet, and prick it a few times with a fork in an artistic manner.

Put it in the baker with a good slow fire for forty-five minutes, and then take it out. If your pals are Frenchmen, they will kiss you. The penalty for knowing how to cook is that the others will make you do all the cooking.

It is all right to talk about roughing it in the woods. But the real woodsman is the man who can be really comfortable in the bush.

Discussion Questions

1. Hemingway's authority comes through in the many details he provides. What details are especially effective in this regard?

2. Hemingway doesn't use many obvious transitions. Yet the essay flows fairly smoothly. How does he achieve that flow?

3. Who is the intended audience for Hemingway's essay? What does he want to say to his audience—that is, what is his thesis?

4. At a glance, Hemingway's tone seems dry and serious. Yet he balances this with humorous asides. Offer two examples. Describe the effect achieved by these contrasting tones.

5. In what ways is this essay still relevant today? Does the essay seem dated in any way? Provide examples.

Professional Model 6.4

On Dumpster Diving
by Lars Eighner

Meet the Writer

Texas writer Lars Eighner is best known for his book *Travels with Lizbeth*, a memoir of being homeless with his dog, Lizbeth. In this essay, taken from his memoir, Eighner describes how to search through trash for food and other useful items.

I began Dumpster diving a year before I became homeless.

I prefer the term "scavenging" and use the word "scrounging" when I mean to be obscure. I have heard people, evidently meaning to be polite, use the word "foraging," but I prefer to reserve that word for gathering nuts and berries and such which I do also, according to the season and opportunity.

I like the frankness of the word "scavenging." I live from the refuse of others. I am a scavenger. I think it a sound and honorable niche, although if I could I would naturally prefer to live the comfortable consumer life, perhaps—and only perhaps—as a slightly less wasteful consumer owing to what I have learned as a scavenger.

Except for jeans, all my clothes come from Dumpsters. Boom boxes, candles, bedding, toilet paper, medicine, books, a type-writer…change sometimes amounting to many dollars: All came from Dumpsters. And, yes, I eat from Dumpsters too.

There are a predictable series of stages that a person goes through in learning to scavenge. At first the new scavenger is filled with disgust and self-loathing. He is ashamed of being seen and may lurk around trying to duck behind things, or he may try to dive at night. (In fact, this is unnecessary, since most people instinctively look away from scavengers.)

Every grain of rice seems to be a maggot. Everything seems to stink. The scavenger can wipe the egg yolk off the found can, but he cannot erase the stigma of eating garbage from his mind.

The stage passes with experience. The scavenger finds a pair of running shoes that fit and look and smell brand-new. He finds a pocket calculator in perfect working order. He finds pristine ice cream, still frozen, more than he can eat or keep. He begins to understand: People do throw away perfectly good stuff, a lot of per-fectly good stuff.

At this stage he may become lost and never recover. All the Dumpster divers I have known come to the point of trying to acquire everything they touch. Why not take it, they reason, it is all free. This is, of course, hopeless, and most divers come to realize that they must restrict themselves to items of relatively immediate utility.

The finding of objects is becoming something of an urban art. Even respectable, employed people will sometimes find something tempting sticking out of a Dumpster or standing beside one. Quite a number of people, not all of them of the bohemian type, are willing to brag that they found this or that piece in the trash.

But eating from Dumpsters is the thing that separates the dilet-tanti from the professionals. Eating safely involves three principles: using the senses and common sense to evaluate the condition of the found materials; knowing the Dumpsters of a given area and check-ing them regularly; and seeking always to answer the question, Why was this discarded?

Perhaps everyone who has a kitchen and a regular supply of gro-ceries has, at one time or another, eaten half a sandwich before dis-covering mold on the bread, or has gotten a mouthful of milk before realizing the milk had turned. Nothing of the sort is likely to happen to a Dumpster diver because he is constantly reminded that most food is discarded for a reason.

Yet perfectly good food can be found in Dumpsters. Canned goods, for example, turn up fairly often in the Dumpsters I frequent. All except the most phobic people would be willing to eat from a can even if it came from a Dumpster. I have few qualms about dry foods such as crackers, cookies, cereal, chips, and pasta if they are free of visible contaminants and still dry and crisp. Raw fruits and vegetables with intact skins seem perfectly safe to me, excluding, of course, the obviously rotten. Many are discarded for minor imperfections that can be pared away. Chocolate is often discarded only because it has become discolored as the cocoa butter de-emulsified.

I began scavenging by pulling pizzas out of the Dumpster behind a pizza delivery shop. In general, prepared food requires caution, but in this case I knew what time the shop closed and went to the Dumpster as soon as the last of the help left.

Because the workers at these places are usually inexperienced, pizzas are often made with the wrong topping, baked incorrectly, or refused on delivery for being cold. The products to be discarded are boxed up because inventory is kept by counting boxes: A boxed pizza can be written off; an unboxed pizza does not exist. So I had a steady supply of fresh, sometimes warm pizza.

The area I frequent is inhabited by many affluent college students. I am not here by chance; the Dumpsters are very rich. Students throw out many good things, including food, particularly at the end of the semester and before and after breaks. I find it advantageous to keep an eye on the academic calendar.

A typical discard is a half jar of peanut butter—though non-organic peanut butter does not require refrigeration and is unlikely to spoil in any reasonable time. Occasionally I find a cheese with a spot of mold, which, of course, I just pare off, and because it is obvious why the cheese was discarded, I treat it with less suspicion than an apparently perfect cheese found in similar circumstances. One of my favorite finds is yogurt—often discarded, still sealed, when the expiration date has passed—because it will keep for several days, even in warm weather.

I avoid ethnic foods I am unfamiliar with. If I do not know what it is supposed to look or smell like when it is good, I cannot be certain I will be able to tell if it is bad.

No matter how careful I am I still get dysentery at least once a month, oftener in warm weather. I do not want to paint too romantic a picture. Dumpster diving has serious drawbacks as a way of life.

Though I have a proprietary feeling about my Dumpsters, I don't mind my direct competitors, other scavengers, as much as I hate the soda-can scroungers.

I have tried scrounging aluminum cans with an able-bodied companion, and afoot we could make no more than a few dollars a day. I can extract the necessities of life from the Dumpsters directly with far less effort than would be required to accumulate the equivalent value in aluminum. Can scroungers, then, are people who *must* have small amounts of cash—mostly drug addicts and winos.

I do not begrudge them the cans, but can scroungers tend to tear up the Dumpsters, littering the area and mixing the contents. There are precious few courtesies among scavengers, but it is a common practice to set aside surplus items: pairs of shoes, clothing, canned goods, and such. A true scavenger hates to see good stuff go to waste, and what he cannot use he leaves in good condition in plain sight. Can scroungers lay waste to everything in their path and will stir one of a pair of good shoes to the bottom of a Dumpster to be lost or ruined in the muck. They become so specialized that they can see only cans and earn my contempt by passing up change, canned goods, and readily hockable items.

Can scroungers will even go through individual garbage cans, something I have never seen a scavenger do. Going through individual garbage cans without spreading litter is almost impossible, and litter is likely to reduce the public's tolerance of scavenging. But my strongest reservation about going through individual garbage cans is that this seems to me a very personal kind of invasion, one to which I would object if I were a homeowner.

Though Dumpsters seem somehow less personal than garbage cans, they still contain bank statements, bills, correspondence, pill bottles, and other sensitive information. I avoid trying to draw conclusions about the people who dump in the Dumpsters I frequent. I think it would be unethical to do so, although I know many people will find the idea of scavenger ethics too funny for words....

Dumpster things are often sad—abandoned teddy bears, shredded wedding albums, despaired-of sales kits. I find diaries and journals. College students also discard their papers; I am horrified to discover the kind of paper that now merits an A in an undergraduate course.

Dumpster diving is outdoor work, often surprisingly pleasant. It is not entirely predictable; things of interest turn up every day, and some days there are finds of great value. I am always very pleased when I can turn up exactly the thing I most wanted to find. Yet in spite of the element of chance, scavenging, more than most other pursuits, tends to yield returns in some proportion to the effort and intelligence brought to bear.

I think of scavenging as a modern form of self-reliance. After ten years of government service, where everything is geared to the lowest common denominator, I find work that rewards initiative and effort refreshing. Certainly I would be happy to have a sinecure again, but I am not heartbroken to be without one.

I find from the experience of scavenging two rather deep lessons. The first is to take what I can use and let the rest go. I have come to think that there is no value in the abstract. A thing I cannot use or make useful, perhaps by trading, has no value, however fine or rare it may be. (I mean useful in the broad sense—some art, for example, I would think valuable.)

The second lesson is the transience of material being. I do not suppose that ideas are immortal, but certainly they are longer-lived than material objects.

The things I find in Dumpsters, the love letters and rag dolls of so many lives, remind me of this lesson. Many times in my travels I have lost everything but the clothes on my back. Now I hardly pick up a thing without envisioning the time I will cast it away. This, I think, is a healthy state of mind. Almost everything I have now has already been cast out at least once, proving that what I own is valueless to someone.

I find that my desire to grab for the gaudy bauble has been largely sated. I think this is an attitude I share with the very wealthy—we both know there is plenty more where whatever we have came from. Between us are the rat-race millions who have confounded their selves with the objects they grasp and who nightly scavenge the cable channels looking for they know not what.

I am sorry for them.

Discussion Questions

1. Describe Eighner's purpose in this essay. Does he explain the scavenging process so that others can also do it efficiently, or is he simply describing the process that he follows because others might find it interesting or important? Does his essay have a purpose larger than that of merely describing a process?

2. Eighner begins his essay with a single-sentence paragraph. He also concludes the essay with a single-sentence paragraph. In each case, what effect is achieved by that strategy?

3. Many of Eighner's paragraphs begin with *I*. What are the advantages and disadvantages of this repetition?

4. Who is the author's intended audience? How has he adjusted his diction to suit that audience? If similar subject matter were directed to a different audience, how might the diction change?

5. What is Eighner's tone? What phrases, sentences, or paragraphs effectively convey this tone? What other tones might different writers adopt for this subject matter?

6. Eighner distinguishes between *dumpster diving, scavenging, scrounging*, and *foraging*. What connotations does each of these terms have for Eighner? What connotations do the terms have for you? What other words might describe what Eighner does? Explain the connotations of those words.

How to Avoid Class Participation

by Karisa Tell

Meet the Writer

Karisa Tell is a self-proclaimed fashionista and physics geek. Her goal in life is to witness someone slipping on a banana peel and/or coin a phrase that sweeps the nation. When not impressing the general public with her wit, she enjoys reading fashion mags (and shortening words).

How many times has your teacher called your name in class when you were least expecting it? A cold sweat glistened on your forehead, your heart seemed to beat erratically, and your stomach plummeted to the floor. Maybe the teacher was just taking attendance, in which case you would just say "here!" and wait for your parasympathetic nervous system to kick in.

But what if your presence in the room had already been established at the beginning of class, and instead your teacher asked you "What's the difference between alpha and beta decay?" Naturally, you would either get the question wrong or give a helpless shrug and an "I dunno…" At this point your face would be bright red, and your classmates would have already decided that you are a complete idiot. If this has never happened to you, know that it will soon, and when it does you will need to be prepared. I can tell you how to avoid this kind of embarrassing confrontation in just a few easy steps.

First of all, when you walk into the classroom on the first day, make sure you do not smile at or say hello to the teacher. Don't even acknowledge his or her presence. Once a unique relationship between you and your teacher has been forged, the teacher will look upon you as her ally in a sea of intimidatingly unfamiliar faces. This will make the teacher more likely to call on *you*.

When selecting a seat, most people would move toward the back of the room, where the teacher can't see them. This is a big mistake. The teacher isn't blind! She can see everyone in the room, and she's going to pay more attention to the kids in the back because they are notoriously the kids who talk all the time, never know the answers, and shoot spitballs at the know-it-all in the front row. You do *not* want that kind of extra attention from a teacher. You also don't want to sit in the front of the room, because then *you* will be the know-it-all being hit with the barrage of spitballs. Plus, if you're a know-it-all, or at least if the teacher thinks you are, she will be more likely to ask you questions because you are supposed to always know the answer. Teachers like to call on smart kids because it makes them look like good teachers when their students get the answer right. It's best to choose a seat some-where in the middle of the classroom. Just make sure you don't sit too far to the front or too far to the back, and you'll be fine.

Usually, a teacher will start out the first class by asking personal questions which are unrelated to the class's subject matter, like "How was your summer?" This question is always followed by complete silence and a lack of response from the students before her. She'll then try to trick you into talking by asking "Who went on a vaca-tion?" Do not raise your hand! By honestly answering a seemingly harmless question, you have just made yourself an easy target for your teacher's probing eyes. Anyone stupid enough to raise his hand is at risk of being called on to elaborate on said vacation.

Another tip is to never twirl your hair, stretch your arms, or scratch your head. You might wonder what harm these simple gestures could cause. Well, if a teacher has just asked a question, she will be look-ing for hands hovering above desk level. She will mistake your hand, casually scratching at your head, for a raised hand, and force you to answer her question. Even if the teacher hasn't asked any questions lately, if you perform the aforementioned gestures, she'll think you have a question or comment to make, and she'll call on you.

The most important rule for participation evasion is to avoid eye contact with your teacher. Some teachers see eye contact and think that you're volunteering an answer. Others call on people by mak-ing eye contact with them. In any case, eye contact with a teacher is never a good idea. It can only lead to embarrassment. Do not make the fundamental mistake of looking down at the floor or at the teacher's last-season shoes. For one thing, sometimes downcast eyes appear to be closed from the teacher's perspective. If this is so, the teacher will reprimand you for sleeping, which would not only be embarrassing, but also could get you in trouble. For another, some teachers purposely call on students who are avoiding eye contact just to be a jerk. I have found that it's best to keep your eyes roving around the area to the left or right of the teacher's head, or even better, on the chalk board. This kills two birds with one stone, the other bird being that you end up, once again, looking like a good student who concentrates on the notes written on the board.

If you have trouble avoiding eye contact, or if your teacher has a habit of humiliating everyone equally, a method that I have found effective is to always take notes. No good teacher wants to interrupt a diligent student at work. If you're really not that diligent of a student, just *pretend* like you're deeply enthralled in your notes, and the teacher will pass right over you. You can…draw pictures of your teacher suffering public humiliation, repeatedly write the words "I hate my life," or just write a note to your good crony across the hall, inserting words like "ionic" and "theorem" every so often for good measure. Any of these tactics should dissuade most normal teachers from bothering you.

In closing, I'd like to point out that this method isn't entirely foolproof (not because I'm not an expert in this area, because I am). It's not foolproof because there is no possible way to avoid all instances of class participation in every class you take. For example, some teachers make a show of greeting every student at the beginning of class. Some arrange the desks in a semi-circle for an atmosphere of optimal discussion. If this happens to you, I pity you and suggest you drop out of school or something.

Hopefully there will come a day when teachers stop horribly embarrassing their students on a daily basis. Until then, keep your hands, shoulders, and even your feet securely anchored down, and *never* look directly into your teacher's eyes.

Discussion Questions

1. Look closely at the order of Tell's suggestions. What guided her decisions about order in this essay?

2. Describe Tell's tone. Which words or phrases effectively convey this tone?

3. Identify phrases or sentences indicating Tell's awareness of her audience.

4. How has Tell used transitions at the beginnings of her paragraphs to smoothly connect each one to the previous paragraph?

Taking Position
by Brooke Kettering

Meet the Writer

Brooke Kettering began writing as a young girl. She wrote on subjects she was passionate about, as she continues to do today. Her many years of practice have enabled her to improve her abilities in all forms of writing.

Her lacrosse routine begins from the toe up. She laces up and readjusts herself to the physical discomfort of the only emotionally comforting thing she has left. The scrolling list of things to do and constant reminders of things she did wrong are put on hold when she enters her haven. The natural wood and open air give her a chance to catch her breath. She rises and feels the familiar pain in her feet as they become stronger; more stable supports. She takes position at the bar with a firm grip, shaking the hand of her familiar friend. *We meet again.* She looks herself in the eye and grins. Suddenly she's transformed into an uninhibited, dramatic actress who can tell a story with a glance, express an emotion with a movement.

Despite her spontaneous transformation, she's thinking the whole way through; thinking exactly how to place her foot and what muscles to utilize. She finishes her first act with an arabesque, the graceful reach that defines dance. She breathes; toes pointed outward, heels together, backside engaged, abdomen strong and supportive, chest raised, back straight, shoulders dropped yet strong.

She stretches out her arms, simultaneously reaching with her foot—counterbalance, body and mind. Takeoff—her foot departs from the solid wood with a more definite destination than a commercial airplane. She keeps her head up, the apex of the rollercoaster formed by the curve of her back. Breathe, tighten, extend, transform.

My routine begins from the toe up. I lace up and readjust myself to the physical discomfort of the only emotionally comforting thing I have left. All I can concentrate on is the duty I need to perform; the task I have before me; the familiar weight that rests on my shoulders. The boundless field and fresh air give me a chance to catch my breath. I prepare and feel the familiar pain of each cleat remolding my feet. I take position at the circle with a steady stance. I readjust my grip on the cold aluminum of my stick, shaking the hand of a familiar friend. *We meet again.* I look my opponent in the eye and grin—this one's ours. I am transformed into a territorial, aggressive competitor; my animalistic instincts surface.

Despite my offensive outburst, I am thinking the whole way through—thinking exactly who to pass to, on which side to cradle, anticipating every move of every player. The play ends with a pass coming toward one of my sides, the ball landing perfectly in my net as if it is the only place in the world for it to be. With a quick glance and even quicker decision, I see an opportunity given only to me. I execute a few quick motions; smoothly and definitively flick my right arm over my left, twisting my body into full force mode, and watch as the ball travels in its intended path. Breathe, get my bearings, smile, and continue right back into the game.

Discussion Questions

1. Describe Kettering's purpose. How does her organizational pattern help her to achieve this purpose?

2. Does Kettering's writing seem to flow smoothly from one phrase, sentence, and paragraph to the next? Why or why not?

3. Find places where Kettering moves beyond mere physical description of processes to include emotional aspects of the processes.

4. Describe Kettering's tone. What phrases or sentences best convey this tone?

Becoming a Poet

by Ben Williams

Meet the Writer

Ben Williams pursues writing and poetics in their many forms. He would like to thank his family, his friends, his challengers and his adversaries for continuing to inspire his responses to the world around him.

I got into poetry for the best reason. The reason that a self-respecting 15-year-old boy should get into anything—a girl. So there I was, a sophomore who had just switched into "Creative Writing." Sometime around there the pain, I mean, the poetry, started.

Technically, I had written before. I'd scrawled the obligatory poetic gestures that are evident in an appropriate eighth-grade English class. I'd learned what alliteration was, and I probably knew consonance and assonance, too. I didn't know poetry though.

That quickly became evident as Mr. Sharkovitz walked in, turned to the class and said, "All right, who knows what poetry is?"

What it is? Um, words? That do things? Sometimes they rhyme? They're, uh, sophisticated? Deep? Black? Go well with coffee? I proceeded to learn more and more about how much I didn't know.

I had this self-righteous sense that I was going to systematically conquer a literary genre with the wits I came equipped with and the pencil I already had in my pocket. Around this time I learned what "trite," "clichéd," and "purple" meant—my writing.

I believed that as long as a thought was pure, as long as I was expressing something I felt, the writing couldn't be bad. I mean, those words had come out of my brain when I was in a poetic mood. I believed words should form on the page as a direct transmutation of my thoughts and feelings. To criticize poetry seemed nonsensical. I mean, how can you criticize somebody's feelings? How can you look at someone's poetry and tell him or her that they're wrong?

It hurt. It burned. But worse, I didn't know how to fix it. Here I was, writing a line such as, "Endless cyclones of torment." Seriously. "Endless cyclones." It was probably the easiest thing in the world for Shark to put a big red line through it and write "purple." Sure, I got that I was wrong. I understood that I had no concept of "endless." I understood that if I wanted to write about torment, I had to show the audience torment, not tell them torment. I got that what I had was wrong, but I couldn't get it right. So I slipped into denial and I fought it.

I tried to stand by my poems, to argue that the idea behind them was more important than the inarticulate way I wrote them. I thought that it was unfair to be held to such a high standard. I mean, give me a break. I just started this poetry thing. I'm a beginner. I'll get better, I promise.

And somehow, I did get better. It didn't get easier, though. If anything, it got harder. Every word my pencil wrote I had to check myself. Test it for weaknesses. Look for any stray word or any vague thought. For a time I wasn't even writing the poems I wanted to write, I was writing the poems I thought wouldn't be ripped to pieces. In retrospect, that was a necessary step.

I had all of these big ideas—too big, really. Ideas based on concepts that sounded good off the tongue but weren't rooted in anything. I wanted to write the poem that would change the world, and it was good that I was taken down a notch.

In class, I would sit on the far side of the room, my back to the window. To my immediate right was an empty desk. To my left was the girl that I mentioned. She was—and is, I imagine—an amazing writer. She didn't have any of the dragging problems I was facing. Directly across from us sat six senior guys. Real jerks, for the most part. But I was biased. Really biased. They were the musicians and slackers who got all the women and were set in their way of thinking. If they didn't like your writing, they told you. Straight up. One especially memorable quote, directed towards another student's play, was, "That was the worst thing I've ever heard. You should probably never write a play again."

Whew. If you wanted to share a poem in that class, it had to be a good one. That left me with two options—say nothing, something I've never been good at, or have something worth saying. I had taken the easy route before. I probably take the easy route most of the time. This was different. This was poetry. Something about the art form struck me. So I worked it.

Helping me through this rough beginning was a poetry group that was offered at Featherstone Center for the Arts by local poet Justen Ahren. This was a small group, made up of my friends and allies. It struck a sharp contrast to the Creative Writing class at the high school. At Featherstone you could put a poem out fearlessly. Criticism was always constructive. Bad poems were valued for their merits and nurtured to health. The yin and yang nature of the two classes slowly improved my writing.

I began keeping a small writing book by my side at all times, writing down poems as soon as they came to me. That's when I wrote my first good poem. I didn't know how good it was at first. Some of the thoughts expressed in it were unclear even to myself, but I had gotten a slightly better eye for poetry and I could see it had a couple merits.

It was inspired by some of the performance poets I had seen recently, and the poem was written so that it lent itself to elocution. It was playful with language with lines like:

wouldn't the world be better

if people were just a bit more like

blankity-blankity-ity-ity-a-li'l-li'l

But it had a certain honest edge to it. I was still frightened to read poems in Creative Writing, so I decided to read it the next time the Featherstone group met.

Especially with poetry, compliments can be hard to interpret. Compliments can be given to the most narcoleptic of poems. Compliments such as "that's the best poem I've heard you read" can mean nothing. There is one compliment that every young poet should strive for—a compliment that this poem happened to earn for me: *Did you really write that?*

And I did write it. Seeing that I was onto something, I kept with it. I smoothed it out. I formed it into six stanzas and kept rewriting and reshaping. Eventually I was satisfied. I had a poem, and just in time.

At the end of each Creative Writing course, a coffeehouse is held in the library. At the coffeehouse every student in the class has to go up to the podium and read something they've written in the class. For a few days, I practiced the poem, having my sister watch my performance and help me find the ways to deliver the lines.

I used to think of myself as being brave, of not caring what people think of me. I'm sitting there at the coffeehouse waiting for my turn to read and I'm sweating. I feel nauseous. I forget how to read. I can feel my voice cracking already. I get called up to the podium.

I stand up from my seat and lose track of time. There are millions of people in the audience. Luckily, I remember how to breathe. With each breath I seem to remind myself that I know what I'm doing, that I have a good poem to read. I tell myself that I'm a poet, that I can write in whatever tense I want to, that I can use periods instead of commas. I get to the microphone, read my poem, and nail it.

I get a grade of 52 points out of a possible 50. People I hardly know tell me that they liked my poem and that they had not previously known that I was a poet. Doom.

Doom because I'm not one, because I suddenly have this public posture as a poet, and I only have one poem. Weeks go by. I keep my writing book by my side constantly, write in it fairly frequently, and get nothing. Maybe four months later, something strikes me, and then boom. I have a second poem. Then I slowly stumble into a third poem, then a fourth.

I have good nights and good weeks, squeezed between bad weeks and bad months. I write 10 or 20 scrawls for every one scribble that survives and lives into a poem. But as the number of scrawls rise, the number of poems rises with it.

Somewhere along the way, I learned a few things. First, that I'm not a poet. I still couldn't tell you what a poet is exactly, but I was, and am, not a poet. I write poetry though, and just as important, I enjoy poetry.

Junior year I took creative writing again. It was ridiculously easier this time around. Shark liked me more as well. He had front row seats to witness my writing improve, and I think he took some well-deserved credit in the fact that my writing improved during his class. The beginning was stormy, but I weathered it. Now the writing came easier. I still had trouble writing good poems, but my bad poems were better than they used to be.

Oh yeah. That girl I mentioned. I kind of forgot about her. I mean, it happens. At some point she stopped being the reason for my writing. I still owe her a lot. She got me into poetry in the first place.

The narrative stops there. Not because it's over. Not because it's caught up to the present, but because the story doesn't have an ending. I want to be a person who creates.

Former poet laureate Donald Hall wrote an essay called, "Poetry and Ambition." The first line is, "I see no reason to spend your life writing poems unless your goal is to write great poems." The essay goes on to state how the problem with a lot of poetry today is that it strives to be sufficient. Hall argues that poets should strive to "write words that last forever." If they fall short of this goal, at least they have pushed themselves to improve. That might be the most refreshing thing about poetry: I can write it till they hammer the nails in.

Discussion Questions

1. Williams's teacher describes his writing as "purple." How would you define "purple" writing? Why should a writer avoid it?

2. When Williams describes reading at the coffeehouse, he shifts to present tense. Teachers tend to discourage such shifts, and for good reason since this often creates confusion. In this case, however, the change works well. Why? What effect is achieved?

3. When Williams first tried his hand at poetry, he didn't know he was beginning a long and arduous process. How would you describe the beginning, middle, and "end" of the process for Williams?

4. Williams admits that he "couldn't tell you what a poet is exactly." How does this uncertainty affect his aspirations to become a poet? (You might want to consult the beginning of the chapter and mention one type of "competence" in your explanation.)

Chapter 7

Definition and Classification

G *roovy! Far out! Out of sight!*
We trust that no matter how much you love the 1970s, these
expressions are not part of your everyday lexicon. Neither are
daddio, swell, dweeb, rad, tubular, or *geek* from other decades. Just as the
hip words you use today will one day sound *awkward—daddio, swell*
and the rest have already lost their *cool.* Or maybe this shift has already
happened and you feel the pressure to keep up.

With each new generation, young people reinvent the language,
infusing it with their own brand of cool. They don't need to consult
slang dictionaries or interview trendsetters; they simply create their
own definitions—perhaps because the language they've been given
is inadequate, or maybe they want to assert their uniqueness. In this
chapter, you will tackle a similar task. Instead of updating the language,
you will "update" your reader's understanding of some concept or idea
that you believe deserves attention. This is not as dull or difficult as it
sounds, so don't have a cow, dude.

Dictionaries provide succinct definitions of thousands of words and
concepts; thus, there's no point in trying to recreate what dictionaries
do very well, which is (1) present a word; (2) classify the word; and (3)
show how the word differs from other words. Instead, you will write an
extended definition in which you present your particular slant on a concept, making a point in the process. Your process may resemble what the
dictionary does—in fact, you may create your own classification system—
but the final product should be more enlightening and compelling. In
short, your purpose will be to offer a fresh perspective on a familiar topic.

Choosing a Topic

Writing topics sometimes arrive at your doorstep if you pause and pay attention. To everything. Notice the way your family greets you in the morning, how your friends and teachers greet you at school. Observe how students carve paths through the hallways, the way backpacks and purses hang on shoulders. Watch everyone rise to recite the Pledge of Allegiance. Pay attention to the hush that ensues when the teacher begins talking—and the furtive glances you exchange with a friend.

How can you turn these ordinary moments into topics for extended definition? You might focus on greetings, for instance, outlining the complexities behind the simple wave, the nod, the "Hey," the finger point. Most of us meander along, barely registering these gestures, when in reality they hold great meaning. Each greeting reveals the very nature of the relationship. In essence, if you pursue this track of thinking, you will define greetings from your particular point of view.

Or study the herds of students grazing the halls. Are they polite, rude, obnoxious, loud? Does the size of a group have any influence on its behavior? Do boys act differently from girls in the hall? Do freshmen act differently from seniors? The answers to these questions can lead to this extended definition of hallway behavior: Since students restrain themselves in the classroom, they need to let loose and assert their identities once they reach the halls.

If you don't want to define the meaning of a behavior, you can focus on a concept to write your extended definition. For instance, when we say "Liberty and justice for all" at the end of the Pledge of Allegiance, what exactly does this phrase mean? What is liberty? What is justice? For *all*? Really? In what ways has the United States honored or not honored this guarantee? Or how do we honor this pledge in our own lives? Why do we bother to stand and recite these words in the first place? Is it just a rote exercise, or does it hold meaning each time?

Another way of finding a topic is to create a list of abstract concepts that hold high interest for you: love, death, friendship, confidence, self-esteem, creativity, intelligence, motivation. Create a list of questions whose answers might reveal meaning. For example, people have been writing and singing and debating about romantic love for centuries, yet love remains elusive. How do you know when you're in love? What is the difference between infatuation and love? Does infatuation always

Writers on Writing

Writing a first draft is very much like watching a Polaroid develop. You can't—and, in fact, you're not supposed to—know exactly what the picture is going to look like until it has finished developing.

—*Anne Lamott*

precede love? Does love involve sacrifice? Does love lead to clarity in thinking or to muddled confusion? What happens biologically when people are in love? Is love healthy or not? These questions are not difficult to devise. And notice their effect. You want to know the answers, don't you? Let that curiosity fuel your own questions.

Using Classification

One of the most common and straightforward ways to define something is to classify it. Animal, mineral, or vegetable? Sweet, sour, or bitter? Big or small? Natural or artificial? Categories help you understand the world—and yourself. When asked to describe yourself on a college admission or job application, you list education, work experience, extracurricular activities, and interests, all in the hope of defining the unique combination that makes you who you are. Rather than limiting you, these categories paint a particular picture of who you are.

Depending on the topic you choose, the classification format may or may not be suitable. If you plan to use classification to develop your extended definition, consider these three guidelines: (1) narrow your topic; (2) be comprehensive; and (3) use a logical order.

Journal Topic

We spend a great deal of time while growing up learning what it means to be "normal." Define normal.

Narrowing Your Topic

When writing a classification essay, focus on *one* unifying feature. For instance, if your topic is local fast-food restaurants, you may choose to classify them based on their speed of service: *The service at restaurant A is lightning fast, B claims to be fast but is only moderately fast, and C is slow but seems proud of this.* The thesis of your essay might be that, ironically, speed may not be the most important criterion in assessing the quality of a fast-food restaurant. Again, you would focus *only* on service, which would effectively unify your essay. You wouldn't mention such factors as nutritional value or location or clientele.

What if your subject can't be classified according to one single feature? For instance, if you decide to classify cliques at your school, you'll want to describe clothes, music, personalities, attitudes, activities, and so on. You'll need to scale down this broad list, but you can still include many of the items if they fit an overarching theme of, say, popularity. "Clique A is least popular—look at their clothes, music, and activities. Clique B is more popular," and so on. In the process of classifying cliques, you will define *popularity*, an elusive concept that inspires heated debate.

Being Comprehensive

Make certain that your classification system includes enough categories. While this advice may seem to contradict the previous advice about narrowing your topic, it doesn't. Say you identify four major branches you can pursue about a topic. You might climb a particular branch and explore its complexity—*including enough categories*—but you wouldn't jump to one of the other three major branches, at least not in a short essay.

If your topic is technology, for instance, you might identify these four branches: a) Does technology improve productivity? b) How does technology affect creativity? c) Does any relationship between technology and leisure time exist? d) Are we too dependent on technology? The first step is to narrow your topic, so you might decide to develop only the first option about productivity. The next step is to consider a thesis and to create a comprehensive yet narrow classification system, a process that will likely occur simultaneously. The outline might ultimately look like this:

Technologies that are:

1. useful but not glamorous

2. merely glamorous but useless

3. both useful and glamorous

4. neither useful nor glamorous

Notice how each category focuses on your perception of *glamorous*, effectively narrowing the topic further. For instance, if you classify college majors, two categories—those that require a lot of homework and those that don't—would be woefully lacking. A more inclusive system on college majors would include those that keep you:

1. so busy you hardly have time to sleep

2. so busy you won't have time for a part-time job

3. busy, but allow time for a part-time job

4. not so busy; you have time for a part-time job and a social life

5. not busy at all; you can pass classes in your sleep

Writing Tip

One of the most effective ways to make your writing appealing to a reader is to vary the sentence patterns. Repetitive sentence patterns tend to lull a reader into boredom. Varied sentence patterns are more likely to engage and stimulate a reader. For example, if many of your sentences begin with the same word, can you use a different word or invert a sentence to achieve more variety? (I is a word frequently overused at the beginnings of sentences.) If all of your sentences are declarative, see if you can recast any of the sentences as questions—but don't overdo that, either. Can some of your sentences be combined into one longer, more complex sentence that is different in form from those near it? Grammatically speaking, if most of your sentences are noun-verb-noun in orientation, can some of them be varied, perhaps by beginning with the -ing form of the verb? These relatively simple sentence acrobatics can make a big difference in how your reader responds to your writing voice.

While this scheme is more inclusive, you may still need to limit your topic. For example, you may want to classify only college majors that lead to a particular type of degree, such as a bachelor's degree or associate's degree.

Using a Logical Order

When you write your extended definition, you'll need to list your categories in some sort of logical order. For instance, suppose you are classifying teachers according to how effective they are. You might create these categories:

1. Teachers who mainly lecture

2. Teachers who lecture and assign worksheets

3. Teachers who use equal lecture and discussion

4. Teachers who rarely lecture and rely on discussion

5. Teachers who rarely lecture and rely on discussion, demonstrations, and activities

Does this classification system focus on a single unifying feature? Yes, as defined by the level of involvement of students. Is the classification system comprehensive? Probably. A little brainstorming will tell you whether most teachers are included in this plan. If not, you might be able to expand the categories.

Finally, what order will you use to describe these categories? Should you present the teachers who mainly lecture at the beginning or at the end of your essay? The answer depends on your purpose. If you intend to argue that teachers who lecture are the most effective, you'll probably begin by showing how demonstrations and activities waste precious class time, then present each succeeding category, until you arrive at your ideal: teachers who lecture. While this logical plan may prove effective, you do have other options. You might show your lecturing teachers first, presenting a flattering picture of their talent and ingenuity, then compare these teachers point by point with teachers in each of the other categories. The particular choice of order is less important than the logic behind the order. Search for the sequence that will best support your purpose.

Including Humor

Believe it or not, papers that rely on classification can be among the most humorous and original you'll write. The key is to invent creative and unusual categories. Instead of using popularity to classify cliques, as suggested earlier, the following categories about cliques in the cafeteria might generate more interest:

1. **Old geezers:** students who spend their lunch hour playing adolescent versions of shuffleboard and bingo

2. **The graying:** students who think they know more than everyone else and constantly offer advice

3. **Certified adults:** students who can't relax, so they finish homework instead of eating

4. **Toddlers:** students who play with straws and spit milk at each other

5. **Diapered:** students dependent on others to teach them how to dress, how to act, and so on

To arrive at these five categories, you probably need to sit in the cafeteria and observe, creating dozens of silly categories that you can pare down to fit your purpose.

If your subject is drivers, you might classify them by how they communicate—through hand gestures, bumper stickers, and so on. Musicians could be classified by the size of their amplifiers or the length of their hair, teachers by how high their belts ride up on their slacks.

Columnist Dave Barry makes a few keen observations as he classifies useless holiday gifts:

- *Cute ceramic knick-knack figurines depicting animals, especially cats*—The way I see it, everybody who wants a cute ceramic cat has already bought one. It is cruel to inflict such objects on other people. I once was present when a holiday guest gave the hostess a ceramic cat, and she stood there, handling it as you would a live grenade, and trying desperately to think of an excuse not to put it on her mantel, which is the only thing you can do with a knick-knack. Eventually, of course, she had to put it on the mantel, and the entire room suddenly acquired an air of cuteness that no amount of expert interior decoration can disguise.

Writers on Writing

In many ways, writing is the act of saying *I*, of imposing oneself upon other people, of saying *listen to me, see it my way, change your mind*. It's an aggressive, even a hostile act. You can disguise its aggressiveness all you want with veils of subordinate clauses and qualifiers and tentative subjunctives, with ellipses and evasions—with the whole manner of intimating rather than claiming, of alluding rather than stating—but there's no getting around the fact that setting words on paper is the tactic of a secret bully, an invasion, an imposition of the writer's sensibility on the reader's most private space.

—Joan Didion

- *Guest soap formed into little balls or fruit shapes*—Nobody uses this soap. The people who live in the house don't use it, because it's for guests. The guests are afraid to use it, because they don't want to mess it up. They end up not washing their hands, which leads to the spread of infections. The government should put a stop to this soon, because it is only a matter of time before somebody starts selling guest soap shaped like cats.
- *Fruitcakes manufactured last April and packaged in cans and allowed to sit in a warehouse until they reach the density of a bowling ball*—These present all the problems of caramel-covered popcorn, with the added problem that they can cause hernias.

(Barry mentions earlier in the column that popcorn, though unwanted, *could* be used as attic insulation.)

With humor, original interpretations and real discoveries may also surface. A comical analysis of cliques may lead you to conclude that so-called cliques don't even exist outside of others' perceptions. In fact, people and groups are unique; they defy classification. In other words, you would classify people—in an outlandish or ironic way—to show that people *can't* be classified.

Journal Topic

Other than tangible goods, what do you want most from life? Spend a few minutes defining your answer.

Developing Your Essay

As you develop ideas for your definition essay, ideas about a possible thesis will probably occur to you simultaneously. Allow this productive process to unfold, and hold back on specifying a precise thesis until the bigger picture begins to emerge. Allow time for your ideas to simmer, in the same way soup ingredients combine to become more flavorful the longer they are allowed to cook.

Say you want to write an extended definition of courage but can't decide which direction to take. During a brainstorming session, you write about people you know who demonstrate courage. You write about public figures. You look for patterns and connections. A vague idea about the structure of your essay begins to take hold, and you settle on this plan: to define courage as it is demonstrated by public and private individuals. As you develop your ideas, you come up with the thesis that courage resides within every one of us, a conclusion that may not have surfaced without such an open-ended process.

If you've completed assignments from earlier chapters, you're already familiar with various options for development. We'll review those options one by one for the sake of clarity, but you'll probably use a combination of these forms.

Assume you zero in on the subject of aging and are nearly ready to write a first draft. You want to define what it means to be a particular age, and you have this thesis in mind: one's mental age doesn't change with time—some people are age fifteen their entire lives; some are stuck at forty. (This idea is adapted from columnist Burt Constable, whose essay appears at the end of this chapter.) Satchel Paige, famed baseball player and street philosopher, once quipped, "How old would you be if you didn't know how old you was?" What follows are different ways you might develop and organize such an essay.

1. **Describe:** Think about the oldest person you know. Describe how that person's physical appearance has changed with age. At the same time, describe what you know about the person's outlook on life, which, in your estimation, has remained stable.

2. **Narrate:** Does a particular event highlight your main point? Did you celebrate a birthday that marked a significant change for you, when you felt you finally caught up with your mental age? Did a time occur when you were ill and feeling much older than your chronological age?

3. **Offer examples:** Are there individuals who embody your main point? For instance, poet Gwendolyn Brooks still had a girl's gleam of curiosity in her eyes at age eighty. Conversely, are there children who are already middle-aged in their demeanor?

4. **Compare and contrast:** Compare the "youngest" old person you know with the "oldest" young person. Compare your present age with some past age. Forecast what you'll be like at age forty and compare that to the present.

5. **Show a process:** *How* do people age? What key events age people mentally? What steps can a person take to avoid becoming "old"?

6. **Classify:** Can you divide people into categories, such as people who accept their age, people who deny their chronological age by dressing youthfully, or people who take vanity to the extreme and insist on plastic surgery?

Before deciding how many of these approaches to use, have a tentative thesis in mind. Write down this thesis at the top of a sheet of paper and brainstorm how your paper will evolve, using each of these approaches. Such a plan will probably help you to refine your thesis.

Whether you decide to use humor or a more straightforward approach, the process of writing an extended definition will clarify your own thinking on your subject. And the final result may spur others to take a fresh view on what they thought was familiar territory.

Journal Topic

You've spent much of your time in school. But defining education might still be a difficult task. What is an education?

Practice

Before beginning the Chapter Assignment, try the following exercises to practice defining and classifying.

1. Define friendship in a sentence or two. Find a partner and critique each other's answers. Revise your definition, incorporating your partner's ideas.

2. In a paragraph, write an extended definition of adulthood, including your views on the subject. If possible, have an adult complete the same task; then compare answers.

3. Assume you plan to write an extended definition of happiness. After reviewing the section "Using a Logical Order" (see page 246), map out a possible outline you might use to develop such an essay.

4. Classify holidays. Be sure to use a single guiding feature in your classification system.

Chapter Assignment

Prewriting

Your assignment for this chapter is to write a definition/classification essay. Use the following suggestions to help you choose a topic and clarify the purpose of your essay.

1. Fill in the blank with five different answers: I wish I knew more about _____ .

2. List three areas in which you have expertise. Define *expertise* broadly. Think about abilities, interests, relationships, outlook, and so on. For example, you might have expertise in skateboarding, or you may consider yourself an expert on being a good son or daughter. Do any of your areas of expertise inspire an extended definition?

3. Once you select a topic, write down numerous ways in which you might develop your essay using description, narration, examples, comparison, showing a process, and classification. Try to do this quickly, without second-guessing yourself. Put your notes aside for a while, and when you return to them, try to discern patterns as you decide how to organize your essay.

4. Once you select a topic, use a graphic organizer (see Appendix B) to help you see the directions your essay might take.

Writing Topics

Select one of the following topics to develop into a definition/classification essay. Feel free to tailor these topics to suit your needs.

1. Write an extended definition of something a person your age is especially qualified to define; for example, a popular style of music, a fashion trend, a slang term, or something else. To write such an essay, you may want to address some of these questions: What accounts for the popularity of this trend or style? What does the trend mean to people your age? Why is it so difficult for adults to appreciate teen trends?

2. Write an extended definition on one of the following: excellence, persistence, passion, vision, determination, success.

3. Write an extended definition on one of the following: failure, weakness, tunnel vision, apathy, boredom.

4. Write about the meaning of winning and losing. Is it ever possible to win and lose at the same time?

5. Write about the meaning of leadership. What constitutes true leadership? Consider using classification to develop the essay.

6. Write about how people find meaning in their lives. In other words, define what constitutes a rich life.

7. Write an extended definition on why we need creativity in our lives. Consider using a classification scheme to outline different types of creativity.

8. Write an extended definition of anxiety. Does anxiety motivate or paralyze?

9. What are the ingredients that make up a bad movie, TV show, or song? Write an extended definition to clarify your answer.

10. Write about what makes a good _____ (fill in the blank). Examples might include car, friend, parent, relationship, school, or neighborhood.

Revision

As you revise and edit your first draft, consider these suggestions.

1. Clarity is always critical in writing. A lack of clarity when writing an extended definition is not the kind of irony you want. With that in mind, read your sentences aloud, one by one, and make sure they convey what you intend.

2. Assess your organizational plan. (You do have a plan, don't you?) Have you made the best decisions about the overall organization? Is a different order more effective? Have you attended to the smaller matters of organization, such as including transitions between sentences and paragraphs?

3. Is your thesis clear?

4. If you used classification to develop your essay, did you (a) focus on a single concept? (b) include enough categories? and (c) use a logical order?

5. What questions do you have for a peer reviewer?

Peer Review

Use these questions to help you evaluate another student's writing. Remember, specific suggestions and examples are most helpful.

1. The essay should reflect the writer's particular point of view, or original definition, of the subject. Highlight two or three examples that reflect this originality.

2. Which passages or examples could be more original? Explain.

3. What are the strengths of the essay?

4. What suggestions can you offer?

5. Point out two or three sentences that are especially effective. Point out a sentence or two that could be clearer.

6. What questions do you have for the writer?

7. Analyze the essay's opening and its conclusion. If both are effective, explain why. If one or both could be stronger, offer the author some suggestions for improvement.

Maybe Your Inner Child is Comfy in Middle Ages

by Burt Constable

Meet the Writer

Burt Constable is an award-winning journalist and columnist for the *Daily Herald* in suburban Chicago.

What age are you?

No, that's how old you are. What age are you?

I believe everyone is born with some ideal age that fits them. Have you ever looked at a tyke in diapers and seen something in his expression that instantly makes you picture the lad as a wizened old man? Have you ever looked in the face of an old woman and seen a twinkle in her eye that reminds you of an impish teenage girl? Looking at footage of George Burns in his 40s, you can tell he wasn't going to feel comfortable with himself until he hit 80. A 16-year-old Andy Rooney surely dreamed of reaching an age when his grumpiness would be considered endearing, almost expected, and not just a character flaw. Conversely, Paul McCartney is always going to be 20, no matter how wrinkly he gets.

Since I can find no esoteric journal or touchy-feely college professor to lend credence to my ideal age theory, I bounce the idea off my columning buddy, Jack Mabley. Jack nods in agreement and fixes his age at 50.

Ah, the middle-aged man. I know lots of middle-aged men. Some are 50, some are 23 and some are 82. Early in his career, Jack became aware of the pressures of rearing a family and the chaos of a newspaper job and knew he could look forward to a more serene life at 50. ("Didn't know—hoped," Jack counters.) His longing for 50 had nothing to do with the fact his boss usually was a 50-year-old man.

"Maybe I'd like to have his office, but I wouldn't want to be like him," Jack remembers.

No, he just had a gut feeling 50 would look right on him. Jack was right. Fifty fit him when he was 35, it fit him when he was 50, and it still fits him.

Other people are hopelessly trapped at age 16, no matter how many marriages, jobs, kids and responsibilities they gather. Then there is the 16-year-old who plays the high school clique game, buys the hippest CD and engages in sophomoric stunts merely to fit in—while in his soul, he longs to wear a cardigan sweater, listen to talk radio and gripe about teens.

Every class has a girl who emerges as the "mom" of the group—curbing unruly behavior, taking confessions from the masses and generally holding civilization together. A friend of mine was a 40-year-old woman in high school, is now a 40-year-old woman in reality and someday will die as a 40-year-old woman.

Those of you whose ideal age is yet to come should look forward to it.

Me? My age is 12. That is the period of my life when I truly felt as if I had a grip on things. (Blissfully ignorant, as opposed to painfully aware ignorant.) That doesn't mean I was happier then. I'm darn happy today, but back when I was 12, I couldn't even fathom these higher levels of happiness.

My body already feels like 80 but my spirit will be 12 forever. Whenever I walk through a doorway, I must resist that urge to hop up and touch the top of the door frame. Many a night my wife has humored me as I, in the guise of picking up the kids' toys, will spend 15 minutes trying to lob a Beanie Baby into the toy box from the other side of the room. (Sometimes she even rebounds my misses for me.) When I finally "swish" my shot, I go so far as to verbalize that crowd noise guys generally make only in our heads.

My wife's ideal age is 30. She was just 24 when I met her, but had the maturity and common sense of someone 30. Now that she is closer to 40 than 30, she still has that spunk and sense of adventure that goes well with a 30-year-old.

"So this would make me a 30-year-old woman living with a 12-year-old boy?" my wife asks.

I interrupt my juggling of dirty sock balls to nod in agreement.

"Yep," my wife concludes. "That sounds about right."

Discussion Questions

1. Constable develops his essay with real and hypothetical examples. What does he achieve by using both? What if he had only used one type of example or the other? How might the essay change?

2. How does Constable define age?

3. In two or three sentences, explain whether you agree or disagree with Constable's definition of age, and why. Supply an original example to support your opinion.

4. Identify Constable's tone. Is his tone serious, whimsical, sarcastic, bitter, comical, or something else? How does he achieve this tone?

Professional Model 7.2

Leave Me Alone

Is solitude such a terrible thing to wish for? I think not.

by Garrison Keillor

Meet the Writer

Garrison Keillor is a humorist, author, and the creator and host of the nationally syndicated radio variety show *A Prairie Home Companion.*

One short weekend, so much to do—an invitation to go swimming at night by moonlight, the Iran protest march downtown with our mouths taped shut, a dance at the Eagles Club with a hot horn band playing '70s funk that propels people onto the dance floor as if shot from guns—but here I am stuck with houseguests who are unable to sit in a room without me for more than 15 minutes. They follow me around like faithful collies. We ran out of conversation on

Friday and they're here until Wednesday. I have had un-Christian thoughts about them. I may have to run away from home.

The problem, dear hearts, is a common one here in the American heartland: an inability to express personal preference in simple declarative sentences, no modifiers.

E.g., "I vish to be alone."

Is this a terrible thing to vish for? I think not. One loves company and then one loves uncompany, just as one enjoys sunshine/darkness, summer/winter, funk/folk, b&w/color, all sorts of dichotomies. Solitude is recognized by most world religions. Hairy-legged hermits sit in prayerful contemplation in their mountain caves and nobody thinks less of them for it. So why can't you or I spend a couple of hours alone in an undisclosed location?

There is nothing odd about wanting to be alone. It doesn't mean that I am spray-painting Nazi slogans on the walls and fantasizing about getting even with them what done me wrong. It doesn't indicate male menopause. It only means that I am experiencing Personal Male Secrecy Syndrome (PMSS), the urge common to all men to climb a tree and sit on a high limb for a few hours. This is a powerful motive in most literary careers. Yes, John Updike had a great gift, but also John Updike preferred not to spend his life at a conference table but rather in a quiet corner with a yellow legal pad and a rollerball pen and write what he wished, nobody looking over his shoulder and saying, "Could we change that 'me' to 'you'?"

America could cut fuel consumption by 14 percent if we made it possible for people to be alone without having to get in their car and drive around town aimlessly on the pretext of running errands. (OK, maybe not exactly 14 percent, but a lot.)

When my daughter was small, we discovered that she loved to be alone in her room with her hundreds of stuffed creatures around her. We could hear her in there, nattering at them, networking with Piglet and Raggedy Ann, creating family groups, constructing elaborate narratives—which is what I may be doing someday in the Good Shepherd Home—and she was happy as a clam.

Having grown up No. 3 in a brood of six, I envied her. As a boy I had to climb on a raft and go floating down the Mississippi for a little downtime, and then there was the Falls of St. Anthony to worry about, and the water intake at the power plant, and enormous barges heading upstream. Solitude was treacherous. You could fall asleep and wind up in St. Louis and have to hitchhike home.

New York is a fine place in which to be alone. To walk into a little cafe with an armload of newspapers and sit at the counter and read them over a bowl of chili and a grilled cheese and a white mug of coffee, and a waitress who says, "What else would you like, love?" —this is heaven. In the papers are dozens of people in serious trouble and you are not one of them. You can soak it all up while you eavesdrop on your neighbors, one of whom is being hounded by her daughter who calls her three times a day to yik-yak, and how do you tell your daughter that enough is enough, already? "I can't turn my cellphone off because then I'd have to worry if my mother is trying to get hold of me. I tell Jessica, I say, 'I've got to go now, honey, and she doesn't hear me.'"

It is crucial in any loving relationship that the partners know when to leave each other alone without having to fill out a privacy application (Reasons for Needing Solitude, Goals of Solo Period, Estimated Time of Reunion). Don't ask, don't tell. Just go in the room and close the door. So long, see you later.

Discussion Questions

1. In a sentence or two, write down Keillor's definition of solitude. Put this in your own words, rather than quoting from the essay.

2. Keillor develops his essay with plenty of examples. Some examples are emotional and personal, while others are logical or hypothetical. In your opinion, which examples are most effective?

3. Keillor begins with a glimpse into his home, where he craves solitude, and ends with him eavesdropping in a public place. Discuss the irony in this contrast. Is it effective?

4. Keillor explains that "there is nothing odd about wanting to be alone," which may strike some readers as defensive. Does he have cause to be defensive? Do we make assumptions about people when they are alone? Explain and include examples.

In Giving I Connect with Others

by Isabel Allende

Meet the Writer

Chilean novelist Isabel Allende has written many best-selling books that have been translated into dozens of languages. As an activist, she seeks economic and social empowerment of women and girls.

I have lived with passion and in a hurry, trying to accomplish too many things. I never had time to think about my beliefs until my 28-year-old daughter Paula fell ill. She was in a coma for a year and I took care of her at home, until she died in my arms in December of 1992.

During that year of agony and the following year of my grieving, everything stopped for me. There was nothing to do—just cry and remember. However, that year also gave an opportunity to reflect upon my journey and the principles that hold me together. I discovered that there is consistency in my beliefs, my writing and the way I lead my life. I have not changed, I am still the same girl I was fifty years ago, and the same young woman I was in the seventies. I still lust for life, I am still ferociously independent, I still crave justice and I fall madly in love easily.

Paralyzed and silent in her bed, my daughter Paula taught me a lesson that is now my mantra: You only have what you give. It's by spending yourself that you become rich.

Paula led a life of service. She worked as a volunteer helping women and children, eight hours a day, six days a week. She never had any money, but she needed very little. When she died she had nothing and she needed nothing. During her illness I had to let go of everything: her laughter, her voice, her grace, her beauty, her company and finally her spirit. When she died I thought I had lost everything. But then I realized I still had the love I had given her. I don't even know if she was able to receive that love. She could not respond in any way, her eyes were somber pools that reflected no light. But I was full of love and that love keeps growing and multiplying and giving fruit.

The pain of losing my child was a cleansing experience. I had to throw overboard all excess baggage and keep only what is essential. Because of Paula, I don't cling to anything anymore. Now I like to give much more than to receive. I am happier when I love than when I am loved. I adore my husband, my son, my grandchildren, my mother, my dog, and frankly I don't know if they even like me. But who cares? Loving them is my joy.

Give, give, give—what is the point of having experience, knowledge or talent if I don't give it away? Of having stories if I don't tell them to others? Of having wealth if I don't share it? I don't intend to be cremated with any of it! It is in giving that I connect with others, with the world and with the divine.

It is in giving that I feel the spirit of my daughter inside me, like a soft presence.

Discussion Questions

1. In this essay, Allende defines the meaning of life—for her. What gives her life meaning? What does her definition mean in practical terms?

2. Great losses often lead to deep discoveries. What did Allende lose? What did she gain?

3. Allende uses description, narration, and examples to develop her essay. Offer one example of each.

4. Who do you suppose is the intended audience of this essay?

Horizontal Slices of Poverty

by Kevin Brewner

Meet the Writer

Kevin Brewner is a writer, teacher, star-gazer and the friend and colleague of this book's authors for many years.

When I reached into my pocket and pulled out the 57 cents, I knew I had to make a decision. I could spend the money on two hamburgers from McDonald's or I could buy a pack of cigarettes. I was broke. I opted for the third time that week to buy smokes, with 27 cents to spare. I could panhandle some money for breakfast—maybe. I guess you could say I was poor.

I'd lost so much weight, the few clothes I had nearly fell off me. Yes, I had a 1964 Oldsmobile 98, but with no money for gas, the piece of junk (all four corners dented, the electric windows working when they felt the desire) just sat in some parking lot—that is if someone hadn't towed the clunker away and sold the rotting vehicle for scrap. I needed a job, but no one was hiring, not even for minimum wage.

At least I had a place to sleep that was warm and dry. Some friends let me roll out a sleeping bag on the floor of their dorm room. Sometimes, they had extra food they would let me have, but none of them were well-to-do either. Another plus to my situation was the fact that I could use the shower on their floor. But if I'd been caught by the dorm supervisor, I'd probably end up in jail. How did I end up in this situation? Just two months before, I was working on a road construction job, making good money. Now, I was losing weight faster than I could imagine. But deep down, I knew many people had lives worse than mine.

My class in downtown Chicago worried my wife. "There are desperate people down there," she'd remind me at least twice a week. "I hope you put your car in a safe place and lock it."

"Yeah, right," I thought. I parked the car in an alley to save money, and the locks didn't work anyway. If some poor soul had crawled into my piece of crap, he or she would have had to have been seeking shelter from the cold. Besides, I'd seen the "desperate" people she thought about: every time I'd go down there, someone near the Pacific Garden Mission would hit me up for my spare change. I had no problems with that; I'd been there before. "And they stink," she said. Yes, they did, but they had run out of friends to lean on.

"Got any change?" some woman asked me once. I looked at her and could see that her dentist wasn't doing a very good job; her three or four teeth were crooked and yellow. She wore three or four ratty coats and kept her hand on her bulging shopping cart. Her boots had holes in the toes and ragged socks poked through. I dug in my pocket and handed her whatever I had on me. Anyway, I'd rather give her the money than some parking garage owned by some stock broker from the North Shore.

"I'm broke," I heard a student say in the hallway to his friend. His nearly new jeans had holes he'd placed there, and his $25 Cure T-shirt seemed only a few days old. "I won't get paid until Friday," he continued. I had to chuckle because I knew he had no clue to what being poor really meant. And probably, neither do I.

Discussion Questions

1. How might this essay be considered an extended definition? What term or idea is Brewner defining for readers?

2. At the beginning of his essay, Brewner states, "I was broke." What details support his contention? Why does he suggest at the end that he has no clue what it means to be broke?

3. Brewner uses description, narration, examples, and comparison to develop his essay. Provide an example of each.

4. If this were a traditional narrative written in chronological order, the reader might get a sense of beginning, middle, and end. What does the author achieve by veering from the typical?

Sidewalks Can Make a Town a Neighborhood

by Carolyn V. Egan

Meet the Writer

Carolyn Egan is an educator and freelance writer living in Connecticut. In her essay, Egan offers a nostalgic description of a means of transportation that is fast becoming scarce: sidewalks.

According to my odometer, the grocery store is exactly 1.1 miles down the road from where I live in an emerging suburb that was a stretch of largely uninterrupted tobacco fields a mere 25 years ago. I walked this distance once in a spasm of self-recrimination, only to find my life at risk at every quirky bend along the route where cars are accustomed to their incautious rule.

My adventure yielded this startling revelation: I need a car to safely navigate my town, because—apart from a few new developments that sit like isolated cocoons—it lacks sidewalks. Most of us drive everywhere, no matter how near our destination. But in my childhood during the 1960s and 70s, the world was still accessible to pedestrians.

Some of my earliest memories are of me scurrying to keep pace with my mother as she pushed my sister in her baby carriage along the sidewalks across town. When I was older, I memorized every crack in the half mile of sidewalk linking my home to my grammar school. No school bus stopped traffic at every block to pick up children at their front doors. Nor did a parade of mothers wait in idling automobiles to cart their children home when the school bell sounded.

When I was little, the world was mine. I knew where the rainwater carved rivers in sand beds at the bottom of the hill before rolling to its final plunge down the storm drain. I knew the best street for a running slide in my winter boots. I knew the smell and look of spring as it quickened green upon the front lawns I passed. And I remember my heart quickening with it, in anticipation.

As I grew, I walked farther. I walked to and from more-distant schools. I walked to my first jobs, to my friends' houses, to the movies. Sidewalks enabled these humming, skipping, thoughtful journeys, during which I came to know the corner stores, the old factory buildings, the smiling ladies hunched over their gardens along the meandering paths that twisted toward home. I knew the seasons of the geese that pierced the indigo sky and the seasons of the squirrels that clicked in solemn contest with hungry birds in gray branches. I knew which dogs would greet me and which would bark a warning; the cats that curled sweet tails around my legs; the mailmen who trudged—heads down—from house to house. All these things I knew and counted on.

I am told that nobody really cares about sidewalks; nobody wants to shovel them. Yet sidewalks—those evenly spaced concrete blocks—stitch a town into a neighborhood. They allow a physical experience of community while beckoning children to explore, to discover, to make friends three blocks away. For kids today, geography is understood from the back seat of a car, rather than through the scents and textures of heart-beating, muscle-flexing, self-motivated expeditions that connect one place to another, one person to another. The destination has displaced the journey.

Parents have become slaves to their children's schedules, terrified to let their offspring out of sight. New houses are huge, enclosing all of life. They're connected by technological portals to the outside world, making an abstraction of everything beyond their walls.

We worry about the safety of our children if we let them loose to wander sidewalks, even while we hear more and more stories of predators on the highways and byways of the Internet. We have forgotten that we cannot protect our children by telling them to hop in and buckle up. Our children do not develop the instincts to discern and avoid danger from the back seat of an automobile. We deprive them of self-mastery by insulating them from very cold and very hot temperatures, from rain, from wind. They do not know who they are without a plan, without a ride. While we encourage dependence in our children by chauffeuring them everywhere, we also encourage in them habits of selfishness and parochialism. Adult maturity is rooted in the unstructured roaming of childhood.

Sidewalks are becoming nostalgic artifacts of a time before three- or four-car families. To me, their absence represents disturbing changes in the way we connect to one another—and the habits, values and capacities we bequeath to our children.

It troubles me to wonder where the sidewalk really ends.

Discussion Questions

1. Most people define sidewalks as slabs of cement. How does Egan define them?

2. If sidewalks disappear, what else may disappear with them?

3. This essay is filled with rich description. Identify three sentences you think work particularly well and explain why. You might consider the use of effective verbs, repeated sounds, rhythmic phrases, and repetition, among other techniques.

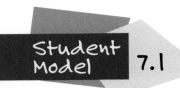

The New Millennium's Little Heroes

by Agnes Milczarek

Meet the Writer

Agnes Milczarek grew up in Poland and has considered herself a serious poet since she was six years old. She enjoys reading, dancing, shopping, and occasionally dressing up in Halloween costumes with her friends, especially when it's not Halloween.

In today's world, a collection of microcosms each spinning to their own tune of hyper-commercialized sugar-coated pop bands, scrolling marquees filled with numbers that can make or break a life, and discoveries whose names are filled with lingo never meant to be understood, save for the hereditary fate they may prevent, it is difficult to catch more than a glimpse of anything human. This "New Millennium" is upon us, marking quantitatively a stage in our progress, in our ability to succeed within the boundaries of what was given to us. At the same time, it is nothing more than a reminder that time is and will keep on flowing, and perhaps that a turning point like this deserves an evaluation not of our achievement in the fields of genetics or in the development of innumerable distractions to place on computer screens, but of the place at which we have arrived in our hearts.

When asked to define a hero nowadays, I must really strain my brain cells to push past the images with which I have grown up. We all learn early about the women's "suffragettes" and yearn to have been a part of that post-WWI movement. Or better yet, to have joined the ranks of Betty Friedan and left the infamous "woman's place" for good, battling the insecurities of the repressed housewife. We envy the Freedom Riders of forty years back and wish we could have marched...or even just sat.

With these images, these tall tales come true to live up to, it's no wonder generations X and Y have been labeled unmotivated. So they search for their role models on TV, or in sports, or in music, because the causes these days run relatively underground. Yet they still exist; the fight against prejudice, homophobia, cruelty, and violence will always exist, because no matter how closely our governments, our nonhuman structures, come to perfection, one guarantee remains: that basic harmful human traits can't change with the passing of a bill.

And when so many other things absolutely have to get done, the most difficult task to accomplish today is to live fully knowing, feeling, and loving others. So I say we take the opportunity this millennium, as we neglected to do in the last, to honor as heroes not only the big names, the stars, the ones that litter headlines, but those little heroes that live and breathe and contribute to our own lives directly: the people that inspire but can still hold to their grain of humility, those that speak not to speak, but to touch. The hero of today need not embody a myth that makes our eyes flicker with excitement, but instead to recognize that we all still have a heart— and then to use his.

I see these people every day in the extraordinary English teachers I have encountered here at school. I have watched one of them over the last couple of years share with her students everything from stories about her days as a lobbyist in the nation's capital to her experiences as a Peace Corps volunteer. Yet while these selfless acts are surely admirable, it is this teacher's ability to know me as an individual, a growing, thinking, sometimes in-over-her-head individual. With just fifty minutes per day of time spent with me, she was able to pick out poems that she knew would inspire me or that were written in a voice similar to mine, and (this is the best part) to label accurately a random occurrence as "an Agnes moment."

She is one of the few people I know who stop to look, to really look, at the expression on a student's face, and to listen, or rather hear, the feelings for which words only stand. A hero like this leads inconspicuously, masked under simple educational good intentions, waking in others what they can't afford to put to sleep.

The message has been sent numerous times by writers, by poets, by people who have trained themselves to decelerate the pace of life in order to *observe*. As everyday corporate life becomes more and more depersonalized, we have to realize that "awake people must be awake" to the lives being led around them; that we must at one point stop mending the wall Robert Frost spoke of; and that every day in Our Town, in any town, will be significant enough, no matter which way you slice it, as long as you stop to see the people hiding behind the clutter of insignificant routine.

So the heroes we need to focus on now are those that are most human. We need a Faulknerian return to the wilderness of the human soul, not a push for the bigger and better. Heroes to me are like good pieces of writing; what matters is not how grandiose or complicated or how famous they are, but how they affect their audience, the individuals which they have made it their point to reach out and to guide. So look for the heroes around you; you can learn a great deal from a person who knows all he or she really needs is the sincerity of a child, the curiosity of a novice, and a big ole human heart.

Discussion Questions

1. In defining a hero, Milczarek has a particular person in mind, yet she spends only a few sentences describing the person. Why?

2. Milczarek suggests that we not look for heroes who are bigger and better. Offer two or more examples to illustrate how society falls into this trap. Also, give at least two examples that match Milczarek's definition of a hero.

3. If you were to write an essay about a hero using Milczarek's definition, whom would you write about?

The Nerdification Proclamation

by Emily Prescott

Meet the Writer

Emily Prescott, a junior, enjoys writing, doodling in the margins of her notebook during physics, and spontaneously leaving positive notes in public places. Her hopes are to one day speak fluent French and own a cat for the sole purpose of naming it after a Jane Austen character.

The last time I did something rebellious was at the Barrington Health Club sometime around 1999. The kiddie pool was built above the main aquatic center, so if a certain five-year-old wanted to throw a bucket of water onto innocent sunbathers below, she could easily achieve her goal.

Eleven years later my rebellion-mobile has had its tires slit, engine cut, and windows smashed. I care more about curfew than my parents do, I've missed maybe three assignments since eighth grade, and I know how to knit. In junior high, while other kids started taking out their rage via vandalism and Plum Grove Junior High dress code violations—I was perfectly content with the occasional adjective-filled, angst-ridden poem. Other than that, I don't own much black, I've never voluntarily listened to heavy metal, and I can't put on a hat without feeling like a hipster.

I know this might come as a shock—but I'm a nerd. Please control your horrified gasps, I know this is a challenging conclusion. Accepting that there is a sizable population of dorks in the world is much like learning about Santa Claus. I promise you, the initial sting goes away with time.

Nerds are great, and for all of you fellow English geeks who have been panicking through the last three paragraphs of intro, that was my thesis. I realize that what I'm trying to say isn't necessarily a breakthrough piece of sociological interpretation, but I also think it's important to appreciate the more awkward sector of a hypothetical teenage pie chart. As a mighty people, we have been crushed by the tyranny of media and culture and it's time for us to live long and prosper.

I think that a common misconception among people who don't identify with social misfits is that nerds don't know they're nerds. Trust me, we're aware, and when I say "we," I'm not trying to speak for this entire group as a whole. In fact, nerds come in many different varieties and flavors. There are theater dorks, math geeks, science nerds, orch-dorks, AP kids, and people who really like clocks. Needless to say, some words just aren't dorky enough. My sincerest apologies if this is disappointing to anybody who's absolutely dying to join the geek squad, but there's no such thing as a football nerd. I'm terribly sorry, but they really just don't exist.

The justification behind my personal nerd label lies in a myriad of various embarrassing and socially awkward characteristics. For one, I have a shelf on my desk dedicated to Harry Potter memorabilia. I realize this could be a lot worse, but my room is also embellished with speech team trophies and a collection of classic literature that's far too extensive for any normal member of Generation Y. I know that there are four little women, five Bennet girls, two Brontë sisters, and only one Mr. Darcy. If all of that doesn't steal me a prom date, I don't know what will.

With this said, I legitimately like being dorky. From experience, I've found that it's extremely hard to find any nerd suffering from an "island of misfit toys" complex. The common media-forced impression of a tall, skinny, pocket-protector-sporting, acne-rocking, seventeen-year-old desperately trying to score an invite to the most happening party of year is an obvious misconception on a lot of levels. To start, I don't even know what a pocket protector looks like. Second, social misfits confident enough to flaunt their nerd-ism aren't incredibly likely to yearn for the fabulous life of being cool.

I recently read an article explaining how people at the top of their class tend to feel less teased and taunted than students who fall somewhere in the middle of their class rank. However it's important to note that intelligence does not necessarily translate to dweeb. For example, one time I multiplied fifteen by two and thought the answer was one hundred and fifty. To assume that all nerds are ambitious, introverted outcasts who spend their weekends taking the ACT over and over again—is a blatant stereotype. Everybody knows that most nerds only take it eight or nine times, I don't get what the big deal is.

The reason I'm saying this is so I can send a message to all the dorks hiding behind computer monitors and chess boards. You guys need to flaunt your sweater vests. And for all the non-nerds, take time out of your day to try something dorky. Go watch hoarders, grab a graphing calculator, or Google some Harry Potter fanfiction. Sure, dorks might spend too much time discussing the fine points of hobbits, express a suppressed desire to serve on the Starship Enterprise, or not know the difference between Kanye and Bruno Mars, but give them a break. Those guys are confusing and equally mundane. So you know what, Mr. Tall and Scary High School Quarterback Guy, you may easily find yourself at a sci-fi convention rocking a pair of Spock ears and a plastic light saber one of these days. Until then, peace out, hang ten, or whatever the cool way of concluding a humorous essay is supposed to be. I wouldn't know, I'm sort of a nerd.

Discussion Questions

1. Prescott explains that nerds "come in many different varieties and flavors." Yet she also identifies commonalities across the different types. Make a list of these common features that are highlighted in the essay. Do these characteristics fit your conception of "nerd"? Explain.

2. Prescott uses humor to define the term *nerd*, and her purpose is mainly to entertain. But what serious messages also come through in the essay?

3. Prescott admits she is far from cool but never quite defines what "cool" means. In a few sentences, how would you define cool? Offer a few examples to support your answer.

Poetic Privacy

by Anthony G. Banks, Jr.

Meet the Writer

Anthony G. Banks, Jr. is from Perris, California. This essay received an honorable mention in the Kaplan/Newsweek "My Turn" Essay Competition.

"...I'm Special.
In all of the world there is no one like me.
No one will ever have my eyes, my ears, my hair, my hands, or my voice.
I'm Special..."

Hundreds of sixth-grade children who have gone to A-Street Elementary have been made to memorize and recite the "I'm Special" poem. A poem which the faculty believes will somehow inculcate a sense of uniqueness in the hearts of the students. However, if the students are all required to memorize the same poem and then watch each other recite that poem one after the other, how special are those children actually expected to feel?

As I finished my turn at the podium, I stepped down and sadly realized that my poem was no different than all of the others. I realized that, to a world divided by stereotypes, I looked no different from any other student and there was seemingly no possible way for me to stand out. Instead of accepting this hindrance and allowing the world to make an impact on me, I chose not to hide beneath the comforting cloak of stereotypes and make an impact on the world.

Where I come from, my town is filled with blank faces with the same stanzas. Blank faces that the world does not take the time to distinguish between. All of the people live their lives like one another, each conforming to the strict controls of their stereotype, forever hoping to be protected from the condemnatory eyes of the world. Unless brutally killed in a tragic accident, no one from my town ever ends up in the newspaper, on television, in the history books, or is, at any length, remembered. To go quietly unnoticed with no purpose on earth is the fate of all who live in my community. It is my life purpose to conquer fate and prove that my poem is unique.

As a whole, since people often label my town as poor, ghetto, and dirty, its people are also labeled as poor, ghetto, and dirty. Among this poor, ghetto, and dirty category are its racial subdivisions. On one small end of the racial spectrum lie the African-Americans. In my hometown, the stereotypical life of an African-American male is to grow up poorly raised, reluctantly go to school, idly remain inactive in the community, have no future plans, and most notably, have little care for what life has to offer. I, on the other hand, am not a poor, ghetto, dirty, stereotypical African-American male. I am much more. I am what my parents have so diligently worked for at mediocre jobs just to tear off the labels that society has adhered to me. I am a student who excels in academics. I am a letterman who strives for progression even when I have reached the top. I am a councilman who supplies the youth with a small voice in a big government. I am a president who attempts to ensure equality at school. I raise money for cancer research. I am a philanthropist who organizes toy drives so that unfortunate children in war-torn countries will not have to sacrifice their Christmas. I am not poor. I am not rich. I appreciate what I have. I am not ghetto and certainly not dirty. I am not classified under any stereotype.

From a disadvantage I have created an empowering advantage. Unlike my peers, I am not afraid of the upcoming changes—going to college, starting a career, or living life as an adult. As I endure my last year of high school, I am sure that no matter what field I choose to enter, my future is a bright one because when I remember everything I gained from this setback I will remember what I regained most of all, a unique poem.

In my poem, my name is not "Special"; my name is Anthony. And every day, as I step away from the shrouding stereotypes of my community, my blank face becomes increasingly defined. The world shall take notice of this and I will no longer be seen as another stereotype but as an exception to the rule—an individual.

Discussion Questions

1. How does Banks define the word *special*? Why is he not satisfied with others' definition of *special*?

2. Banks insists he won't be classified under any stereotypes. Why? How do stereotypes limit one's perspectives, from both within and without?

3. Do you think Banks's message applies only to his world? Or is his message universal? Explain.

4. Imagine that Banks asked you to be a peer reviewer of his essay. What suggestions about imagery would you offer him?

5. What kinds of stereotypes are present in your town or school? In what ways are they accurate or inaccurate?

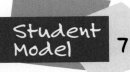

Student Model **7.4**

A Gift in Disguise
by Ryan Patrick Kelley

Meet the Writer

Ryan Patrick Kelley is from Hope, Rhode Island. This essay was a runner-up in the Kaplan/Newsweek "My Turn" Essay Competition.

It's the 18th time I washed my hands today and it's only 9:30 in the morning. I can't eat; I can't sleep; I can't think. Everyday life has become impossible.

As odd as it may sound, four years ago this was my life.

Late in the eighth grade I was diagnosed with OCD. OCD, or obsessive-compulsive disorder, is an anxiety disorder characterized by patterns of senseless thoughts and behaviors beyond the sufferer's control. OCD occurs in a spectrum, from mild to severe. If severe and left untreated it can destroy a person's capacity to function at school, at work, or even at home. In my case, the OCD was the result of an untreated strep throat infection. As my antibodies were dispersed in an attempt to fight the infection, they had an adverse effect. The doctors told me that instead of my antibodies attacking the strep infection, they were affecting a portion of my brain that controls rational thought. The normal individual has between 200 and 300 antibodies of this type in their body at any given time. I had over 2,700 when my OCD was at its worst.

My days at school were torture. Where I once saw friends and fun, I now saw strangers and germs. I didn't feel like I could trust anyone. Doorknobs, shoes, restrooms, and things that came in contact with the ground or other people were off limits. I couldn't touch my notebooks or pencils. Eat lunch? Not a chance! I was completely handicapped. I cannot describe it any other way. The constant use of anti-bacterial alcohol gel left my hands raw. Washing wasn't restricted to thoughts of being dirty. I tried to wash away bad thoughts by cleansing my hands. Touching the garbage, of course, was not an option. If it even came into my sight, I had to wash my hands or, in some cases, take a shower. Before I realized it, I was taking in excess of ten showers a day. My skin soon became so dry, it began to crack open and bleed. This terrified me. An opening in my body? Any germ, any disease could enter without resistance. Before long my school day had to be shortened. Gym class was completely terrifying. I was exhausted, completely exhausted. The energy I used to put into everyday life was now depleted from struggling against thoughts and compulsions seemingly beyond my control.

Home was no sanctuary. I felt my favorite possessions were contaminated. Sports cards that I cherished all my life could no longer be in my sight. My clothes were one of the biggest problems of all. Unlike hands, clothes couldn't be washed every ten seconds. When I had an exceptionally bad day, the clothes I wore became "contaminated" and in some cases, could never be worn again. If I felt a certain shirt was contaminated and it found its way back into my closet, not only that shirt but the two adjacent garments then became contaminated in my mind and were discarded. Not only couldn't I eat at school, but also at home. When my mom tried to tempt me with food, I would obsess about what her hands, the plate, and the fork had previously touched. Sometimes I felt the food had been poisoned or was spoiled. Small everyday tasks became all-day projects. Getting ready for school became a two-hour ritual. Spending a majority of my time at home resulted in the contamination of most parts of the house. Finding a safe place to sit was becoming impossible. What little of a life I had left was crumbling.

A psychiatrist I call "My Angel" diagnosed and treated me. She and I still meet a few times a year. For a short time I saw a behavioral therapist who helped me learn strategies to cope with the OCD. Slowly I learned to fight the thoughts and feelings that had been controlling my body and my life for so long. To this day I have and will always have OCD, but we have learned to co-exist. Thankfully, my symptoms have disappeared.

I lost a lot to OCD, but I gained more. I came out of this experience a better person—a person who takes nothing for granted. I am lucky enough to have the opportunity to attend college. This is an opportunity of which I intend to take full advantage. There were good days and bad days as I battled OCD. Persistence and staying focused helped me through the rougher days. I know these qualities will serve me well throughout college, my career, and the rest of my life. OCD helped me learn empathy for people with disabilities. Someday I hope to help others with OCD. Psychology will be my major in college.

OCD turned my life upside down. Courage comes in all shapes and sizes. Meeting each day during that turbulent time in my life took every ounce of courage I could muster. Persevering through OCD and overcoming it turned me around. I now especially appreciate the small pleasures in life that were once threatened and nearly taken away from me. Savoring every part of every day makes life much more meaningful. In that way, OCD has been a blessing to me. That merciless disease helped me to value my life in a way I could have never imagined previously and set me on a path to help others similarly afflicted. OCD gave me a valuable gift.

Discussion Questions

1. If you had read about OCD in a medical journal, you would have learned about its symptoms and causes. What does Kelley's extended definition of OCD supply that a medical dictionary would not?

2. Kelley writes that school was torture and that home was no sanctuary. Identify one supporting example for each of these claims. How did Kelley ultimately learn to view his world as less threatening?

3. Explain why Kelley entitles the essay "A Gift in Disguise."

4. If you were to write your own essay using Kelley's title, what would you write about?

5. Kelley uses the word *courage* to describe his battles with OCD. Explain why this is a fitting word.

6. Imagine that Kelley asked you to be a peer reviewer of his essay. What suggestions about imagery would you give him?

Chapter 8

Argument

magine reading this editorial about teenagers from your school in the local newspaper:

> Teenagers today have no respect for privacy and property. I live on Fairfield Avenue, a few blocks west of the high school. Not a day goes by when I don't find a candy wrapper or soda bottle on my lawn—or even a worksheet or other homework. And the language I hear, not just from the boys, is abhorrent. Why young people need to rely on vulgarity is beyond me. I shouldn't be surprised though. They are merely parroting what they hear in their trashy music and TV shows and movies. If vulgarity is what they want to fill their heads with, this is their right, I suppose. But they should have the decency not to shout that vulgar language in front of my house. The littering, the loitering, and the foul language are bad enough. But I save the worst for last. Because of the new parking configuration at the high school, students now use my street as a shortcut. I timed this shortcut and compared this with the old route and found that the shortcut saved students only 31 seconds. If they used the 31 seconds saved to pick up trash, I'd be happy. But they don't. They speed down my street (saving an extra few precious seconds?), revving their engines, shouting obscenities, and polluting what used to be a quiet street. They need to be taught some manners.

Before reading further, jot down your initial reactions to this editorial. Do you sympathize with the writer? Does the writer present a convincing argument? If you were one of the students littering and loitering, would you stop?

Your reaction was influenced by several factors, of course. Maybe your own grandparents live on such a busy street; maybe you're also bothered by casual vulgarity. On the other hand, maybe you once had a fierce argument with such a neighbor, or perhaps you know what it's like to be rushed at lunchtime. Put aside these personal biases and try to objectively assess the effectiveness of the editorial. To do so, you need to ask a few questions. Who is the intended *audience*? What is the specific *purpose* of the editorial? Has the writer presented a *logical argument*?

Let's look at audience and purpose. Does the writer hope one of the rowdy teens in question will read the editorial and stop littering and cussing? Does the writer hope to encourage other annoyed neighbors to join in stopping the teens, or to pressure the principal or a city council member to intervene? It's difficult to tell, isn't it? Most likely, the writer needed to vent and didn't carefully consider audience and purpose, which is a problem. How can he or she present a convincing case without precise aims? Furthermore, is the writer most concerned with littering, loitering, language, or speeding? In such a short editorial, a limited plea to a particular audience would have been far more effective.

Is the argument logical? The thesis is clearly stated at the outset: Teens have no respect for privacy and property. The writer concedes that teens have the right to use foul language, as long as they are not shouting it aloud so that it disturbs others. He or she also gives the precise timing for the shortcut to school, thus backing up the argument with facutal information. Thus, the writer attempts to appear as a reasonable person with an argument based on fairness and objectivity. But take another look at the first sentence: "Teenagers today have no respect for privacy and property." Since the writer doesn't qualify this remark, it appears that *all* teenagers are indicted. The writer makes the same sweeping claim with the suggestion that teen music and television are trashy. Certainly some is trashy, but only some. These generalizations are inflammatory; they make the editorial sound more like attack than argument, which tends to put readers who disagree on the defensive. As a result, these readers will call into question every other claim, including the accuracy of the driving experiment.

"Well," the neighbor may protest, "everyone has a right to an opinion." People usually resort to this claim when they haven't made their case, when they haven't taken the time to develop their ideas, when they haven't done their research. People who spew opinions without support or who scream their biases while sneering at the facts reveal a curious

Writers on Writing

An article is often gossip. An essay is reflection and insight. An article often has the temporary advantage of social heat— what's hot out there right now. An essay's heat is interior. An article can be timely, topical, engaged in the issues and personalities of the moment; it is likely to be stale within the month. In five years it may have acquired the quaint aura of a rotary phone. An article is usually Siamese-twinned to its date of birth. An essay defies its date of birth—and ours, too.

—Cynthia Ozick

and sometimes dangerous hypocrisy. What they really seem to want is an end to the discussion or argument, and an acknowledgment that their opinions count more than the facts and more than others' opinions. If everyone has a right to an opinion, this means that all opinions should be heard, that all opinions matter, not just one's own.

How could this disgruntled neighbor have made a more convincing case? In this chapter we'll show you how to build a fair, balanced, and logical argument on some controversial issue of your choice. For instance, should your high school offer more or fewer off-campus privileges? Should the minimum driving age be increased? Should teachers allow students to use cell phones in class? Should colleges rely more on a portfolio rather than test scores when admitting students? Or you can address more serious issues. Should minors be given contraceptives without a parent's consent? Should the government allow and encourage stem cell research? Start thinking about an issue you'd like to explore, and as you forge through this chapter, you can begin to formulate your argument. You'll also learn how to identify and dismantle arguments that *seem* fair and logical but crumble under scrutiny.

Journal Topic

Make a brief list of strong beliefs you have. Then, this next step may be a bit uncomfortable but it's just for practice, pick one of those beliefs and argue against it.

Using Logic to Persuade

Many politicians, advertisers, and media conglomerates are masters at creating an *image* of fairness. Some politicians, for example, will often try to taint their opponents with backhanded compliments: "He was a fine governor—in a state that limits the power of the governor." Or they might say something without really saying it, leaving themselves room for denial: "I never said my opponent was a racist; I simply worried that the voters may view him that way." Moreover, these politicians may deal in hypothetical assumptions that attack their opponent's character: "Would you vote for this person if he fathered an illegitimate child?" This is a significant *if*, and a damaging one, even if the candidate in question is innocent of the charge.

Media giants own television and radio stations, newspapers, and other sources that allegedly provide objective news. Tracing the lines of ownership, however, can provide a telling glimpse about the reliability of a source. Advertisers are more transparent in their efforts to appear fair, when in fact their arguments are patently biased and skewed: "Buy this product, and people will like you."

How can you avoid these blatant misuses of logic? Approach your essay with a sporting attitude. Just because you're creating an "argument" doesn't mean you have to adopt a win-at-all-costs attitude. You are not debating, you won't be shouting at anyone, you don't need to win. You are not the cable channel pundit who cuts off his guests when they are gaining the upper hand. To attack is easy; to convince, as you've likely discovered, is deliberate and sometimes painstaking, like building a popsicle-stick bridge that won't collapse under the slightest pressure. Instead of pointing a finger at your audience, present an open palm of ideas: *This is my thesis, here is my evidence and support, and wouldn't the world be a better place if we adopted these ideas?* Think of yourself as an attorney presenting closing statements to the jury.

Here are some key suggestions to help you use logic appropriately and maintain a respectful tone:

1. Avoid insults. Don't call your opposition "lily-livered" or "boil-brained" or "onion-eyed." While this may be entertaining, you don't score points for cleverness at the expense of solid support.

2. Don't indulge in name-calling. You may believe that people who listen to Nickelback and Miley Cyrus have poor taste in music, but labeling these fans as "losers" or "morons" doesn't strengthen your case.

3. Be careful when using sarcasm. Sarcasm can be alluring, as enticing as that extra helping of double-fudge layer cake, but it is better when consumed sparingly. The overuse of sarcasm will affect your tone, making you seem like a cold, scolding grouch instead of a reasonable but impassioned thinker.

4. Likewise, be careful with irony and exaggeration. In this case, consistency is key. If your tone is ironic, be clear about this. If you mean to exaggerate, be lavish—but avoid clichés. For instance, to convince school administrators to allow older students more freedom, you might exaggerate the restrictions and "hardships" older students have had to endure: starchy gym uniforms, hallways secured by the CIA, endless lines in the cafeteria waiting for servings of the mystery meat of the week, and so on.

5. Avoid absolutes such as *always*, *never*, *all*, and *every*. If you declare or suggest that *all* teachers are boring, you create an overwhelming burden of proof (and, in this case, you alienate the main reader of your paper).

6. Consider humor. Some topics don't invite humor, and you want to be careful about offending readers. When used appropriately, however, humor can ease defenses.

7. Demonstrate that you understand the opposing point of view. Your argument will be more persuasive if you show understanding and empathy for those you disagree with. For instance, if the neighbor in our opening editorial had acknowledged that students have busy schedules these days, she would likely have established some rapport with those students.

Avoiding Fallacies

Working under a deadline, students sometimes resort to what we'll call *quick-logic*, reasoning that is constructed hurriedly and sloppily, and that sinks like a rock in quicksand when examined. Scholars who study language call these lapses in reasoning **fallacies**. Listed here are several types of fallacies you should avoid. After you complete a first draft of your argument, use the list to help you identify fallacies that may have slipped into your reasoning.

1. **Circular argument:** A friend calls about last-minute tickets he won to a concert, and you suddenly need the family car. Having no time to think of reasons to convince your parents, and wanting to be evasive because the concert is far from home, you blurt out, "You have to let me use the car tonight because I really, really need it and you just have to let me." You haven't given a reason for being allowed to use the car, only repeated the plea.

   Definition: repeating the main point without supplying reasons.

   > The tardy policy is unsound because it doesn't work.

   > High school students should be allowed to venture off-campus because this would give them more freedom.

2. **Begging the question:** You complain to your guidance counselor that your grade is low in one class because the teacher treats you unfairly. You offer specific evidence, but the counselor advises you to do extra credit and says, "Even if you didn't mean to be, *it's clear* that you have been disrespectful." As you leave the office, the counselor's "advice" makes you wonder, or begs the question, *How have I been disrespectful?* Contrary to your counselor's claim, your disrespect is not clear, at least not to you. Phrases that assume, such as "It's clear," signal false logic that begs the question. Other such phrases include *it is obvious, everyone knows,* and *without question.*

Definition: making assumptions without supplying support.

> *It is clear that* restrictions placed on teens encourage rebellion.

> *As everyone in our town will agree,* the mayor has done a terrible job.

3. **Faulty analogy:** Your dad orders you to clean your room. Here's your ill-advised response: "I'm treated like a slave in this house. Even real slaves get to do what they want in their own rooms." You think your analogy will prove your point. In fact, analogies merely illustrate rather than prove points. Moreover, your analogy is faulty because in reality, your situation is far from that of a slave.

Definition: a weak or silly analogy that falls apart when examined.

> If we don't topple this dictator he will become like a bicycle without brakes.

> Lowering the drinking age is like releasing dogs from their leashes.

4. **Post hoc fallacy:** You start working at an ice cream shop on Tuesday. A week later the shop offers five new flavors. You claim that your being hired is directly responsible for the introduction of new flavors, only because your being hired preceded the new offerings.

Definition: suggesting A caused B because A occurred prior to B.

This is similar to the fallacy of *false cause* in which one suggests, without evidence, that one event causes another. This is also similar to the *non sequitur fallacy,* which means, literally, "it does not follow in sequence." When using a non sequitur fallacy, one suggests a connection that doesn't exist between two events or ideas.

> Allowing students to wear hats in school will lead to gang problems.

> Wear these jeans and you'll be attractive.

5. **Either/or fallacy:** Someone mentions that several students at a rival school are friendly. You have always believed the opposite. If you refuse to acknowledge the possibility that even a few students at this school are friendly, you are probably reasoning under an either/or fallacy.

Definition: suggesting that only two options exist in dealing with an issue.

> You either support this war or you support the terrorists.
>
> Students who don't go to college will undoubtedly fall behind their peers.

6. **Red herring:** You think your school ought to offer a filmmaking club. In a letter to the principal, you draw attention to vandalism occurring in the school, suggesting that the vandalism would decrease with the addition of new clubs. You are using *vandalism* as a red herring—a brightly colored, smelly fish that distracts people's attention away from the topic at hand.

   Definition: deflecting attention from the main argument and highlighting an irrelevant point.

   > There has been an increase in teen violence in the suburbs, so we should enforce a uniform policy.
   >
   > Why do people keep bringing up charges of corruption and incompetence? This candidate has nice hair and teeth.

   Political ads will obviously be more subtle than the last example, but the message is the same, enhanced by soft focus and peppy music.

7. **Trick question:** You enjoy frustrating your sister by asking her trick questions. No matter which way she answers, you will catch her in a trap.

   Definition: phrasing a question in such a way that no direct answer is desirable.

   > Is everyone at that school still preppy and arrogant?
   >
   > Does your mother know you cheat?

8. **Name-calling or labeling:** Two of your friends are spending more time with each other than with you, and you're becoming jealous. Rather than explaining that you're hurt by being left out, you label them both jerks, hoping to convince others to agree with you.

   Definition: focusing on the personal rather than the broader issue.

   > It is a known fact that this candidate has been treated for clinical depression, so she doesn't deserve your vote.
   >
   > Look, it's a politician reading to children in class. We should vote for him.

9. **Argument to the people** (also called *ad populum*): You want to convince your teacher to extend a project deadline. Instead of supplying logical reasons for an extension, you unwittingly use the

"argument to the people" fallacy: "*Good* teachers are flexible with their assignments."

Definition: appealing to emotional biases while ignoring the issues.

> If you love this country, you'll support this bill.

> If you want safe neighborhoods, you'll adopt this new measure.

After perusing the list of fallacies, you may have several reactions and questions. For instance, although fallacies are false arguments, do they ever work in persuading an audience? Sure, sometimes. Since this is a chapter on argument, and fallacies sometimes persuade, then why shouldn't you use them? Consider the deliberate use of fallacies as a form of cheating, a technique to downplay the complexity of a problem, a way of sidestepping the real issues of an argument, like intentionally distracting a referee at a critical moment in the game. The chance of winning increases perhaps, but the victory is a hollow one, fostering resentment rather than honest discourse. Also, smart, perceptive, and careful readers will notice fallacies and dismiss your argument. Of course, we're referring here to the deliberate use of fallacies. Lapses in logic are bound to occur every so often, which is why having others critique your work is critical. Other readers may notice and point out fallacies you may have missed, enabling you to strengthen your argument.

Building a Valid Argument

Say you want to argue that the minimum driving age should be changed from sixteen to seventeen, a proposal with which many state legislatures have been wrestling for years. How do you proceed? You can present pieces of evidence—examples, statistics, relevant quotes—that build and lead to your conclusions, a technique called inductive reasoning. Or you can present your conclusions first and then attempt to apply these conclusions to your argument, an example of deductive reasoning. While you don't always need to be conscious of which type of reasoning you're using, and you probably will use both, a brief discussion of the distinction may prove helpful.

Writers on Writing

Writing is hard work. A clear sentence is no accident. Very few sentences come out right the first time, or even the third time. Remember this as a consolation in moments of despair. If you find that writing is hard, it's because it *is* hard. It's one of the hardest things that people do.

—*William Zinsser*

Inductive Reasoning

Inductive reasoning is a process in which you present particular information in a particular order to draw a general conclusion. In other words, you move from the specific to the general. When using inductive reasoning, you take the reader on a guided tour, with a certain destination in mind: "On your left, notice all the rash decisions made by sixteen-year-olds. On your right, tally the accident rates for sixteen-year-olds... As you can see, sixteen-year-olds should not be trusted behind the wheel." As you present your mounting evidence, keep the following tips in mind:

1. When quoting someone, don't change the context or meaning of the quote. For example, when a movie critic writes that a movie is "engrossing—for the first five minutes," don't simply report "engrossing," as a DVD sleeve might do to entice buyers.

2. Be fair when presenting statistics (and be at least slightly wary when statistics are cited to you). If the percentage of students smoking at your school doubled in the past year, but only five people out of 3,000 smoked to begin with, you should mention this relatively low number. You could write that, although the number is low, it might indicate a trend.

3. Don't ignore solid and relevant evidence that contradicts your argument. In fact, view this evidence as offering an opportunity to clarify your point. Ignoring contrary evidence suggests that you're either unaware of the evidence (and thus, that you haven't done your research), or that you're trying to conceal it because you don't know how to refute it.

4. Present evidence from reliable sources, which becomes trickier when using the Internet. (See the section "Finding Sources on the Internet" in Chapter 9, pages 335–337, for more information on Internet research.) Blogs are usually less reliable than pages from a university site; someone's profile page is probably less reliable than a nationwide medical organization. When using books and magazines, find the most current editions. If using personal sources, establish the expertise of your source. For instance, if your psychologist aunt supplies information about sleep and dreams that you want to cite, be sure to mention her credentials.

5. Discern opinion from fact. If you state that the crime rate is down this year, make sure that your claim is supported by evidence, such as police statistics, and not just your observations.

Deductive Reasoning

With **deductive reasoning**, you move from the general to the specific. You begin with broad conclusions or premises, and attempt to apply those conclusions to your argument. For example, you might remind readers of the limited privileges provided to sixteen-year-olds: they can't vote or sign binding contracts; they can't see R-rated movies; and they can't stay out too late because of curfew regulations. These restrictions exist for good reasons, to allow sixteen-year-olds time to mature before handling adult responsibilities, responsibilities that bring greater consequences. Therefore, you might argue, changing the minimum driving age to seventeen simply reaffirms our customary thinking regarding teenage behavior.

If you've ever had to work through a mathematical proof, deductive reasoning probably sounds familiar. The "proof," in this case, takes the form of a syllogism, which is outlined next. A **syllogism** is a type of deductive reasoning that includes three steps: a major premise, a minor premise, and a conclusion. In college, entire courses are devoted to the study of such matters; what follows is a brief introduction meant to help you write an argumentative essay.

Major premise: State a broad idea.

Minor premise: Offer a specific case of the broad idea.

Conclusion: If both premises are true, conclusion is valid.

Here's an example of a valid syllogism:

> **Major premise:** Medical doctors earn high salaries.
>
> **Minor premise:** Dr. T is a medical doctor.
>
> **Conclusion:** Dr. T earns a high salary.

If we create a syllogism for the driving issue, it might look like this:

> **Major premise:** Teens are not awarded full adult privileges in our society because they need time to mature.
>
> **Minor premise:** Sixteen-year-olds are teens.
>
> **Conclusion:** Sixteen-year-olds should not be awarded full adult privileges.

Should you try to create such concise syllogisms every time you use deductive reasoning? You'll have to answer this for yourself, but probably yes—at least until you feel confident in your reasoning skills. Over the years, teachers likely have given you some indication of your skill level, posting red flags such as "does not follow" and "I don't get this." Or they may have complimented you on your solid use of evidence. Regardless, time spent outlining syllogisms can help you identify fallacies and other lapses in logic. More specifically, syllogisms help achieve three aims:

1. Syllogisms encourage a precision of language.

   Let's look one more time at the syllogism about sixteen-year-olds. While the syllogism holds up, it fails to account for teens older than sixteen. The major premise should probably read: "*Young* teens are not awarded full privileges...." Also, with precise language comes precise thought; you'd probably want to account for why seventeen-year-olds—who are also still teens—should be allowed to drive, which may lead to a discussion on the merit of meting out privileges gradually.

2. Syllogisms help prevent false leaps in logic.

   Sometimes a minor premise doesn't logically follow the major premise, or the conclusion isn't supported by the premises.

   Major premise: High school seniors should apply to college early.

   Minor premise: Mary applied to college early.

   Conclusion: Mary is a senior.

   Although both premises are accurate, they are not necessarily related. Mary could be a junior or sophomore, which would make the conclusion invalid.

3. Syllogisms help point out false and unreasonable assumptions.

   Major premise: All teachers want to help students.

   Minor premise: Mr. Y is a teacher.

   Conclusion: Mr. Y wants to help students.

   Although the logic is sound, which makes the syllogism technically valid, the major premise is unfounded, making the entire syllogism worthless. Do *all* teachers want to help students? Maybe not. If one or both of your premises are untrue, your conclusions mean nothing.

Emotional Appeal

While logic may convince you to exercise regularly and eat nutritious meals, you don't always *feel* convinced, which is why you need to consider emotions as well as logic when crafting an argument. For example, a logical argument might include a sentence like this: *To ensure good health, the body needs a variety of nutrients, such as carbohydrates, fats, and proteins.* An emotional appeal will include much of this information, but it will be more likely to grip the reader through the use of imagery and figurative language: *A body is like a furnace that needs constant attention to keep it burning bright.*

Logical and emotional appeals are sometimes so intertwined that it's impossible to separate them, though you may lean more heavily on one appeal over the other. Many other chapters in this text deal extensively with techniques that appeal to the reader's emotions, but here are a few reminders of how to appeal effectively to emotions:

- Be aware of connotation.
- Appeal to the senses.
- Use figurative language.
- Adopt a clear tone.
- Tell a story.
- Offer examples.

Organizing Your Essay

Here's an outline you may want to follow to structure your essay.

Introduction	Engaging opening
Thesis	Your purpose in writing the essay
Body	Opposing positions and your response to them
	Your evidence: facts, statistics, examples, stories
Conclusion	Thesis (worded differently)
	Vision of future

Formulating a Thesis

If you wanted to ask someone you didn't know well to a dance, you probably wouldn't blurt out your request in a rush. You'd start with small talk and calmly lead up to the big question because you want to prepare the person to listen, to make the person receptive to your ideas. Since this is not a dating manual, we'll allow your imagination to fill in the small talk and, instead, attempt to apply our sappy analogy to the essay at hand—suggesting that you need to find a way to make your reader *receptive* to your ideas.

There may be instances when you boldly state your thesis in the opening sentence because you're confident that your audience is already receptive. More often, however, you will need to set up your thesis by first drawing in your reader. Many writers and teachers visualize this process as an upside-down pyramid or a funnel: begin in the broadest terms and gradually narrow your focus until you're ready to unveil your thesis. You can paint a picture with description, offer a story or an example, cite statistics or experts, ask questions, and so on. Beginning with a dictionary definition, as you have probably tried a time or two, might not be the most engaging opening. You will have plenty of room to define terms along the way.

In a short essay, you can set up a thesis in a paragraph. If the essay is longer or the thesis is complex, the set-up may require several paragraphs. Here's an example from an *Atlantic* article by Carl Elliott:

> Back in the old days, long before drug companies started making headlines in the business pages, doctors were routinely called upon by company representatives known as "detail men." To "detail" a doctor is to give that doctor information about a company's new drugs, with the aim of persuading the doctor to prescribe them. When I was growing up, in South Carolina in the 1970s, I would occasionally see detail men sitting patiently in the waiting room outside the office of my father, a family doctor. They were pretty easy to spot. Detail men were usually sober, conservatively dressed gentlemen who would not have looked out of place at the Presbyterian church across the street. Instead of Bibles or hymn books, though, they carried detail bags, which were filled with journal articles, drug samples, and branded knickknacks for the office.
>
> Today detail men are officially known as "pharmaceutical sales representatives," but everyone I know calls them "drug reps." Drug reps are still easy to spot in a clinic or hospital, but for slightly different reasons. The most obvious is their appearance.... The average drug rep looks like a supermodel, or maybe an A-list movie star. Drug reps today are often young, well groomed, and strikingly good-looking. Many are women. They are usually affable and sometimes very smart.... Their job is to persuade doctors to prescribe their drugs.

Can you identify Elliott's thesis from these two paragraphs? Probably not. Because his argument is a complicated one—the essay is quite lengthy—Elliott uses many paragraphs to familiarize the reader with this world before introducing his thesis, which appears in the sixth paragraph: "For better or worse, America has turned its health-care system over to the same market forces that transformed the village hardware store into Home Depot and the corner pharmacy into a strip-mall CVS."

Dealing with Opposing Arguments to Your Thesis

Once you've set up and stated your thesis, you may want to briefly address opposing arguments. Demonstrate that you understand these arguments, then calmly and swiftly refute them. Why *briefly* and *swiftly?* You simply want to defuse major objections at this point, but you don't want to delay the presentation of your evidence for too long. Besides, as you present your case, you will address objections along the way.

Presenting Your Evidence

Present your evidence: facts, statistics, examples, stories, and any other data relevant to your thesis. Review the tips for presenting evidence outlined earlier in the section "Building a Valid Argument." Gradually devise some sort of organizational plan when filling out the body of your paper. Do you first present minor examples that lead to more significant ones? Do you follow a chronological pattern? Do you begin with the personal and then broaden to the community, then the city, then the entire society? Do you begin with amusing anecdotes and build to more serious examples? There are no wrong answers to these questions, but if you don't pose them, your essay will likely be disorganized, and readers may struggle to follow your argument.

Crafting Your Conclusion

Conclusions are difficult. You want to return to your thesis, but you certainly don't want to use the same phrasing. The reader has followed your argument for several pages and is now quite informed on the topic; therefore, you can now be more sophisticated with your wording. If in your introduction you were the expert carpenter addressing someone who didn't know the best way to use a hand saw, in the conclusion you are now speaking to a not-so-naïve apprentice. Moreover, you want to leave your audience with some vision of what the world will be like if your ideas are adopted. In essence, you want to inspire.

Choosing a Topic

There's no reason to be walking around for days muttering, "I can't think of a topic." If you spend ten minutes perusing a newspaper or magazine, you'll probably find a dozen ideas. Of the dozen, one or two might be intriguing enough to write about, or they might inspire other ideas. To test this strategy, we turned to our local paper, the *Daily Herald*, and found a story on the front page about how schools are monitoring Internet use by students. Some schools are considering using an alarm system: Every time students enter a site they've been warned not to use, a loud buzzer sounds, alerting the teacher and exposing five shades of embarrassment on the face of the vilified student. You could write about this very issue, interviewing school officials, teachers, and fellow students, to find out which schools use the technology and how it works, then discussing the ethics of such use.

Or the article might inspire other general questions. How far should a school go in regulating student behavior? Should schools teach issues like character and integrity? Should schools play a role in encouraging abstinence? Should drug tests be administered to athletes? If you want to broaden your scope further, you might write about individuals who must endure public scorn over a crime they committed: they must display placards on their lawns or license plates on their cars that reveal the nature of their crime. Most of these ideas about topics would probably not have occurred to you had you not picked up the newspaper.

Another productive method for finding a topic is to spend ten minutes writing down all the things that bother you—about home, school, work, government, or the world. Your gripes can be small or global. If you're a contented person, find a disgruntled friend to assist you. Or interview people. Ask them about injustices they see in the world, what they would change if they could. Since people your own age are likely to have views similar to yours, consider talking with older neighbors or relatives, too.

You might arrive at a topic by beginning broadly and then narrowing your focus. Pick a general subject that interests you:

Broad Categories

Personal

Social

Political

Legal

Educational

Ethical

Medical

Say you decide to write about personal issues that relate to your age group. Branch off from there and make a list of particular topics to write about. Although you will ultimately need only one topic, develop the list. You might be surprised by what you find when you scratch beneath the surface. Here's an example:

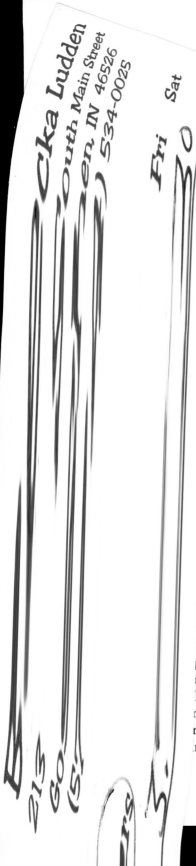

acebook)

rimination against teens

hildren's entertainment

rricular activities or sports

as a requirement

on parenting

the media

ore time with technology
ople

s in public areas

selection to a single issue
sertions about that issue.
able opinion that can be
. Here are a few assertions
n the preceding list:

igned for free access and
y regulated.

enforce strict Internet use,
backfire.

should be located in a public
n.

er social networks should
proval when a minor opens

ecome habitual, especially
ther addictive people.

similarities in these assertions? (1) They are all
pported or refuted. (2) They all contain the word
of that word (as with the last assertion). (3) They
he more specific, the better. (4) They are all rea-
r words, they avoid absolutes such as *every*, *never*,
rds that create an overwhelming burden of proof.
nternet use should not be regulated *at all*. You'd

Writing Tip

Have you ever woken up knowing that you just had a vivid dream, but you can't remember the dream itself? Or maybe you can remember the dream for a couple of minutes, but when you begin to tell someone about it later you find that the details have vanished? Ideas for writing work similarly. If an idea for a poem, essay, school assignment, story, or screenplay flashes across your brain, you need to write it down immediately. If you don't, it might be lost forever.

Even if it's not a full idea—maybe it's just an image or a catchy phrase you would like to use or develop—write it down right away.

Some writers carry a notebook at all times. Other less formal writers just grab anything, jot down the idea, and stick it in their pocket or purse (or tap it into their iPad). Where you record the idea isn't as important as how quickly you do it.

Even if the idea or image is the coolest notion you've ever conceived, and you are absolutely certain that you will never forget it, write it down quickly. Otherwise, just like those dreams, it may disappear.

have to explain why even the most unsavory of sites should be freely accessible to anyone, including small children.

Are these opinions also legitimate assertions?

- The television should be turned on when you do homework.

- School is boring.

- People should listen to the oldies station.

You'll notice that none are assertions. Although two contain the word *should*, they all deal with personal tastes. I like jazz—you like country. I can devour an apple pie in one sitting—you can barely look at apple pie. I watch baseball—you prefer soccer. There's no use trying to convince you to like jazz, apple pie, or baseball. Your tastes are different from mine, and tastes are not something you can logically argue about. You might alter these statements to *make* them arguable. For instance, you can argue that country music has had a great influence on many other types of music. Or you can try to convince someone that apple pie is not a healthy dessert—or that soccer is better for cardiovascular health than some sports. But let's agree to respect our differences in tastes and not waste time arguing over them.

What about these statements?

- Child abusers should be punished.

- Drunk driving must be stopped.

- Police officers should not abuse their power.

These statements *sound* arguable. But who would argue against these statements? Police officers *should* abuse their power? When creating an assertion, ask yourself whether the statement will generate genuine discussion, genuine argument. If not, it may not be worth writing about.

Finally, while deciding on a topic, keep in mind that your personal beliefs don't need to match your argument. That is, you can argue for a position with which you do not agree. You probably won't be inclined to do so, but if you're looking for a challenge, defending the opposition's side can often help to clarify your own beliefs.

Journal Topic

The principal has granted you one modest wish. You can change one school rule—as long as you can write a brief and convincing argument for your case. Go ahead.

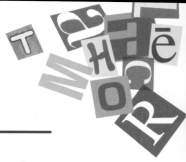

the Chapter Assignment, try the following
ormulating and critiquing an argument.

s in the following statements. More than one
, so be ready to defend your answer.

that females are better suited for household

bey their parents when they're young or suffer
er in life.

:tatorship will bring democracy to that country.

you that diets don't work.

a bad idea because people will have to pay more.

en would support this idea.

spaper or magazine, or watch a few commercials
identify four fallacies.

on a familiar issue. Here's an example:

: Busywork often creates resentment and
tudents.

: Worksheets are busywork.

orksheets create resentment and defiance.

task of supporting or refuting this assertion:
r listeners than males. He makes a list of points
lop his argument. As he scans the list of points he
e realizes he has used inductive reasoning. What
: like?

he following vague statements into assertions. The
an example.

ent needs to be cleaned up.

're serious about cleaning the environment,
rk our cars and find alternative ways to get

b. School is not fun.

c. Many teens have part-time jobs.

d. Many homeless people are in big cities.

e. Marriage is a good idea.

6. You decide to develop an argument on this assert
should be viewed as opportunities rather than disapp
a brief opening that might be used to set up this ass
the following options: paint a picture with descrip
offer examples; cite a source; or present facts.

Chapter Assignment

Prewriting

**Your assignment for this chapter is to write
essay. Use the following suggestions to help you
and clarify the purpose of your essay.**

Select an issue you want to write about and write an
issue. If you're having difficulty with this, review the se
a Topic" or select one of the following assertions. Writ
at the top of a sheet of paper, then draw a line down th
page, creating two columns. On one side, write down a
think of that will support the assertion: evidence, logic
the other side, write down anything you can think of
assertion. Spend at least ten minutes generating ideas.

Writing Topics

**Choose your own topic or select one from the f
develop into an argument essay.**

Write a well-developed argument for *or* against
you've chosen. Some topics will require more research
consider this when selecting. Be particularly mindful
you intend to persuade.

chool should be less strict.

hool needs major changes.

t cut programs because of financial concerns, the
ed.

uld not be allowed in public schools.

ve more rights in the church.

restrict the graphic details they present on televi-

should be legalized.

gh school level should emphasize teamwork and
ore than winning.

cies must be enacted soon.

n to express their emotions more freely.

ot be a game.

too much time on their appearance.

ated person has an advantage in the workforce over
ut a college degree.

s, which impose restrictions on gun ownership, need
tly enforced.

educe crime in big cities, we need to reduce poverty.

ve a useful function.

and edit your first draft, consider these sugges-

on technique: read your paper aloud, or find someone
to you. Holes in logic sometimes become apparent
ur own essay. As you listen, consider the following
on your answers to these questions, revise and rewrite

clear? Is it presented early?

acknowledge and deal with opposing arguments?

primarily on logical or emotional appeals? Offer one
ch.

4. Do you rely on inductive reasoning? If so, do you
   evidence fairly? Explain.

5. Do you use deductive reasoning? If so, write down
   you use.

6. Have you avoided fallacies? Use the list of fallacies
   to help you answer this question.

7. What sort of organizational plan did you use for th
   essay? Does a pattern hold it together?

Peer Review

Use these questions to help you evaluate anot
writing. Remember, specific suggestions and exam
helpful.

1. Has the writer presented a valid and convincing
   specific when you point out convincing or unconvin

2. What evidence is most effective? What evidence s
   weak?

3. What other points should the writer address?

4. How does the writer deal with opposing arguments
   is this strategy effective? How might it be improved

5. How well does the overall organization work? Can
   better way to organize the essay?

6. How has the writer specifically appealed to the inter

7. What questions do you have for the writer?

I Have a Dream

by Martin Luther King, Jr.

Meet the Writer

Martin Luther King, Jr. African American inspired the Civil Rights Movement of the 1950s and 1960s. He received the Nobel Peace Prize in 1964 for his use of nonviolent protest to bring about change. King was assassinated in 1968. His birthday is observed as a national holiday each January.

Five score years ago, a great American, in whose symbolic shadow we stand, signed the Emancipation Proclamation. This momentous decree came as a great beacon light of hope to millions of Negro slaves who had been seared in the flames of withering injustice. It came as a joyous daybreak to end the long night of captivity.

But one hundred years later, we must face the tragic fact that the Negro is still not free. One hundred years later, the life of the Negro is still sadly crippled by the manacles of segregation and the chains of discrimination. One hundred years later, the Negro lives on a lonely island of poverty in the midst of a vast ocean of material prosperity. One hundred years later, the Negro is still languishing in the corners of American society and finds himself an exile in his own land. So we have come here today to dramatize an appalling condition.

In a sense we have come to our nation's Capital to cash a check. When the architects of our republic wrote the magnificent words of the Constitution and the Declaration of Independence, they were signing a promissory note to which every American was to fall heir. This note was a promise that all men would be guaranteed the unalienable rights of life, liberty, and the pursuit of happiness.

It is obvious today that America has defaulted on this promissory note insofar as her citizens of color are concerned. Instead of honoring this sacred obligation, America has given the Negro people a bad check; a check which has come back marked "insufficient funds." But we refuse to believe that the bank of injustice is

bankrupt. We refuse to believe that there are insu
great vaults of opportunity of this nation. So we h
this check—a check that will give us upon deman
dom and the security of justice. We have also com
spot to remind America of the fierce urgency of n
to engage in the luxury of cooling off or to take th
drug of gradualism. *Now* is the time to make real t
Democracy. *Now* is the time to rise from the dark
ley of segregation to the sunlit path of racial justic
to open the doors of opportunity to all of God's ch
time to lift our nation from the quicksands of racial
solid rock of brotherhood.

It would be fatal for the nation to overlook the
moment and to underestimate the determination o
sweltering summer of the Negro's legitimate discor
until there is an invigorating autumn of freedom an
is not an end, but a beginning. Those who hope tha
needed to blow off steam and will now be content
awakening if the nation returns to business as usual
neither rest nor tranquility in America until the Neg
citizenship rights. The whirlwinds of revolt will conti
foundations of our nation until the bright day of just

But there is something I must say to my people
warm threshold which leads into the palace of justic
of gaining our rightful place we must not be guilty o
Let us not seek to satisfy our thirst for freedom by d
cup of bitterness and hatred. We must forever condu
on the high plane of dignity and discipline. We must
creative protest to degenerate into physical violence
again we must rise to the majestic heights of meetin
with soul force. The marvelous new militancy which h
Negro community must not lead us to a distrust of a
for many of our white brothers, as evidenced by their
today, have come to realize that their destiny is tied
tiny and their freedom is inextricably bound to our fre
not walk alone.

And as we walk, we must make the pledge that w
ahead. We cannot turn back. There are those who are
devotees of civil rights, "When will you be satisfied?"

be satisfied as long as the Negro is the victim of the unspeakable horrors of police brutality. We can never be satisfied as long as our bodies, heavy with the fatigue of travel, cannot gain lodging in the motels of the highways and the hotels of the cities. We cannot be satisfied as long as the Negro's basic mobility is from a smaller ghetto to a larger one. We can never be satisfied as long as a Negro in Mississippi cannot vote and a Negro in New York believes he has nothing for which to vote. No, no, we are not satisfied, and we will not be satisfied until justice rolls down like waters and righteousness like a mighty stream.

I am not unmindful that some of you have come here out of great trials and tribulations. Some of you have come fresh from narrow jail cells. Some of you have come from areas where your quest for freedom left you battered by the storms of persecution and staggered by the winds of police brutality. You have been the veterans of creative suffering. Continue to work with the faith that unearned suffering is redemptive.

Go back to Mississippi, go back to Alabama, go back to South Carolina, go back to Georgia, go back to Louisiana, go back to the slums and ghettos of our northern cities, knowing that somehow this situation can and will be changed. Let us not wallow in the valley of despair.

I say to you today, my friends, that in spite of the difficulties and frustrations of the moment I still have a dream. It is a dream deeply rooted in the American dream.

I have a dream that one day this nation will rise up and live out the true meaning of its creed: "We hold these truths to be self-evident; that all men are created equal."

I have a dream that one day on the red hills of Georgia the sons of former slaves and the sons of former slaveowners will be able to sit down together at the table of brotherhood.

I have a dream that the state of Mississippi, a desert state sweltering with the heat of injustice and oppression, will be transformed into an oasis of freedom and justice.

I have a dream that my four little children will one day live in a nation where they will not be judged by the color of their skin but by the content of their character.

I have a dream today.

I have a dream that the state of Alabama, whose governor's lips are presently dripping with the words of interposition and nullification, will be transformed into a situation where little black boys and black girls will be able to join hands with little white boys and white girls and walk together as sisters and brothers.

I have a dream today.

I have a dream that one day every valley shall be exalted, every hill and mountain shall be made low, the rough places will be made plain, and the crooked places will be made straight, and the glory of the Lord shall be revealed, and all flesh shall see it together.

This is our hope. This is the faith with which I return to the South. With this faith we will be able to hew out of the mountain of despair a stone of hope. With this faith we will be able to transform the jangling discords of our nation into a beautiful symphony of brotherhood. With this faith we will be able to work together, to pray together, to struggle together, to go to jail together, to stand up for freedom together, knowing that we will be free one day.

This will be the day when all of God's children will be able to sing with new meaning.

My country, 'tis of thee
Sweet land of liberty,
  Of thee I sing:
Land where my fathers died,
Land of the pilgrims' pride,
From every mountainside
  Let freedom ring.

And if America is to be a great nation this must become true. So let freedom ring from the prodigious hilltops of New Hampshire. Let freedom ring from the mighty mountains of New York. Let freedom ring from the heightening Alleghenies of Pennsylvania!

Let freedom ring from the snowcapped Rockies of Colorado!

Let freedom ring from the curvaceous peaks of California!

But not only that; let freedom ring from Stone Mountain of Georgia!

Let freedom ring from Lookout Mountain of Tennessee!

Let freedom ring from every hill and molehill of Mississippi. From every mountainside, let freedom ring.

When we let freedom ring, when we let it ring from every village and every hamlet, from every state and every city, we will be able to speed up that day when all of God's children, black men and white men, Jews and Gentiles, Protestants and Catholics, will be able to join hands and sing in the words of the old Negro spiritual, "Free at last! free at last! thank God almighty, we are free at last!"

Discussion Questions

1. King begins his essay with the phrase "Five score years ago," which means 100 years. Why doesn't King use the simpler number?

2. At other times, King does use simpler language. Find two examples and explain why he does this.

3. Analyze the "insufficient funds" analogy. What does the analogy mean? Why is it appropriate?

4. Does King rely primarily on inductive or deductive reasoning? Provide examples to support your answer.

5. Notice how King discusses freedom and injustice on both a personal and national level. Provide two examples of each. What does King achieve by including both?

6. Who is King's audience? What does he want them to believe or do?

7. King often uses repetition to create refrains pleasing for their musicality. Analyze one of these refrains, paying attention to sound and content. Discuss any patterns you notice.

8. Why does King include the lyrics to "My Country 'Tis of Thee"?

Now You Take "Bambi" or "Snow White"—That's Scary!

by Stephen King

Meet the Writer

Best-selling author Stephen King is well known for horror stories, many of which have sold more than 350 million copies worldwide. A number of King's books have been made into films. He lives in Maine.

Read the story synopsis below and ask yourself if it would make the sort of film you'd want your kids watching on the Friday- or Saturday-night movie.

A good but rather weak man discovers that, because of inflation, recession and his second wife's fondness for overusing his credit cards, the family is tottering on the brink of financial ruin. In fact, they can expect to see the repossession men coming for the car, the almost new recreational vehicle and the two color TVs any day; and a pink warning-of-foreclosure notice has already arrived from the bank that holds the mortgage on their house.

The wife's solution is simple but chilling: kill the two children, make it look like an accident and collect the insurance. She browbeats her husband into going along with this homicidal scheme. A wilderness trip is arranged, and while wifey stays in camp, the father leads his two children deep into the Great Smoky wilderness. In the end, he finds he cannot kill them in cold blood; he simply leaves them to wander around until, presumably, they die of hunger and exposure.

The two children spend a horrifying three days and two nights in the wilderness. Near the end of their endurance, they stumble upon a back-country cabin and go to it, hoping for rescue. The woman who lives alone there turns out to be a cannibal. She cages the two children and prepares to roast them in her oven as she has roasted and eaten other wanderers before them. The boy manages to get free. He creeps up behind the woman as she stokes her oven and pushes her in, where she burns to death in her own fire.

You're probably shaking your head no, even if you have already recognized the origin of this bloody little tale (if you didn't, ask your kids: they probably will) as "Hansel and Gretel," a so called "fairy tale" that most kids are exposed to even before they start kindergarten. In addition to this story with its grim and terrifying images of child abandonment, children lost in the woods and imprisoned by an evil woman, cannibalism and justifiable homicide, small children are routinely exposed to tales of mass murder and mutilation ("Bluebird"), the eating of a loved one by a monster ("Little Red Riding-Hood"), treachery and deceit ("Snow White") and even the specter of a little boy who must face a black-hooded, ax-wielding headsman ("The 500 Hats of Bartholomew Cubbins," by Dr. Seuss).

I'm sometimes asked what I allow my kids to watch on the tube, for two reasons: first, my three children, at 10, 8, and 4, are still young enough to be in the age group that opponents of TV violence and horror consider to be particularly impressionable and at risk; and second, my seven novels have been popularly classified as "horror stories." People tend to think those two facts contradictory. But...I'm not sure that they are.

Three of my books have been made into films, and at this writing, two of them have been shown on TV. In the case of "Salem's Lot," a made-for-TV movie, there was never a question of allowing my kids to watch it on its first run on CBS; it began at 9 o'clock in our time zone, and all three children go to bed earlier than that. Even on a weekend, and even for the oldest, an 11 o'clock bedtime is just not negotiable. A previous *TV GUIDE* article about children and frightening programs mentioned a 3-year-old who watched "Lot" and consequently suffered night terrors. I have no wish to question any responsible parent's judgment—all parents raise their children in different ways—but it did strike me as passingly odd that a 3-year-old should have been allowed to stay up that late to get scared.

But in my case, the hours of the telecast were not really a factor, because we have one of those neat little time-machines, a video-cassette recorder. I taped the program and, after viewing it myself, decided my children could watch it if they wanted to. My daughter had no interest; she's more involved with stories of brave dogs and loyal horses these days. My two sons, Joe, 8, and Owen, then 3, did watch. Neither of them seemed to have any problems either while watching or in the middle of the night—when those problems most likely turn up.

I also have a tape of "Carrie," a theatrical film first shown on TV about two and a half years ago. I elected to keep this one on what my kids call "the high shelf" (where I put the tapes that are forbidden to them), because I felt that its depiction of children turning against other children, the lead character's horrifying embarrassment at a school dance and her later act of matricide would upset them. "Lot," on the contrary, is a story that the children accepted as a fairy tale in modern dress.

Other tapes on my "high shelf" include "Night of the Living Dead" (cannibalism), "The Brood" (David Cronenberg's film of inter-generational breakdown and homicidal "children of rage" who are set free to murder and rampage), and "The Exorcist." They are all up there for the same reason: they contain elements that I think might freak the kids out.

Not that it's possible to keep kids away from everything on TV (or in the movies, for that matter) that will freak them out; the movies that terrorized my own nights most thoroughly as a kid were not those through which Frankenstein's monster or the Wolfman lurched and growled, but the Disney cartoons. I watched Bambi's mother shot and Bambi running frantically to escape being burned up in a forest fire. I watched, appalled, dismayed and sweaty with fear, as Snow White bit into the poisoned apple while the old crone giggled in evil ecstasy. I was similarly terrified by the walking brooms in "Fantasia" and the big, bad wolf who chased the fleeing pigs from house to house with such grim and homicidal intensity. More recently, Owen, who just turned 4, crawled into bed with my wife and me. "Cruella DeVille is in my room," he said. Cruella DeVille is, of course, the villainess of "101 Dalmatians" and I suppose Owen had decided that a woman who would want to turn puppies into dogskin coats might also be interested in little boys. All these films would certainly get G-ratings if they were produced today, and frightening excerpts of them have been shown on TV during "the children's hour."

Do I believe that all violent or horrifying programming should be banned from network TV? No, I do not. Do I believe it should be telecast only in the later evening hours, TV's version of the "high shelf"?

Yes, I do. Do I believe that children should be forbidden all violent or horrifying programs? No, I do not. Like their elders, children have a right to experience the entire spectrum of drama, from such warm and mostly unthreatening programs as *Little House on the Prairie* and *The Waltons* to scarier fare. It's been suggested again and again that such entertainment offers us a catharsis—a chance to enter for a little while a scary and yet controllable world where we can express our fears, aggressions and possibly even hostilities. Surely no one would suggest that children do not have their own fears and hostilities to face and overcome; those dark feelings are the basis of many of the fairy tales children love best.

Do I think a child's intake of violent or horrifying programs should be limited? Yes, I do, and that's why I have a high shelf. But the pressure groups who want to see all horror (and anything smacking of sex, for that matter) arbitrarily removed from television make me both uneasy and angry. The element of Big Brotherism inherent in such an idea causes the unease; the idea of a bunch of people I don't even know presuming to dictate what is best for my children causes the anger. I feel that deciding such things myself is my right—and my responsibility.

Discussion Questions

1. Does the name Stephen King carry weight as you read this essay? Would your reaction to the essay be different if you thought the essay was written by accountant Stephen King? Explain.

2. Does King rely mainly on inductive or deductive reasoning to make his case? Provide examples to support your answer.

3. King uses *Hansel and Gretel* and *Bambi* to make a point. What point does he make?

4. Who is King's audience? Does he make a convincing case? Explain.

5. Do you agree with King's contention that there should be a "high shelf" for younger children, to keep some viewing material out of their reach? If so, what current movies would you place on this shelf? What "questionable" movies would you allow children to watch? If you don't agree with the high shelf, explain why.

No Heart for the Homeless

by Stuart D. Bykofsky

Meet the Writer

Stuart Bykofsky is a columnist for the *Philadelphia Daily News*.

I am about to be heartless. There are people living on the streets of most American cities, turning sidewalks into dormitories. They are called the homeless, street people, vagrants, beggars, vent men, bag ladies, bums. Often they are called worse. They are America's living nightmare—tattered human bundles. They have got to go.

I don't know, exactly, when they got the *right* to live on the street. I don't know, exactly, when I *lost* the right to walk through town without being pestered by panhandlers. I do know I want them off my sidewalk. If you think I am heartless for saying that, can I send them to live on *your* sidewalk?

I am fed up with the trash they bring into my neighborhood. The pools of urine in apartment-house lobbies disgust me. I am fed up with picking my way down sidewalks blocked by plastic milk crates, stepping over human forms sprawled on steam gratings.

I also am fed up with newspaper columnists who periodically have a good cry in print over the plight of the street people—and the average citizen's callous reaction to them. I have yet to read that one of these columnists has taken a street person home for a bath and a meal. That happens only in movies like "Down and Out in Beverly Hills."

What are we, the heartless, supposed to do? In the Sermon on the Mount, Jesus urged his followers to "give to everyone who begs from you." The horde of the homeless turns this plea into a joke. Walking to work this morning, I was approached eight times: "Mister, I'm hungry." "Can you help me out?" "You have any spare change?" "Got a quarter?" But what would a quarter do? If I really mean to help, I should follow Jesus and give a dollar to everyone who asks. That would be $8 on my way to work—and $8 on the way home, because they are still there. That's $80 a week.

Early on, I felt pity for those in the streets, but their relentless begging has forced me to change *my* habits, my attitudes. Panhandlers have taught me to suspect anyone approaching me on the street. "Can I ask you something, sir?" a casually dressed man asks. Maybe he's a tourist needing directions. Maybe he just wants to know the time. No. He wants access to my pockets. Tired of being hit like a money-access machine, I'm now deaf to people in the street. I'm not happy about that, but there it is.

I am amazed by their persistence. Since I walk the same route every day, I pass the same street people on the same gratings, or curled in the same makeshift, cardboard shelters. Every time I leave my apartment building, I mean *every time*, I am panhandled by begging sentinels more steadfast than Gurkhas. Every time, I ignore them. I wish I could make them disappear.

At 6 feet 3 and 185 pounds, I'm not frightened when one shuffles up to me, dull-eyed, asking alms. They do frighten my elderly neighbors. It is psychological assault. Why should they have to put up with it?

Don't tell me that's the price we pay for living in a democracy. Tell me why they are allowed to make the street their home—day and night, hot and cold—when I can't park a car at the curb for an hour without paying a meter. How is that possible? I find it ironical that my tax money keeps the street—their home—paved and clean. That makes me their landlord. I want to evict them.

Vagrancy laws: No one has reliable statistics about their numbers across America, but authorities agree the homeless fall into three categories: (1) the economically distressed, who would work if they could find work; (2) the mentally ill, who can't work; (3) the alcoholic, the drug-addicted and others who won't work. Police once routinely arrested people sleeping in the streets, or the parks, or the railroad stations, as vagrants. Vagrancy laws were struck down because it shouldn't be a crime to be out of work. That seems right to me. No one should be arrested because he or she has no money. But by the same token, no one should be allowed to set up housekeeping on the sidewalk.

This is the nub of the problem. If I don't want them sleeping on the sidewalks, what is to be done?

People sleeping on the streets depress property values, decrease tourism, tarnish a city's reputation and inhibit customers from entering shops. In subtle ways, we already are paying the price for the homeless. I would rather pay higher taxes and get these people off the streets.

The unemployed are the easiest to help because they are able and willing to work. If they want a job, but society is unable to provide a job, then government should provide money for food and shelter to be delivered through welfare or a workfare program.

The mental patients, the "harmless schizophrenics," were turned loose when the courts decided no one should be locked up just because they were sick. Communities were to provide local facilities. Big surprise: they didn't. But some level of government must. The mentally incompetent who now have the "freedom" to die on cold streets must be steered to decent tax-supported homes or institutions that will care for them.

The drunk, the addicted and the just plain shiftless present an entirely different problem. They say they are on the streets because they have nowhere else to go. We must take that excuse away from them. New facilities do not have to be built. Every community has factories and warehouses that have closed down. Nearly every community has abandoned houses. These can be converted at minimal cost into a shelter that provides light, heat and plumbing. Call them tax-supported flophouses, call them almshouses, I don't care.

People can't be *forced* to live there, of course. They have their rights. But so do we. Once we have made shelter available, we have the right to say this: the streets are not for sleeping anymore.

Discussion Questions

1. What does Bykofsky hope to achieve with his first sentence? Is the first sentence effective? Explain.

2. Identify how Bykofsky uses both inductive and deductive reasoning. Provide examples.

3. Bykofsky admits he has "no heart for the homeless," but in fact, he does show compassion. Provide evidence of this compassion.

4. Select any one paragraph and write a brief rebuttal.

5. Bykofsky argues that he has the right to walk through town without being pestered. Do you agree that this is a right? Why or why not?

6. Bykofsky argues that homeless people create societal problems. What are those problems, and what is his solution? Explain why you agree or disagree.

7. Bykofsky adopts a bold stance and risks appearing cold and heartless, which is why he supplies plenty of logical reasons for his argument. If you wanted to adopt a bold stance on some issue at school, what would you write about?

Frightening—And Fantastic

by Anna Quindlen

Meet the Writer

Anna Quindlen is the author of many best-selling works of fiction and nonfiction. She won the Pulitzer Prize in 1992 for her *New York Times* column. The following article was published in the September 18, 2006 issue of *Newsweek* magazine.

In May, as part of a program to prepare them for college, the seniors at my daughter's high school heard from a nationally recognized expert on date rape. In August, as part of their introduction to life on campus, the students at the liberal-arts college she is now attending heard from a nationally recognized expert on date rape--the same expert, offering the same warnings about the perils of sexual assault.

Those perils are real. So are the dangers of binge drinking, drug use, unsafe sex, Internet predators, bicycling without a helmet, riding in a car without a seat belt and smoking cigarettes. And perhaps it's also a little dangerous to say of all of the above: enough!

I'm the world's biggest fan of education and information. I was happy that my kids learned early how the seed and the egg got together, at school and from their parents. I like the idea of lung-cancer patients' visiting classes to show teenagers just how glamorous smoking can be once you've had chemo. Every time I hear that little snicking sound that means my kids are belted in, I feel a faint sense of well-being, even though they're not really kids anymore. I've always wanted them, and their friends, to have all the information necessary to make smart choices and avoid dangerous situations.

But for a long time I've had the uncomfortable feeling that the result has been a generation enveloped by a black miasma of imminent disaster. It's not that they hear about the dangers of drugs: they hear about them in school presentations, public-service announcements, print ads, TV movies, "After School Specials," cable documentaries and, of course, from responsible mothers and fathers. They've heard about them in elementary school, middle school, high school and college.

The net effect could be that the drumbeat of danger becomes persistent white noise, unremarked, unheard, unheeded. But that wasn't my concern when I realized that my daughter was going to hear the same warning about date rape in summer that she'd just heard in spring. Once, someone asked me what single quality I most wanted to pass on to my children. Without hesitation I replied, "*Joie de vivre.*" Love of life. That sense of waking up in the morning and thinking that there may be good things ready to happen.

That fantastic feeling is easily lost in a frightening tide of bad tidings. Once, people drifted into unexamined marriages with illusions about a lifetime of romance, or torrid sex, or two hearts that beat as one. Today people plan weddings dogged by divorce and adultery statistics, hearing ubiquitous warnings that marriage is hard work and they might want to try couples counseling even before the ceremony. While once everything was unspoken, now it seems that everything is out there.

Or everything but this: that lots of marriages are happy or at least contented, and pulling in harness can be more satisfying than going it alone. That amid the guys who try to pin you down at a party, it is not so unusual to find one who lights you up and makes you laugh. That sometimes people do stupid things and take stupid chances and get away with it without ruining their lives. A life of unremitting caution, without the carefree--or even, occasionally, the careless--may turn out to be half a life, like the Bible with the Ten Commandments but no Song of Solomon or Sermon on the Mount.

A little more than a decade ago, one of my sons told me very sadly that he didn't understand how he was ever going to have children. At first I thought he meant that he didn't know how he would afford them, or have the patience to raise them. It turned out that he couldn't figure out how he could someday impregnate a woman. When I told him that a day would come when it would be safe to have sex without a condom, he looked at me as though I had lost my mind. Clearly he'd gotten the message. But he'd gotten only the deprivation, not the joy.

So this is a plea for parents to remember to have That Talk with their kids. No, not the one about smoking cigarettes or driving under the influence. That's the one they will certainly get. What they need to hear occasionally is about the pleasures, not just the perils. Even when we talk about September 11, we can tell a tale of human goodness as well as evil, a tale of those who saved strangers as well as those who murdered them. For all the sleazebags who will try to lure a kid into a car, there are many Good Samaritans who are just concerned when they see a 12-year-old trudging along the road in the rain. I suppose we live at a time when we can't afford to let them accept the Samaritan's ride. But we also can't afford to have them think that Samaritans no longer exist. All these lectures, lessons and cautionary tales can't be to preserve a lifetime of looking over one shoulder. As Oscar Wilde wrote, "We are all in the gutter, but some of us are looking at the stars."

Discussion Questions

1. Quindlen fears that young people have grown up "enveloped by a black miasma of imminent disaster." Do you agree? Have you been bombarded with messages about danger? Have these insistent messages shaped your thinking about the world, as she suggests?

2. List several passages in which Quindlen uses logic to persuade. Make another list of emotional appeals. Which list is more convincing? Does this essay need both?

3. To give you practice in identifying fallacies, rewrite any three sentences from Quindlen's essay, adding a different fallacy in each sentence. How would the essay be weaker if these fallacies were included in the original article?

4. As discussed in the chapter, Quindlen deals with opposing arguments to her thesis. (a) What is her thesis? (b) What opposing arguments does she acknowledge? (c) What is achieved by dealing with opposing arguments?

The New Face of Bullying

by Jackie Schiffer

Meet the Writer

Jackie Schiffer enjoys singing, writing, reading, baking, and playing a wide variety of instruments. She lives with her parents, brother, and sister.

2000, a year that for many marked the greatest changes in their lives, was a year that marked my life with horror. I was a victim of severe bullying when I switched schools. I was terrorized by the girls in my class who would leave the lunch table when I sat down, mimic me, take books, folders, and homework out of my desk, and then they wrote a book about all the things they didn't like about me. These girls targeted everything that meant anything to me and ripped any shred of confidence I had until it was nothing. They taunted me saying that I was a "teacher's pet," "a freak," and "incessantly ugly." There wasn't a night for four months where I didn't cry myself to sleep. And even worse, I lived those four months in complete silence for fear of what might happen if I spoke up. All this happening to a ten-year old little girl just for switching schools?

To better understand bullying, we must first analyze what is causing the problem. Then we must determine a solution for bullying and how we can eliminate it from our schools.

Bullies are much more common and serious in today's society than one would imagine. According to the findings of *Are We Safe?: The 2000 National Crime Prevention Survey*, up to "75% of children have been victims of bullying during their school careers." Experts and students agree that bullying is no laughing matter.

Bullying is everywhere in our children's lives. Modern-day bullying is not your typical "big-guy stealing milk money from the smart-guy with thick glasses." According to an April 25, 2001, article in the *Journal of the American Medical Association*, while boys are more likely to engage in physical fights, girls resort to psychological and verbal violence such as rumors, which was definitely the case with me.

Violent bullying is also rampant in our society. *The Courier-Journal* of Louisville, Kentucky reported on May 26, 2004 an incident where two boys from Westport Middle School engaged in a fight on a school bus and one of the eighth graders brutally punched, beat, and knocked the other boy unconscious.

An article in *The Chicago Sun-Times* on February 17, 1999, reported the story of sixth grader Derek Zak who was "beaten senseless by another student" in Oak Lawn/Hometown District 135. Derek's family filed a lawsuit against Hometown School because the school didn't follow its bullying policy and remove the bully, who was a previous offender, from the classroom, nor was Derek's substitute teacher warned of potential problems with the bully. The school also failed to provide proper medical care or call Derek's mother to tell her of the beating. Derek faced a concussion and was hospitalized. Since this time, the alleged bully has merely been removed from the school.

And bullying is far more rampant today due to recent technological advancements. Websites, blogs, and instant messaging allow bullying to be done faster and become more widespread. These forms of bullying are particularly serious because there is virtually no way to control it. "Cyber Cruelty," a story in *The Fort Worth Star-Telegram*, reported on the case of 14-year-old Alyssa A. of Wyckoff, New Jersey. Alyssa was cyber-bullied for two weeks by a classmate, who swore at her and told her she was "ugly," "stupid" and "useless." Alyssa ended up having to turn to her parents and school administrators. Also reported in the article was that Internet SAFE, an agency that monitors online behavior of children, found 42% of kids report being bullied online.

The *Are We Safe?* survey found that "About half of parents in this survey see bullying as no problem for their children." The North Carolina Department of Juvenile Justice and Delinquency Prevention Center found that only "39% of parents with a child in grade six or higher are more likely to say they fear for their child's safety."

Nels Ericson of the Office of Juvenile Justice and Delinquency Prevention reported in a June 2001 article that those who bully and are bullied appear to be at greatest risk of experiencing the following: loneliness; trouble making friends; lack of success in school; skipping/dropping school; and involvement in problem behaviors such as smoking, drugs and drinking. In addition to the risks of students engaging in "problem behavior," homicide and suicide are more rampant among bullies and the bullied.

CBS' 48 Hours ran a segment titled "The Mind of A Shooter" about the 1995 school shooting in Lynville, Tennessee, in which then 17-year-old Jamie Rouse shot two teachers and a student. At 25, Rouse felt much of the incident could be attributed to bullying. He stated, "I was desperately unhappy—and it started when I was a child, bullied by classmates for being small and too quiet. Things got worse in high school, where I was ostracized by kids who thought I worshipped the devil." Rouse strongly believes that the bullying he faced vastly contributed to his shooting rage.

Experts have also concluded bullying was one of the key causes of the 1999 Columbine High School shootings. Drs. Patricia Marks Greenfield and Jaana Juvonen of the American Psychological Association attribute the radical behavior of the Columbine shooters, Eric Harris and Dylan Klebold, to bullying in A Developmental Look at Columbine. Much of the boys' behavior is attributed to their outcast-ing because of behavior similar to that of Rouse.

The resolution to solve bullying must be multilateral. Various organizations have done case studies on bullying and are seeking to raise awareness. These organizations include the American Medical Association, the American Psychological Association, the National Parents and Teachers Association, and the United Nations World Health Organization. After the Columbine High School tragedy, many schools developed a Zero-Tolerance Policy toward bullying. While a bullying policy is important, it is still crucial to deal with each case individually, which a Zero-Tolerance Policy does not allow. The Daily Herald reported on August 24, 2004 that the Naperville, Illinois, school district found success in surveying the student population on bullying and targeting bullying using various means. Some of these means include using national anti-bullying programs such as Manners Matrix, Peaceful Playgrounds and Quest Educational Programs; the use of posters and positive media; character building programs; and using alternate methods to promote self-confidence and positive social behaviors such as the use of motivational speakers and using groups such as "Dare to Be Different," which uses dance and acting to address social problems such as bullying. Manners Matrix is the national anti-bullying campaign that has seen the greatest deal of success due to its "Manners Matrix Method," a collaborative survey that allows schools to see the following: "How frequently ten different behaviors are occurring at school, which students are being targeted, severity of impact, how students responded, location, time of day, who did it, what students see happening, attitudes and beliefs, along with information from the parents, teachers, and even bus drivers!"

While today, it is still difficult for me to speak of the bullying I faced at age ten, I have overcome what once damaged me. I feel it is my duty to speak out against the horrors that too many are forced to live with. Bullying is on the rise; statistics from the Carolina Institute for Conflict Resolution's website show that every seven minutes a child is bullied. As a serious social problem, bullying must be stopped before the implications on the future of our society become too detrimental. No one should be forced to live in silence when we all have so much to say, to do and become in this world.

Discussion Questions

1. Schiffer frames her essay with a personal example. What effect does this have on your reading of the essay?

2. Schiffer uses examples to develop her argument. Which two examples do you find most effective and why?

3. Review the solutions Schiffer offers. Pick one and describe how the solution might be applied at your school. Be specific and practical.

Conquering Close-Mindedness
by Lauryn Bruck

Meet the Writer

After high school, Lauryn Bruck moved to Washington, D.C., to study International Politics and Foreign Policy at Georgetown University. When she graduates, she hopes to work in the Capitol and maybe someday run for political office.

After processing shock, fear, and raw wonderment, I realized that I was literally nose-to-nose with a six-foot-seven, four hundred pound Maori tribal leader. I mean, this guy's mom definitely paid the extra thirty-nine cents to super-size him when he was born. If that wasn't enough of a culture shock to knock my Donald Duck suspenders right off, pressing noses with his five brothers, which is a custom in their culture, definitely accomplished the task.

For the next two days of my three-week stay in New Zealand last summer, my tour group of multi-cultural club members and I were wined, dined, entertained, and educated by these Jolly Green Giant sized tribal men. Although their appearance was dramatically different from mine, over the course of the night, I recognized that their lifestyle, morals, values, and goals were remarkably similar to my own. Maori life is centered around community and hard work, and many of the hardships that they had to overcome were the same ones that I had to conquer. They were incredibly kind and hospitable to us, and fascinating in their uniqueness.

What you may not know about this experience is that I didn't want to go to New Zealand. I threw a pretty nasty temper tantrum about the whole thing. But don't worry, the injuries to others were minimal and my mom was released from intensive care in only three short months. Before the trip, our chaperone had shown us a picture of a man from the Maori tribe, and I simply wrote him off as a barbarian. After surviving an eighteen hour flight where my Adderall wore off after hour 3 and the flight attendants had to bring out the tasers to calm me down, I wasn't very happy with the idea of wasting a night staying in smelly grass huts and watching a bunch of oversized men in loin cloths jump around like cavemen, unless I could join them of course, but the whole loin cloth thing probably wouldn't have gone over well. I mean, I wasn't paying thousands of dollars for something I could see at a Green Bay Packers game. However, the experience was unlike anything I had expected it to be. I found out that the Maoris were actually much more civilized than those psycho Cheesehead Packers fans. From the moment we opened the door to meet them, I realized that my arrogant stereotype of the Maori tribe was pathetically naïve.

We have all found ourselves in a situation where we have wrongly judged something or have been too scared to try something new because we had a close-minded attitude. As president of the multi-cultural club, I thought that it would be appropriate to educate all of you new members of the club on the dangers of not keeping an open mind. Close-mindedness rips opportunities right out of our hands just like Britney Spears ripped the decency out of every nine year old girl across the United States. It leaves us with a skewed and limited view of the world around us, comparable to John Travolta's view of the World in the Nobel Peace Prize winning TV movie, *The Boy in the Bubble*. There is so much value in this world scattered amongst what seems to be trivial that we have to be open-minded or we will never discover the many things in life that we need to find, like Adderall, self-inflatable whoopie cushions and Michael Flatley, Lord of the Dance.

In order to better understand this outbreak of close-mindedness, we will examine several causes of this disease, some problems that come out of close-mindedness, and finally pop some highly addictive pills to cure ourselves of the epidemic of close-mindedness that has swept our society.

One of the most prominent causes of close-mindedness is the fear to step outside of our comfort zones and experience something new. Now, I'm not saying to dress up like a gopher and hijack the Planter's Peanuts truck just because you've never done it before. Do something constructive, like pinning up sexy pictures of Kramer in Grandma's bedroom to cheer her up. Oh, honey, thank you so much. He looks just like my first boyfriend back in the 1760's! *Oh if only grandpa had never come along....* A second cause of close-mindedness is that many of us are guilty of possessing naïve perceptions and prejudices which cause us to write off the unknown before we even attempt to understand it.

The first and foremost of the wide array of problems caused by close-mindedness is that it denies us access to important experiences that will teach us valuable lessons. False perceptions also serve to limit our appreciation of the world around us.

Although close-mindedness has caused an array of serious problems, there are several ways to prevent them from happening. The most obvious way to conquer close-mindedness is to use Preparation H. But if that doesn't work for you, try being open to new things. If you are afraid to do something because you are unsure about its outcome, conquer your fears and experience something new. However, in order to accomplish this, we need to get rid of unfair and prejudiced judgments which may block our enthusiasm to try something that we never have before.

The very root of the cause of close-mindedness is the unwillingness of most of us to step outside our comfort zones. It is human nature to possess the fear of the uncertain; however, taking risks is a necessity to discovery. In order to avoid a lawsuit, I must warn you that some risks, such as getting coffee from McDonalds, should only be attempted by trained professionals because the skills involved to not spill your coffee are not the skills possessed by just any ordinary citizen. And although the consequences of a spill are only understood by Harvard's top law students, we must at least try to understand the concept. If we spill something hot on our lap, we will get burnt. Succeeding is just as much about risk-taking as it is about talent and determination. Fear blinds us to the necessity and value of experiencing something new. If we never put ourselves on the line, then have already chosen a very bland future. Take my example, I put myself on the line and cut my hair into the super trendy, yet sporty mullet last year. It instantly became a ground breaking trend with followers such as the super sexy Billy Ray Cyrus and the sleek and suave Travis Tritt. And if I hadn't taken this chance with my hair, everyone in Tennessee wouldn't have a hairdo right now.

False assumptions about the unknown also build a barricade in front of new occurrences. And you know what they say about assumptions: they make a buttocks out of you and me. Sorry that's the PG version of the analogy. John J. Emerick, in his book, *Be the*

Person You Want to Be, wrote that "If you hold limiting beliefs, you will create barriers and obstacles to support those beliefs, thus creating true limitations." It is so easy to just write off something unfamiliar instead of facing the fear that we may not have complete control over. So many of us will insult a person or idea that we don't understand as an excuse to not learn more about it. If everyone lived their lives cynically, dismissing everything as stupid, no one would ever become well-rounded. No one would ever take interest in anything other than their own goals and we would lose all of the encouragement and support that a community can bring us.

Both the fear of the uncertain and false assumptions contribute to the largest problem that has come out of close-mindedness. The greatest thing that a person who is close-minded will lose is the valuable experiences that come from being open-minded. Take someone as open-minded as Barney, the big purple dinosaur, who by the way should also be on Adderall. Imagine if he was too afraid to finger paint, play with extremely well behaved children, and teach America's youth a profoundly positive message. If he never conquered these childish fears, then he never would have been able to make the ground shaking contribution to the intellectual community that he is world renowned for. We should all take a minute out of our day to admire Barney's unwavering bravery. He was able to stare into the faces of those smiling, polite children, which is especially remarkable after living such a cushy life eating plants and surviving the destruction of his entire species.

There is so much to learn and observe that we simply cannot afford to be close-minded if we want to gain a greater understanding of our world. Professor C. George Boeree from Shippensburg University said, "If you want to understand the entirety of reality, you will need to add all possible perspectives together." If we do fall victim to the fear and judgment that make up close-mindedness, we are limiting the perspective that we can gain about our society. Experiences with different cultures open up the mind to different ways of life while at the same time teaching the observer more about his or her culture. However, different ethnic groups such as carnies should be avoided at all costs. Small men, BIG problem. They are the monster that is lurking under your bed that laugh like cracked-out clowns and eat your stuffed animals.

Although close-mindedness seems almost impossible to fix, there are several surprisingly easy ways of opening the closed door in millions of people's minds. The most obvious way to open up your mind is to try something new. Whether your experience is unforgettable or something that you want to forget, like the whole taser incident on the plane, the experience has still taught you very valuable lessons about who you are, who other people truly are, and how everyone interacts with each other; and in my case to never forget my Adderall again. Going into an uncertain experience is always nerve-wracking; and even if the experience is a complete failure, it is still very valuable. Failure is human nature, and for me second nature; however, it is also our best opportunity. When someone fails at something, such as looking good in a mullet—serious in the front, party in the back— they can look back and see their exact mistakes and learn from them in a more memorable way than any other way to learn something.

Another very effective and obvious way to remain victorious over close-mindedness is to give up judging and making false assumptions about certain situations. Human pride is one of the longest-lasting materials that can build a barrier in front of discovery. Pride and misinformation also often times come hand in hand, just like Celine Dion and crippling migraines come hand in hand. If everyone gave up judging then they would have no excuse not to go out and explore the world. They would also have no fear to learn about the uncertain and gain a better understanding of our world.

Ever since my visit with the Maoris, I vowed that I would never let a stereotype cause me to miss out on an amazing opportunity. My stay with them was definitely life-changing. I was so fascinated by this encounter with a completely different culture and so horribly embarrassed by my bad attitude before the experience that I knew from then on, I must keep an open mind to everything to never risk missing anything as wonderful as those thirty-six hours again as I hope all of you multi-cultural club members will keep an open mind and not miss an opportunity to learn about different cultures by waxing my back for me after the meeting. I realized that there is a whole entire world out there that holds so much more than my own. So go ahead, open the closed door in your mind and see what there is outside. Hopefully Celine Dion isn't out there caroling.

Discussion Questions

1. Bruck uses humor to make a serious point. What is that point? How does humor help?

2. Bruck pretends that her audience is a group of multicultural club members. What is the effect of using this method? Who is Bruck's real audience?

3. If you wanted to urge an audience to venture beyond their comfort zone, what approach would you adopt as a writer? Offer a brief example.

8.3 **Student Model**

The Siesta Solution
by Jennifer Ford

Meet the Writer

Jennifer Ford is from Rochester, New York. This essay was a runner-up in the Kaplan/*Newsweek* "My Turn" Essay Competition.

The media has stereotyped the "kindergarten teacher" as a jacket-zipping, shoe-tying, apple-juice-distributing babysitter. The media is blind: she is a genius. Unique to only the kindergarten teacher's lesson plan is the inclusion of a napping period, a mandate to lie down and engage in peaceful sleep. This napping period provides an outlet for stress, a chance to recharge, and a playground for the subconscious mind. (And people wonder why kindergartners are so agreeable, obedient, and creative?) Superintendents of today's society, I implore you: why limit this practice to only the young and helpless? Would not the majority of high school students, who are balancing heavy courseloads, sports, musical studies and part-time jobs, benefit similarly from the privilege of in-school-nappy-time? Have the state education regulators overlooked the health benefits and stimulation opportunities granted by midday sleep? Are we as students being denied our rightful privilege to recharge our batteries?!

No, really, I'm dead serious. I propose new legislation dictating an additional requirement in school policy: naptime. In my own experience as a high-school student, I have become far too well acquainted with the wee hours of morning, either from pulling all-nighters to finish assignments or from sheer restlessness because my teenage biological clock is urging wakefulness. In essence, this very same clock prods my eyelids to droop and my mind to wane each day at around 1:30 p.m. I am not alone. I have witnessed many class-mates suffer humiliation and even ridicule as a teacher awakens them during class. This degrading treatment is misplaced: sleepy students are victims of a sleep deprivation brought about by society's sched-ules. Move class time to 10 o'clock at night, when most students are brilliantly multitasking (doing homework while simultaneously conducting six instant messenger conversations) and improvements would ensue. However, a rearrangement of the school day deems unfeasible for teachers who crash around 9:30 p.m. Thus, the solution is simple: legalize sleeping in class, and channel this sleeping into an allotted time slot.

I anticipate your doubt. Marvelous ideas take a while to catch on. However, I state with confidence that a half-hour-napping period is not at all radical in comparison with policy that already exists within the school district. Take gym class: I spent two weeks participating in a unit designed to sharpen my athletic skills in picnic games: bocce and beach ball tossing. Physical education was designed to boost midday energy levels and combat America's tendencies for obesity. Obviously, those motives have gone awry, as exemplified by my spending a class period playing "keep-the-ball-from-rolling-over-your-side-of-the-square." Interestingly, enrollment for the "stress manage-ment" unit in my high school's gym curriculum is the highest com-pared to the attendance lists for all other physical education units. Why? Because subconsciously, students are pining for a siesta! They need a break, a chance to lie down and close their eyes and breathe slowly. The effects of that half-hour recharge period are profound: thought is clearer, heart rate is steadier, and attitude is refreshed.

To ignore my demands for school-sponsored sleep is to shoot oneself in the foot. Why is it that DWI is deserving of legal conse-quences, costly protest campaigns, and rehabilitation programs, yet

DWD (driving while drowsy) goes undetected and unremedied? The effects of sleepiness parallel the effects of drugs and alcohol: judgment is impaired, reaction time is slowed, and attention is unsteady. To combat the dangerous circumstances of driving among sleep-deprived teens, the school system should offer students a chance to get the shut-eye they need. How hypocritical: state law mandates that every school provide an area and time for students to eat lunch but the provisions and protections stops there. Sleep, a bodily function equally important as replenishing the body's food storage, is not guaranteed through school policy. Heck, it's not even allowed.

Fellow citizens, let's take a clue from our kindergarten teachers, who stimulate and rejuvenate students daily through slumber. Let's take a clue from our Southern Mexican neighbors, who arrange their daily schedules around a midday snooze and meal. Let's take a clue from the multitude of high-school students who amble into school every morning, barely conscious and highly unmotivated due to their lack of sleep. Let's solve this whole dilemma of drowsiness and incompatible biological clocks and dangerous driving conditions and attention-deficit disorders with one whopping simple solution: the Siesta Solution.

Discussion Questions

1. Ford creates a vivid picture of the life of a busy high school student. What other example could Ford add to show this bustle?

2. Had Ford adopted a more serious tone, would she have been more or less convincing?

3. Propose a different solution to combat the drowsiness felt by many students.

4. If you read this essay aloud, you'll notice that Ford achieves pleasant rhythms by varying the lengths of her sentences. Point out two examples of this rhythm. Ford also uses devices such as alliteration to create pleasing sounds. List two examples of alliteration.

5. Ford makes good use of imagery to bring her argument to life. List three examples of imagery. What does Ford achieve by using this imagery?

Is This What Life's About?

by Elizabeth Shaw

Meet the Writer

Sixteen-year-old Elizabeth Shaw is from Alexandria, Virginia. This essay was published in *Newsweek*'s "My Turn" column.

My alarm starts to ring at 6:30 a.m. In a few minutes I'm awake enough to find the OFF switch. After a few more moments hiding under the blankets, I slide out of bed and into the bathroom. Most mornings I look into the mirror and see puffy eyes and colorless cheeks. As I wash my face, I promise that I will get more sleep, but I know I'll be up late again tonight.

I get dressed and gather my books together. When I'm lucky, I grab a quick breakfast before rushing out the door for my 45-minute commute. During the day I fly from one class to the next, using my spare time to finish my homework. In my classes I labor through quizzes, tests, labs, lectures, presentations and projects. Can I help it if I catch a nap in a class or two?

Once the school day is done, I'm off to a practice, club or volunteer organization. Sometimes these extracurricular activities are fun, but they always take a lot of time and effort. It's 7 or 8 o'clock before I get home at night. After 12 hours of running around, I still don't have time to unwind. I wolf down my dinner, usually microwaved soup or cold cereal, by myself as my family has already eaten. Then I stagger off to complete my day with more studying.

There's no feeling quite like sitting down at 8 o'clock at night to start four hours of homework. I don't pick my favorite or the easiest assignment to do first anymore. I start with the work that will be collected and graded for content. Then, as I approach exhaustion, I tackle the assignments that just have to be completed. Forget about understanding; I'll figure out the material before I take the test. For now, I just need to finish so I can go to bed. When midnight chimes and I'm face down in a textbook at my desk, I make one last attempt at some assignments and then call it quits. I drag myself off to the shower, then I crash into bed for a few hours of rest before the beginning again.

This cycle continues week after week, broken only by weekends full of homework and chores. I don't mean to overdramatize. I don't have the most hectic schedule or the most work. Some of my friends get up at 4 a.m. to go to swim practice and then attend a full day of school. Somehow, they have the energy for another practice in the afternoon before starting their homework. Why do we do this to ourselves?

We're not addicted to stress and not all of us are overachievers. The numerous teens who push themselves academically have their own personal justifications, but nearly every high-school student who works into the early morning hours is after one thing: acceptance to a "good" college.

Pressure to attend a prestigious university comes from every-where. School administrators, guidance counselors and parents make it seems as if my life will be over unless I get into a good college. If I want to get a decent job, make money and generally succeed in hav-ing a happy life, I'd better attend an illustrious school. As a junior in high school, I feel I am being drowned by college information. A year ago the SAT's and "Early Action" were concepts and vague terms that had little to do with me. Now they're part of my daily vocabulary. TV news has stories about competition for college or how expensive it is. My home is bombarded by mailed brochures on special pro-grams and schools. Everywhere I turn, someone is shoving colleges into my face.

These messages about college also cause a panic in parents. My mother has become obsessed with the progress of my as-yet-unwritten college application. She questions how good anything I do will look to colleges. Is it better for me to join the crew team or tutor elementary-school kids? Can I do both? Recently, my mom and I were looking over the application to Stanford University, where I'd like to apply. There was space on the form to fill out information on inde-pendent research or on special awards. Realizing that I had no labo-ratory experience or special awards I sighed and admitted to myself that I needed to look at other schools. My mother, never a quitter, began madly making plans. "What about that Westinghouse project? Could you do something with that? And this summer, you can do an internship then." I objected and said that I wanted to relax this summer. She shocked me with the intensity of her reply: "You had fun last summer. You can't do that again this year."

When I talk to my friends, they tell me about similar conversations in their homes. They're being shipped off on college tours or enrolled in classes to raise their SAT scores a few more points. Yet as much as we complain about our parents, we are equally obsessed. We try to do every after-school activity we can while still getting perfect grades. We try to live up to impossible levels of perfection in order to appease the unseen gods in the college admissions offices.

But what happens if, in spite of all my efforts, I am not accepted by any well-known school? In talking with adults, I've learned that it doesn't really matter what college you attend. People often end up pursuing careers completely different from what they studied in school. More than not attending a good school, adults seem to regret not enjoying high school for what it was—the last years of adolescence. When I look at my classmates, I see people who sometimes worry too much about achievements they can list. There is plenty of time to work as an adult, but childhood is short. Overworking as teenagers might get us into good colleges, but what sort of memories will it make?

One night recently, I decided for once to get enough sleep. I skipped the organizational meeting for crew (I'm cox in a varsity eight) and headed to a park with my friends. Then I went home and had dinner with my family and talked to them about what was happening in their lives. Early in the evening, I got into bed for a long night's rest, not even bothering to start my homework. I realize I did nothing "productive"—nothing that would help my GPA or fill in a blank on some application. But I know that I lived, and I know that is more important.

Discussion Questions

1. What is Shaw's thesis and who is her audience?

2. Identify how Shaw uses both inductive and deductive reasoning.

3. Do you find Shaw's argument convincing? Explain. Offer your own examples to support your opinion.

4. Shaw makes use of description, examples, and narration to help make her point. Offer one example of each.

5. Shaw states that "pressure to attend a prestigious university comes from everywhere." Do you think this is an exaggeration? How might Shaw have qualified this remark to allow for exceptions? Would her argument be stronger or weaker if she had offered exceptions?

6. Shaw uses clear and effective nouns and verbs. List three examples of each and explain why these nouns and verbs are effective.

Chapter 9

The Research Paper

esearch paper! Term paper! Note cards! Bibliography! These
are some of the most intimidating words that students encounter
in their high school English experience. The terms don't need
to be that scary.

First of all, we should clarify a frequently misunderstood issue.
Research is not writing, and writing is not research. They are two
different activities requiring different skills. All too often, a student
assumes that if she has produced a massive research project, complete
with perfectly executed documentation, she must be an excellent writer.
Wrong. Good writers can create sloppy, meaningless research projects,
and good researchers can write research papers that are dreadful to read.

Research is merely a way to generate or gather information that
may then be written down. It's similar to remembering. You may recall
a fascinating episode or detail from your past, but that isn't the same as
writing it down. Research works the same way. You may peruse source
material or gather information in other ways, but the writing hasn't
happened until…you write something.

So, when you have a research project in front of you, please realize
that research and writing are separate parts of the project. To successfully
complete the project, you will need to be adept at both skills.

In this chapter, you will learn the process of writing a research
paper. The first steps of this process involve research; the latter steps
involve writing. Here are the steps you will be following, along with a
brief explanation of each:

1. Generate **a thesis:** A good thesis will guide your research project
   and be very helpful when you are mired in sources written by
   experts in the field you are researching.

2. Develop **a preliminary outline:** Simply guess at the main, obvious topics that you will include in your paper, and write them down in outline form, using Roman numerals (I, II, III, IV, V, etc.) to number the topics you plan to cover. This should take ninety seconds or less.

3. Create **a preliminary Works Cited list:** Find some sources that you might use and write them down in correct citation form.

4. Take **notes:** Using your preliminary outline as a guide, find the information in your sources that seems relevant to your thesis. Write down that information in organized notes, using a form that makes sense to you.

5. **Write a final, ultradetailed outline:** For this step, organize your notes into headings, subheadings, and sub-subheadings, and so forth. When you have finished this outline, the research part is over and the writing part begins.

6. **Write a rough draft:** Transform that ultradetailed outline into sentences and paragraphs. In parentheses, make note of the source you used for each quote, statistic, or specific piece of information. These are your citations.

7. **Edit your rough draft and prepare a final copy, complete with a Works Cited page:** Go over your paper thoroughly, looking specifically for errors in spelling, sentence structure, and conventions, and adding the components necessary for research writing.

Now let's discuss how to accomplish each of these steps in ways designed to minimize frustration and help you create a satisfying finished product.

Journal Topic

Write about a subject you are curious about. What do you want to know about this subject? If your response becomes a series of questions, that's fine.

Generating a Thesis

The thesis of your research paper is similar to the thesis statements that you have created for other writing projects; however, the thesis of a research paper may be more technical. For most of the other writing genres included in this book, you have probably written about topics that involve you, your life, your interests, and your experiences. A research project, on the other hand, may involve learning and writing about material that does not hold the same degree of personal relevance. In fact, it might not be relevant to you at all.

For your own well-being, do some soul-searching and try very hard to find ways to make the subject interesting and relevant to you. Your work becomes easier if you can find personal meaning and satisfaction in it. For example, if you are assigned to write about a historical topic, you may want to choose an event that had an impact on someone in your family (such as a great-grandfather who served in World War II, for instance) or that occurred in your home state or local area. If your assigned topic is to research the life of a prominent person, choose someone you personally admire or find interesting. If your topic is scientific in nature, think about the practical applications of the science to your own life. How does it improve, complicate, or otherwise affect you? Finding your personal connection to the subject matter will make the process of writing about it more gratifying.

If the subject you plan to research is something you have a special interest in, you may have already done some reading or thinking about it, and therefore you have a head start. On the other hand, if the subject of your research project is completely foreign to you, then spend a little time with a general source—maybe an encyclopedia or even a relevant video from the library—trying to get a feel for the topic as a whole.

Then find *your* niche. What can you and only you say about this topic better than anyone else? How can you write about this subject in a way that your teacher hasn't seen over and over? Ask yourself these questions:

- What do I find most interesting or compelling about this topic?

- Why is this topic important, at least to some people?

- Is this topic similar to other ideas or subjects that I'm already familiar with?

- Why might this topic matter to me, now or at some future point?

Then, using the guidelines presented earlier, write a workable thesis that will serve as the primary focus for your project.

Developing a Preliminary Outline

Creating a preliminary outline is one of the easiest steps in your research process. It's impossible to do it wrong, as long as you do it.

Based on what you already know about your topic, guess what the main sections of your paper will be about and write them down in one, two, or three word subtopics. For example, if you are writing about a college, you might guess that you will include sections on entrance requirements, graduation requirements, financial aid possibilities, living arrangements, and a couple of other things that specifically interest you. The preliminary outline might look like this:

   I.   Entrance Requirements

   II.   Financial Aid

 III.   Places to Live

  IV.   Available Activities

   V.   Majors in Engineering

  VI.   Graduation Requirements

If you are researching the life of a particular artist, you might easily assume that you will include information about the artist's place of birth, sources of inspiration, most famous works, and something about the circumstances of the artist's death. That outline might look like this:

   I.   O'Keeffe's Early Life

   II.   Sources of Ideas

 III.   Most Famous Works

  IV.   Late Life and Death

A relatively informal outline like this will serve as a map for you after you find some potential sources. An occasional source of frustration for students arises when they have stacks of dense research material in front of them, and they are not sure what is important and what is not. A preliminary outline will help you when you get to that point. You look for information relevant to the topics on your outline, and you can bypass everything else. You still, however, should be open to adapting your outline. For example, if you are reading through your sources, and you notice a lot of information on a particular topic that you originally did not include, and now you think that it would be a worthwhile addition, go ahead and add it. Along the same line, as you're reading source material, you may notice that one of your subtopics really doesn't have much information on it, or it doesn't seem as important as you originally thought. Go ahead and scratch it out. That's why it's called a *preliminary* outline.

Your outline will continue to evolve as you progress through these early planning stages. Your thesis may also continue to evolve as you learn more about your topic and discover the best way to organize your findings.

Creating a Preliminary Works Cited List

Your teacher will probably require a minimum number of sources for your project. To ensure that you end up meeting this number, your preliminary Works Cited list will probably need several more sources than your teacher requires for the final paper. In other words, if your assignment is to have five sources in your final product, you will probably want to have a dozen or so in your possession for the preliminary Works Cited list. This provides you with the luxury of discarding sources that are less worthwhile or that duplicate information you've already found elsewhere.

Do you want to be an efficient researcher? If you love exploring libraries and browsing at your own pace, then don't worry about efficiency. Just follow your own creative path, and you will most likely end up with a very good set of sources. It may take you longer that way. But who cares? You love this stuff! If, on the other hand, you want to gather your sources in an efficient but thorough manner, you may try asking your librarian for help. The Internet is also a good resource, although you'll need to make sure the sites you visit are reliable. See the next sections for more tips on using libraries and the Internet.

Finding Sources at a Library

If your topic is fairly broad, you will need to find some books about it. If your topic is very contemporary, periodicals will probably be more valuable to you than books. The books you find on a contemporary topic are likely to be valuable, but they may not be very plentiful. Go to the library catalog and enter your subject. If you get a workable number of hits, that's great. If you get too many, choose the most recent works, especially if your topic is scientific or technical in nature. If your search returns too few sources, try a broader search. For example, if you are researching colonial furniture and you come up with a small number of potential sources, try searching for colonial architecture, colonial life, American furniture, or furniture history.

Book sources tend to provide you with large amounts of information, much of which will be outside the parameters of your thesis. Periodicals and other documents tend to be more focused, and when they are relevant to your thesis, they will likely be very valuable.

Because each library's collection tends to be organized a little differently, be sure to recruit a librarian's help as you search for materials. Our advice here is necessarily general. Ask a librarian for help with finding periodicals and other sources.

Librarians sometimes experience frustrations with how students perceive the requirements of research papers. Consider these comments from a blog post by librarian Barbara Fister of Gustavus Adolphus College about what she sees when helping college freshmen with research projects:

"The first year 'research paper' has always sent a mixed message. You're supposed to be original, but must quote someone else to back up every point you make—while in constant fear that you'll be accused of stealing from them. The obscure rules of citing sources only exacerbates the confusion and focuses attention on mechanics.

"I hate it when students who have hit on a novel and interesting way of looking at an issue tell me they have to change their topic because they can't find sources that say exactly what they plan to say. I try to persuade them otherwise, but they believe that original ideas are not allowed in 'research.' How messed up is that? The other and, sadly, more frequent reference desk winch-making moment involves a student needing help finding sources for a paper *he's already written*. Most commonly, students pull together a bunch of sources, many of which they barely understand on a topic they know little about, and do their best to mash the contents up into the required number of pages.

"In other words, librarians know about the struggle to balance your own ideas with the research you find. They can help with the latter, but, as librarian Fister suggests, it's your responsibility to maintain your voice and be original—even in a research paper."

Remember that librarians don't know everything, but they know how to help you find information on just about anything. A librarian's job is to help you discover information; your job is to put the information to work.

As you work in the library, avoid the temptation to read the sources you find. That's right. Don't read them…yet. Your library time is probably limited, and you want to be efficient, right? Use your library time to *find* sources. Use other time to actually read them. If you become absorbed in the first source you find, you might run out of time at the library. Find sources now; read them later—unless, of course, you have unlimited library time. Then do it however you please.

Finding Sources on the Internet

Beware the Internet—but use it, too! The Internet can be a rich source of information for researchers, if it's used wisely. Used unwisely, it can be a sorrowful source of inefficiency. Because the Internet is usually so fun and friendly, precious research minutes can slip by while you're dawdling over a site that offers a lot of flashy images but very little substance. (Do yourself a favor: close any instant messaging windows you may have open and focus on the task at hand.)

Online research can be roughly divided into two arenas: the open Internet and subscription services. Your school or public library may subscribe to any number of services that can be useful to you, depending upon the focus of your research. These subscription services are delivered via computer, so they look like the Internet, but they are actually paid for by someone at the receiving end. Your library may have online subscriptions to a variety of helpful research outlets.

Online subscription services may require passwords or other codes to use the services. Your librarian can provide those for you, as well as help you understand how to access the information on the subscription service.

The open Internet, or World Wide Web, is the vast, interconnected medium that allows you to search, surf, and click your way to sites devoted to almost every conceivable topic. The most common way to begin research on the Internet is to go to your favorite search engine and type in some terms. This will generate a list of sites that may be useful to you or may be complete garbage. The first site provided by a search engine is usually the subject's official website, which might be useful or might be filled with biased information. The second site listed on a search engine is usually an open-source encyclopedia, such as Wikipedia. These sites are sometimes reliable, but not always.

Here's a research tip that can help you efficiently find reliable sources. Consider using a social-bookmarking site such as Delicious or Diigo. The primary purpose of these sites is to help Internet users organize their bookmarks online so that they are available on any computer connected to the Internet. Users bookmark sites they find valuable, and that's the beauty of this for you as a researcher. You can search a site like Delicous or Diigo much like you would a search engine site like Google or Bing. However, if you conduct a search in a social-bookmarking site, you are more likely to find valuable sites because the most common search returns are those bookmarked by actual people who designated them as valuable enough to bookmark.

Because anyone who purchases or obtains a domain name can operate a website, and some of these people and organizations are flaky, many websites that purport to be about one thing actually turn out to be something quite different. Distinguishing valid, reliable websites from those that are less valuable is an important research skill.

For example, a website with an address (URL) ending in *.gov* or *.edu* probably deserves a look. Those sites are sponsored by either a government entity or educational institution, respectively. Those that end in *.com* or some other extension *may* be responsible and valuable to you, but be wary. Look at the bottom of the home page. Is the site authored by a respectable institution or credible individual, or is it authored and maintained by someone who is simply a devotee of the subject? Devotees or fans of a particular subject may create worthwhile websites, but they may also be crackpots. Since most of us are trying to be efficient researchers, why spend time on the site of someone whose expertise is suspect? Stick to the websites generated by people or institutions with reputations that are obviously beyond reproach.

You should also be aware of political or philosophical biases inherent in a given website. (This is also true of print sources.) Although everyone is entitled to an opinion, your research is supposed to be relatively objective. Use your highest level of skepticism when evaluating what you read on websites, and remember that what is presented as fact may be merely one person's opinion.

After finding a useful website, you don't have to read and absorb the whole thing right away, and you don't need to print out the entire site. If the site has a Search feature, enter some key words or synonyms from your thesis to see if they generate any hits within the site. If a particular Web page has a lot of text, use an Edit/Find command the same way to see if it leads you to relevant sections of the page. If those simple approaches do not generate worthwhile leads within a particular site, you probably ought to go to another site for the sake of efficiency. (See the Practice section on pages 350–351 for more tips on Internet research.)

Writing Your Works Cited List

Let's take stock of where you are in this process. You have a thesis, so you know what you're writing about. You have a preliminary outline, so you know the main sections of your paper. You have located some sources, so you have some material to include in your paper. (You still haven't read your sources yet. That's fine. You're still in the organizing mode.)

Now it's time to work through a research step that will save you time later, and that simultaneously will create a worthwhile organizational tool for you. It's time to write your preliminary Works Cited list. The basic idea is that you will take the publication information from each source you have gathered and transform it into a perfectly cited entry.

Your first step is to identify what types of sources you have chosen. This usually isn't too tricky. All you are really doing is taking each source and asking yourself, *What the heck is this?* Is it a book? A periodical? An online source? Your citation will be different depending on which source it is. To make your job easier, you can usually find an example citation for virtually every type of source you might come up with—even for interviews you conduct over the telephone, for programs on DVD, and so on.

Who decides how a citation should be formatted? Various individuals and organizations have created formats that suit their own purposes. Each one is different from the others. Be sure you know whether or not your teacher is expecting you to use a particular style for your project. The most common citation styles are those devised by the Modern Language Association (MLA) and the American Psychological Association (APA). MLA format is the most commonly used in writing and English classes, so that is what we will refer to throughout this chapter. Your teacher may specify a different format for you to use. If not, consult Appendix A of this book to find examples of MLA citation style.

Be aware, too, that some word-processing programs and websites provide a citation function. That's nice, if it follows the same citation format that you're required to use. You just plug in the information required, and it creates the citation for you. It's not so nice, however, if the program uses a format other than the one required by your teacher. You can also find online resources to help you with citations. For example, the Purdue Online Writing Lab (OWL) is an excellent resource.

When writing your citation, you'll need to know the following:

- If a book, does it have one or more authors? Is it written by a corporation or some other institution? If it is an anthology put together by an editor rather than a book by a single author, are you using the entire book, or one of the pieces within it?

- If a periodical, how frequently is it published? On what pages can the article you are using be found?

- If an Internet site or online subscription service, what is the URL? What date was it launched? On what date did you view or print it? Who is the author or sponsor of the site?

For additional guidelines and examples for how to cite your sources, see Appendix D. This appendix will show you some of the intricacies of creating a perfectly cited entry, such as:

- How do you indent entries?

- How should titles of works be formatted (underlined, italicized, or enclosed in quotation marks)?

- When do you include page numbers, and when are they omitted?

- What do you do when you have more than one source by the same author?

- What do you do when you have more than one source with the same title?

- Do you need a period at the end of each entry?

The best advice for creating your preliminary Works Cited list is simple: Follow the format. Follow it carefully. Don't guess. Don't improvise. Very little guesswork or improvisation should be involved. If you tend to be a creative person, now is *not* the time to prove it. Just be a good soldier and follow the form. Remind yourself about the purpose of this step. It's not really research, and it's certainly not writing. It's simply detailed organization. Also keep telling yourself that later on you'll be glad you did this step now.

You will know you are finished with this step when you have a neat, alphabetized list of all your sources that closely follows the requirements of the citation style.

Taking Notes

Before delving into all of those sources, take another look at your thesis. Based on your new awareness of the sources you have collected, do you need to tweak your thesis? Do your sources seem like they can help you with the thesis you have generated? If not, feel free to revise your thesis before working in depth with your sources.

Once you are satisfied that your thesis is just right, it is time to dig into the materials you have collected, searching for information that is relevant to your thesis. As you find those bits of information, you will need a note-taking system to keep your information organized.

You may be saying to yourself, *Eh. I'll just highlight stuff and then write it down in order for my rough draft.* That's a shortcut that won't work. You will soon forget why you highlighted what and how you intended to use it. (Besides, you shouldn't be highlighting or writing in borrowed books!)

Notes can be written down in any number of formats. Perhaps your teacher has a specific way to do it. If not, use a system that makes sense for you. Maybe you will use index cards. Perhaps you will use a notebook or legal pad, or just type your notes into a document on your laptop. The medium itself isn't that critical. The most important aspects of your note-taking system are (1) that you can write down the most relevant phrases and sentences from your sources, and (2) that you have a method for keeping track of which source the information came from.

Writers on Writing

A writer can spend years hoping to discover shortcuts to make the act of writing less arduous and slow. He will find that no such shortcuts exist. If we grow as human beings, looking upon the complex world with a maturing eye, the process of writing can only grow more difficult.

—Harry Mark Petrakis

For example, if you're using note cards, you may write down *one* important phrase, quote, or sentence from one of your sources on a card. Elsewhere on the card, you may write down the author, title, and the page number where you found the material. You don't need to write down the entire bibliography entry on the card, unless you really love doing that. You simply need to jot down enough information about the source so that you can properly credit it in the body of your paper.

Now is also the time to include a brief notation about where you might use the piece of information in your final paper. Take a look back at the preliminary outlines on pages 332–333. If you are researching a specific college and you find something about the scholarships available at the school, write down that information and label it *II. Financial Aid.* Later, this will help you efficiently find the information for each section of your paper. (Be sure to note both the Roman numeral and the heading. You might end up changing one or the other of them, and if you have written down both elements, you're much less likely to confuse yourself.)

Your note card might look like this.

II. Financial Aid

Iowa State University has three forms of financial aid: need-based, scholarships, and student employment.

www.admissions.iastate.edu/finance.php

You can easily adapt the note-card approach to legal pads, word-processing documents, or spiral notebooks. Whatever method you use, proceed like this, skimming through each of your sources, ignoring material irrelevant to your thesis and writing down the juicy parts with organizational labels that will help you know where you found the information and where you intend to use it.

For some assignments, your opinions and personal perspectives will be important components. When that is the case, you should write down your own ideas as notes, too. They can be labeled *My Opinion* or *Personal Idea* and labeled with a Roman numeral and heading so that they end up in the proper section when you organize your notes.

Remember that your preliminary outline is preliminary. You can change it. As previously mentioned, if an element in your outline seems less important than you originally thought, feel free to dump it. If your note-taking process uncovers an area of interest that you originally left off your preliminary outline, go ahead and add it.

Writing a Final, Ultradetailed Outline

The next step is hard intellectual work. You are now ready to develop an outline with depth and detail. In this step, you will make many of the important decisions about the final shape of your paper. You will include all of the facts, data, and ideas that you have generated as a researcher.

Begin this step by familiarizing yourself with the notes you have taken. If you have taken them over an extended period of time, you may need to refresh your memory about exactly what you have accumulated. Take another look at your preliminary outline. Do you still like the order of the elements? If not, switch things around. It's still preliminary, but not for much longer.

Take a deep breath. Set aside some time. Minimize the possibility of distractions. Go to work on the next step: putting together everything that goes together. If you have carefully labeled and organized your notes, the payoff begins now. For example, if your topic is a specific college, put all of your material labeled *II. Financial Aid* together in one stack. If your notes are index cards, you can easily manipulate them into piles. If you have taken notes in a notebook or legal pad, you may want to actually cut them apart with scissors. (It's a good idea to make a copy of your notes while they are still intact, in case something accidentally gets cut the wrong way, or if you have written on the back sides of your paper). If your notes are in a word-processing format, you can cut and paste them into the order you like. However you do it, keep track of the source of each note for the purpose of citations.

Continue to sort your notes until you have nestled each item with material from the same outline level—all of the IIs together, for example. Then it's time to organize the sections. Choose one of the sections, probably the one you like or understand the best. Read over all of the notes for that section and decide on the best way to organize the section.

To help organize each section, ask yourself these questions:

- *What is the main idea of this section?*

- *What are the supporting examples?*

- *What are the subcategories?*

- *If I'm including my opinions, what are my thoughts based on the material in this section?* (Your own opinions will require separate notes. If you haven't already done so, write them down now and add them to the notes with a label indicating that you are the originator of the idea.)

- What is the most effective way to order this material?

Once you have a mental grasp of the section, write it down in outline form, including every level of detail that you can. Here are the possible levels of detail:

I. Main Idea of Section

   A. Supporting examples

      1. Subcategories

         a. Detail

            (1) More detail

               (a) Even more detail

You probably will not need to go beyond six levels of detail, but don't be surprised if you do reach this level of detail in some of your sections. This is a demanding intellectual task, but it's very important because it forces you to understand the ways that the ideas and material for each section connect to, support, and illuminate each other. If you slop through this stage, your paper will not communicate its ideas very well. As long as you're going to all of this work, you might as well generate a project that makes as much sense as possible, right?

You may wonder whether or not to write your outline in sentences or in phrases. Perhaps your teacher will have a requirement about that. If so, follow it. If not, then it doesn't really matter much. Because the outline is simply an organizational plan of ideas, it's not completely necessary to express those ideas in sentences at this stage. If you choose, however, to write your outline in sentences, you may discover an advantage: If you wrestle some of these ideas into sentence form now, you have given yourself a head start on the next step—writing a rough draft. If that seems like an added level of unnecessary work at this point, then just write your outline in phrases. It will still turn out fine.

Continue going through your notes until you have organized and outlined every section. You now have a final, ultradetailed outline. Everything that is going to be in your paper should be in this outline. Yes, everything. If in doubt, put it in. If you have any leftover notes, treat them the same way you do the leftover food that's been in your refrigerator for a couple of days: Find a way to use it, or bid it goodbye.

Journal Topic

You're asked to write a research paper that will be due in four weeks. What excites you about this task? What worries, frustrates, or annoys you? Be specific.

Writing a Rough Draft

For the scope of this project, your time as a researcher is now finished. If you have followed all of the steps up to this point, you have accomplished an important scholarly mission. After choosing and refining a focus, you have found material previously written on the topic. (You have literally "re-searched.") You have extracted the parts most relevant for your purpose and have made sophisticated decisions about how best to organize them. Perhaps you have also added your own opinions or commentary.

You are now ready to be a writer. Everything you know about writing effectively is in your tool belt. The experience you have gained from writing other pieces will be helpful to you. If research seemed like a strange, mystical endeavor, you will be glad to be back in familiar territory.

For some essays, you have relied upon your memory as the source of material. Some previous academic projects with smaller parameters may have required you to explain or discuss material you have learned about, and your memory provided you with the details. Pieces of writing based on your own experiences were generated almost exclusively by using your memory as the source. This research project is too big to hold in your memory. To use a techno-metaphor, your final, ultradetailed outline will now serve as your "external memory." You don't have to remember anything because you already wrote it down in an outline in the order you want it to appear in your paper.

As you did in the previous step, choose the section of your outline you want to work on first. Read over the section, noticing and reflecting upon how the different elements and levels work together. Now write it down in a paragraph or more. Take your time.

Write the section in the simplest, plainest language that you can, with the full acknowledgement that some of the material may be complex. Pay particular attention at the beginnings of sentences to provide transition words or phrases that show the relationship between the sentences. If one sentence provides an example of something mentioned in the previous sentence, you might write "For example." If a sentence contains a variation on an idea mentioned in the previous sentence, you might begin with "Another...." Each sentence in each paragraph should somehow build upon or reference the preceding sentence. Your job is to make it easy for a reader to follow the flow of your thoughts. If a reader can't do that, your writing has no reason to exist.

Including Internal Documentation

As you write, you will obviously include material that you found in sources written by other people or institutions. It is your responsibility, as the author of this paper, to properly provide credit to the authors whose ideas you have included. Including the work of those authors without proper documentation is a serious academic crime called **plagiarism**.

Avoiding plagiarism is pretty easy to do. Simply provide documentation for the ideas you use from other authors. The Works Cited list you have already created takes care of some of that. It shows your readers that you acknowledge consulting other works as you have prepared your research. It even shows your readers everything they need to know to locate those sources and investigate them for their own purposes, if they so desire.

A Works Cited list isn't enough, however, to completely absolve yourself of plagiarism. You must include internal documentation: within the text of your paper, you must document, or cite, the specific ideas or words of other writers that you have used. (Please note that the term *citation* is used both for the items in the list of sources you have used and for the internal documentation used within the body of your paper.)

In general, you must provide citations in three situations:

1. Any direct quote

2. Any statistic

3. Anything that paraphrases a specific idea or is not common knowledge

Let's consider each of these in a bit more depth. Direct quotes occur when you use the exact words of another writer in your work. Of course, the vast majority of your research paper should consist of your own words, phrases, and sentences. In some instances, however, another writer may have written about an idea in such a compelling or important way that you want to use his words. That's fine to do as long as you enclose the words in quotation marks and provide a citation. In fact, your teacher may require you to use a certain maximum or minimum number of direct quotes.

Statistics also require citations. Because statistics are usually the result of some type of study or research project, the circumstances of how the original researcher arrived at the numbers may be of value to those reading your work. It's probably not necessary for you to provide a description of those circumstances, but it may be important to your reader. For that reason, a citation is necessary. For our purposes, statistics are any expression of "something per something," such as teachers per student, dollars per year, or hours per day. These statistics may be in the form of percentages, ratios, or other numerical comparisons.

The other situation requiring a citation is not as clear-cut as direct quotes and statistics. Anything that is not common knowledge requires a citation. So, what is *common knowledge*? Any information found in more than one source can usually be considered common knowledge and therefore does not need a citation. For example, if you are researching Iowa State University, one of your sources may say that the school is located in Ames, Iowa. Another source will probably also say that Ames, Iowa, is the location. There you have it. More than one source contains the same information; therefore, it is common knowledge and does not require a citation. If some other source says the school is located elsewhere, that would require a citation. (It might also require you to jettison that source because it's flat out wrong.)

Just as we saw with writing a Works Cited list, writing internal citations requires very little guesswork or creativity. Those organizations that devise documentation formats—Modern Language Association (MLA) and American Psychological Association (APA), for example—also design internal citation formats that complement their approaches to Works Cited lists.

Citation formats have become greatly simplified over the past decade or so. For the most part, all you need to do is put some parentheses at the end of the sentence requiring a citation. Within those parentheses, include the barest amount of information to enable a reader looking in your bibliography to find the full citation for the source that originally contained the cited information.

For example, let's say you're writing about President Harry Truman, and you are using this source:

> Daniel, Clifton Truman. *Growing Up with My Grandfather*. New York: Carol Publishing Group, 1995.

If you decide to use the author's description of how Truman used a silent glare to silence his critics, which is found on page 62, you might have the following sentence and citation in your paper:

> Harry Truman could convey disappointment to generals and grandchildren alike using only a silent glare (Daniel 62).

Similarly, if you choose to use some of the author's exact words imbedded in one of your sentences as a direct quote, the result might look like this:

> Generals and grandchildren alike discovered that Truman "turned stone-cold silent when someone close to him disappointed him" (Daniel 62).

So, what exactly goes in those parentheses? Usually, it will be an author's last name and a page number. More accurately, it will be whatever comes first in the Works Cited entry for that source. If the source doesn't have a specific author, the first element of the citation might be a title. In that case, be sure the title appears exactly the same way it is presented in the Works Cited list. If the title, for example, is in italics in the Works Cited list, it should also be italicized in the citation. If the title requires quotation marks, those quotation marks should also appear in the citation.

In some special circumstances, however, this general rule obviously won't work. For example, what if you have more than one source by the same author, or you have several Works Cited entries with the same title? In that case, add a second element from the Works Cited entry to the citations from each of those sources so that your reader can distinguish between them. If, for example, you're using an additional source by Daniel, the citation would look like this: (Daniel, *Growing* 62). Using a shortened version of the title is acceptable.

Here's another variation on the previous example. If the sentence that you write includes a specific reference to the source, all you need in the parentheses is a page number:

> Truman's grandson Clifton Truman Daniel remembers that Truman "turned stone-cold silent when someone close to him disappointed him" (62).

In the preceding brief example, the source is subtly inserted rather than introduced, which in this case, is probably sufficient. The sentence and quote flow together smoothly. In most cases, however, you should consider this simple guideline to ensure seamless transitions between the research you present and the rest of your paper:

1. Introduce **your source**. If the person you're quoting is an expert in some area, for example, mention this.

2. Insert **the source**. Use quotation marks if using exact words.

3. Briefly **comment on the source**.

Here's an example that builds on the previous one.

> Generals and grandchildren alike discovered that Truman "turned stone-cold when someone close to him disappointed him" (Daniel 62). In a similar vein, Indiana University historian Robert H. Ferrell argues that Truman's personality was "direct, interested, concerned, and filled with information" when speaking to potential supporters on the campaign trail (278). Someone who witnessed both circumstances might conclude that Truman had wild mood swings, when in fact, the two observations demonstrate that Truman was *calculated* in his attempts to influence others.

This is such an important point that we're going to belabor the obvious. In the preceding example, notice how the second source is *identified* ("Indiana University historian"), and how the sources are followed by a *comment* from the writer ("Someone who witnessed both circumstances..."). The commentary is original, the *writer's* idea. When writing a research paper, the writer is not a puzzle-maker assembling pieces. The writer collects and sorts, but she also compares, synthesizes, hypothesizes—*she thinks*—all the while maintaining a fresh voice.

What if your source is not a printed source with page numbers? Simply use the first element of the source's Works Cited entry in the citation. The fact that it has no page numbers will signal your reader that the source is in a nonpaginated format. For example, if you are researching rescues by teen lifeguards each year, you might use the Lifeguarding section of the American Red Cross website, which includes statistics related to drowning and near-drowning incidents. The MLA citation for that site looks like this:

> "Summer Safety." The American National Red Cross. *American Red Cross*, 2011. Web. 22. Apr. 2011.

Notice that the citation does not include a page number, because the website has no actual page numbers. If you need to create an internal citation for this source—for instance, if you use a statistic from the website in your paper—your citation would look something like this:

According to the American Red Cross, "Almost half (48%) said they had nearly drowned at some point in their life" ("Summer Safety"). This surprising statistic shows the importance of lifeguards and CPR training.

Although no page number is given, a reader can easily access the website by finding the source in the Works Cited list.

Our final advice about documentation is that you should have at least one citation for every item in your Works Cited list. Remember when you were creating the preliminary Works Cited list, and you chose more sources than were actually required? You must now eliminate the sources you did not cite. Also, whenever you cite a source in the body of your paper, that source must appear in your Works Cited list. See Appendix D for more information on documenting sources.

Editing Your Rough Draft and Preparing a Final Copy

Now that you have the solid body of an essay, you still need to spiff it up. Let's consider the introduction. A reader who picks up your research paper and endeavors to read it is making a commitment to spend a sizable amount of time and intellectual energy with your work. Your introduction should motivate that reader and shape his reading experience. You can do that by establishing a friendly but professional tone. A research paper is not the place to try out your most dramatic or hilarious opening gambit.

Write an interesting first sentence. Then segue into a paragraph that sets up the body of your paper. Be sure to include a sentence or two that previews the main sections of your work. Check to be certain that the first sentence of your first body section flows smoothly from your introduction.

Writers on Writing

Write while the heat is in you....The writer who postpones the recording of his thoughts uses an iron which has cooled to burn a hole with. He cannot inflame the minds of his audience.

—*Henry David Thoreau*

After you are satisfied with your introduction, let's work on the conclusion. Take another look at your introduction. Does it contain the seed of a good conclusion? Can you rephrase that first sentence or some of the other opening material, or somehow reference it again at the end of your paper? If so, that makes your reader feel really smart: "Hey, that's that same idea I read about ten pages earlier! I remember that! Now I understand it in a new and more enlightened way! Thanks, Brilliant Research Paper Writer!" If you can provide your reader with a conclusion-reading experience like that, you've probably made a pretty good impression.

Finally, check your transitions between paragraphs and especially between each section. Provide a word or phrase at the beginning of each paragraph that somehow refers back to the previous paragraph. This is how you create the sense of flow that is so valuable to skilled writers.

Now is also a good time to take a close look at your direct quotations. Do they seem smoothly integrated or simply "stuck in"? As mentioned earlier, each direct quotation should include brief identifying information about the original source, as well as an explanation of its significance. Of course, each direct quotation should also include proper documentation.

If your teacher requires that you include headings, please don't rely on those headings to serve as transitions. Readers don't really read headings; they notice them. Headings are processed differently in a reader's mind than the text of your sentences.

Your Works Cited list may also require some fine-tuning at this late stage. Several steps ago, when we were still calling it a preliminary Works Cited list, you had entries that were in perfect shape, according to the format you were following. Before attaching that Works Cited list to your final paper, you should check the following items:

- Is it alphabetized correctly?

- Have you used correct indentation?

- Are the elements of each entry in the correct order?

- Is the punctuation correct for each element in the entry, including a period at the end?

- Have you used quotation marks and italics (or underlining) correctly for both the internal citations and in the Works Cited list?

If you have followed these steps, you have survived a scholarly, academically responsible, thorough process resulting in a piece of work of which you can be proud. Maybe it will even serve as the basis of a lifelong interest for you.

Even if that isn't the case, you have undergone a series of steps—some involving research and some involving writing—that will serve you well any time you need to gather, synthesize, and report information. This is a skill set that will probably pop up more than you would expect in the course of your life. Although this is a rigorous process, the next time you face a similar project, you will do so with less fear, anxiety, and confusion. You now know from experience that as long as you work efficiently and wisely, you can effectively manage a project of this scope.

Practice

Before beginning the Chapter Assignment, try the following exercises to practice the steps involved in writing a research paper.

1. On a separate sheet of paper, organize the following points into a coherent outline.

   Thesis: Colleges should rely more on a portfolio of a student's work than on a student's standardized test scores.

   Test scores don't reveal a student's work ethic.

   Demonstrate how portfolios can be cost-effective.

   Test scores don't provide a complete picture of a student's aptitude.

   Portfolios better reveal work ethic.

   How to convince colleges to adopt portfolio assessment.

   Portfolios provide a more accurate assessment of a student's aptitude.

   Demonstrate how portfolios predict success in school.

   Test scores don't show motivation.

   Portfolios reveal motivation.

   Tests don't show the results of a sustained effort.

   Portfolios reveal the results of a sustained effort.

   Demonstrate how portfolios reveal character, something a test score never will.

2. Which of these statements would need to be documented? In other words, which statements require a citation?

   a. Presidential elections in the United States are held every four years.

   b. In 1911 Henry Ford wrote, "Automobiles will change the landscape of this country."

   c. One recent survey revealed that 23 percent of high school students nationwide have smoked a cigarette in the past month.

d. President Truman ordered that an atomic bomb be dropped on Hiroshima in 1945.

e. Numerous studies show that the rate of nonviolent crimes across the United States has decreased in the past decade.

f. Ernest Hemingway attacked F. Scott Fitzgerald in many publications.

g. Congress will enact new immigration legislation, according to the *New York Times.*

3. Once you have a few possible research topics in mind, try the following tips for searching online. Keep in mind that websites and URLs change frequently, so these are just a few examples of the search engines you might use.

a. Go to the Google News website (http://www.emcp.net/google-news) for the most updated news on a particular subject.

b. If you want to search through a variety of search engines at once, you might use a search engine such as Dogpile (http://www.emcp.net/dogpile).

c. If you want to see your results in clusters, you could search a site such as Yippy (http://www.emcp.net/clusty).

d. Go to Delicious (http://www.emcp.net/delicious) or Diigo (http://www.emcp.net/diigo) and enter some search terms. Compare the results to the same search using Google or Bing.

e. Try phrasing questions in the form of statements, and add an asterisk: "The frontal lobe is responsible for *" Yes, you need to put quotation marks around the entire phrase. As a result, the search engine will look for perfect matches—and then complete the statement.

f. If you need a definition for a term, say, acetylcholine, go to Google and type, "define: acetylcholine."

g. If you want to limit hits, put a minus sign in front of a word. For example, if you want information about the country Jordan but receive results instead for basketball player Michael Jordan, type: Jordan -Michael. (Be sure to include the space before the minus sign.)

Chapter Assignment

Prewriting

Use the following suggestions to help you choose a topic and clarify the purpose of your research paper.

Since you'll be spending several weeks working on your research paper, choose your topic carefully. Once you decide on a topic, consider doing the following:

1. Make a list of key words or phrases related to your topic that you might use during a search. For example, if your topic is schizophrenia, the following terms might prove useful: psychosis, mental illness, treatment, paranoia, delusions, and hallucinations. If the phrases don't come easily, find someone to help you brainstorm.

2. Make a list of ten to fifteen questions you'd like answered about your topic. This may help guide your research.

3. Find a teacher or other adult who has more knowledge about your topic than you do, and interview this person for a few minutes. Ask your questions. Express your curiosity. Also ask about recommended sources.

Writing Topics

Select one of the following topics to write a research paper. You'll need to narrow your focus, of course.

1. **Personal issues:** friendship, romance, marriage, divorce, identity, self-esteem, generosity, kindness, aggression, shyness

2. **Political issues:** local or national politics, party system, proposed laws, injustice, civil rights, homelessness, immigration, economics

3. **Historical issues:** war, the military, milestones, presidents, government, religion

4. **Psychological issues:** learning, memory, sleep, dreams, hypnosis, brain function, mental illness, therapy, personality

5. **Sociological issues:** group pressure, obedience, rebellion, conformity

Revision

As you revise and edit your first draft, consider these suggestions.

1. Now that you have a first draft in hand, create an outline that accurately reflects your paper. This outline may or may not resemble your preliminary outline or your ultradetailed outline. Is every paragraph inserted in the right place? Does each section lead logically to the next? Does a different order make more sense?

2. Study your paragraphs. Do you devote one main idea to each paragraph? Can you combine some paragraphs—or break up longer ones into smaller chunks? Have you included clear and effective transitions between sentences and paragraphs?

3. Is your thesis clear? Does every sentence serve to support that thesis? If not, can you cut any sentences? Do you need to add more support? If so, where?

4. Have you relied on a variety of sources to support your thesis? If you happen to rely too heavily on a single source or two, can you find ways to support your thesis by using more material from other sources?

Peer Review

Use these questions to help you evaluate another student's writing. Remember, specific suggestions and examples are most helpful.

1. Research papers have a reputation for being dull. What has the writer done to defy that reputation and to maintain your interest? Be specific.

2. What is the thesis? Is the thesis stated clearly? Has the writer provided enough evidence to support the thesis? Explain.

3. Is the organizational plan clear and effective? What changes would you suggest?

4. Offer three or four other suggestions that might improve the paper. You might address sentence structure, transitions, development, and clarity.

America: Made in China

by Mark Wiemer

Meet the Writer

Mark Wiemer became interested in writing at a young age thanks to many summer days spent reading with his mom. He enjoys crafting lyrics for bands he performs with and experimenting with aspects of acoustics and sound. Mark expects that writing will continue to be a passion of his in the future and plans to indulge in compositions breadth, incorporating writing into as many aspects of his life as possible.

There used to be a time in America when everything that *could* be made in America had a factory to make it. From steel to jeans, America was known for its high product output and high quality products. The general motto of most employed individuals could be seen as, "Make your product however you please, just as long as it meets demand, works, and does the job for a long time." The workplace was also very different. White collar jobs were just as important as other positions, but lacked as high a demand because blue collar work was enough to provide for the American family.

Two major events happened in the last ten years which sent America into the new age of employment—the Internet was implemented not only in the United States, but around the world, and the World Trade Organization inducted China as one of its members. Nandan Nilekani, of Infosys Technologies, a new Indian corporation responsible for outsourced American jobs, was quoted in the book *The World is Flat* as saying, "Tom, the playing field is being leveled" (Friedman 7). This is what could be described as the general feeling of many unemployed individuals who see their jobs swept away due to China's economic colossus as snow plowed from the streets by plows.

America's reaction to these events was as unnoticed as when an individual is first infected with a virus. Over time though, the complications of this "virus" became noticed by those whose jobs were the first to leave the country, blue collar workers. Because of the ease of moving their work out of the country, blue collar work was immediately struck down by outsourcing to China. Corporations gazed at the cheap labor force of China and the profits they were making as a dog would savor the sight of a steak on the kitchen counter. Their intent was not to decimate the American workforce; rather, it was to provide for cheaper costs and larger quantities of goods which could easily be produced and shipped out of other countries. The Chinese are also very hard workers, and the unemployment rate is astounding. This meant that a cheap, hardworking labor force was available around the clock; the corporations loved the idea of twenty-four-seven production.

Despite these advantages, outsourcing labor to China has not yielded a large advantage for the United States. Corporations went to China seeking, in short, wealth. They thought of China as a pot of gold but had their hopes smoldered by the ill promises of a get-rich-quick pyramid scheme. Outsourcing American work to China has affected the United State's economy in a negative way because it has given way to the degeneration of American jobs, has made America's advantage in ingenuity unoriginal, and has opened America up to a weakened dollar and economy.

The Government can be partially to blame for the outsourcing of America. Despite knowing the issue is real, there have been little efforts done by the government to resolve the problem. As revealed by "The Outsourcing Bogeyman," "Dennis Hastert, meanwhile warned that 'outsourcing can be a problem for American workers and the American Economy'" (Drezner 1). So if they understand outsourcing as a serious threat to the well-being of America, why do they allow it to continue?

Corporate executives are aware of the problem as well, and have brought the issue before Congress to make them aware of it. We can see that "In a January testimony before Congress, Hewlett-Packard chief Carly Fiorina warned that 'there is no job that is America's God-given right anymore" (Drezner 2). This statement clearly illustrates that corporations are aware of the problem, yet still outsourcing has continued. The government has tried to occupy criticizing fingers pointed their way by throwing legislation for them to hold. Congress did this by throwing "a $328 billion spending bill before the U.S.

Senate [in January of 2004 which] would prohibit government contractors from outsourcing work overseas, a provision [which] could affect companies such as International Business Machines Corp" (Bloomberg News 1). Hiding behind their legislation, Congress claimed to have seized the problem, but as Daniel Drenzer of *Foreign Affairs* found, "Forrester Research estimates that 3.3 million white-collar jobs will move overseas by 2015"(2). If an expected 3.3 million jobs, white collar alone, are expected to be eliminated from the country, where are the workers going to go? Unlike jobs that once vacated can be filled by other employees, these jobs will be filled by individuals outside the country. How can we expect all these individuals to find jobs? What are the means going to be to support themselves or their families?

Some support has been raised by those directly affected by manufacturing. Non-profit organizations such as S.A.M. (Save American Manufacturing) have acted as special interest groups to raise awareness of the effects of outsourcing to China.

Although these organizations have helped to gain awareness of the issue, they are neither large enough nor vocal enough to strike the majority of America out of its naive daze.

While the Government has been sitting with the issue of outsourcing like a benched athlete at a baseball game, passively watching America lose to China, blue and white collar jobs have been leaving the country. Why is it that Americans are becoming unemployed at such a critical rate? The answer is that there is no possibility of Americans competing with Chinese labor rates, ethics, or standards of living while still maintaining a place in America's economy.

American workers are used to a salary that will allow them to meet general necessities such as electrical and heating utilities and other amenities such as food and as well as consumer goods such as videos, music, and other entertainment amenities. In China, a vast majority of the workforce expects only enough money to buy food. The pay in China is cents on the dollar, meaning that corporations can afford to pay 20 or more Chinese workers to one American. This (as one can imagine) turns into large profits for corporations, which can then direct those profits to building rent, executive salaries, and other avenues. Unfortunately, Americans have another issue to deal with as well which strikes at a moral level. Unlike America, there are no labor laws in China which protect the rights of employees at the workplace. This means that workers in a Chinese position may go through a workday underpaid and overworked.

Regardless of where the money goes, it was thought that turning to China was a way to ensure instant wealth. We can see that this is not the case though, based off of an interview with Richard D. Goulet, who was interviewed by Carol Kleiman of the *Chicago Tribune*, who stated that "In the last three to five years, I realized that outsourcing was being used to reduce with no commitment to quality…and I've found that companies that outsource are no more valuable in terms of the stock market than those who don't" (2). Despite referring to the stock market, Goulet's statement strikes at the core of what America, and corporations need to realize about outsourcing to China. Contrary to the consumer thinking they are receiving better prices, and the corporations believing they are making more profits, neither is true.

If jobs are leaving the country to outsourcing to China, then how are unemployed Americans expected to make money to buy these "cheap" items from China? It is currently predicted, according to a November issue of the *CQ Researcher Online* that "China's $1.6 trillion economic output is expected to triple in 15 years, overtaking the United States by 2039" (Katel 1). Furthermore, if the American public has no means of work to buy the products, how are corporations "taking advantage of outsourcing" supposed to move their products off the shelves and into Americans' hands? Americans have to realize that outsourcing doesn't only move jobs from the country, but actual currency as well. When we pay China to do work that American workers could do, we are literally taking money out of circulation in the American market. Most money lost from U.S. circulation, the blood of the American economy, has been bled out from all the cuts corporations have made by outsourcing American work to China.

As much as we hope it wouldn't be the cause, much of outsourcing to China by corporations has been for the financial enhancement of top ranking officials. As Karen Shoffner of the *Lake Zurich Courier* found, "Alan Tonelson, a research fellow at USBIC's education foundation, described U.S. trade policy with China as 'Outsourcing Deals' mainly for multinational corporations"(1). These deals have ended with huge salaries for corporate executives, yet no return for employees or the American economy. Yet, we cannot blame outsourcing alone on greed; we also have to look at other factors that have chained America's hands to China.

With the advent of the Internet, the world quickly grew smaller as communication across oceans could happen in seconds rather than days. Countries which were seen as exotic, third world countries only ten years ago, have become as "plugged in," both in terms of technology and the world scene, as bustling American cities. As Thomas Friedman exasperated during a trip to India, "No, this definitely wasn't Kansas. It didn't even seem like India. Was this the new world, the old world, or the next world?"(4). Although Friedman's statement isn't directed toward the country of China, its implications are. Friedman is pointing out that countries like China who once seemed to be light years behind American ways, have turned full circle as a person fresh from plastic surgery into something new and extremely dynamic. Once coined "third world countries" have become technological oases in the midst of the world.

Not only has technology placed America at the mercy of China, but so has legislation. Corporations, even if *trying* to keep work in America, have been forced to move their work to China to compete with other nations, including China, who is able to undercut American wages and product prices. For example, as noted in *The World is Flat*, "The free software movement has become a serious challenge to Microsoft and some other big global software players"(119). Because of the legislation the government has imposed on American business, domestic corporations are forced to compete globally, meaning they *must* keep their prices at a low rate. If they keep their prices high due to American wages, taxes, and other expenses, there is no doubt that corporation will suffer adverse affects which may lead ultimately to the corporation becoming disembodied. Tying back into legislation, one can reason that if Congress could propose a solution to the problem it would help American business regain the foothold it had a decade ago. Congress could also halt all trade with China until there was evident proof that they had stopped "floating" their currency against the American dollar. As pointed out by Ted Fishman, the author of *China Inc.*, and an economic analysis, "China's seventh place [world economic] rating may be too low because China pegs its currency to the dollar"(10). What Fishman is stating simply means that when the value of the American dollar rises, Chinese currency will as well, but when the American dollar depreciates, so does China's currency. This means that China artificially puts its currency just slightly under the American value to always have the cheaper rate, but also receive as much money as possible. Another way Congress could help to resolve outsourcing issues would be to impose laws regulating the amount of foreign goods imported to the U.S. from China, allowing America to return to a time before outsourcing to China, when corporations would be undercut by American small business, not entire countries.

Small business used to be the enemy of corporate America in terms of undercutting prices. When something was too expensive to buy from a large company, one could be sure a small business would make the good, and at a reduced rate as well. With corporate America reducing its prices and outsourcing to China though, it has left small business in a quandary. How low can they sell a good before not making a profit? As Karen Shoffner points out, "The bottom line is that a growing number of U.S. domestic manufacturers across the individual spectrum find themselves competing against finished goods that cost less than the cost of the U.S. firm's raw materials" (2). How are small businesses expected to compete with rates like these? As fulfilling as it may seem for Americans to buy goods at prices considered "steals from China," all that euphoric pleasure amounts to the substance of a split balloon...nothing but air. One who asks why would find the most honest answer from Joseph Fehsenfeld. When interviewed by Karen Shoffner, he simply stated that "The impact is negative to the economy, to the middle class. We can't support the standard of living we had before if we embrace the open market" (2). If Americans expect outsourcing to continue, and watch America's jobs sail away and register for Chinese citizenship, then they must be prepared to become unemployed, and remove a truss of their standard of living.

Outsourcing to China is not an evil, but it is not a necessity. Its existence can be compared to smoking. One starts the habit through peer or political pressure and slowly becomes addicted. He keeps hungering for all the nicotine of incoming goods at reduced prices and quick profits. Thriving off these hypnotic economic peaks, feeling the rush of being something electrified, until the current staves its luster, because now the adverse effects are becoming obvious. Like losing the lungs to cancer, the lifeline of the economy is blocked off, and the damage will become irreversible if we fail to subdue the problem soon. Outsourcing U.S. jobs to China is unnecessary. Unless China is the only country capable to make a certain product, there is no reason to outsource U.S. work there. The government needs to realize this and propose legislation which will limit the amount of imports from China. This would allow more jobs to remain in the country, making it possible for the American people to provide for their standard of living. Outsourcing to China has had a hostile effect on the U.S. workforce and economy.

Works Cited

Bloomberg News. "Senate Weighs Outsourcing Curb." *Chicago Tribune* 22 Jan. 2004, sec. Business: 4. *NewsBank Inc.* Web. 22 Nov. 2005.

Drenzer, Daniel W. "The Outsourcing Bogeyman." *Foreign Affairs.* May-June 2005. Web. 1 Dec. 2005.

Fishman, Ted C. *China, Inc.* New York: Scribner, 2005. Print.

Friedman, Thomas L. *The World is Flat.* New York: Farrar, Staus, and Giroux, 2005. Print.

Katel, Peter. "Emerging China." *The CQ Researcher Online* 15.40 (2005). Web. 17 Nov. 2005.

Kleiman, Carol. "Outsourcing a Matter of Many Sides." *Chicago Tribune* 11 Mar. 2004, sec. Business: 2. *Newsbank Inc.* Web. 22 Nov. 2005.

Shoffner, Karen. "Local Manufacturers say China Trade Policy hurts." *Lake Zurich Courier* (2005): 1-2. *American Economic Alert.* Web. 17 Nov. 2005.

Discussion Questions

1. Identify Wiemer's thesis. How does he support or prove his thesis?

2. How much emphasis does Wiemer place on his own opinion? Are his personal perspectives subtly incorporated, overtly spotlighted, or not at all apparent?

3. Identify specific points in the writing where Wiemer has attempted to maintain your interest in a potentially dull topic.

4. Evaluate Wiemer's organizational plan. Sketch an outline that reflects his strategy for organizing his arguments.

5. Identify at least five effective transitions used at the beginnings of paragraphs to link to the preceding paragraphs.

6. Evaluate Wiemer's Works Cited page. What are the various types of sources used? Does each source seem credible? Has he used a satisfying number of sources? Why or why not?

7. Wiemer refers to one source—Thomas Friedman's book *The World Is Flat*—more frequently than any other source. Is this appropriate? Why or why not?

8. Is Wiemer's paper too technical in any places? If so, how could he make it more accessible?

Chapter 10

Writing About Literature

Let's face it. **Writing about literature** is one of the most daunting composition tasks you're likely to face in high school. Most writing tasks ask you to draw upon your own expertise and experiences. You have the upper hand. Your audience, most notably your teachers, will assume that you know what you're talking about when it comes to your own life.

But when you write about literature, the rhetorical situation changes. If your audience is primarily your English teachers, they know a lot about the subject matter because they have been studying and teaching literature for years, sometimes decades. Not only that, but they may already have entrenched opinions about the literature under study. So, as you approach the job of explaining your reaction to a poem, novel, play, or story, your work is cut out for you. How do you make your writing satisfying to a sophisticated audience who may know more about the subject than you do?

The best piece of advice we can offer is to make your writing original. What can you and only you say about this work? What literary angle can you write about that thousands of other students haven't already covered? Maybe it seems as though we just made a daunting task into an impossible one. Actually, we just made it easier, but it will require some thought on your part.

The nature of your approach will depend somewhat on the nature of the assignment. Has your teacher given you a very specific topic to write about, or has she provided the option of coming up with your own topic? Is there an expectation that you will use only the primary text for supporting your thesis, or does your teacher expect you to incorporate research into your writing as you develop your thesis?

"Thesis? What thesis? We have to come up with a thesis for this, too?" Yes, you do. Development of a viable thesis is especially important when writing about literature.

Choosing a Literary Thesis

Regardless of how your assignment is presented to you, a good starting place for this essay is your own honest reaction to the work. This, of course, requires that you have read the story, chapter, poem, play, or novel and have made a sincere attempt to understand its primary themes or issues. If you try the shortcut of turning to critical works or the Internet *before* formulating your own opinions about the work, your thinking is likely to be uninspired, contaminated, or confused.

If you have an open-ended assignment that leaves you free to choose your own topic, here are some questions to consider:

1. Compare and contrast characters in the work. Which characters are similar? Which characters are so different that they are essentially opposites?

2. How do descriptive details in the work combine to create the setting?

3. If the action takes place in more than one setting, compare and contrast the various settings.

4. What are the most obvious characteristics of the work? For example, is the piece extremely short or extremely long? Does it have huge amounts of dialogue? Does the point of view shift dramatically? Choose one of these characteristics and write about how it fulfills the author's purpose.

5. Which characters are similar? Which characters are so different that they are essentially opposites? What does this tell us about the author's purpose?

6. Does the author use a recurring motif or image? Cite examples of this recurrence and explain their significance to the work.

7. How is this work representative of or significantly different from other works by the same author or in the same genre?

8. How is this work representative of its time? How have perceptions of its cultural aspects shifted?

9. Describe your personal involvement with this piece. What incidents from your own life affected the way you experienced this work? How does your own philosophy or bank of personal experiences prevent this work from appealing to you?

10. Was this piece of writing influential on other writers or artists? Was it popular during its time? Why or why not?

11. Is the content or theme of this work morally acceptable to you? Why or why not? (Since morals vary from person to person, this topic is as much about you as it is about the work under study.)

If you have read the literary work under study with good intentions and you feel like you don't "get" it, there is actually a kernel of good news in that fact. What exactly didn't you get? How did the writer's style or approach inhibit your understanding? Was it the way he wrote the sentences? Was it the way the story or poem unfolded? Was it the fact that a character did something so beyond your reality that it was difficult for you to accept or understand? If so, you have generated the seed of a very useful literary analysis. For example, a thesis derived from a frustrating reading experience might look something like these:

> The plot of Faulkner's "A Rose for Emily" is presented out of chronological order, needlessly confusing the reader.

> Nick Adams is so traumatized by his war experience that the story "Big, Two-Hearted River" would be better told by a more reliable narrator.

> In John Updike's "A&P," Sammy's decision to quit his job might be brave, but it's not very wise.

Each of these theses is arguable. A thoughtful reader might disagree with you, and that's fine. As long as you execute your analysis with support and sincerity, you should be able to create a fine piece of literary criticism.

If your task is to write about a topic your teacher has chosen, at least you know the parameters of your assignment. Common topics may include:

- How does a character change within the story or novel?

- How does the setting influence the story or novel?

- What is the theme of the story, novel, or poem, and how is it developed throughout the work?

- What is the author's tone, or attitude, toward some aspect of the story, novel, or poem?

Another type of teacher-generated question includes the opportunity for personal reflection or opinion. These prompts are writer-friendly because they allow you to write about the literature in ways that are unique to you.

- Which character do you most or least closely resemble? Why?

- Which character do you admire or despise? Why?

- How would you approach the story's conflict or dilemma similarly or differently from a character you've chosen to examine?

- Do you agree or disagree with the poem's message? Why?

Still another approach that teachers use is to make the assignment more open-ended. Again, these assignments allow you to build upon your own experiences and expertise as you write about the literature under consideration.

- Choose an aspect of this work and explain its relevance for you.

- Write about a character that you find interesting.

- Choose a quote from this work and explain why you agree or disagree with it.

Your responses to these questions and prompts won't give you your specific thesis, but they can get you thinking along the right lines. From this brainstorming, you'll need to write a specific, arguable thesis that emphasizes your ideas about your chosen piece of literature. The tips about creating a thesis statement that you learned in Chapter 1 (see pages 12–16) are still relevant when writing about literature.

Once you have an idea for a thesis, scratch out a brief preliminary outline. This will take about ninety seconds, and it will include your guesses about what subtopics your paper is likely to include. Specific examples supporting your thesis will likely be one of the subtopics. (For more advice on writing a preliminary outline, please take a look at pages 332–333 in Chapter 9.)

If your assignment involves incorporating critical material from other sources, the research and writing advice in the rest of this chapter will be relevant and valuable for you. If, however, the scope of your assignment only involves writing your own interpretations of the literature supported by quotes and other material from your primary source, further research is not necessary.

Use everything you know about good writing as you create this literary essay. The lessons you have learned about how to craft a thesis, develop an argument, provide smooth transitions, and use descriptive language should be employed. An essay about literature should be just as rewarding for your reader as any of your other writing.

Journal Topic

What was one of your least enjoyable reading experiences, and why?

Using the Historical Present Tense

When writing your literary analysis, maintain the present tense in describing events that occur in the piece of literature. This is sometimes called *historical present tense*. In the narration chapter, we discouraged the use of present tense. For literary analysis, present tense is the standard approach, as you'll notice when you read literary criticism.

Past tense: Macbeth *saw* a dagger, which *was* either a hallucination caused by sleep deprivation or an example of supernatural powers at work.

Historical present tense: Macbeth *sees* a dagger floating in the air, which *is* either a hallucination caused by sleep deprivation or an example of supernatural powers at work.

A logical person might ask, *Why should I write in present tense about something that was written hundreds of years ago, in a story that took place even longer ago than that?*

Here's the philosophy behind using present tense for literary analysis: When we read a literary work like *Macbeth*, the story—along with its characters, plot, and setting—is happening in our imaginations *in present tense* as we read. Your version of *Macbeth*—the one in your imagination—is slightly different from that experienced by any of your classmates or your teacher. The immediacy of your reading experience dictates that you should write in present tense. Not only that, but when you reread *Macbeth*, you will re-create another, slightly different version of the play than you created the first time you read it. (Rereading *The Catcher in the Rye*, a well-known novel by J. D. Salinger, every few years is an excellent example. Reading that book during your high school years is a very different experience from reading it as a thirty- or forty-year-old. The book doesn't change, but the versions of it that you create in your mind are different because your banks of life experiences have changed.)

This use of present tense has a beneficial effect upon your reader. Because you're writing in present tense, the writing will transfer the immediacy of your reading experience to your reader with some extra "zing" that would not be there if you were plodding along in past tense.

Entering the World of Literary Research

If part of your literary essay assignment is to include support generated by critics, you are in for an intellectually demanding but rewarding experience. The world of the literary critic is sparsely populated. Its inhabitants have, in most cases, spent their careers reading literature, thinking about literature, and writing about literature. While the rest of us have gone about our lives doing other things, the critics have been crafting thoughtful analyses of literature. While critics may admire or despise certain works or writers, their primary purpose is to analyze the literature rather than to rate it in an oversimplified "thumbs up" or "thumbs down" fashion.

When we step into the critic's world, it might appear foreign, maybe even hostile. We know the words the critics are using, but the ideas are very abstract and can seem vague, irrelevant, or archaic. In some cases, the critics might even appear to be full of hot air, and you may feel that they go into far too much detail to make a point that the universe could do just fine without. But let's begin by giving them the benefit of the doubt. Let's assume that we can learn something from their careers spent in reflection upon great works of literature. As you become used to dealing with literary criticism, don't be surprised if you begin to admire the way many critics approach their craft. The writing of critics such as Cleanth Brooks can be literature in itself.

Finding Literary Criticism

How do you find valid criticism for the work about which you are writing? Let's begin with that thesis you have so carefully crafted. Use it to guide your search for relevant criticism. Remember, you're not trying to find everything ever published about the work or its author. You're trying to find a few good sources that support your thesis, a considerably smaller task. If you become lost in a sea of literary criticism, look at your thesis. Bear in mind that you may not actually find material that specifically supports your thesis. You may have to be satisfied with criticism that merely relates to it in some way. Even then, you might need to be creative and resourceful in how you envision your research material interfacing with your thesis.

Twenty-first century, techno-savvy students tend to want to hop right on the Internet and pop some key words into their favorite search engine to see what surfaces. Although in general we are great believers in the Internet as a research tool, we have to issue a caution here: save yourself some heartache and resist the urge to surf when it comes to literary research. Most of the literary "research" you will find on the open Internet is either garbage or the work of someone who knows about as much as you do. Many tribute sites pay homage to a particular writer, book, or genre. That doesn't mean that the sites' creators have any more expertise or intelligence than you do; they just have an enthusiasm. Skip those. Your search engine results may also lead you to papers written by other students in either high school or college. Skip those, too. Those papers can be useful in a limited way—perhaps guiding you toward other potential sources or revealing what research work has

Writers on Writing

I find that sometimes my thinking or rather my fancy takes the shape of verse and sometimes the shape of prose, and sometimes it may be a tale or it may be a confession or it may be, well, an opinion. But I don't think they are different. I mean I don't think of them as being in watertight compartments, and I think it's mere chance that a fancy of mine or even an opinion of mine should find its way into prose or into verse. Those things are not essential. You might as well say, you might as well speak about the fact of a book having a gray or a red binding.

—*Jorge Luis Borges*

been thoroughly covered by other writers—but they are usually not worth the effort you put into finding them. Your research time would be much better spent searching for sources in a more productive vein.

Here are the two main things to remember about finding relevant literary criticism: Gale is golden, and librarians are golden, too. Both can be found online or in a bricks-and-mortar building.

Gale Research products are an extraordinary resource for literary criticism. Depending on which Gale products are available to you, don't be surprised if you find everything you need in one or two volumes. The hardest thing about using them is cracking the code for the index. (If you need help with this, consult a librarian.) Once you understand how the index works, and it's not overly difficult, you will discover that a lot of the work is already done for you. You will find abstracts and extracts of criticism on virtually any significant author or work of literature ever written in any language. A close second in terms of research efficiency are critical collections edited by Harold Bloom. These frequently contain the best criticism available on a particular title or author.

As mentioned earlier, another valuable resource available to you in person or online is your friendly neighborhood (or school) librarian. Don't expect a librarian to do all of your work for you, but a wise researcher like you will ask how to find resources on your particular topic. Students sometimes become frustrated with librarians because of a simple misunderstanding of the librarian's role in a research process. Librarians don't know everything, but they do know how to find out pretty much everything. Don't become dismayed when a librarian doesn't know the exact answer to your focused question. Instead, be grateful when you are given the librarian's best professional advice on how *you* can discover the answer. A librarian is more like a treasure map than a treasure chest.

Now you have gathered some sources. Let's call these your tentative sources. An effective way to use your time is to narrow down the number of sources you're working with. Skim each one. Look over the chapter titles and article headings. If the source looks potentially relevant to your thesis, keep it. If it seems to be irrelevant, dump it.

When you have narrowed down your sources to a manageable number, which may depend on the requirements of your teacher, then begin to read them a little more thoroughly but still essentially skimming them. If any of the sources, upon this closer examination, seems like a dead end, dump it.

The sources that survive this narrowing-down process will provide the literary criticism for your paper. Making photocopies of the relevant pages of the sources, as well as their title pages and copyright information, is a good idea at this point.

Before reading your newfound critical pieces, go back to your preliminary outline. How does it look to you after spending some time with the critics? Do you have a section or two that seems like it needs to be expanded, tweaked, or dropped? Does each section seem like fertile ground for discussion? Do the critics have commentary on these issues? Do you still think it's important to cover these issues in your paper? Touch up your outline, promoting it from preliminary to final. Then it's time to enter…the critic's zone.

Reading Literary Criticism

You now have a set of sources that has passed a couple of cursory examinations. It's time to get serious. Choose the source that is least scary. If it's an article, glance through the whole thing. If it's an entire book, locate the chapter or section that seems most relevant. (If the entire book seems relevant, your thesis is probably too broad.)

Get a sense of whether the whole article or section is relevant to your thesis, or if only a passage of it is particularly juicy. Read those juicy sections carefully and thoroughly. (Here's an insider's tip: For most scholarly writing like this, some portion of it—usually toward the beginning—is devoted to hashing over what other critics have said about the topic. That may be useful to you if you're looking for other sources, but it makes for deadly dull reading. Skip it. In fact, whenever your critic references another critic, you can usually skip that, too.)

Read the most relevant criticism again. Summarize, in no more than four words, each section's essence in the margin of your photocopy. Or write the applicable heading from your preliminary outline in the margin of your copy of the article. This will enable you to easily find the most useful passages of criticism again when you need them. Work your way like this through each of your sources, noting the most relevant sections and briefly summarizing them in the margins.

Literary criticism can be frustrating for a number of reasons. One of the primary causes of frustration is that you may be hoping to find a critic who says exactly what you want to say in your paper. Wouldn't that be nice? It's probably not going to happen. Instead of the critics writing about what you want them to write about, they have their own ideas. You are in search of the critical commentary that supports or overlaps your thesis in some way. That's the best you can hope for.

Be concise.

Let's say, for example, that you're interested in writing about the portrayal of women in Flannery O'Connor's novel *Wise Blood*, and you can't find a piece of criticism dealing with that specific topic.

Then you look at a book entitled *New Essays on Wise Blood,* edited by Michael Kreyling and published by Cambridge University Press. You see a critique entitled "The Woman without Any Bones: Anti-Angel Aggression in *Wise Blood,*" by Patricia Smith Yaeger. It's worth a look, right? But this essay's focus isn't exactly on your topic. It deals primarily with O'Connor's "curious refusal to allow herself to be gendered," but as the author seeks to illuminate that idea, she simultaneously has a lot to say about the female characters in *Wise Blood.* Those comments, while they're not central to Yaeger's thesis, are very useful for yours.

As you work your way through the criticism, keep your thesis in front of you on a piece of paper or note card. Glance at it frequently as you read. Constantly ask yourself, *Is this relevant to my thesis?* Your instincts about finding useful material will grow sharper as you continue this process.

When writing an in-class essay in any subject area, or answering an essay question on a test in any subject area, keep two goals in mind: focus and elaborate.

Focus means that you should confine yourself to answering the question that the test or prompt requires and not stray off topic. Frequently, a suggested approach to the answer is embedded in the prompt. For example, imagine you are faced with this question from American history: *Discuss the positive and negative results of the 1945 Yalta Conference that helped end World War II.* In this case, you know that you should go beyond simply stating that the Yalta Conference helped end World War II. The question assumes that you know at least that much. The question also demands that you provide positive and negative outcomes of the conference, so be sure to have some of each.

Elaborate means that you should give details. In other words, say everything you know about this subject while still maintaining the focus on the question. Students sometimes try to outguess essay questions and write the minimum amount necessary to get all the points. Instead, you should write in as much detail as possible.

Remember that your purpose in this writing situation is to convince your audience (in this case, your teacher) that you know the material extremely well. Focusing on the requirements of the prompt and writing with elaborate detail helps you to accomplish that purpose.

Developing Your Literary Analysis

Let's take stock of where you are in this process. You have thoughtfully refined your thesis to a workable idea that is not too narrow and not too broad. In fact, it's perfect!

You have developed a preliminary outline, and you have adjusted it to reflect any changes you deemed necessary after skimming your sources.

You have found exactly the right number of worthwhile sources, and you have read each of them a few times, and now you're relatively sure you know the critics' main points and how they connect to your thesis and a section of your outline.

At this point, you are pretty much finished with the *research process*. It's time to get on with the *writing process*. If finding and reading those sources seemed like a visit to the local quicksand beach, rejoice! You're back on solid ground as a writer. Everything you know about writing is ready for you to put to use. You can approach the task of developing your literary analysis in one of two ways. The first way is to simply set aside the critics for awhile. Write *your* analysis. Develop your ideas about the thesis. What did you realize as you read and thought about this work? Follow your final outline, and write your way through each of the subtopic headings. When you have finished this process, it's time to go back and blend the critical commentary with the ideas that you have written about. Skim through the critical essays you collected, referring to the notes you wrote in the margins to find the relevant passages. At this point it should be fairly simple for you to insert a few carefully chosen quotations from these other critics in your own essay, along with parenthetical citations to show where the quotations came from. As you look at the criticism now, you should see it a bit differently. Before, you were looking at the criticism as a reader, someone trying to *comprehend* it. Now you are looking at the criticism as a writer, someone focused on *using* it for your own purpose.

The other approach to developing your analysis is to write it one outline section at a time. Begin with the section with which you're most comfortable, and then write what *you* have to say about it. Then include relevant quotations from other critics to supplement your own ideas. Either one of these approaches yields a similar writing product; your choice simply depends on your own preferences. Don't forget that the criticism you use in your paper needs to be properly cited, as you learned in Chapter 9 in the sections "Writing Your Works Cited List" (pages 337–339) and "Including Internal Documentation" (pages 344–348). (See also Appendix D.) As you work the literary criticism into your paper, be sure to use only the pithiest, most powerful and relevant parts. Perhaps you will quote full sentences or even an entire paragraph written by a critic, but that is not necessary and probably not even a very good idea. After all, the critic was writing those sentences as part of a work with a different purpose. You are lifting grafts of the critic's work to suit *your* purpose. His sentence structure may not suit your purpose. So, again, take only the most salient phrase of the criticism and craft a sentence of your own that includes it. If you absolutely must use whole sentences to capture the idea of the critic, then your duty as a writer is to smoothly integrate that quote into your own writing.

For example, critic Elizabeth Meese wrote this sentence in her essay about Zora Neale Hurston's use of oral language in *Their Eyes Were Watching God*: "One of Janie's greatest lessons about language centers on its power to deconstruct and to construct, to kill or to give life" (67–68). That's a fine sentence, and it serves Meese's purpose perfectly. However, if you are writing about a somewhat different topic—let's say the characteristics of the narrator in that same work—Meese's sentence may augment your purpose as well. You can embed the most powerful part of Meese's sentence in your writing like this:

> One way that Janie's narration is important is due to "its power to deconstruct and to construct, to kill or to give life" (Meese 67–68).

A sentence like this effectively and efficiently uses the essence of the critical commentary to support and illuminate *your* purpose. Again, remember to provide a citation referencing Meese's original essay.

Let's consider a different example. In an interview published in *The Best of* Spitball, *the Literary Baseball Magazine*, W. P. Kinsella, author of *Shoeless Joe*, responded this way to an interviewer's question about whether it was important for a writer to have an emotional tie to a particular setting:

> Oh, yeah. I think it can't help but help if you have a place that you have feelings for. I've never had any feelings for a place before I went to Iowa. I lived in Alberta, was raised in Alberta, and it's a horrible, cold, ugly place. And I've lived on the coast, and I do like it very much here in the Pacific Northwest, but I don't have a terrible affection for it. I could move away from here and not feel any regrets. I like Iowa very much, though.

Kinsella definitely answers the interviewer's question. Let's say, however, that you are interested in how the setting of Iowa is developed in the novel *Shoeless Joe*. You might write a sentence like this:

The charm of Iowa in Kinsella's book may be based on the fact that Kinsella "never had any feelings for a place before [he] went to Iowa" ("The Spitball Interview" 65).

Again, you have taken a relevant phrase that was originally uttered for a somewhat different purpose and validly used it as a means of developing your own analysis and properly cited it, giving credit to the source in which you found it. (For a review of how to cite your sources, see the section "Including Internal Documentation" in Chapter 9, pages 344–348.)

Try to plan so that, after writing your way through all of this—explaining your own ideas with support and illumination from the work of critics—you have a day or so to set aside your work before editing it. When it's time to edit—a process different from both research and writing—keep in mind that you want this particular piece to be as engaging for a reader as anything you have ever written. The fact that it is literary research doesn't mean it has to be stodgy, stiff, or boring. Allow your writing voice to speak. The voice may be moderated a bit because of the inclusion of critical commentary, but it should still be uniquely yours.

Before we end this chapter, we want to draw your attention to a few key terms mentioned throughout this section: *blend, mesh, fully integrate*. In other words, it's not enough to cleverly insert comments or ideas from critics in the right places. The lines must flow organically to and from the body of your own work. If this sounds confusing, here's a simple guideline from the previous chapter on research:

1. **Introduce your source.** If the critic you're quoting is an expert in some area, mention this. To infer that the source is a critic—or to occasionally label the person a "critic"—is usually sufficient.

2. **Insert the critic's ideas.** Use quotation marks if using exact words.

3. **Briefly comment on the critic's ideas.** A simple transitional phrase is often enough.

To understand the effectiveness of this guideline, study the first three paragraphs of the professional model on Raymond Carver at the end of this chapter. (By the way, reading the essay alone, without reading the story by Carver, may be confusing.) The sentences in those paragraphs blend and mesh gracefully. Though the result seems effortless, the integration requires careful attention. Here's an excerpt from that essay's third paragraph:

> Detachment, in fact, is one of the fictive stances by which Carver achieves startling effects. As James Atlas says, the stories' "minimality gives them a certain bleak power." Because the endings of the stories are truncated, the reader-as-literary detective must often supply the conclusion.

We said at the beginning of this chapter that writing about literature is daunting. Following the steps you've just learned will lead you to the completion of a scholarly piece of writing that may spark a lifelong interest for you in a particular book, author, or genre. You can truthfully consider yourself to be an expert on your thesis. At a minimum, this process will provide an intellectual experience that will serve you well in college or any time that you are required to develop sophisticated ideas that take into account work previously accomplished by others.

Practice

Before beginning the Chapter Assignment, try the following exercises to practice the steps involved in writing about literature.

1. Pick a novel or poem you've discussed in one of your classes. Write down one major theme that runs through the work and offer an example that highlights that theme. Remember to use the historical present tense.

   The Great Gatsby examines how wealth can corrupt people. For example, Tom Buchanan, because of his status, is allowed to have affairs, as long as he conceals the affairs according to the customs of the rich.

2. Make a list of similarities and differences between two fictional characters. Analyze the list, trying to discern any intriguing connections that might be worth exploring in an essay. Write a thesis statement for each connection that you identify.

3. Analyze the following poem by William Wordsworth. Focus on theme. What does Wordsworth seem to be saying about childhood and growing up?

   ### My Heart Leaps Up When I Behold

   My heart leaps up when I behold
   A rainbow in the sky:
   So was it when my life began;
   So is it now I am a man;
   So be it when I shall grow old,
   Or let me die!
   The Child is father of the Man;
   And I could wish my days to be
   Bound each to each by natural piety.

Chapter Assignment

Prewriting

Your assignment for this chapter is to write a literary analysis. Use the following suggestions to help you choose a topic and clarify the purpose of your essay.

With a particular literary work in mind, take another look at these questions reprinted from the section "Choosing a Literary Thesis." Choose three that you feel might work for you to develop, and then write for one minute on each of those topics. Do any of them seem like fertile territory for you? If not, try three more.

1. Discuss how a character is different from the other characters in the work.

2. How do details in the work, such as figurative language, dialogue, or imagery, combine to create the setting?

3. Contrast the work's various settings.

4. What are the most obvious characteristics of the work's form? Is it extremely short or extremely long? Does it have huge amounts of dialogue? Does the point of view shift dramatically? Choose one of these characteristics and write about how it fulfills the author's purpose.

5. Which characters are similar? Which characters are so different that they are essentially opposites? What does this tell you about the author's purpose?

6. Does the author use a recurring motif or image? What are examples of this recurrence, and what do they reveal about the author's purpose?

7. How is this work representative of or significantly different from other works by the same author or in the same genre? (This obviously presumes that you are familiar with some other works.)

8. How is this work representative of its time? How have perceptions of its cultural aspects shifted?

9. Describe your personal involvement with this work. What incidents from your own life affected the way you experienced this piece? How does your own philosophy or bank of personal experiences prevent this work from appealing to you?

10. Why was this piece of writing influential on other writers, artists, or its time? Was it popular during its time? Why or why not?

11. Is this work morally acceptable to you? Why or why not? (Since morals vary from person to person, this topic is as much about you as it is about the work under study.)

Writing Topics

Your teacher may want to assign the topic for this chapter. Otherwise, if you are allowed to select your own topic, consider choosing the thesis that offered the most possibilities for you in the Prewriting exercise. If your teacher requires literary research, be sure to follow the steps described in this chapter.

Revision

Before submitting your final literary research project, use the following checklist.

1. Have you consistently used the present tense when discussing the work?

2. Have you included citations for all direct quotes and ideas from other authors?

3. Is your Works Cited page alphabetized, indented correctly, and punctuated correctly?

4. Is your thesis clear? Have you fulfilled its promises?

5. Are your direct quotes smoothly integrated into your own sentences wherever possible? Do you comment on each quote, or use a transition after the quote?

6. Do you understand everything you have written? If not, where do you need to simplify or clarify?

Peer Review

Use these questions to help you evaluate another student's writing. Remember, specific suggestions and examples are most helpful.

1. Identify the writer's thesis. Is it clear? Where in the essay is it introduced?

2. Does every example support the thesis? Point out specific places where the examples do or don't support the thesis.

3. If you've read the work discussed in the paper, offer additional examples to support the thesis. If you haven't read it, try to find a place where an example could be made more clear.

4. How has the writer organized the paper? Is it easy to follow? If not, can you offer suggestions about how to improve it?

5. Has the writer used effective transitions? Provide examples.

6. What other suggestions do you have for improving this paper?

To get the idea of how literary criticism works, the Professional Essay section in this chapter involves two pieces. First you will read a short story by Raymond Carver called "Popular Mechanics." Following the story is Professional Essay 10.1, a literary critique entitled "Physical and Social Laws in Ray Carver's 'Popular Mechanics,'" by Norman German and Jack Bedell. Notice that these critics use footnotes instead of internal citations. The latter is better suited for current use.

Popular Mechanics
by Raymond Carver

Early that day the weather turned and the snow was melting into dirty water. Streaks of it ran down from the little shoulder-high window that faced the backyard. Cars slushed by on the street outside, where it was getting dark. But it was getting dark on the inside too.

He was in the bedroom pushing clothes into a suitcase when she came to the door.

I'm glad you're leaving! I'm glad you're leaving! she said. Do you hear?

He kept on putting his things into the suitcase.

Son of a bitch! I'm so glad you're leaving! She began to cry. You can't even look me in the face, can you?

Then she noticed the baby's picture on the bed and picked it up.

He looked at her and she wiped her eyes and stared at him before turning and going back to the living room.

Bring that back, he said.

Just get your things and get out, she said

He did not answer. He fastened the suitcase, put on his coat, looked around the bedroom before turning off the light. Then he went out to the living room.

She stood in the doorway of the little kitchen, holding the baby.

I want the baby, he said.

Are you crazy?

No, but I want the baby. I'll get someone to come by for his things.

You're not touching this baby, she said.

The baby had begun to cry and she uncovered the blanket from around his head.

Oh, oh, she said, looking at the baby.

He moved toward her.

For God's sake! she said. She took a step back into the kitchen.

I want the baby.

Get out of here!

She turned and tried to hold the baby over in a corner behind the stove.

But he came up. He reached across the stove and tightened his hands on the baby.

Let go of him, he said.

Get away, get away! she cried.

The baby was red-faced and screaming. In the scuffle they knocked down a flowerpot that hung behind the stove.

He crowded her into the wall then, trying to break her grip. He held on to the baby and pushed with all his weight.

Let go of him, he said.

Don't, she said. You're hurting the baby, she said.

I'm not hurting the baby, he said.

The kitchen window gave no light. In the near-dark he worked on her fisted fingers with one hand and with the other hand he gripped the screaming baby up under an arm near the shoulder.

She felt her fingers being forced open. She felt the baby going from her.

No! she screamed just as her hands came loose.

She would have it, this baby. She grabbed for the baby's other arm. She caught the baby around the wrist and leaned back.

But he would not let go. He felt the baby slipping out of his hands and he pulled back very hard.

In this manner, the issue was decided.

Discussion Questions

1. What conclusions can you make about this story? Consider both its plot and the unique elements of its form. As you think about these issues, *you* are the literary critic.

2. How does this story affect you? How does it make you feel? How are those effects accomplished? Exactly how does Raymond Carver use language to make his mark upon a reader?

3. Why do you think the story is titled "Popular Mechanics"?

Physical and Social Laws in Ray Carver's "Popular Mechanics"

by Norman German and Jack Bedell

Meet the Writer

Norman German and Jack Bedell are professors in the English Department at Southeastern Louisiana University in Hammond, Louisiana. This essay was published in *Critique* magazine.

> And yet let no admirer…resent my saying that at the first reading what most impressed me was not so much what was in the book as what was left out of it. —*Looking Backward*

The reviewers of Raymond Carver's 1981 collection of stories, *What We Talk About When We Talk About Love*, praise his "laconic and spare"[1] style for its "fierce compression"[2] and liken it to that of Anderson, Hemingway, Cheever, and Updike.[3] Apart from these labels, only one critic, Robert Houston, attempts to explain the reason for the style.

Houston says that "Carver's characters never have 'epiphanies.'… Yet there *is* revelation, a revelation that Carver locates not in the characters but in the reader.…"[4] Since Carver does not editorialize, the reader must discover for himself the morals—or, if you prefer, meanings—of the stories. Carver is, however, involved in morality, unlike his characters, who have experienced what David Boxer and Cassandra Phillips call "Carverian dissociation."[5] Carver's narrative art is detached from the emotions of his characters, but he disguises his concern for man's moral deficiencies so as to intrude as little as possible between the fiction and the reader. The actions of the characters are sufficient to carry his themes.

Detachment, in fact, is one of the fictive stances by which Carver achieves startling effects. As James Atlas says, the stories' "minimality gives them a certain bleak power."6 Because the endings of the stories are truncated, the reader-as-literary detective must often supply the conclusion.

A case in point is "Popular Mechanics," at little more than a page long, the shortest short-short story in *What We Talk About*. Ambrose Bierce's definition of love in *The Devil's Dictionary* ("a temporary insanity curable by marriage") might aptly have served as an epigraph to the story, for, despite its misleading title, its theme is the deterioration of love.

Puzzling though the title "Popular Mechanics" may be, Carver is not overly subtle or obscure about its intended meaning. The title, also the title of a magazine for do-it-yourselfers, should conjure up in the reader's mind, by story's end, physical laws such as "for every action there is an equal but opposite reaction." Before the tug of war begins between the young husband and wife for the baby, "they knocked down a flowerpot that hung behind the stove." A passage from Robinson's "Mr. Flood's Party" may serve as an informing contrast: "As a mother lays her sleeping child / Down tenderly, fearing it may awake, / He set the jug down slowly at his feet / With trembling care, knowing that most things break." The flowerpot should have reminded the parents in Carver's story that they, too, live in a world where most things, even children, break.

The man tries to "break [his wife's] grip" by holding "on to the baby and [pushing] with all his weight." Here, the greater force is bound to win. Next, he works "on her fisted fingers with one hand and with the other hand he gripped the screaming baby up under an arm near the shoulder." Obviously, he is trying to gain an advantage through leverage.

As the child slips from her, the wife catches "the baby around the wrist and [leans] back." The husband then feels "the baby slipping out of his hands and he [pulls] back very hard." In the tug of war, the woman first has the advantage, then the man, then the woman again, based on laws involving force, mass, and leverage.

The conclusion of the story is understated: "In this manner, the issue was decided." Based on mechanical laws, what can the reader know about the outcome of the contest of wills turned into a contest of strength?—that the husband "won," and that the baby lost. The grim conclusion, the breaking or dislocating of the baby's arm, occurs in the reader's mind, after some thought. The metaphor Carver works in the story is that of the baby as wishbone. And wishbones break. W. D. Snodgrass uses the same image in poem 3 of the sequential title poem to *Heart's Needle*, when the divorcing parents lift the child over a puddle by pulling it in opposite directions: "The child between them on the street / Comes to a puddle, lifts his feet / And hangs on their hands." The persona later calls the child "love's wishbone." An argument for influence, or extreme fortuity, can be made based on the fact that a similar incident is mentioned in Snodgrass's poem: "I tugged your hand, once, when I hated / Things less: a mere game dislocated / The radius of your wrist." Earlier, working a different image, Snodgrass says, "something somewhere has to give."

The final line of "Popular Mechanics," "the *issue* was decided," is a gruesome pun implying that the *argument* as well as the fate of the parents' offspring (issue) was decided. These two "popular mechanics" deal with their marital problem much as do-it-yourselfers might fix their cars: not with finesse, but by force. In the heat of the moment, both peaceful legal means and concern for the baby are forgotten.

Carver seems to be retelling and altering the story of Solomon and the two mothers (who were also prostitutes) to highlight a disconcerting fact of contemporary culture. In I Kings 3, two women have babies born three days apart. One woman's baby dies, and she exchanges her dead baby for the other woman's living baby. The just woman goes before Solomon with her complaint. Wisely, Solomon suggests dividing the baby with a sword and giving each woman half of the child. The just woman, with true motherly concern, urges Solomon not to slay the child, but to give it to the other woman, who in her turn says, "Let it be neither mine nor thine, but divide it."

In Carver's story, the baby's welfare is obviously not the "issue." Had the parents been tested by Solomon, they would have been served an equal share of their baby. In updating the story, Carver exposes a trait common to all in some degree, a selfish cruelty that often causes innocents to suffer. Interestingly, Snodgrass's "Heart's Needle: 3" concludes, "Love's wishbone, child, although I've gone / As men must and let you be drawn / Off to appease another, / It may help that... / Solomon himself might say / I am your real mother."

Ironically, the parents adore the icon of their baby but are careless with the baby itself. Early in the story, the husband is about to pack the baby's picture in his suitcase when the wife sees it and takes it to the living room. The argument over the baby's image turns into a struggle over the real baby, who, though identified as a boy, is usually referred to as "the baby," "this baby," or "it" ("She would have it, this baby"), thus disturbingly impersonalizing the child as an object to fight over—to the parents, a victory symbol and little else.

As Carver's other stories testify, this kind of squabble is too often the decadent result of "true love." In the opening sentence of "Popular Mechanics," the ideal of marriage is contrasted with the reality via a meteorological metaphor: "Early that day the weather turned and the snow was melting into dirty water." What was snowy pure is now corrupt.

In the expository first paragraph of the story, the light that seeps in on the characters from the outside world is fading rapidly. As the light dims, the civility of the parents wanes. After packing his belongings, the man need only turn off the light to put an end to this segment of his life. At the climax of the fight, when the baby is endangered, "the kitchen window [gives] no light."

Volume of sound is inversely proportional to amount of light in the story. The darker the setting gets, the louder the characters become. Yet, despite the shrill voices of the parents, the reader senses a histrionic air, a faking or exaggerating of emotions. Impervious to his wife's ravings, the husband simply keeps packing. Both have screamed at the other so often that they are immune to hostility—immune, even, to the baby's genuine screaming. The only remnant of true vitality in the house is the flowerpot behind the stove, and it is broken through carelessness. The breaking pot symbolizes the breakup of the marriage. Another reading is that the flowerpot contains no life—at least no plant is mentioned. Tucked away "behind the stove," away from the light, any once-potted flower would long since have withered. The empty pot is like the house, a lifeless hull.

The bedroom, the kitchen, the living room—places of warm familial gatherings and intimacy—constitute the story's settings. In a typically Carverian liminal emblem of people on the verge, the author situates the woman "in the doorway of the kitchen." Before and after this scene, the narrator says, "Streaks of [dirty water] ran down from the little shoulder-high window that faced the backyard" and "The kitchen window gave no light." In both passages, the window-as-threshold reminds the reader of the intimacy-distance dichotomy that Carver works throughout the story.

The turning off and on of lights and emotions in the story represents the ease with which contemporary lovers step in and out of marriages. The violence and hatred of the characters are the "popular mechanics," or *modus vivendi*, of present-day relationships. Here and in many of his stories, Carver paints a dark vision of the present state of human relations.

NORTHWESTERN STATE UNIVERSITY OF LOUISIANA

Notes

1. James Atlas, "Less is Less," *The Atlantic Monthly*, 247, 6 (June 1981) 97.
2. Meredith Marsh, "The Mutability of the Heart," *The New Republic*, 184, 17 (April 25, 1981) 38.
3. David Boxer and Cassandra Phillips, "*Will You Please Be Quiet, Please?*: Voyeurism, Dissociation, and the Art of Ray Carver," *Iowa Review*, 10, 3 (1980) 81.
4. Robert Houston, "A Stunning Inarticulateness," *The Nation*, 233, 1 (July 4, 1981) 23.
5. Boxer, 77.
6. Atlas, 97.

Discussion Questions

1. Do these critics explicitly state their thesis? If so, where? Is it repeated or reinforced anywhere else?

2. Do the references to other writers, critics, and stories with whom you may not be familiar seriously inhibit your understanding of this essay?

3. Notice the variety of ways that these authors incorporate Carver's words, phrases, and sentences into their text. How many different ways do they "attach" Carver's words to their own?

4. If you were assigned to write an essay about "Popular Mechanics," where would you begin?

Fate is Fate

by Mitch Dinterman

Meet the Writer

Mitchell Dinterman is a dedicated student and varsity athlete. Outside of school, his social life and extracurricular activities such as basketball, drum line, and volunteering occupy any extra time he might have. And although his plans for the future remain undecided, his search for the right school and major continues.

Fate is the decider of our lives, leading us step by step until the end. The wish of every human being is to have the access and the power to control his fate. Unfortunately, this is not the case, and our fate, in fact, is elusive to everyone. When we attempt to access what is inaccessible, we only become more confused. As a result, we fall further from the answer. By falling out of reach, we are only proving ourselves incapable of knowing our fate. This common struggle is seen through the life of Joseph K. in Franz Kafka's *The Trial*, where he, too, cannot come to understand his fate despite the great efforts exerted. He then struggles until he reaches the end and finally confronts death. In *The Trial*, Franz Kafka shows that man is continuously persecuted by an inescapable destiny. As Joseph K. is dragged along by his unavoidable fate, he exemplifies a key Everyman obstacle and consequently loses his sense of self-assurance and composure.

No matter our wish for our destiny, escaping fate is simply impossible. Throughout the book, Kafka drives to illuminate this underlying focus: that fate is unalterable. Critic R. G. Collins is even more bleak: "Because everything has its own contradiction within itself, it ultimately reduces life to an optical illusion; our progress towards meaning is nothing but a trick" (55). There is no hope, then, in trying to alter the course of events because life will always lead to the end. In attempting to make sense of "the illusion," the situation only becomes more unattainable—not only unattainable, but strange, as K. heads to his first interrogation. "K. turned toward the stairs to make his way up to the Court of Inquiry, but then came to a standstill again, for in addition to this staircase he could see in the courtyard three other separate flights of stairs and besides these a little passage at the other end which seemed to lead into a second courtyard. He was annoyed that he had not been given more definite information about the room" (Kafka 35). K. is given a simple task, to arrive at a certain location and on time, but when he arrives he confronts an odd obstacle. As the trial progresses the characteristics of his situation become bizarre and unplanned. The sequence of events becomes more and more staged. As the events become concrete, K. sees survival as impossible. "K. now saw himself continually threatened by mistakes intruding into his work from all sides which he was no longer able to circumvent" (Kafka 198). In fact, survival can only be achieved through constant alertness and commitment, which is a feat unfeasible for man.

Juggling both his trial and his job at the bank, K. is unable to succeed. David Grossvogel simply points out that "Once more, K. is outside an event that concerns him but that he cannot penetrate" (193). The truth that K. is searching for is never known or influenced by anyone. K. can fight and defend himself all he wants but he would only be wasting his efforts. "The Court can never be dislodged from that conviction. If I were to paint all the Judges in a row on one canvas and you were to plead your case before it, you would have more hope of success than before the actual Court" (Kafka 150). Kafka uses a painting in Titorelli's explanation to emphasize K.'s impenetrability. Once a painting has been created, there is no way to make changes. In K.'s situation, there is no way to change the opinions of the officers. In addition to informing K. of the uselessness in trying, Titorelli warns K. that real acquittals only occur in legends. Therefore, escaping his fate would be impossible; even searching for the answer would be useless.

Beyond being inevitable, K.'s fate is also disguised and distances him from the truth. Frederick J. Hoffman interestingly reveals that "At no time is the crime specified; at no time are the officials or minions of the Law made to look like monsters or grotesques. They are common variants of the human condition, of which K. is himself the central image" (192). These officials, who may seem like monsters to K., never appear as anything but normal men; these men are able to skillfully maintain a watch on K. And although the crime is never announced, K. takes no initiative in seeking the answer. Instead, he assumes that his fate would be stated to him:

> "Dear Uncle," said K., "it's no use getting excited, it's as useless on your part as it would be on mine. No case is won by getting excited, you might let my practical experience count for something." (Kafka 97)

In this passage, K. speaks in an impassionate tone to show his resigned attitude toward his trial. As his fate is disguised and never revealed, K. is left hopeless. He never once looks past the appearance of a situation to find the true meaning. "Must I, he thought, let myself be confused still worse by the gabble of those wretched hirelings?—they admit themselves that's all they are" (Kafka 7). Joseph K. only sees the warders as what they present themselves to be, and truly believes that they are nothing more than miserable and worthless men. K. does not treat the warders as if they know what K. only wishes he knew, and this is a result of his lack of comprehension. If Franz Kafka had wanted the warders to appear grotesque, they would be scarier and have a much different effect on K. Kafka has the ability to portray the warders however he wishes, but he chooses the image of common men. In doing this, he disguises the warders and continues to disguise K.'s fate until the end. Because fate is disguised, man is incapable of knowing his fate. This decision is important in showing K.'s interpretation to be limited and weak.

This lack of understanding is not visible to man until the very end when he acknowledges his failure to know the truth. This is seen in both the parable, "Before the Law," and in K.'s life. In the parable, the man waiting outside the Law "perceives a radiance streaming inextinguishably from the door" (Kafka 214) just before he dies. The man's vision of light represents his realization of his incapability to enter the door of the Law. Similarly, in *The Trial*, as K. walks to his death, the moonlight shines on him. Soon after K.'s awareness of the moonlight, he apologizes to his escorts for struggling earlier in their walk. "'I didn't mean to stop,' he said to his companions, shamed by their obliging compliance" (Kafka 226). K. is finally acknowledging the impossibility of survival. "K. now perceived clearly that he was supposed to seize the knife himself, as it traveled from hand to hand above him, and plunge it into his own breast" (Kafka 228). In both cases, just before death, the fate is realized and accepted.

As K. does end up dying, the argument is made that fate is not only determined, but also dark and cynical. Harold Bloom extracts an important line from a diary belonging to Franz Kafka that was used throughout the writing of *The Trial* and also led to the characterization of Joseph K.: "For I have gone the tiniest step upward, won any, be it the most dubious kind of security for myself, I then stretch out on my step and wait for the Negative, not to climb up to me, indeed, but to drag me down from it" (13). Likewise, each time K. catches a glimpse of the light or takes a step in the positive direction, he is drawn back into darkness.

To highlight these themes, Kafka utilizes many additional rhetorical strategies. His frequent misinterpretations serve as signs of his increasing incapability to see the truth. One of K.'s most obvious struggles is his conversation with the bank president and the Italian client. Despite his knowledge and background with the Italian language, K. can only nod as if to understand what is being said behind the Italian's thick mustache. Soon K. realizes that there is very little chance of communication between himself and the Italian. Here Kafka also uses the image of water to emphasize K.'s incomprehension by saying "the words mostly came pouring out in a flood" (Kafka 200). Another situation demonstrating K.'s inability to realize what is in front of him, representative of his fate, is when he visits Leni in Dr. Huld's office. "That picture was painted when he was young, but it could never have been in the least like him, for he's a small man, almost a dwarf...He is an Examining Magistrate...That's all invention...Actually he is sitting on a kitchen chair, with an old horserug doubled under him" (Kakfa 108). K., who knows something about art, thinks he understands this portrait but does not. He misreads it as a great judge but Leni informs him what the painting truly portrays. Later, as K. enters the cathedral, the lighting makes it impossible for him to distinguish something as simple as a column from a statue. "From a distance it looked like an empty niche intended for a statue" (Kafka 206). Ultimately, K. is lost.

Through imagery also, Kafka is able to emphasize and further develop the hopelessness K. has obtained. Walter Sokel offers this insightful example: "Even by such an apparently minor feature as the use of the image of water does Kafka point to that reversal of evaluation. In K.'s waking life, which is his trial, only the negative side of the image of water is allowed to appear" (81). In fact, Kafka uses the dark side of water, seasickness, to convey bewilderment, helplessness and terror in a world stripped of comprehensibility, familiarity and protection: "He felt as if he were seasick. He felt he was on a ship rolling in heavy seas. It was as if the waters were dashing against the wooden walls, as if the roaring of breaking waves came from the end of the passage, as if the passage itself pitched and rolled and the waiting clients on either side rose and fell with it" (Kafka 72). In the Court offices, K. feels nauseous and hopeless and not until he gets outside does he feel better. This helplessness, directly correlated with the image of water, comes from K.'s attempts to control his destiny. Through this symbol of water, Kafka expands on K.'s incapability to evade fate: "The water, glittering and trembling in the moonlight, divided on either side of a small island, on which the foliage of trees and bushes rose in thick masses, as if bunched together" (Kafka 226). This scene is very symbolic as K. is like the island, surrounded by the hopelessness the water carries. Like the bushes and trees, he is stuck with all other people, grouped together as one, possessing the same troubles brought on by fate. K. looks down the length of this river on the way to his death, and the hopelessness that his fate carries now returns. K. is unable to escape the unfortunate significance of the dark image of water and is then executed.

But one year before K.'s execution, he is arrested; throughout the entire trial, K. believes himself to be innocent. While talking to the priest, K. finally decides to rebel. "'But I am not guilty,' said K.; 'it's a mistake. And, if it comes to that, how can any man be guilty? We are all simply men here one as much as the other'" (Kafka 210). K., in trying to avoid his fate, is guilty. Therefore, by saying that all men are deserving of the same treatment, K. proves that no man is innocent. Guilt has become our fate, a fate in which we are all deserving. Harold Bloom adds this psychological interpretation: "Joseph K. has no con-sciousness of having done wrong, but just as Freudian man nurtures the desire to destroy authority or the father, so even Joseph K. has his own unfulfilled wishes against the image of the Law" (18). K. has convinced himself that he is innocent and that guilt is not a possibility, but the truth is he is guilty like any other Freudian man. Attempting to destroy or ignore authority does nothing; guilt is omnipresent and should never be doubted because we are all deserving in some way.

While guilt is bound to find us all at some point, this guilt comes with many complications. A.E. Dyson maintains that "There is noth-ing in him of human generosity or religious vision; he has no natural or supernatural resources against the charge of 'guilt.' In this, his mentality colours events, contributing more to the nightmare than at first we might suspect" (71). Guilt builds upon these nightmares and adds to the extreme darkness and helplessness that come with the inevitability of fate. As K. converses with Block, Block informs him of all the talk and conspiracies about the hopelessness of his fate. "And one of the superstitions is that you're supposed to tell from a man's face, especially the line of his lips, how his case is going to turn out. Well people declared that judging from the expression of your lips you would be found guilty, and in the near future too" (Kafka 174). The trial's fate and guilt have gradually taken K.'s confidence away from him, absorbed K.'s personality and have become his constant expression. Before the trial reaches any definitive result, the outcome is apparent to all; the trial is a foregone conclusion.

What pushes K. along increasingly faster to the end is his very own loss of confidence and composure. K.'s loss of self-assurance begins with insecurities when he is arrested. Frederick Hoffman notes that "This introductory shock is of the utmost importance to the impression the novel will ultimately have. It suggests to the intrusion of the absurd into a world protected on all sides by familiar assurances and securities" (190). K. no longer lives in a world of securities; Kafka started the story with the intrusion to leave plenty of time for K. to become even more insecure. K.'s insecurities only increase as the inability to answer basic questions becomes clear. Dyson then further develops this idea, suggesting that "He is plunged into a position where he finds himself alone and isolated, not knowing the rules, not knowing if there are any rules; life itself at stake, and no 'path or friendly clue' to be his guide" (61). K. is made to feel uncertain and frustrated similar to the feeling of a nightmare, without anyone to seek help from or to consult when needed.

K. experiences a nightmare of his own one night as he is leaving the bank; he finds the warders receiving yet another whipping:

> All the next day K. could not get the warders out of his
> head; he was absent-minded and to catch up on his work had to
> stay in his office even later than the day before. As he passed the
> lumber-room again on his way out he could not resist opening
> the door. And what confronted him, instead of darkness he had
> expected, bewildered him completely. Everything was still the
> same, exactly as he had found it on opening the door the previ-
> ous evening (Kafka 89).

K. has now become completely insecure and has lost any confidence he had remaining. His situation grows around him, absorbs him and moves him even further away from normality. The strongest likelihood is that his situation may lead to madness and a loss of composure. According to R.G. Collins, this composure may be inevitable: "More truly, the nature of man's dilemma is struggle—this is the contradiction peculiar to it. We are hopeless, but cannot help struggling" (56). K. and man, who have lost composure and confidence will struggle until death completes their fate. This struggle is seen as K. is being taken to his execution site. "Into his mind came a recollection of flies struggling away from the flypaper till their legs were torn off. The gentlemen won't find it easy" (Kafka 225). Kafka successfully uses a fly to characterize K.'s situation. The tiny creature is so bothersome and will struggle to free itself in a perilous situation. But in the end, the fly is helpless in size and strength in comparison to the fly paper. Likewise, K. cannot allow himself to die without struggling, but his efforts are useless, for his destiny will not change.

In *The Trial*, Franz Kafka shows that man is continuously persecuted by an inescapable destiny. As Joseph K. is dragged along by his unavoidable fate, he exemplifies a key everyman obstacle and consequently loses his sense of self-assurance and composure. No matter what transpires in K.'s life or man's life, significant or insignificant, life will always end the same way. There is nothing anyone can possibly do to alter his fate. Man shares this struggle and as a result constantly worries, grows increasingly anxious and eventually loses all confidence. Man is guilty of this and Kafka effectively proves through K.'s story that fate is something that is completely inevitable. The harder man tries to ignore this and create his own fate, the more blinded he becomes and the quicker his fate seems to absorb him, leading him straight to death.

Works Cited

Bloom, Harold. Introduction to Franz Kafka's *The Trial*. Ed. Harold Bloom. New York: Chelsea House Publishers, 1987. 1–22. Print.

Collins, R. G. "Kafka's Special Methods of Thinking." *Mosaic 3*, No. 4 (Summer 1970). Rpt. In Franz Kafka's *The Trial*. Ed. Harold Bloom. New York: Chelsea House Publishers, 1987. 41–56. Print.

Dyson, A. E. "Trial by Enigma: Kafka's *The Trial*." *Between Two Worlds: Aspects of Literary Form*. New York: Macmillan, 1972. Rpt. in Franz Kafka's *The Trial*. Ed. Harold Bloom. New York: Chelsea House Publishers, 1987. 57–72. Print.

Grossvogel, David I. "*The Trial:* Structure as Mystery." *Mystery and its Fictions: From Oedipus to Agatha Christie.* Baltimore: The Johns Hopkins University Press, 1979. Rpt. in Franz Kafka's *The Trial.* Ed. Harold Bloom. New York: Chelsea House Publishers, 1986. 183–197. Print.

Hoffman, Frederick J. "Kafka's *The Trial:* The Assailant as Landscape." *Bucknell Review* IX, No. 2 (May 1960): 89-105. Rpt. in *Twentieth-Century Literary Criticism.* Ed. Dennis Poupard and Paula Kepos. Vol. 29. Detroit: Gale Research Inc., 1988. 190–193. Print.

Kafka, Franz. *The Trial.* Trans. Willa and Edwin Muir. New York: Shocken Books Inc., 1935. Print.

Sokel, Walter H. "The Three Endings of Josef K. and the Role of Art in *The Trial.*" *The Kafka Debate: New Perspectives for Our Time.* New York: Gordian Press, 1977. Rpt. in Franz Kafka's *The Trial.* Ed. Harold Bloom. New York: Chelsea House Publishers, 1987. 73-94. Print.

Discussion Questions

1. This kind of essay is often difficult to appreciate if you haven't read the primary source, in this case, Kafka's *The Trial*. But this essay provides a rich glimpse into that source. After reading the essay, what are your impressions of the book?

2. Read the first two paragraphs again. In as few words as possible, write down Dinterman's thesis.

3. Dinterman introduces, then comments on, the ideas of other critics he uses to support his thesis. Identify what you believe is the strongest use of this critical support. In particular, identify the transitions used, both before and after the source is inserted.

4. Take a look at the transitions used throughout the essay. List two that work well.

5. If you were a peer editor of this essay, what two suggestions would you offer? Be specific.

Chapter 11

Writing the College Application Essay

magine for a moment that you are a college admissions officer. Your work today consists of perusing the contents of a stack of files. Each file contains the transcript, standardized test results, application form, resume, and other materials relating to a student who has applied for admission to your school. In addition, each file also contains an essay written by the student in response to a prompt provided by the college. You hope that those materials will provide you with a profile of the student's aptitude as well as some insights into the student's personality, work ethic, and interests as you seek to discover whether this student is a viable candidate for admission to your school.

You choose a file. The student is in the top half of her class, and she has participated in many activities. Her college entrance exam scores are respectable, but many students have higher scores. At this point, you're thinking, *This student is a Maybe. I'll look at her essay.*

The first page of this essay has the student's name and the words "Application Essay" centered at the top. You say to yourself, *That's not a title; it's a label. Not a strong start here.* As you read the essay, you find that the student has written about how her part-time job gave her experience in dealing with many types of people. You shift in your chair because you have read dozens of essays on this topic over the years. In fact, it's probably the topic most often chosen by students, second only to revelations gained on various vacations and morals learned from recently deceased relatives. You're pretty sure that this essay will be completely predictable in its approach and organization, and you're right. The writing is actually quite competent. This student probably received mostly A's and B's on her papers in high school.

As you finish the essay, you find that your opinion of this student has not been enhanced by reading this essay. She is still a Maybe.

You choose another file. This student ranks in the middle of his class at an academically rigorous high school. He scored reasonably well on his college entrance exam, but many other applicants scored better. In high school, he has been involved in one sport, and he served on student council, but he did not hold a leadership position in either of those activities. At this point, you're thinking, *This student is also a Maybe. Let's look at his essay.*

You pull the essay from the file. At first glance, you notice that it has a catchy title, and it's neatly prepared. The paragraphs look about right—not too long, not too short. As you begin to read the essay, you notice that the student is a reasonably accomplished writer. Not only does he use fresh, vivid, detailed language, but his sentences are engagingly complex, and the essay has that elusive sense of flow.

The content of the essay tells you some important information about the student. He is interested in archery, although his school doesn't offer it as a sport or club. *Hmm,* you think. *I don't know if I've ever read an essay about archery.* As you continue to read, you discover that archery is not only an interest of this student; it also taught him some important life lessons as he mastered the sport and applied it in a variety of contexts. By the time you finish reading the essay, your understanding of this student has been greatly illuminated; you realize that he is a strong, mature individual with integrity, determination, and unique perspectives. He is also a strong writer. On the basis of his essay, he is no longer a Maybe. He's a Yes.

Writers on Writing

First I determine roughly how much I hope to achieve during a single writing session, aiming fairly high. Then I try to write or type swiftly and continuously, without agonising over the expression of each sentence. I don't worry about whether I am writing entirely without style, grace or accuracy. I just write, and cover the page. When I have finished, I leave it. I take a breather—by walking the dog; picking up the children; making the tea; watching TV; or going to bed. Later, or the next day, I take a look at what I have written. Now is the time to scrutinise it.

—*Susan Sellers*

Journal Topic

In a paragraph, describe your ideal college. What qualities do you think this ideal college seeks in its potential students?

These hypothetical scenarios are provided to show you that your approach to your college application essay can be crucial as you seek to fulfill the essay's purpose: helping you to gain admission to a particular college or university.

Essay Topics

The college admission essay is usually written on a topic provided with the school's admission materials. The Common Application is the standardized admission application used by dozens of American colleges and universities. Its essay prompts tend to be straightforward. Here are some recent examples:

- Evaluate a significant experience, achievement, risk you have taken, or ethical dilemma you have faced and its impact on you.

- Discuss some issue of personal, local, national, or international concern and its importance to you.

- Indicate a person who has had a significant influence on you, and describe that influence.

- Describe a character in fiction, an historical figure, or a creative work (as in art, music, science, etc.) that has had an influence on you, and explain that influence.

- A range of academic interests, personal perspectives, and life experiences adds much to the educational mix. Given your personal background, describe an experience that illustrates what you would bring to the diversity in a college community, or an encounter that demonstrated the importance of diversity to you.

- Topic of your choice.

Some schools provide notoriously wacky essay prompts. For example, the University of Chicago has used these unusual prompts in recent years:

- University of Chicago alumna and renowned author/critic Susan Sontag said, "The only interesting answers are those that destroy the questions." We all have heard serious questions, absurd questions, and seriously absurd questions, some of which cannot be answered without obliterating the very question. Destroy a question with your answer.

- Have you ever walked through the aisles of a warehouse store like Costco or Sam's Club and wondered who would buy a jar of mustard a foot and a half tall? We've bought it, but it didn't stop us from wondering about other things, like absurd eating contests, impulse buys, excess, unimagined uses for mustard, storage, preservatives, notions of bigness…and dozens of other ideas both silly and serious. Write an essay somehow inspired by super-huge mustard.

- How do you feel about Wednesday?

As different as these choices may seem, each has the same intent: To provide the college with an understanding of you, your outlook, your writing ability, and your viability as a student at their institution. Obviously, these questions have no specific right answer. The rightness of the answer is determined by how favorable an impression of you it makes upon its reader. Similarly, there is no formula. The college application essay is as distinct and highly individualized as each writer who approaches the task.

Essay-Writing Tips

With that in mind, we offer here some ideas to keep in mind as you write your college admission essay. Before you even look at prompts, have in mind some key personal characteristics that you would like the school to know about. Consider the traits of a successful college student: perseverance, curiosity, diligence, discipline, and so on. What can you write about that will unquestionably demonstrate that you possess one or more of these traits? If one of the prompts lends itself to such a discussion, choose that one. Otherwise, if an open-ended, write-your-own-question option exists, that might be the way to go. Maybe one of your earlier essays dealt with an image of yourself that you would like to convey. If so, you probably have a viable head start.

Keep in mind that those who review your application materials will know quite a bit about you from the other materials you provided. Consider using the application essay as an opportunity to demonstrate something *else* about you. Of particular importance may be activities, interests, or experiences that are important to you but that were separate from your academic experience. For example, perhaps you are accomplished at something for which your school does not have a program. Maybe you are a dedicated equestrian, and you spend a lot of time training in that area. If your high school does not include an equestrian club, your involvement and expertise in that area may never be known to the college admissions officials.

When you sit down to write an essay, rather than striving to write the perfect first sentence, jot down five possible first sentences, all of which are drastically different from each other. After you've written five or six possible openings, walk away. Let the dust settle. When you return, see whether one opening seems more compelling than another, or if one of them inspires yet another beginning. Even if you deem all five unworthy, at least you've approached the beginning from several angles, which may help you decide on the tone for your essay. And you'll know how you don't want to start your essay!

Writers on Writing

Re-examine each sentence that you put on paper. Is every word doing new work? Can any thought be expressed with more economy? Is anything pompous or pretentious or faddish? Are you hanging on to something useless just because you think it's beautiful?

Simplify, simplify.

—*William Zinsser*

Perhaps you are involved in humanitarian, voluntary, or mission work that is separate from your school life. If so, it may not be reported on your other forms and application materials. Consider using it as the basis of your application essay.

As you write your essay, be particularly mindful of your tone. An authentic tone is very important. Write with sincerity, but do not cross into melodrama. If you are writing about an episode or situation that is inherently emotional, describing your emotions in great detail is not a good idea. A better approach is to provide great detail about the event or situation itself and allow those details to evoke an emotional reaction from your reader. Your attitude toward the subject under discussion should be very clear, but any emotional reaction from your reader will arise naturally from your descriptions and not because of any emotions you may have experienced. In fact, you may risk alienating your reader if you expect him to react a certain way just because you did so. Allowing your reader to experience what happened through effective detail and description is more likely to result in your intended effect. If your reader has an emotional reaction, that's fine, but you can't force it upon him.

Similarly, your writing should reveal how your mind and heart work. Allow your reader to understand how you processed the subject under discussion. How did you first perceive it? How did your perceptions evolve and become more sophisticated? How did your various actions result in increasingly valuable realizations? In fact, it's quite possible that you will actually learn something about yourself as you write this essay. If so, be sure to include that as part of the essay's development.

Presenting your essay in the neatest, clearest format is always a good idea. (However, we do know a student who responded to an open-ended essay in an unusual format. The question said to use the essay space on the application to reveal something about himself. This student stapled candy wrappers and magazine photos of various American vice-presidents on the application form with no explanation whatsoever. Although the college accepted him, we can't really recommend this unorthodox approach for everyone.) Use your best sentence craftsmanship, subtle but effective transitions, and vivid language that takes risks. Submit your typed essay on clean paper in a font that is easy to read.

If you submit your essay through an online application process, be sure to edit and check your spelling carefully before you click Send. This is a step that many students forget to do.

Writers on Writing

A redundant word is an unnecessary word. Considering the high price of newsprint and book stock, we ought to watch for redundancies and pluck them from our writing as if we were plucking ticks off a dog's back. Redundancies, like ticks, suck the blood from our prose.

—*James J. Kilpatrick*

In addition, if your application materials stipulate a word count, be sure to follow it. Write as much as you can in early drafts. During the editing phase, make wise choices about what will most appeal to your audience and best fulfill your purpose.

In summary, these are the most important considerations to keep in mind when writing your college application essay:

1. Reveal something about yourself that will enable the admissions officials to see you as a unique individual.

2. Use details and description to enhance your reader's understanding of your experiences but not necessarily of your emotions.

3. Write in an authentic, sincere voice.

4. Demonstrate how your mind works as you become involved with a compelling situation, individual, or idea.

A well-written application essay will put you in the best possible light when that college admissions officer sits down with your file. If you have captured the best and most important aspects of yourself in the essay, and the college rejects you, that school may not be a good match for you. On the other hand, a college that selects you because your essay reveals that you are the kind of person who can be successful at that school is likely to provide you with a rewarding post–high school experience.

In the following essay, the dean of admissions from Pomona College in California describes the process of reviewing application essays.

Don't Be Bland
by Bruce Poch

For admissions officers, reviewing applications is like final-exam week for students—except it lasts for months. Great applications tell us we've done our job well, by attracting top-caliber students. But it's challenging to maintain the frenetic pace without forgetting these are all real people with real aspirations—people whose life stories we are here to unravel, if they will let us.

The essay is a key piece of learning those life stories. I live near Los Angeles, where every day screenplays are read without regard for human context. The writer's life and dreams don't matter—all that matters is the writing, the ideas, the end product. On the other hand, in reading essays, context does matter: who wrote this? We are driven to put the jigsaw puzzle together because we think we are building a community, not just choosing neat stories. When I pick up a file, I want to know whether the student has siblings or not, who his parents are, where he went to high school. Then I want the essay to help the rest of the application make sense, to humanize all the numbers that flow past. I am looking for insight.

A brilliantly written essay may compel me to look beyond superficial shortcomings in an application. But if no recommendation or grade or test score hints at such writing talent, I may succumb to cynicism and assume the writer had help—maybe too much. In the worst cases, I may find that I have read it before—with name and place changed—on the Internet, in an essay-editing service or a "best essays" book.

The most appealing essays take the opportunity to show a voice not rendered homogeneous and pasteurized. But sometimes the essays tell us too much. Pomona offers this instruction with one essay option: "We realize that not everything done in life is about getting into college. Tell us about something you did that was just plain fun." One student grimly reported that nothing was fun because in his family everything was about getting into college. Every activity, course choice and spare moment. It did spark our sympathy, but it almost led to a call to Child Protective Services as well.

Perfection isn't required. We have seen phenomenal errors in essays that haven't damaged a student at all. I recall a student who wrote of the July 1969 lunar landing of—I kid you not—Louis Armstrong. I read on, shaking my head. This student was great—a jazz trumpeter who longed to study astronomy. It was a classic slip and perhaps a hurried merging of two personal heroes. He was offered admission, graduated and went on for a Ph.D. in astrophysics. He may not have been as memorable if he had named "Neil" instead of "Louis" in his essay's opening line. Hey, we're human, too.

An essay that is rough around the edges may still be compelling. Good ideas make an impression, even when expressed with bad punctuation and spelling errors. Energy and excitement can be communicated. I'm not suggesting the "I came, I saw, I conquered" approach to essay writing, nor the "I saved the world" angle taken by some students who write about community-service projects. I'm talking about smaller moments that are well captured. Essays don't require the life tragedy that so many seem to think is necessary. Not all admission offers come out of sympathy!

Admissions officers, even at the most selective institutions, really aren't looking for perfection in 17- and 18-year-olds. We are looking for the human being behind the roster of activities and grades. We are looking for those who can let down their guard just a bit to allow others in. We are looking for people whose egos won't get in the way of learning, students whose investment in ideas and words tells us—in the context of their records—that they are aware of a world beyond their own homes, schools, grades and scores. A picture, they say, is worth a thousand words. To us, an essay that reveals a student's unaltered voice is worth much, much more.

When you work a math problem incorrectly, you just hit the calculator's clear button or erase your figures and start over. Because writing is more personal than most other academic or intellectual activities, you may hesitate to discard your words, even when you realize that a piece of writing is not your best work. You have invested something of yourself in those words, and it is painful to throw them away.

Although parting with words that you have worked on for hours or days is painful, that is exactly what you must do when you discover that your efforts have resulted in a piece of writing that is unlikely to satisfy you or your reader.

Maybe you only need to discard parts of your writing. Perhaps the introduction is salvageable, but you know the rest of it has problems. In that case, keep the introduction and rework the rest of it. On the other hand, if the introduction is the problem, then delete that section and keep the rest.

You owe it to yourself and your readers to present only the best work you can produce. You are truly a writer when you discard inferior work and set yourself to the task of producing better work.

Practice

Before beginning the Chapter Assignment, try the following exercises to help you select a topic for your college application essay.

1. Think of a friend of yours who wants to go to a college that requires an essay for admission. Begin that essay for your friend. Write approximately a paragraph.

2. On a sheet of paper, create two columns. In the left column, list your strengths. In the right column, list your goals. When you're done, draw lines connecting which strengths will help you achieve which goals.

3. Get together with a family member or friend, and ask this person to describe your strengths. For each strength, think of an example.

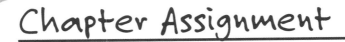

Chapter Assignment

Prewriting

Your assignment for this chapter is to write a college application essay. Use the following suggestions to help you choose a topic and clarify the purpose of your essay.

1. Create a list of goals you hope to have achieved before completing college. What will you need to do to accomplish those goals?

2. Make a list of your strengths. Include skills, attitudes, personal qualities, and anything else you can think of. Once you're ready to write your first draft, a little modesty may serve you well, but for now, give yourself a great pat on the back and let loose with praise for yourself.

3. Find the application essay prompts for the schools you want to attend. Students tend to freeze while thinking of an opening, so instead of sitting down and trying to determine *the* opening you will use, quickly and without censoring yourself, write *several* possible opening paragraphs. When you look back on these paragraphs after several days, you may find a few gems in them.

4. Discuss something that you feel passionate about. Later, when you begin to write your application essay, see if you can find a way to let these passions surface.

Writing Topics

Find the essay prompts from several colleges you want to attend and select one to be the focus of your essay.

Revision

As you revise and edit your first draft, consider these questions.

1. Have you directly answered the essay prompt? Does the essay fit the school's length requirement?

2. Will your opening capture the interest of an admissions counselor?

3. Have you used effective verbs? Study your sentences, one by one, before you decide. Also, review the section "Using Effective Verbs" in Chapter 2 (pages 52–54) for advice on this task.

4. Does each sentence and paragraph flow into the next? Consult the section "Using Transitions" in Chapter 4 (pages 135–137) for help.

5. Is the essay organized in a logical way? Might a different order work better?

Peer Review

As you read this essay, put yourself in the shoes of a college admissions counselor. Use the following questions to help you evaluate another student's writing. Remember, specific suggestions and examples are most helpful.

1. Does the essay provide you with a favorable impression of this candidate? Use specifics to explain why or why not.

2. What reservations do you have about this candidate, based on what you've read?

3. What passages work particularly well?

4. Focus on clarity. Which sentences could be phrased more directly or clearly?

5. What other suggestions do you have for improving this essay?

6. What questions do you have for this applicant?

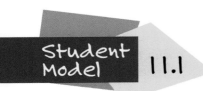

Silhouettes

by Katherine Berger

Meet the Writer

Katherine Berger's application essay helped her become a sociology and French double-major who enjoys reading and theorizing about current sociological issues even when she's not in class. She is currently studying abroad in Dakar, Senegal, where she enjoys playing soccer in the street with the kids in her neighborhood.

A caricature artist would jump at the chance to draw any of my four great-grandmothers as they appear in their yellowed portraits, displaying uncharacteristically distinguished features. Toothy smile, firm jaw, rough hands, wit-filled eyes—each feature begs the telling of a story. When told, I've seen each woman puff up and pull right off of the page. After some such storytelling event, I sit alone and trace their silhouettes with my pointer finger, hoping that as their shape becomes more familiar to my touch I will gain access to their thoughts as well.

Bertha's smile mirrored her spunk as her first black-buttoned boot hit the gangplank in Germany, a 13-year-old explorer ready to discover America for herself. Adeline's jawbone forever hardened in the wake of her third buried baby, knowing as she and her husband let dinner pass them by and onto 10 others, that perseverance, not worry, would see them through another winter as cold as last. Julia's hands lost their femininity through the work that filled the time between learning to spit and to survive a dust storm, developing confidence that on this Kansas frontier she could master anything the terrain threw at her. Last, Adella Katherine, my namesake and the recipient of my most ardent curiosity, for her story is told through the confident poise with which she wears her plumed hat, and the secret held within the eyes that peer out beneath the brim.

I have not wasted time in tracing their shapes; had I not, I could not take pride in the same prominent features that I see staring back at me from the mirror. But I was wrong in looking any farther than myself to learn of their hopes and joys and sorrows. In acts of love to the great-granddaughter they never knew, they wove their experiences through the marrow of my bones in a way less tangible than genetics. Written under my skin are Bertha's inner child, Adeline's courage, Julia's grit, and the secret behind Adella Katherine's eyes, her faith. They are incredible women of yesterday. I can be an incredible woman of today.

So I, along with these unearned traits, face each new day of what will be *my* story. As family, friends, teachers, and pastors pour into me, and I into them, I wonder what I will pass to my great-granddaughter when my life is simplified into one word.

Discussion Questions

1. Consider Berger's purpose in this essay: gaining admission to a college. What strategies did she adopt to fulfill that purpose? If you were a college admissions officer, what would you consider the positive and negative aspects of Berger's candidacy based on this application essay?

2. Berger obviously wants her audience to know some of the characteristics she shares with her great-grandmothers. Beyond those, what do you learn about Berger from the way she structures this essay and explains her topic?

3. Notice how Berger varies her sentence patterns. Do any of her sentences begin with the same word? Does she balance simple and complex sentences? What is the effect of this variety?

Personal Geography

by Alex Beata

Meet the Writer

Alex Beata lives at home with his parents, sisters, and the family dog. He is a casual writer, and his main academic interests lie in geography and other social studies. He could see himself as a college professor in ten years.

Geography has long been a keen interest of mine. As a child, I could lose myself in an atlas or an old copy of *National Geographic* for hours on end, mesmerized by the colorful pages and exotic names. As I grew older, my knowledge deepened, and I began participating in the "Geo Bee." I won the school-level competition five years in a row and advanced to the state level each year. I have placed 4th and 10th in the State of Illinois *National Geographic* Bee.

In searching for a career, something that will help to define my life, I believe that I must follow my passions. Only then will "work" cease to be work, but rather a daily adventure pursuing what I love. As someone who has routinely received globes and maps for birthday gifts, I clearly know where my passion lies. Now I have only to harness that energy and apply it to pressing current issues.

My lifelong pursuit of geography has deeply shaped my thinking. Geography has unveiled the true variety of cultures and peoples on this earth, and it has taught me to appreciate the common bonds of nature and humanity that unite us across cultural divides. Geography has shown me that all people are connected, even if by seemingly impossible ties, and that the decisions we make as individuals and as societies have far broader impact than we may first imagine. It is therefore imperative that we as a global community work together to overcome common problems and to build a better world. I understand that as Americans, we are just one of many peoples to inhabit this earth, and that our particular worldview is just one of many perspectives. Geography has taught me to respect and understand these perspectives, and to acknowledge both the diversity and broad commonalities of the world and its people.

Over the coming decades, resources such as oil and water, and their management, are going to be front-and-center on the domestic and international stage. Continued human growth and expansion will further tax natural resources, and the need to understand and design sustainable methods of balancing both human and environmental concerns will grow. People from across the globe are becoming closer every day through new technologies. As the global community matures, knowledge of the world and all its people will be more and more essential.

The only academic subject that can comprehensively span all these concerns is geography. It is my professional aspiration to one day help make intelligent, competent decisions in these matters. Each generation has a responsibility to leave for its children a better world than it received; I feel called to contribute to that task. Thus, what was once a childhood interest has now led me to a life's ambition. I trust that The George Washington University will give me the intellectual and professional foundation to achieve this goal.

Discussion Questions

1. Consider Beata's purpose in this essay: gaining admission to a college. What strategies did he adopt to fulfill that purpose? If you were a college admissions officer, what would you consider the positive and negative aspects of Beata's candidacy based on this application essay?

2. How does Beata seek to set himself apart from other applicants?

3. Beata obviously wants his audience to know about his passion for geography. Beyond that, what do you learn about Beata from the way he structures this essay and explains his topic?

The Zen of Clams

by Nicole Perry

Meet the Writer

Nicole Perry grew up on Martha's Vineyard, where she enjoys summers lifeguarding at one of the local beaches. An avid dancer and Scholastic Art Award winner, she balances her creative interests by participating in softball and cross country at her regional high school. Nicole plans to pursue a bachelor's degree in English.

"Could I get a hot dog without the actual meat, just some ketchup on a bun and maybe a little relish?" my mom asked.

The vendor stared back at her and laughed under her breath. Slowly, the squat woman reached for a bun, pausing for a minute to shake her head as she shoveled on some condiments and handed the pathetic looking meal over to my mom, all the while giving her that same condescending, belittling glance from the side of her eyes.

I hate that look. In an instant, it makes me maliciously protective of my mom, and I want nothing more than to snap back at the vendor: "Excuse me, allow me to point out that you work at a hot dog stand for a living and you're wearing a cardboard hat and an apron with a dancing soda can on it, so stop acting as if my mom is some sort of circus freak. Wipe that smug look off your face, and give the woman her damn ketchup and bread!"

I restrain myself to nothing more than a dirty look. A few moments later, as my mom and I eat our food at a nearby bench, I turn to her and sigh, "Mom, you are so weird. Honestly, just when I think you couldn't possibly be any stranger, you go and top yourself."

How ironic that the same attitude I give my mom every day about her "unique" beliefs and odd behavior, is also the attitude that I despise when it comes from other people.

Could it be then, that in reality we possess the very traits that we find undesirable and annoying in others? The characteristics we ascribe to our enemies could in fact be some of our own. And if that were the case, then essentially, no one is exempt from being labeled selfish or backstabbing or a liar. Perhaps we all possess these flaws, and above all, possess the inability to see these flaws within ourselves.

I remember last summer when my mom called me into the kitchen and asked me to pour the night's clams into a pot of boiling water.

"You called me all the way in here to dump a bag of clams into a pot of water that is four inches away from you?" I asked with a rude look of disbelief.

"Well I don't want to take on the negative karma of the clams' souls by aiding in their death." My mom always explained things with innocent patience, as if it were perfectly normal to fear clam karma. I gave my mom my familiar roll of the eyes and grabbed the heavy bag.

"You are so annoying, mom. Why can't you just be normal for once? You go to some hippy weirdo church in the woods of Chilmark, you meditate on a pillow in our basement closet, and now you won't even make dinner." I dumped in the clams, splashing hot water on the stove and stomped off.

What a hypocrite I am to judge my mom's beliefs and accuse her of being weird, all the while going to bed at night worrying about the bad clam karma on my soul and hoping that I didn't dump any sinners into that boiling pot of water.

I think that by recognizing the flaws within ourselves, we could be more understanding of those same flaws in others. Could this not be the start to eliminating hate and resentment? Isn't it what Gandhi meant in his hopes for peace by suggesting focusing on self-improvement instead of trying to improve the world?

It's hard for me still to criticize my mom when I face the fact that I was eager to eat the food she claimed was blessed by her guru, Sadu Ram, during my AP final exams. Not only that, but even when I have a house of my own, I will most likely still buy organic tampons and brown recycled napkins. Furthermore, when my mom isn't looking, I sometimes eat her dried kelp and aloe plants because deep down I do believe in their healing power.

If people could admit certain flaws and traits about themselves and embrace them as a part of who they are, then maybe when they see those same traits in others, they will be accepting and understanding. Could it be that the cause of all the world's hatred is nothing more than hypocrisy? And is the cure to end hypocrisy, or simply to accept the fact that we are all hypocrites?

It still bothers me sometimes that my mom didn't want to take on the bad karma of those clams, yet had no problem allowing me to do so, and it seems hypocritical. Perhaps this is why she is always so patient when I scoff at her beliefs and give her those icy stares, all the while becoming more and more like her each day.

Maybe it's that my mom knows that she, just like me and the rest of the world, are all hypocrites, and that by including herself in that massive group of flawed beings, she accepts and loves them all the more.

Discussion Questions

1. Perry begins with dialogue. Is this effective? What is achieved by this opening?

2. One purpose of the college application essay is to shed light on the writer. What do we learn about Perry from this essay?

3. What are the main lessons Perry has learned through her interaction with her mother? None of these lessons seem preachy. How does Perry avoid this trap?

4. If you were a college admissions officer, would you accept Perry to your school? Why or why not?

Writing Online

Most writers like to believe their writing will last a while, even if it's merely a matter of weeks. For instance, you may have saved copies of the essays you wrote this semester, maybe sharing a few with friends and family, relishing the praise your teacher lavished upon you. Maybe you've considered entering one of your essays in a contest or used one as a college admissions essay. Perhaps you have a place where you collect such essays and skim through them once in a while, which is a stark and sometimes painful reminder of how far you've come in your writing.

All of this suggests a deliberate, often slow process: gathering ideas, pounding out sentences, printing a hard copy, waiting for the paper to be graded, perhaps revising and waiting again. Writing for an *online* audience, however, streamlines and often changes this process. You compose, you post, and the message is transmitted to one person or blasted to potentially millions of people, who may respond within seconds. Speed is expected and prized. In fact, one of the original online messaging tools was called IM, short for *instant messaging*. How much of this speedy communication constitutes good writing is questionable. How much of it will last is unclear.

On the other hand, we're inspired and encouraged by the way writers have adapted to this new medium. If you've ever posted or commented on a blog, updated your status on an online social network, or written on a microblogging site that limits your posts to a certain number of characters, you're already aware that your online writing can be shaped by the technology you're using. Here's a little secret: some adults are concerned that today's students are forgetting how to write "correctly" because of an over-reliance on text message abbreviations, emoticons, and acronyms. Are those concerns valid? Sure. But we suspect that most student writers know the difference between how communication is encoded in a text message and how a similar message might be delivered in more formal writing.

The goal of this chapter is to help you think about ways your online writing can be more effective. Until recently, technology-based writing for many students was a nonschool activity. People kept in touch with friends and family through text messages, status updates, instant messages, and email, but writing for school rarely involved those kinds of communication. Well, times are changing. Increasingly, teachers are making use of Internet platforms such as listservs, social networks, and blogs in their classes. Regardless of how expert you may feel using particular technology platforms, you need to be able to adapt your writing depending on the situation you're in and the purpose you're trying to fulfill.

Good writers consider their audience when writing. This is also true for the kinds of writing you do online or through text messages. For example, if you're sending a text message to a family member or commenting on a friend's status update, you can throw in some abbreviations or emoticons and the person on the other end is likely to know exactly what you mean and how you feel about it. You know some people well enough that you have consciously or unconsciously agreed on some language shortcuts and codes that save time and carry your messages efficiently. Others outside your social circle might not understand the shortcuts, but that's OK because you're not writing to or for them.

As long as people communicate with each other, they will create their own variations in the language they use with each other. That's natural. But as we said, these types of technology-based communications are becoming more common in schools and workplaces. You need to know how to use them clearly and purposefully in those settings and not just default to text-speak any time you're using technology.

For example, let's say a teacher asks you to read an article or blog post and to comment about it online. Obviously, your teacher wants to see your thoughts expressed in academically appropriate language. If you write your response using the kinds of shortcuts that make perfect sense to your friends or family, it's possible that your teacher won't know what the heck you're talking about.

In the future, you may be asked to post updates on projects in a social network or wiki as a part of your job or volunteer work. Again, you want your writing to sound professional and to create a positive, clear impression of your thoughts, so you do not want to use those shortcuts just because the writing happens to be online.

In this chapter we will explore how to write effectively using common Internet platforms such as blogs, microblogs, social networks and communities, and wikis.

How is Online Writing Different?

Good writing is good writing, correct? Just because you intend to post the writing online instead of turning it in for a class doesn't mean that you can get sloppy with grammar and neglect to proofread—right? We hope you agree, but we do want to acknowledge some key differences.

1) Online writing tends to be more informal and conversational.

As you can tell from reading this text, we don't take issue with informality. For example, in the last sentence, we could have written, "As you can *discern* from reading," but *discern*, a perfectly fine word, strikes us as a bit stuffy here. The decision over tone and word choice is intertwined with purpose and audience—and yes, technology. Know your purpose and recognize your audience, and the informality will work for you.

2) Online writing is sometimes anonymous.

Because of this anonymity, the tone is often meaner and cruder. People feel free to engage in personal attacks or make offensive statements they would never dare to utter when speaking face to face. Not only are such Internet attacks cowardly, but we're confident that such writing achieves little. The attackers are like a pack of yapping dogs. They make a lot of noise, but there's no thinking in the barking. We urge you not to add to the din, even if you're allowed to be anonymous. A more measured response will ultimately hold more power than a rambling rant.

3) Online writing is interactive.

This is true communication with a real audience. With nearly every assignment, teachers try to simulate such authenticity, but with online writing, there's no need to pretend. It's an exciting time to be a writer, to have the capacity to connect with audiences beyond your immediate world.

Journal Topic

Pretend today is your birthday and that you're feeling reflective about growing up. Furthermore, you want to post your feelings online. Write a paragraph on how *this* birthday is different than previous ones.

How is Online Writing the Same?

We want to briefly revisit the "Defining Good Writing" section from Chapter 1 because the ideas are still important and easily forgotten when writing for an online audience.

1. Good writing is worthwhile.

Do you have something important to say? Will others enjoy or learn something from your writing? Are you allowing your particular voice to shine through? Are you taking risks?

Recently, a TV show was created based on themed tweets on Twitter. While television may not be the ultimate marker for "worthwhile," the idea that a series of 140 characters posted over time could be developed into a broadcast program is nonetheless impressive.

So don't be afraid to think big. Not only can you create worthwhile sentences and paragraphs, you can create an entire site that invites others to contribute, which in turn creates a community of sorts. We'll discuss this idea of community in more detail later.

2. Good writing is developed.

Have you provided enough details? Have you offered enough examples? Will your reader need more? There's nothing wrong with brevity, especially with online writing. But you also want to provide fresh insights that make your reader think and feel. We list specific examples of this throughout the chapter.

3. Good writing is organized.

Is your writing focused? Is there logic to the order you've chosen in each paragraph or post? Even in short posts, sentences should align smoothly, one idea leading logically to another.

4. Good writing is clear and concise.

Will your writing be understood? Have you chosen your language precisely? Have you taken out unnecessary words? Is your focus purposeful and sharp? While chatting, some people feel the need to add LOL or HA HA after the message, fearing their meaning will not be clear. One worthy goal: craft messages with such clarity that you can banish silly acronyms forever. This need for clarity often becomes apparent *after* a message is posted and responses flood in.

5. Good writing is polished.

Have you made an effort to use appropriate grammar, syntax, and punctuation? Have you proofread your writing? While we are now armed with a Send button that can flash our thoughts in an instant—and we've all seen how this can become a compulsion—the thoughts still require a degree of shaping and care before they're unleashed to the world. Pausing to proofread will avoid that embarrassing message you wish you'd never sent.

We'll discuss the value of abbreviations in more detail later, but a quick note here. Some abbreviations take about as much time or longer to create than the original word, and many smack of immaturity and annoy readers. Whenever possible, when space is not limited, you will want to avoid abbreviations, such as "prolly" ("probably"), "ur" ("you are"), and a host of others that have infiltrated online writing.

With these ideas about good writing fresh in mind, let's see how they apply to specific online writing platforms and situations. One quick note of explanation: Most online platforms are created by businesses, and from time to time as a company changes its business model, a site may be closed down or merged with another site. Because of that, we usually use generic terms to discuss these platforms. For example, currently the best known and most used microblogging site is Twitter, but that could change, and there are other microblog sites. For these reasons, we use the term *microblog* instead of *Twitter* or any other company name.

Microblogs

Microblogs are sites such as Twitter that allow you to say anything—but you are confined by a limited number of characters, usually 140. Everyone understands that when you're working within those constraints, shortcuts are necessary. It's perfectly fine to leave out some letters and punctuation when you're posting to a microblog. Anyone using that platform is probably doing the same thing. It's part of that platform's communication system. Your writing on a microblog site can be considered clear and polished even if you substitute "&" for "and" or "w/" for "with." Those are acceptable shortcuts on microblog sites because they save characters that can be used elsewhere to make your message more meaningful. For instance, if you write *Trying to find latest stats on college admission trends for stdnts w/learning disabilities. Can anyone help w/sources? Pls RT.* on a microblog site, everyone knows exactly what you mean: *I'm trying to find the latest statistics on college admission trends for students with learning disabilities. Can anyone direct me to a good source? Please Retweet.* If you had written out *statistics, with, students,* and *Please Retweet,* you would not have had room for *learning disabilities,* which is the key term in this message.

Obviously, you still want your writing to create a positive impression, especially when your posts are related to school or work, so your writing on this kind of site should try to achieve a balance between the word limits of the site and your desire for your writing to be clear and polished. (And remember, depending on how your account is set up, even your personal communication may be viewed by people outside your academic and professional circle.)

What are ways that microblogs can be useful to you? Posting your thoughts in a sentence or two can be a useful way to focus your mind before sitting down to work on a project. Of course, you can do that without posting it to a microblog, and maybe that's better in some ways. But if you are working with others, or are involved in a community of like-minded people, posting your ideas to a microblog can let them know what you're doing or thinking about. If they do the same thing, your work together can proceed more smoothly, even if you're not physically in the same location.

You can also stay in touch with the leading experts of many fields who are active on microblogging sites. While it may be difficult to communicate with them through other means, they may take a moment to communicate with you in one of these quick communication forums. Even if they don't, you can still keep up with their thoughts and activities as inspiration for your own.

If you have a question about almost anything, you can post it on a microblog site, and you will receive responses. Depending on how you phrase the question, it's possible to hear from others who can provide answers or direct you to information through other means. Some writers find that the limitations of microblogs actually enhance their creativity as they write "poetweets" or "twaiku." We have also seen novels, stories, and memoirs posted one tweet at a time.

In some cases, your post may be re-posted by others to help spread your information or question, but those re-postings also require additional characters. If your original post uses all the available characters, someone who wants to help you by re-posting will need to edit your original message. It's better if you control your writing than having someone else do it. Let's say you post, *I'd like to interview people who are involved in community service in my town. Can anyone suggest good people to contact? Please RT.* That's 132 characters. Someone who wants to help by re-posting your message will need to edit it. (Why? Their post will include not only your message but also your user ID. That takes up characters.) It's important to limit your message to the shortest number of characters, and if possible, leave unimportant words at the end so they can be easily deleted. This version is only 96 characters, which leaves room for your user ID in the re-post: *Need to interview local people involved in community service. Anyone know good contacts? Pls RT.*

Your microblog posts may include links to Internet sites. Some of those URLs can be ridiculously long and eat up valuable characters. If you encounter that problem, some microblog sites will ask you if you want to shorten the URL. Alternately, if your microblogging site doesn't prompt you automatically, a much shorter URL can be generated by using any of a number of services such as tinyurl.com or bit.ly or tiny.cc. Shortening a URL has no effect on the tone or meaning of your message and frees up characters for your actual writing.

Engaging in an extended conversation via a microblog site is not polite online etiquette, unless your conversation will be of interest to or involve others. A back-and-forth conversation between you and another person about something routine is poor microblog etiquette because each post takes up a spot in their feed of most recent posts. When you log on to a microblog site, you are shown a certain number of the most recent posts, usually no more than 100. Whatever percentage of that number is taken up by someone else's personal conversation is replacing other more recent posts that might be of more interest. One-on-one conversations about routine matters can still take place on microblog sites, but it's best to do them through a private channel rather than through the public feed.

Writing directly into an online blog space is a little risky. Some sites are notoriously unforgiving when you try to revise. If you hit Back or Backspace, your work can disappear. Instead, begin your blog post as a word-processing document. Write, revise, and save all of your ideas offline and then copy them into your online blog when you're ready. You can write notes to yourself in the offline draft about where to insert media and hyperlinks. Later, once you've pasted your draft into the blog space, you can add the media and html codes and begin working with those other online elements. Adding media and hyperlinks is best accomplished while working online, but most techno-glitches are likely to occur as you add these media elements. If your text is saved elsewhere, it's easy to paste it in again if something goes wrong.

Blogs

A **blog** (short for "web log") is an online journal. Maintaining a blog is an excellent way to reflect on the events, situations, and controversies in your life. Your blog space can be designed to reflect your personality, and what you add to your blog can be shared with subscribers, a few friends, everyone, or kept private, depending on the site that hosts your blog. If you are asked to write a blog as part of a school assignment, your teacher will likely provide some guidelines for you about how your blog should be set up and what it should include. For your personal blog, you will decide what to include.

How can you make your blog worthwhile so that your readers will be engaged in what you write, perhaps comment on your ideas, and visit your blog again when you add new posts? In this section, we will provide guidance on what to write about, how to make your blog visually interesting, and how to get readers involved.

What should you write about in your blog? For a blog that is part of a class assignment, your teacher will give you some parameters, but your goal is to make your blog purposeful, relevant to class, and worthwhile to read. Write about what you think of the material covered in class. Your teacher wants to know your take on the activities, units, or readings covered. You are a unique individual, so your blog post should be unlike anyone else's. For example, if the blog is for your literature class, you could write about your personal reaction to stories you are reading or about specific literary characters you can relate to. (See Chapter 10 "Writing about Literature" for more ideas.) If the blog is for a history or social studies class, you can write about how current or historical events discussed in class affected your family or ancestors. If this is a blog for a psychology or science class, write about how you apply various concepts in your own life.

For your personal blog, avoid a diary-style chronicle of what you did each day. A more worthwhile approach is sharing a sense of what you're thinking about and how you feel about the events in your life. Provide depth and description. If you only have one or two sentences to share, you can do that with a status update or tweet, but for a blog, keep going until you have at least two paragraphs on whatever topic you've chosen. Tell stories. Ask yourself questions. Answer those questions. As you go through your day, have your radar out for possible blog topics. Things that make you stop and think or that affect you emotionally are usually good topics for a blog post.

Because a blog entry is usually a concise piece of writing, it should maintain a single focus. Include everything you can say about the topic, including any relevant background, but resist the urge to explore related topics. Save those for additional blog posts. Most blog posts are shorter than 500 words, or about three to four paragraphs. It's fine to make yours longer, but think about it from a potential reader's perspective. A reader wants to spend a few minutes with your ideas, perhaps comment on what you've written, and then move on. If your writing is much longer than 500 words, a reader might be tempted to skip your blog and move on to something else online.

Tone is an important consideration for a blog post. In general, blog readers appreciate a tone that is light and positive. If your topic lends

Writers on Writing

Everything that you see, hear, feel, touch, overhear, read, dream, imagine, remember is a potential subject.... The way the subject becomes clear is by collecting concrete specifics about it, and you can collect specifics by observing and by asking why, who, what, when, where, how. The most ordinary things—oranges—can be a subject.

—*Don Murray*

itself to that, the tone will probably take care of itself. But if your topic is controversial, managing your tone is even more important. Although your attitude should be clear, avoid using your blog as a space to rant. A blistering tirade can feel good to write, and it can be a valuable starting place, but a reader doesn't usually gain much from reading it. Even if your take on a particular topic is negative, look for ways to provide balance in your writing. Very few situations are 100% negative. Pay particular attention to the ending. If most of the post has a critical tone, see if you can find a way to end on a positive note. If you're writing about a problem, suggest a solution. If you're writing about a personally difficult situation, write about what you are learning from it.

An advantage to online writing is that you can design your blog to be appealing even before a reader begins to look at your words. Incorporating visual elements such as photos, artwork, widgets, or videos is easy and pleasing to the eye. The process is different for each blog site, but virtually any site will accommodate these visual elements for your blog. Try adding a visual element toward the top of your blog to attract attention. If you only have one media visual element, use it at the top. If you have more than one, use the most significant, intriguing, or provocative visual at the top, and then insert the rest in appropriate places throughout your blog.

Using Videos in Blogs

Videos can be useful additions to your blog post, but they should be used wisely. The best way to include a video is to *embed* it directly in your blog post, rather than provide a link that requires a reader to click away from your blog to view the video. That reader might not make it back to your blog! If the video is embedded in your blog, the reader stays on your page, either views the video or not, then continues reading your words.

Videos can be included fairly easily, but the process depends on where the video is located. If the video is stored on your computer, your blog site will provide a process to upload it. If the video is located elsewhere online—for example on YouTube, Hulu, or Vimeo—you will need to use an embed code to place the video in your blog. The embed code can usually be found near the onscreen video, sometimes with a Share button. Using the embed code will directly place the video in your blog; using the URL will simply provide a link to the video. Those links are visually unappealing. Including the actual video looks much better.

Videos should be used to enhance the points you make in your writing. They should not distract from your ideas. If the video is merely there as a design element and isn't necessary for understanding or visualizing what you're writing about, embed it at the end. However, if your blog topic is focused on a particular video, it should appear toward the top of your blog post. For example, if your blog post is focused on controversial comments made by a celebrity or politician, embed the related video toward the top of your post so that a reader can view it and continue to read your thoughts about it. If your blog post is focused on a specific athletic move or moment in a game, that video highlight should also be embedded at the top so that your readers can view it and then have in mind exactly what you're picturing as they read your reactions.

Using Widgets in Blogs

Widgets work similarly to videos, and they can also be used to enhance your ideas. Examples of widgets include RSS feeds, polls, slideshows, and many other applications that provide embed codes. (An RSS feed allows users to subscribe to and/or publish regularly updated material. RSS stands for Really Simple Syndication.) Again, place widgets in your blog in places where they enrich your reader's experience with your ideas rather than distracting from them. For example, if your blog focuses on a scientific topic—weather, for example—you can embed live webcams from remote locations that show exactly what's going on at this moment relevant to your topic. If your blog is focused on art, various photo sites and museums provide embed codes for slide shows that you can include in your blog. If you want readers to take a survey, you can design it on a survey site and then embed it in your blog, then update the blog later with the results. You can also embed your microblog updates as a running RSS feed in your blog.

Using Hyperlinks in Blogs

Just as online writing now requires us to think differently about how we use language and images and other design elements, reading online is also a different experience than reading in a page-based format. An advantage to writing online is that you can easily provide a rich, interactive experience for your reader. Adding hyperlinks to your blog post is an excellent way to accomplish that. A hyperlink is a clickable link to another online location that is embedded in your words. You can typically create a hyperlink simply by highlighting part of your text and clicking on a "Link" icon, sometimes represented by a picture of chain links. For example, if you are writing about a particular restaurant, you can embed the URL for its official website at the point where you first mention the name of the restaurant. You can do the same for a government agency, philanthropic organization, movie or book, or virtually any other topic that has online material.

Another way to use hyperlinks is to connect your current blog post to a previous post. Let's say you just attended a concert, and you want to blog about it. Yes, you can provide a hyperlink to the website for the band you just saw, but you can also provide a link back to a previous blog post of yours if you're making a comparison between this concert and a previous concert you wrote about. Write a few words about the other concert and then embed a hyperlink that takes your reader to your previous post to learn more.

The disadvantage of using hyperlinks is that they can disrupt the flow of communication as your reader moves from your blog to a linked website and then, you hope, back to your blog. This disadvantage is a trade-off with the advantage of providing relevant material for your reader. For example, if you discuss a specific sports team in your blog post, you can set links to the team's website, as well as the league's website. This is an easy way to provide your readers with more background information about your topic without you needing to write it. Again, it's possible that readers who click a link will become so engrossed in the other website that their train of thought will be broken, and they won't return to your post. However, it may still be worth the risk to provide the links. In fact, blog etiquette dictates that if you mention a topic that has a website devoted to it, you should provide a link to the site. Some blog sites insert these links automatically.

On days when there's no pressure to awaken at a particular time—on weekends, let's say—rise from your bed early and lie down on a couch. Don't shake off your drowsiness. Have a pad of paper and pen ready (or your smartphone open and thumbs flexed) and think/dream about what you'd like to write today. By the way, REM sleep stages increase in length as sleep progresses, so in the morning, you've probably just emerged from a REM period, a time rich with imaginative dreamscapes. As you lie on the couch, you're not in REM, but your mind is still in an imaginative mode, and ideas tend to gush. With pen in hand, don't analyze. Just try to keep up. Close your eyes but stay awake. Then wait. When you feel like writing something down, do it, and if you can keep your eyes half shut or closed while doing so, that's even better. This little trick is especially effective when you're searching for writing ideas: *What do I want to say? What can I post next?*

Blog Comments

Be sure to organize your blog post so that it ends with an invitation for your readers to respond by posting a comment. This can be as simple as "So, what do you think about all this?" But a better approach is to make your invitation specific to the topic and issues you raise in your blog post: "Do you think most people are greedy or generous?"; "What are some ways you have helped other people lately?" When people respond to your blog, you know they've thought about your ideas and want to share their reactions with you and others. By specifically asking your readers to respond, you are more likely to generate comments than if your blog post simply ends with a standard conclusion.

What if some idiot writes an inappropriate comment on your blog? If it's a school-related blog, be sure your teacher knows about it, but don't be surprised if the teacher sees it before you do. Comments are easy to delete.

For your personal blog, you can set the preferences so that you approve comments before they're unveiled to the public. For most blog sites, those who want to comment are required to register before they can post anything. If a user posts something threatening or inappropriate, you can delete the comment, block the user, and report the incident to the website manager.

Here are sample posts from our own blogs, which we hope you find instructive.

My Old Man's Wisdom
by Tony Romano
25 April 2011
TonyRomanoAuthor.com

A note first to any young person reading this. The expression "my old man" may sound archaic or crude or quaint in a "swell" kind of way. But I've always been fond of "my old man." To me, it's nothing less than an endearment. I'm too young to have ever used the expression, but when I was a kid, the older guys in the neighborhood would do so freely and matter-of-factly, nothing affectionate in their tone, only in my longing to use the words myself, though I never have.

My dad is nearly 91 years old. Until he was about 70, he never had a headache—or a cough, or sore throat or upset stomach. Nothing. When he got his first cough, this was momentous. Anyway, because of congestive heart problems of late, he is in and out of hospitals, the frequency becoming sadly troublesome lately. During his recent long stay last week, I got to spend a few hours with him without my mom hovering. When I arrived, quite early so I could intercept the doctor and try to get him out of there, I sauntered into his room and found him fast asleep. I waited outside his room so as not to disturb him. While I read a newspaper, I noticed a woman approaching his room with some contraption and rose to stop her from the critical task she was about to undertake, which turned out to be less than critical. She needed to weigh my old man. Now. This couldn't wait apparently. I'm usually fairly timid but I looked her in the eye and told her the weight business would have to wait because the poor guy hadn't been sleeping well and there was no way we were going to wake him for this. She turned away, said she'd come back later, which she never did because she was at the end of her shift. I felt like Michael Corleone from the movie, *The Godfather*, needing to protect his ailing father, which was reinforced when I stopped another woman from bursting in to take out the garbage, a task that apparently must get done before 8:00 am. She left too, and my chest puffed out.

Later, after my old man had awoken, and during a spell when he was feeling more like his old self, he offered these pearls: "No think too much." I took this in. What else, I asked. "No eat too much. No work too much." Hospital? I asked. He pfft-ed. "Hospital no good." Sleep? His eyes widened. He appreciated my encouragement. "No sleep too much," he pronounced. He gazed out the window, satisfied, his 100-pound frame barely filling the bed. Then he turned to me and pointed. "Everything too much no good." As he spoke, I was trying to live in the present. I really was. But I tore off a piece of "Your Daily Menu" from the hospital cart because I was afraid I'd forget, and wrote down his advice. I was hoping he wouldn't notice, but he was content, pleased that I was writing down his words. For posterity, he probably thought. And he was right. *Everything too much no good.* A perfect book title. I yearned for more, but I could tell he would tire soon. I looked up from my paper. "That's all," he added, his hands smoothing the sheet at his chest, dismissing any more pronouncements. He nodded and offered a crooked smile. "I tell a good a ting," he said. And he did.

WhatsNotWrong?

by Gary Anderson
January 25, 2011
WhatsNotWrong.wordpress.com

The phrase "What's Not Wrong?" comes from a game-like activity I enjoy doing with my classes. It stems from the realization that it's usually easy to make a list of what *is* wrong at any given time. We have no problem articulating what is wrong with the world, our health, our schedule, the people around us, the government, and on and on. But when we are asked to name one thing that is *not* wrong, sometimes we struggle with that.

Here is how I do "What's Not Wrong?" in class the first time. I write the question "What's Not Wrong?" on the board in enormous letters. (I like to use the Spanish upside-down question mark at the front end of it. Wouldn't it be nice if English did that too?) I also give each student a small piece of paper. Old page-a-day calendars are perfect for this, especially if one side is blank. Then I tell the class, "Right now, we're going to have a little dose of positivity. It's easy to think of things that are going wrong in our lives and in our days. That's easy. Your challenge right now is to write down one thing that is absolutely, incontrovertibly *Not Wrong*–anything that is going well for you, any thing you're happy about or pleased with, or something that makes you smile inwardly or outwardly. Write it down anonymously. Don't show it to anyone. Give it to me when you're finished. Go."

Then the questions begin: "What if we can't think of anything?" "What if I'm having a really bad day?" "Can we write down something that is true, like 2+2=4? Truth is not wrong." I just smile and say, "Do your best, and do it quickly."

Some students take to it right away; others struggle mightily. I wait until every student has given me a paper with something written on it. Then I sit down in the front of the room and read them aloud, prefacing most of them with the question "What's Not Wrong?"

Sometimes students write about a recent strong test score or achievement in an activity or sport. Some write about upcoming vacations or events planned with friends. Some mention recent or upcoming milestones: removal of orthodontia, birthdays, anniversaries. Some write about rainbows, or goldfish, or their own personal avatar of happiness.

After spending a few minutes listening to the not-wrong-ness in the room, no one is able to continue with a negative attitude, at least outwardly.

The next time we do "What's Not Wrong?" several days later, most students are able to come up with an idea more quickly. Before too long, students start to ask, "Can we do 'What's Not Wrong?' today?" Sometimes I say yes, but if it doesn't fit the daily schedule, I say, "You know, you really don't need a teacher or class in order to tell yourself what's not wrong. You can do it any time any place."

"What's Not Wrong?" has turned out to be a memorable experience for many students. Imagine my surprise to hear from a former student who conducted a What's-Not-Wrong segment every Thursday morning on her radio talk show. A group of former students held an informal reunion and found themselves playing "What's Not Wrong?" I was thrilled when one of them emailed to tell me about it. Another former student posts a "What's Not Wrong?" idea on Twitter from time to time.

So, why title my blog "What's Not Wrong?"? Because I want to focus on good things here. There is enough badness in the world, and I don't want to add more. Of course, sometimes I'll be compelled to write about problems that I'm working through or frustrations that are vexing me. I realize that no one wants to read rants, so by naming this blog "What's Not Wrong?" I am reminding myself to focus on solutions, not problems. To concentrate on events worth celebrating and finding my way to the positive aspects of difficult situations.

Thanks for your time in reading this. Your comments and questions are always welcome.

Social Networks and Communities

Let's face it. A lot of what goes on in large social networking sites like Facebook is pointless fun, but what people post can also be annoying or boring. Social networking sites, however, are rapidly becoming an important method of communication in school and business settings, replacing email as a preferred method of relaying messages and information to other people. Successful communication in a social network setting is an increasingly important academic, occupational, and personal skill. Moreover, social networks have played an unprecedented role in political campaigns and protests, a testament to the power of words. We have even seen social networks play a role in world events that changed the course of history.

In some cases, a social network is just that: a network where people are connected within one online platform. They can contact each other easily and keep track of each other's activities, if everyone posts updates about what they're up to.

Social networks are at their best, however, when they morph into online communities. Consider the connotations of each word: *network* and *community*. Which one sounds more appealing? Each has its place, but a "network" simply implies connection, while a "community" suggests that those involved are committed to a common purpose and dedicated to building something that benefits all of its members. This might sound idealistic, but the way we think about the sites we belong to affects the ways we write when we visit them, and purposeful writing is the key to all successful social networks and online communities.

If all we're concerned about is the ability to communicate publicly or privately within a certain site, then we tend to use the media simply to report facts or share small talk: *Here's what I'm doing. What are you doing? Isn't that nice? Have fun.*

On the other hand, when a network is dedicated to a purpose shared by its members, powerful writing can take place. Our words contribute to and build a community centered around a common interest or purpose. When we bring that mindset to our writing in an online setting, we tend to write with more depth and reflection. We are more conscious of how our words may be affecting people who are also members of this community.

Writing Tip

Throughout the day, jot down ideas that you think might be worth sharing with the world, or type some quick notes to yourself on your phone or other electronic device. For example, if you notice that most of your classmates dress similarly, you might write a note about the lure of conformity. If you notice people driving recklessly, maybe you can write a note about behavior patterns while driving and how that pattern magically changes when people step out of their cars. At the end of the week, you'll have about seven notes, enough perhaps to get you started on an online post.

Online communities can form around social networking sites, blogs, discussion forums, or bulletin board sites—any place where members can share information (including multimedia such as photo albums and videos) and comments with one another. Knowing how to effectively express yourself in those various forums will allow you to be a responsible, respectful, valuable member of an online community.

Let's deal with status updates first. A status update is a quick statement about your current mood or activity. The purpose of a status update is simply to let people know what's going on with you at the moment. It's not intended to be the start of a big conversation or discussion. Some people get confused about that, however. You do not need to start a "discussion" about your current mood or activity, unless you believe a lot of people will actually have something significant to say about it. Starting a discussion for a status update is like calling a meeting and then saying, "I'm doing my homework right now. I need to focus." Or setting up a conference call where you tell everyone, "Hi. I'm having a great day. Hope to see you soon."

Starting a discussion is a good idea when you want to gather input about a specific issue relevant to members of the online community. When you start a discussion, provide a balanced view of the issue you're interested in, then specifically ask community members to respond. It's also a good idea to make the discussion visually appealing using some of the techniques mentioned in the section on blogs. How is a discussion different from a blog? A blog is focused on you; a discussion is focused on an issue. Obviously, some overlap can exist between the two formats. When you're trying to decide between writing a discussion starter or a blog post, here are the guiding questions:

- Is my purpose to gather information and ideas from other members? If the answer is Yes, start a discussion.

- Is my purpose to reflect on a situation or issue? If the answer is Yes, start a blog.

- If the answer is Yes to both questions, maybe you should do both.

The sense of community within a social network is really built through comments that members make on each other's posts. In general, those comments should be positive, although it's fine to disagree with someone's ideas, as long as the disagreements are expressed respectfully and clearly. Worthwhile comments frequently take the form of questions as they seek to ask other members to clarify or develop the ideas in their posts.

Good comments are also specific. It's OK to paste a relevant part of the original post in a comment in italics or quotation marks and then write your comments underneath that quote. When responding to a video, it's a good idea to refer to time markers, as in "The speaker in this video contradicts himself at 2:32. Which idea does he really believe?"

Journal Topic

Write a note of about 200 words on some change you'd like to make at your school. Pretend that your school has a website that welcomes such messages and that your words will be read by the entire school, including the principal and staff.

Wikis

Wikis are a specific type of online community in which users work collaboratively to author and edit information on a website. The most well-known example, of course, is Wikipedia, an online encyclopedia written entirely by users. Since the technology behind a wiki allows users to *add* or *change* information, wikis require a certain kind of etiquette. Changing the work of others in a wiki platform should be done only with very good reason. Some wikis also require users to sign up as a member and get the permission of other members before making changes.

Think carefully about the purpose behind your involvement in any wiki you're using. Is your role to add information, or is your role to edit or change what others have added? If your role is simply to add information—perhaps your own perspective on a class discussion—then changing what others have written would be a major blunder, even if you have the technology available to do so. If, however, the wiki's purpose is to create a group project or presentation, then it's probably fine to change what others have written, especially if the wiki tracks and records those changes, who made them, and the reasons for the changes.

The basic points of wiki etiquette:

- If users are working together on a group project where each user is supposed to contribute, then changing the work of others may be understandable.

- It's also OK to edit the work of other users if *they have specifically asked you to do so.*

- Adding information is always OK.

Online writing is both the same and different from other kinds of writing that we do. The needs for organization, development, clarity, purpose, audience awareness, and correctness are just as important for online writing as for other types of writing. However, those goals can be accomplished more expertly if we use the tools of technology wisely. Interactive capabilities, design elements, and a more dynamic relationship with readers provide the opportunity to use writing in ways that go beyond crafting effective sentences and paragraphs. But those sentences and paragraphs are still the foundation on which all good writing is built, online or on paper.

Practice

1. One of your teachers has created a classroom blog in which you must participate. In a paragraph, respond to this question the teacher has posted: "In what ways are the friendships you have developed in high school different from your friendships in elementary or middle school?" If this were a real school blog, your classmates would read your answer, so keep that in mind as you complete this.

2. Assume you've been keeping a personal blog for the past few months. What would your entry be for the last few days? You can simply make a list of possible topics you might write about.

3. Try this exercise in tone. Let's say you want to write online about a recent disappointment in your life. Write two versions of the entry you might write. Version A should be a tirade, written entirely in a negative tone. Version B should be more balanced. Each version can be just a few sentences. This is an exercise. We don't recommend posting the tirade.

4. Write a microblog post about some recent event at your school. Use a maximum of 140 characters. This can be a fifteen-second task if you merely describe the event. The challenge is to make the entry engaging. Consider word choice, tone, and humor.

Chapter Assignment

Prewriting

Your assignment for this chapter is to write entries for a blog. Use the following suggestions to help you choose a topic and clarify the purpose of your blog.

1. Make a list of possible themes you might like to focus on in a personal blog. For example, if you dance or play a musical instrument, your blog could center on creativity. If you have expertise in some area, such as camping or biking, your blog could explore that interest and provide a forum for sharing your knowledge with others. Or you can choose a more general theme: what it's like to be a student, or what it's like to live in a certain area.

2. Make a list of five questions you'd like to ask the world. The questions should be clear, direct, and answerable. Don't worry about phrasing or clarity or length at this point.

3. Make a list of sites and short videos you'd like to share with others.

Writing Topics

Select one of the following suggestions to develop your blog. Feel free to tailor these topics to suit your needs.

1. Start a personal blog. (See Prewriting #1 for ideas.) Include at least three separate entries and make sure each entry is at least two paragraphs in length (a total of around 300 words). Also, each entry should have a single focus. And remember, just because your entries are focused doesn't mean you can't infuse them with humor when appropriate. Readers appreciate efforts you make to include humor. Whether you actually post the entries and continue your blog is your decision. Once you start, you may find that you enjoy the process. At the end of each entry, list a site to which you can send readers that would enhance what you've written. For example, if your blog's focus is sports, you can send them to a sports news site you visit frequently.

2. Imagine that one of your teachers has started a classroom blog. One of the course requirements is that you post a class-related question from time to time. Write five such questions based on recent class

activities and experiences. Feel free to ask your teachers for help. For example, your history teacher might have discussed the question: "What twentieth-century invention is overrated?" Select one question and write a blog entry in which you answer the question in three or more paragraphs, or about 400–500 words.

3. Write twenty microblog entries over the next few days. If you think you might actually post the entries on Twitter or a similar site, check out the requirements and follow them closely. If you're not worried about any particular requirements, follow this one: use no more than 140 characters for each entry. (Remember, individual letters *and* spaces count as characters. See pages 414–415 earlier in this chapter for advice on abbreviations and on conserving valuable space.) In terms of content, some of the entries might direct viewers to favorite sites or videos others might like. (See the previous Prewriting #3.)

4. Think about a national or international news story from the past week. If you're stumped, skim through an online newspaper or other news site. Then write a blog post of 200 words or less on your reactions to this story. Repeat this procedure for four other news stories for a total of five blog posts.

5. If you completed Prewriting task #2, take each of the five questions and work on phrasing them in a way that will elicit the greatest chance for a response. You might preface the question with a personal note. You might edit for clarity. Work on having your voice come through in as few words as possible. Consider posting the questions on a microblog site, such as Twitter.

Revision

Revision takes on added urgency when you know your writing may reach a potentially large audience. Before sharing your work with the world, if that's what you choose to do, consider these questions:

1. Is your tone appropriate for your audience? Are you too formal or too casual?

2. Will your writing offend? This is not to suggest that you can't include bold sentiments, but are your views reasoned and reasonable?

3. Is your language lively and engaging? Have you taken time to include effective verbs, effective imagery, and figurative language?

4. Are your views original? Have you made an honest effort at including an authentic voice? If you've borrowed ideas or reposted the work of others, be sure to offer citations of the source to avoid plagiarism.

5. What questions do you have for a peer reviewer? Be specific.

Peer Review

Use these questions to help you evaluate another student's writing. Remember, specific suggestions and examples are most helpful.

1. What main points does the writer convey?

2. Does the writer seem knowledgeable about the subject matter?

3. Is the tone personal and inviting? What are some examples of an inviting tone? Are there any places where the tone does not seem to fit?

4. Is anything in the writing that some people might find offensive?

5. Does the writer invite you to respond? Are you likely to add a comment to this blog? Why or why not?

6. What suggestions do you have for the writer?

Running On Ice

by Mary Fons

Paper Girl
maryfons.com/blog

There's a volunteer at the theater who is a runner. This is something he came to later in his life; I don't think he ever ran much as a younger man, but now he's committed to it. I asked him tonight how his running has been going and he said that he ran today in fact, clocking two miles in right about 15 minutes, which is very good. We chatted about running in cold weather and I told him how before I got sick I used to run quite a bit and that I used to run in the wintertime. It was my favorite time to run.

What stories will we tell as we age? I used to run in the wintertime in Chicago. I would get up so early, back when I lived with T. and L. on Margate Terrace. I would pull thermal tights from my dresser drawer and find my fleece headband, put on my wicking t-shirt and my University of Iowa sweatshirt and run to the lake which was so close to where we lived. I would crunch over the icy grass (what was left of it) and I would run out to the piers. No ships dock at those piers, but there are lighthouses there. Back then I would run like my life was on fire. The fire would meet the ice out there on the lake and I would look at the skyline against a sea of gray and silver and feel totally alone in the world, just watching my breath slip out in little clouds.

I was a younger woman. There was much I hadn't seen. But looking at that girl from where I sit now, I think she may have known more than I do. She seems brilliant and perfect. Oh, that we would see ourselves as perfect while we are.

We are.

On Being a "Market Kid"

by *Mary Fons*

Quilty with Mary Fons

quiltersclubofamerica.com/blogs/mary_k_fons

When we were in Houston 10 or so days ago, I was remembering being a kid with a mom in the quilt industry.

My father wasn't around, so mom was a single mom, and when she had to go out of town, Gramma stayed with us or a quilting friend from the guild would come for the weekend. That was when we were younger. As my older sister got into her teens and could drive and be responsible enough to take care of any emergencies that might arise, we made it on our own. Mom went and taught all over the country (and then all over the world) so that she could keep us in school clothes and lunch money.

And she went to Fall Market every year. That was one trip that was on the calendar in perpetuity. We knew that Halloween week-end, Mom would be out of town. When I was at Market a few weeks ago, I heard many people, moms and dads alike, lamenting the fact that they were missing their kids' costumes. They said that little Joe or little Suzy would never forgive them for missing Superman or the Fairy Queen, and I realized that I was a "Market Kid."

"They'll forgive you," I reassured those who were concerned. "I never really did Halloween, and I turned out okay."

Indeed, I think I turned out okay, but I really dislike Halloween. I don't know if I disliked it before and that's why it didn't bother me that much that Mom couldn't take us all trick-or-treating or if Mom couldn't ever take us trick-or-treating and that's why I never dress up, decline to go to Halloween parties, and skip the whole thing. It should be mentioned that I went into the theater. So I guess I did like to dress up. But I did it in a professional way, not just for kicks and a Twix bar.

Hang in there, Market kids. I heard a rumor that the lady who owns and runs Fall Market has booked Halloween weekend for the next five years straight.

Boo!

Discussion Questions

1. What do these two blog posts have in common? What can you conclude about the writer? Would you continue reading her blog updates? Why or why not?

2. What are several effective uses of imagery in "Running on Ice"? What does the imagery achieve in each case?

3. Do you sometimes think that your old self was smarter in some ways than you are now? Explain.

4. In "Market Kid," Fons suggests that sacrifice and hardship help shape a person. How did they shape Fons? How has sacrifice or hardship shaped your attitudes?

5. If you were to comment on one of Fons's blog posts, what would you write?

Professional Model 12.2

Moderation, Guilt, and Social Media

by Meredith Stewart

In For Good
inforgood.wordpress.com

It's been clear to me for several months that I haven't been putting in the work reading and writing longer pieces which give me a deeper satisfaction than the momentary pleasure of an @ reply. In thinking about how I might make more space for that kind of reading and writing, I realized I was spending more time than I was comfortable with scrolling through tweets and reading Facebook status updates. Not bad practices, but best consumed in moderation.

The problem is I'm bad at moderation. I'm an "eat the marshmallow" kind of person. But I'm also a person powerfully influenced by inertia. If the marshmallow's in the other room, I'm not likely to get up to go get it.

These aren't traits I particularly love about myself, but I have found I can use them to my advantage, primarily by acting in bursts of self-control that then make action or abstention (whichever I'm aiming for) more attractive and easier options down the road.

So, I decided to limit the number of people I followed on Twitter and to reduce my friends on Facebook. I recognize that's a controversial action, especially given its potential for hurting others' feelings, but it seemed a good way to achieve the goal I was aiming for while reducing the amount of self-control I would have to consistently exert.

I even thought about deactivating my Facebook account altogether, but when I did, this popped up:

I find the ways Facebook taps into human emotions to encourage users to stay members and to friend as many people as they can fascinating and maddening. Facebook benefits from having people participate in the site, and they've tapped into human emotions—guilt, loneliness, desire to be part of a group—to try to retain members.

Un-friending people on Facebook was hard, since I'd already culled through my friend list earlier in the year, going from 800 to around 350. I consistently found myself asking, *but what if I need this person in the future?* I realized this was probably a bad standard because a) I was trying to address interactions in the present and b) It reduced my friends to what they could do for me.

I started to ask instead, *Do my interactions with this person make me think? Do those interactions regularly bring me joy, rather than just distraction or amusement?* Those questions helped me cut the list to under 200.

I emailed a friend about my social media pruning. Her response has me wondering if guilt around connecting or not in social media was more prevalent in women. Ideally, I'd be the kind of person who could resist distraction on her own accord, but I'm not and so I'm trying not to feel guilty about creating the external structures to get the work done that I want/need to.

Do you feel guilty about the ways in which you limit your social circle online?

Do you think guilt over limiting one's circle/interactions on social media is more prevalent in women or felt more strongly by them? (I recognize the potential for gross over-generalizations in this question, but I still think it's worth asking.)

What strategies help you interact online without doing so at the detriment of other areas of your work and life?

Discussion Questions

1. What reasons does Stewart offer for limiting her Twitter and Facebook activity? Do you think her actions will help achieve her goal? Explain.

2. Stewart examines the reasons she participates in social networks. If you participate in social networks, what are your reasons? If you don't participate, why not?

3. At the end of her post, Stewart lists several questions for her readers. Answer any one of those questions.

Professional Model 12.3

Capture the Conversation

by Michele Norris

Grace Notes Blog
michele-norris.com/category/grace-notes

On her website, National Public Radio commentator Michele Norris started a conversation with her readers by inviting them to respond to her book, *The Grace of Silence,* a memoir that shares her personal reflections on race in America:

"At some point all of us face the question: How well do we really know the people who raised us? Or, how well do we really understand our racial legacy or our family history? . . . Tell us about your discoveries and your journey to learn more about your family history. You can also tell us about your experiences, thoughts, triumphs, laments, theories or anthems."

The chapter discusses ways in which online writing can create a sense of community. If you go to Norris's site, you'll get an idea of how this can happen. What follows are two reader responses to Norris's blog post.

Comment by *Neli Moody*
Subject: *Two Rivers*
http://michele-norris.com/your-stories/neli-moody-two-rivers/
My story is the story of America. My maternal ancestor fought in the Revolutionary War. I have seen the papers from this time. My father's people were slaves and I have seen the census of 1870 when they had the name of their slaveowner, a name that had changed ten years later. I was born in a city above the Ohio River, a city known for its underground railroad to freedom. The spirits of my ancestors seemed to swirl around that river and a black person's life was determined by which side of it one lived on. Researching my history continues to be an emotional journey. But America is a place where rivers meet and join and flow to the sea. Each history is the story of America.

Comment by *Arlene Lee*
Subject: *Birthday Present: you are black, sorta?*
http://michele-norris.com/your-stories/arlene-lee-birthday-pres-ent-you-are-black-sorta/
There is much more to the story but the words do capture the moment. My mother raised me to be white and I am, at least by self-identification I guess. She died a couple of days before I turned 50 this past fall. On the eve of my birthday I was going through some of her papers and found her birth certificate. My mother immigrated to this country from Peru in 1958. In her papers were her original birth certificate and a fake one that she used to come to the United States. She had changed from black to white, illegitimate to legitimate and became 8 years younger. The context for all this is important but for me the bottom-line was a sense of tremendous sadness that she never felt she could share this with me. It breaks my heart that we never had a chance to talk about it, that she didn't feel she could trust her only child to understand and that she didn't feel she could ever come out of hiding. Both of those things make me sad, the lack of trust and the apparent belief that the world hasn't changed so much since 1958 that her race would be a non-issue. It clearly is an issue. And now, I have a new prism through which to see things.

Discussion Questions

1. In her comment, entitled "Two Rivers," Neli Moody writes of how an accident of geography can dictate a person's fate. She writes: "The spirits of my ancestors seemed to swirl around that river [the Ohio] and a black person's life was determined by which side of it one lived on." Moody doesn't offer specifics about what happened on either side of the river, but what do you imagine?

2. The second commentator, Arlene Lee, describes how her mother hid her true identity from her family for all of her life. Why do you think her mother felt the need to hide her true self? What does Lee mean when she says that she now has "a new prism through which to see things"?

3. Respond to Michele Norris's call for stories. How well do you know your family's history? Do you wish you knew more? How has your family history shaped your identity?

Testing

by Kaval Kaziz

From Ordinary to Waterlily
kaziz.edublogs.org

I log into my email expecting to see the regular spam emails and a few from colleges that have too much time on their hands. As I scroll through and click on each email I want to delete, I notice one from the College Board. *Subject: Your SAT scores are in!* I do not know why there is an exclamation point, because this is definitely not a very exciting moment for me. Next to the actual SAT, this is a very stressful moment. I hesitatingly click on the website and input all of my information, and my score does not please me. In fact, I think I might cry.

Basically, standardized testing may work for some people and it's a good basis to have but it shows nothing to colleges. We put so much emphasis on standardized testing such as the SAT and for Texas, the TAKS test, but really, what does it show?

The standard tests ask the SAME questions every time and there are always tricks. And now you are thinking, "Well if there are tricks then why not learn them and beat the test?" But unfortunately it's not that simple. One would need to take expensive classes and take the test about a million times to learn everything there is to know. And once a student knows the information, Voila! A near perfect, yet completely meaningless score is right at their front door. The standard test barely tests students on actual concepts. Not much background information is necessary and this is why standardized tests, such as the SAT and TAKS, are stupid.

On the other hand, curriculum based tests actually prove in a score whether or not certain material has been taught and retained, and the application of that knowledge. Curriculum based tests would be tests such as exams. Exams show that what a student has learned in the classroom is actually understood. Facts and concepts and theories and history and background information are necessary to do well on exams. The curriculum tests show a productive view of a student's learning and test-taking capabilities. More emphasis should be put on class averages and exams rather than TAKS scores.

Discussion Questions

1. How would you describe the tone of this blog post? Angry? Frustrated? Good-natured? A combination of several tones? What words or phrases help to convey tone?

2. In paragraph 3, Kaziz attempts to answer an objection from the reader: "And now you are thinking...." What effect does this technique have?

3. Where does Kaziz use exaggeration? Is the exaggeration effective?

4. If you were to comment on Kaziz's blog post, what would you say?

Student Model 12.2

War on Freedom

by Zahira Rodriguez

Language (F)Arts
zahrodriguez.edublogs.org

Freedom. It is the topic for most fights between parents and teens. Teens want every inch of it they can get and parents hate everything that word stands for. Why is giving a teenager a little freedom so dang complicated? Maybe it's because teens and adults speak, and HEAR, a different language. You tell me, a teenager, "freedom" and I think of about a million dreams of mine. To list a few, I think of car keys, no dress codes, dying my hair blue, to be up on a mountain and yell at the top of my lungs, to stick a pencil in my hair and call it style, to wear snow boots in the summer and a skirt in winter, to eat dessert first, to go to a concert with my boyfriend without my mom calling every 5 minutes to "check on me." Parents, on the other hand, hear the word freedom from their teens and think of a thousand nightmares. Drugs, sex, bad mouthing, gangs, spray painting, wrecks, that one story of a teen on the Lifetime channel who went to a party and got raped, heartbreak, their kids calling from jail or juvie, bankruptcy, debt, hospital bills, the ER.

Why such a disconnection? Why do teens think freedom means losing common sense, and parents think it leads to death? It all leads to trust. Do parents really trust their teens to give them some freedom? Do teenagers really trust their parents enough to tell them something they might not like to hear? Not at all. There are parents checking their children's text messages to makes sure they are "staying out of trouble." Granted, there are also teens pregnant at 16. Why can't we find middle ground?

It's extremely important to have parents that trust you, so that as a teen you feel comfortable talking to them about anything. I have a friend who has crashed her car twice. Her mom hasn't found out of either. When I asked her why she's hiding it, she gave the usual reply I hear from my friends at least once a week, and often time find myself saying: "Are you kidding, my parents would kill me." This fear teens have of admitting to parents when they make a mistake breaks the trust parents and teens should have. But why are teens so scared? It once again leads to the different languages teens and parents speak.

Teens see parents as these merciless, cruel creatures unable to understand or listen to anything we say. Parents see teens as these fragile children needing guidance and (UNWANTED) advice on everything, who will always make the wrong decision because that is just what teenagers do. If parents would just be willing to listen to their kids and give them a chance to prove them wrong, the incessant fighting may stop. If teens would try to trust their parents to understand when a mistake is made, and not be afraid to talk to them about it, maybe the old relationship they had before they turned 13—where everyone wasn't mad at everyone all the time—might come back.

Discussion Questions

1. Rodriguez lists several things that come to mind when she hears the word *freedom*. What would be on your list?

2. Rodriguez also lists what many parents of teenagers think when they hear the word *freedom*. What would be on the list of most parents you know?

3. Do you agree that trust is key to bridging the gap between teens and parents? Explain. What is another solution?

4. If you were to post a reply to this blog entry, what would you write?

What Does It Take?

Lindsey Washall

Deliciously Awkward
lindseywashall.blogspot.com

I'll begin this post by stating for everyone who will read it that what I have to say here has no conclusion. I suppose that it's more of a "brain dump" of something that I had on my mind for a little while today.

I was looking at some of the photography and graphics work that I have done over the past year and was comparing it to the work of some budding "artists" (it will soon become clear why that word is in quotes) that I made the acquaintance of in Savannah, GA over the summer...and my question is, what really makes someone an artist?

Wikipedia defines an artist as "a person engaged in one or more of any of a broad spectrum of activities related to creating art, practicing the arts and/or demonstrating an art." And while the term "artist" traditionally refers to the field of the visual arts, I am also curious about the other fields that are more broadly considered arts as well. Among these could be the culinary arts or performance art. At what point does a person have the grounds to say that they have surpassed the point of being a dilettante and have reached the point of being an artist?

And is being an artist a permanent state of being once you've reached it? Or is it something more like a phase that you can drift in and out of? For instance, during the school year the majority of my photography is portraiture and concert photography that I do for a profit, but whenever school is not in session I have the time to create my own ideas and stage them just to my liking. Is it only in that time when I should consider it art? Or is it all a form of art because I do consider my for-profit work to have my own unique spin on it?

That's all I have for now... I could consider the subject for much longer and pose many more questions, but I'll leave it at that.

Discussion Questions

1. Washall lists several questions that she genuinely wants answered. Pick one or two of the questions and offer your answers.

2. What's the effect of Washall not supplying her own solution to this blog?

3. If you were to write a similar blog, what questions would you like answered?

4. Many teachers would probably frown on the reliance on Wikipedia for a school essay. Do you think the reference to Wikipedia in a blog is appropriate?

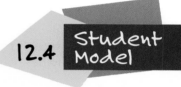

12.4 Student Model

Love Isn't Blind

Aly Freeman

I'm Just Me
alyfreeman.edublogs.org

"Young love never lasts. You're going to grow up and change."
"Don't get ahead of yourself."
"Love is blind but young love is even blinder."
"Love isn't real until you're older and you see a person for who they really are."
"You guys are getting pretty serious; don't do anything you'll regret."
…BLAH, BLAH, BLAH!

Any of these phrases sound even remotely familiar to you? Maybe not if you've never had a serious relationship in high school, but for a lot of us, we hear this from our parents a lot more than we like. Truth is, as teenagers, being faced with doubt and insecurities doesn't really do us a whole lot of good. Parents, want some advice? Let us do our thing and we'll figure the rest out on our own. Now I'm not saying go ahead and let us do drugs then get drunk so we spend the night throwing our guts up and learn a lesson, but when it comes to love, well that's just one big mystery we gotta decipher on our own.

Parents (or should I say "most" parents) all think the same thing when their teenage child gets into a serious relationship. It goes a little something like this, "Oh my God, what the hell are they doing? What the hell should I do? They don't even know what love is. Is it time for the talk!? I don't want them to get hurt." Now, a lot of times the screaming inside their heads doesn't come out that way (the way it's originally formed), but instead comes out in the form of the quotes I wrote up there. ^ Parents tend to try and ease into the topic of "serious relationships" and then proceed to warn us of (insert 1 million ridiculous things here). Well the truth is, young love has a bigger chance of surviving than you think.

For example, my Grandma and Grandpa met when they were 14 and have been happily married for like almost 60 years! Now you might be thinking, yeah yeah, that's a generation thing, times have changed! Well, I also know of a friend of mine whose sister is 21 and who has only ever had one boyfriend (who she met her senior year of high school) and they are most likely going to get married. I go on to point out that "young love" is really the most "pure" love there is. As kids, who don't have to worry about bills—or paying for anything for that matter—we aren't weighed down with the world's evil influences. I say this because when we see someone we like, we don't judge them on their income or political beliefs, or whether or not they want to have kids someday or not. We see them for who they are right then, in the prime of their life, with no worries. So you think young love is blind?—Well I say it's the other way around.

Discussion Questions

1. Freeman maintains that young love is pure. What evidence does she provide? And do you agree?

2. Does Freeman have a particular audience in mind in this blog post? Evidence?

3. Freeman provides several examples to support her argument. Which one is the most effective and why?

4. How would you respond to this blog post?

Air Glory

Lilly Rotter

Of This Still Life
ldrotter.blogspot.com

I really wanted that iPod.

My sister and I were carelessly leaning up against a fencepost, anticipating the six o'clock drawing for an iPod nano at the 2007 Lifest Christian Music Festival. I stared up at kids swinging through air on the "Air Glory," a giant crane that harnessed in two riders at a time to free fall from high up, set up in the middle of a dusty horse arena. We listened to the screams of the fallers and the nervous giggles of those getting harnessed. It was an odd looking contraption that towered 100 feet above us, designed to give riders the thrill of a lifetime. As its metal beams reflected the glimmer of the setting sun onto my face, I had not a care in the world. But then a sudden scream filled the air, so potent that it grabbed the attention of everyone in the area. I waited for the harness to catch, for the girl to be swung back up into safety.

But the rope never caught her.

The terrifying thud left the entire arena silent. One second… two seconds… No one moved. No one made a noise. I stood there in complete horror, my mouth gaping in disbelief. As the dust settled the crowd suddenly began to panic. Doctors quickly identified themselves and ran in to help, security ordered ambulances, and all I could do was stand there, numb.

On that day, sixteen-year-old Elizabeth Mohl died, and I had to watch. I cried about it for days, not able to make sense of it. Why did this happen? How could someone so seemingly invincible be gone in an instant? That fall changed the way I view my life. It is not a burden, an obligation, or a responsibility, but rather it is a gift. I have been gifted with so many talents and opportunities. Every day I embrace what it means to be alive, and on those days where everything seems to be a chore, I remind myself how very fortunate I am to be living in this beautiful country, healthy and young. This experience has taught me to set goals and reach for my highest expectations, because I never know if today is going to be my last.

Suddenly that iPod didn't seem all that important.

Discussion Questions

1. In order for her readers to feel the horror she felt while watching this tragedy, Rotter needs to supply details. Which details place you there at the fencepost with Rotter?

2. Describe a time when your perspective changed because of something you experienced.

3. When we read blogs, we form impressions about the writer. What impressions did you form about Rotter? Provide examples from the blog to support your answer.

Thinking Like a Writer: Creative Nonfiction

If you've made it this far in the text, you're probably already thinking like a writer. You're carrying a notebook or note cards with you.
You're searching for the darn pen you could have sworn was in your
jacket. You're searching for a stray pen, wondering how demented you'll
seem if you ask the supermarket clerk for one, just for a second, because
you have this idea, and you're afraid that if you don't get it down it will
slip away like rainwater. You're staring at napkins with indecipherable
scratches you've made on them that you *know* were important at the
time but now can't figure out why. You're losing focus at times, even
when your best friend speaks directly to you, because something this
friend said triggered an idea you'd like to jot down for the paper you're
writing this week. You're bolting from your bed just as you're getting
comfortable because some actor on television blurted out a line that
might help with next week's paper. You're wondering what your teacher
thought of the last paper you handed in and considering sending an
e-mail, worded casually to belie the urgency you feel. You're wondering
about a classmate's reactions, too, because you've found someone you
can trust, who isn't harsh with criticism and who enjoys your writing.
In fact, you write sometimes with this person in mind. But you don't
want to be a pest, so you wait, and endure, and tell yourself not to betray
how much this writing business means to you. You're paying attention
a little differently now when you read, too. You mark phrases you wish

you'd written and write down words you'd like to use yourself. Every so often you run to the dictionary. You're beginning to notice writing contests as well and are considering sending work out to them.

Even if this description doesn't capture you well, you're at least familiar with the pressure of wondering where the next idea will come from. The guideposts provided throughout this book have probably helped in this regard—they have focused your options and have compelled you to search along specific avenues. But the guideposts may have felt limiting at times, which is inevitable—and ultimately enviable. No writer, at least no writer we know, sits down at a desk and decides to write an extended definition or a process paper. More likely, and more realistically, a writer begins with some version of this: *What do I want to say?* Now that you've written an extended definition or a process paper or some other papers suggested in this book, you should be better able to express what you want to say. This is not necessarily due to what you read in the text, but because you took the time to assemble words on a page. This chapter will provide you with a variety of ideas on how to more creatively express what you want to say, along with suggestions about sharing your work with others.

Journal Topic

Describe a specific achievement or task that reflects your work ethic.

Realizing You're a Writer

Once you say to yourself, *I am a writer*, you will begin to notice a need to produce writing, a desire to wrestle your thoughts and ideas into meaningful sentences and paragraphs. A writer, for example, may go to a movie. But she isn't quite finished with that experience until she writes her thoughts in the most vibrant language possible. Then she looks for a place to share those thoughts, perhaps in a blog post or other online forum, or simply by showing her creation to other people. A writer may be moved by an image in a newspaper, magazine, or work of art and accept the challenge of articulating what is so compelling about that image in a piece of writing that is organized, developed, descriptive, and—yes—has a thesis. That writing can then be shared in any number of ways. Or, a writer may have an opinion on an event or situation in her world, community, or school. She then writes that opinion in a well-crafted, forceful piece and looks for opportunities to present it to others.

At first, you may feel compelled to follow traditional forms as you write under your own direction. That's fine—but when you are ready to improvise, go for it. For most school assignments, the form determines the subject. For example, if the assignment is to write a narrative, the writing you produce will most likely be a story told in chronological order, with a beginning, middle, and end (see Chapter 3). If the assignment is to write a comparison, you will probably organize in point-by-point or block-by-block (see Chapter 5). However, when *you* decide on the topic, you will also decide on the form. You might find yourself writing creatively in the form of a recipe, open letter, diary entry, grocery list, or in almost any fashion that involves words. For instance, if you want to write about the time you decided to break off a relationship, you might write an open letter to others who find themselves in a similar predicament. Most topics will suggest their own forms. The organizational shape of your work will emerge naturally from the subject matter.

Opportunities to publish your writing exist all around you. Many publishing outlets are looking for your voice. In fact, they need your writing to provide material to their readers. Anthologies, magazines, online and print zines (small independent magazines), blogs, and other websites all can provide venues for your writing. Whether you want to write stories, poems, screenplays, opinions on current topics, daily summaries of your life and thoughts, or reviews of movies, books, or bands, the opportunity exists for you to write and publish those materials, and readers are out there for you. If you can't find a good niche for your writing, it is relatively easy for you to launch your own publishing venue, online or in print. For example, Figment.com is an online community for high school-age writers who want to share their work and respond to the work of others. See Chapter 12 for more ideas about sharing your work online.

When you acknowledge your identity as a writer, you will begin to notice places to submit your writing. Your school may have a newspaper, literary magazine, or other forum. Even if it's not an official publication, perhaps some people in your school are producing zines focused on a particular subject or outlook. If not, maybe you should start one.

Writers on Writing

This is the first secret of good writing: We must look *intently*, and hear *intently*, and taste *intently*…we must look at everything *very hard*. Is it the task at hand to describe a snowfall? Very well. We begin by observing that the snow is white. Is it as white as bond paper? White as whipped cream? Is the snow daisy white, or eggwhite white, or whitewash white? Let us look very hard. We will see that snow comes in different textures. The light snow that looks like powdered sugar is not the heavy snow that clings like wet cotton. When we write matter-of-factly that *Last night it snowed and this morning the fields were white*, we haven't said much. We have not looked *intently*.

—*James J. Kilpatrick*

Magazines such as *Teen Ink* and *Polyphony H.S.* are looking for writing from high school students. If you are interested in writing reviews about movies, music, or books, it's easy to post these yourself on Amazon.com, the Internet Movie Database (IMDb.com), or any other website that includes reactions from readers.

Before submitting your work to a magazine or website, thoroughly familiarize yourself with the publication to develop a keen sense of your audience. For example, *Newsweek* publishes a "My Turn" column that invites readers to send in an essay of about 800 words on some topic close to their hearts. One such piece appears at the end of this chapter in Professional Model 13.3, "My Black Skin Makes My White Coat Vanish," by Mana Lumumba-Kasongo. Read a few "My Turn" essays and you'll learn what the editors look for: an engaging voice that expresses a strong opinion or shares a personal experience. As you work your way through this chapter, you'll notice that many of the ideas discussed will help you write such an essay.

Conveying *tone* is one of the most important aspects involved in writing your own ideas in your own voice. As you remember from Chapter 1, tone is an author's attitude toward her subject matter. If you have chosen to write about a particular topic, you must have some particular feelings or attitude about that topic, and you want your reader to realize and understand those emotions and perspectives, and perhaps even share them. Careful attention to *diction* (the words you choose) is an important consideration in developing your tone. Another important way to employ tone is to structure your writing so that its revelations are presented in an order and manner that guides your reader to realizations that are in sync with your tone.

You may also find that the development of your writing includes a blending of the strategies described in this book. A single piece of writing may include a narrative section, an extended definition, and a discussion of a relevant process, or some other combination of strategies. For example, if you discern a need in your community for more soccer fields, you might decide to write a piece for your local or school newspaper. In that piece, you might include a paragraph or two detailing the times you have waited interminably for access to a field (narrative). You might then write a section in which you discuss the concepts of *sportsmanship* and *community* (definition). Finally, your piece might end with a discussion of exactly how your community could go about adding more soccer fields (process).

Writing Tip

If you're able to write with music playing, find a song that lasts about seven minutes. Use the song for an exercise in timed writing, trying to get as many words as you can on the page before the song ends. You can try this exercise at any point in the writing process, but the results will probably be most productive once you've selected a topic. If music interferes with your writing, try a stopwatch instead.

Writing Creative Nonfiction

A more artistic type of expository writing is called **creative nonfiction**. We tend to view creative nonfiction as "essays that rock." At its best, creative nonfiction is a fully developed prose piece exploring factual or true matters through the innovative use of rhetorical and literary devices. In other words, the purpose of such a piece is not merely to convey one theme or thesis. Its purpose is to illuminate the primary idea through the use of sophisticated (but not necessarily complex) language and development. Effective creative nonfiction pieces also convey a sense of mood that may not be present in more traditional essays.

Many creative nonfiction pieces employ techniques commonly used by fiction writers. A creative nonfiction writer may focus on the setting of his piece to firmly establish a sense of place, as well as to create a mood that serves his overall purpose. The people involved in the situation are treated almost like characters in a story, and they are presented to readers in much the same way that a fiction writer introduces and develops his characters.

Consider this opening paragraph from Nathaniel Philbrick's *Mayflower*:

> For sixty-five days, the *Mayflower* had blundered her way through storms and headwinds, her bottom a shaggy pelt of seaweed and barnacles, her leaky deck spewing salt water onto her passengers' devoted heads. There were 102 of them—104 if you counted the two dogs: a spaniel and a giant, slobbery mastiff. Most of their provisions and equipment were beneath them in the hold, the primary storage area of the vessel. The passengers were in the between, or 'tween, decks—a dank, airless space about seventy-five feet long and not even five feet high that separated the hold from the upper deck. The 'tween decks was more of a crawlspace than a place to live, made even more claustrophobic by the passengers' attempts to provide themselves with some privacy. A series of thin-walled cabins had been built, creating a crowded warren of rooms that overflowed with people and their possessions: chests of clothing, casks of food, chairs, pillows, rugs, and omnipresent chamber pots. There was even a boat—cut into pieces for later assembly—doing temporary duty as a bed.

Nearly every writer has been given the advice, "Write what you know." This seems to me to rely too heavily on the narrow, limited ego and conscious mind I've already slandered. I prefer another piece of advice I have heard, "Write what you need to know."

— *Susan Power*

Notice how Philbrick chooses particular words to emphasize the oppressive mood of this setting: *leaky, dank, airless, claustrophobic, thin-walled, crowded.* His approach is not appreciably different from how a fiction writer would approach a similar task.

In his book *Ava's Man,* journalist Rick Bragg presents his grandmother in language that would be right at home in a work of fiction:

> She was old all my life. Even when I was sitting in the red dirt, fascinated with my own toes, Ava's face had a line in it for every hot mile she ever walked, for every fit she ever threw. Her hair was long and black as crows, streaked with white, and her eyes, behind the ancient, yellowed glass of her round spectacles, were pale, pale blue, almost silver. The blind have eyes like that, that color, but Ava could see fine, Ava could see forever. She could tell your fortune by gazing into the dregs of your coffee cup, and swore that if the bottoms of your feet itched, you would walk on strange ground. She could be gentle as a baby bird and sweet as divinity candy, but if her prescription was off, or if she just got mad, she would sit bolt upright in bed at three o'clock in the morning and dog-cuss anyone who came to mind, including the dead. Some days she would doze in her rocker and speak softly to people that I could not find, even by looking under the porch. Now I know I was just listening to her dreams.

Although Ava was a real person, this description renders her as a "character" who then plays her part throughout the rest of Bragg's book. Bragg's description also provides us with the beginning of a sense of his admiration for Ava; in other words, his tone begins to emerge in this paragraph.

Although a creative nonfiction piece may be primarily in one mode or another—narration, process, or argument, for example—you should feel free to explore in writing whatever avenues open along the way. Feel free to digress, as long as it suits your overall purpose and contributes to the overall effect you intend for your reader. Ultimately, as you prepare the final version of your creative nonfiction, you will ask yourself: *Does this piece work? Does the writing achieve its purpose? Does the diction match the tone? Is the writing appropriately gauged to affect its intended audience?*

Journal Topic

Write about confidence. In what situations do you feel most and least confident? Explain.

Writing Satire and Parody

Two enjoyable stances to adopt in your own writing include *satire* and *parody*. **Satire** is ridicule or criticism of a particular target using gentle, humorous, or indirect diction. When writing satire, tone is extremely important. A reader can either immediately or gradually realize your attitude toward the subject matter.

Perhaps the most famous example of satire in the English language is Jonathan Swift's 1729 essay *A Modest Proposal* in which he satirically "proposes" the cannibalization of Irish children as a fitting extension of British treatment of the Irish in the eighteenth century. Swift's target—the British aristocracy—are symbolically identified as *landlords* when he writes, "I grant this food will be somewhat dear, and therefore very proper for landlords, who, as they have already devoured most of the parents, seem to have the best title to the children." Swift recommends that "a young healthy child well nursed is at a year old a most delicious, nourishing, and wholesome food, whether stewed, roasted, baked, or boiled." If taken out of its satirical context, his essay seems barbaric. When considered in context, it still seems barbaric, and that is exactly his point and attitude: The British treatment of the Irish was barbaric. Swift's tone and diction match his purpose.

American satirists Mark Twain and Will Rogers, as well as their more contemporary counterparts, such as Kurt Vonnegut, Jon Stewart, Chris Rock, and Sarah Vowell use the powerful and famous as their most tempting targets, frequently with hilarious results. Rarely do these writers go for

Writing Tip

Writers keep journals for a variety of purposes: for posterity, for personal satisfaction, or simply for brainstorming ideas. Most journals are private and are not meant to be read by others. But consider working on a different kind of journal as well, a journal with a specific audience in mind: your parents, a relative, a friend. The next few years are probably going to be defining ones for you. Perhaps you want to create a record of this time for someone. The advantage of keeping such a journal is manifold: you will probably be more persistent because you have a specific purpose; your sense of audience will be razor sharp; you will create a gift for someone that will mean much more than the pair of socks you were considering. If you don't leap on this idea today or tomorrow, tuck it away and think about writing a journal one day for your children. What were you thinking about when your son took his first step, when your daughter tackled the dog? Wouldn't you like to receive such a journal?

easy jokes. On the contrary, their writing is carefully crafted to produce both humor and satire.

Parody ridicules an artistic work by imitating some of its features and exaggerating others. Films such as *Scream* and *Scary Movie*, and their seemingly endless sequels, are actually parodies of a film genre that includes horror movies like *Halloween*, *Nightmare on Elm Street*, and numerous others. Many Mel Brooks films are also parodies: *Blazing Saddles* is a parody of westerns; *Spaceballs* is a spoof on outer space epics; *Young Frankenstein* is a takeoff on classic monster movies.

In writing, parody copies some of the most obvious features and exaggerates other features of a genre, piece of writing, or particular author. Writers with a distinctive voice make especially good objects of parody—William Shakespeare, Ernest Hemingway, and William Faulkner, for example. Perhaps worth noting here is the idea that parody need not be used only for negative, critical purposes. Parody can also be a form of tribute. Parodying an admired author or artist is a creative mixture of honoring and teasing.

Anyone familiar with the work and style of Ernest Hemingway can identify and enjoy the aspects of his work parodied by Susannah Indigo in this short piece:

Across the Freeway and Into the Cheese

The thing about living in the tunnels was that you could stay hungry for a long time and barely notice because of all the dancing in the dark. Hunger was good discipline for a prairie dog and you learned from it. Cy learned it a little too well and this was well and good, but Cy was not well.

"We could take him to Harry's Bar and American Grill for good food and drink," Lady Marmot suggested, looking sadly at Cy's furry body slumped just under the swinging chandelier at the far end of the Lost tunnel.

"No, Harry's Bar is too far," I told her, checking Cy's slow pulse. "This is not a moveable beast."

"What shall we do?"

"We'll leave him here and cross the Big Road to the place with the numbers. A fine plastic dish of nachos with extra onions and a lemon-lime slurpee will do the trick." The place with the bold numbers was not exactly Harry's, but then, what was?

"Oh no, not the Big Road. Not again. Couldn't we just go across the river and into the trees?" she asked.

"No."

"Why not?"

"It's been done."

I held her close and she smelled like hope and fear mixed with dirt. She had the aroma of a woman who can look at you and make you believe you can save her and you know you can't but you try anyway and maybe tomorrow, with any luck, you'll still be alive to take her to Harry's.

"Must we go?"

"We must."

If that was how it was then that was how it was but there was no law saying that Lady Marmot had to like it and we both knew it.

"Hold my paw," I said, and she grabbed on as though it mattered.

We ran. The traffic never stopped. We ran as though our lives depended on it. When we hit the yellow lines I felt a glimmer of hope. The threats were many in the dirt-side world, but none could make you a man quite like the promise of roadkill.

When we made it to the cheese she kissed me hard. I knew then that we'd make it back and I knew I would make Cy well and this was well and good, but I also knew that when this was done I would have to face writing the hard stories about up in the dirt. I kissed her hard anyway. It wasn't exactly love, but then, what was?

If you have a subject that you would like to satirize or parody, follow these simple steps:

1. **Identify your subject as precisely as possible:** Is it a particular person? If so, what exactly about this person is worthy of your efforts? His policies, persona, attitude, or accomplishments? If your target is an idea or attitude, what are the exact contours of the problem created by it? If you want to write a parody of the work of other writers, define for yourself whether your interest is in a particular author, a specific story, or an entire genre.

2. **Determine your purpose:** Do you want to write a gently teasing tweak of your target? Do you want to write in scathing language so that your object is utterly humiliated? Is your purpose to convey an attitude that is superior to that of your target, so that a logical person will adopt your views? This process of determination is critical because it has enormous implications for your tone, diction, and overall approach.

3. **Identify your target points, perhaps in an informal outline:** What are the obvious and subtle points that you want to address in your writing? What exactly bothers you about your target? A satire says something meaningful and leads a reader to a new awareness. Be sure you have something meaningful to offer. Otherwise, it's just a rant. A parody must be focused on identifiable points of comparison, or your work will be confusing. (If a reader has no familiarity

with Ernest Hemingway, Susannah Indigo's sample parody probably seems pointless.)

4. **Have some fun while you write:** Let your emotions and attitudes toward your topic fuel your first draft. Later, during editing, you can rein in your emotions, if that is more appropriate for your purpose.

5. **Put away your draft for a few hours or a few days:** The editing of a satire piece can require some distance. After you have cooled off and the writing is no longer such a direct expression of your immediate emotional state, ask yourself these questions: *Does it still work? Does the diction match the tone? Will the audience understand both the content and the intent?*

If you enjoy writing and want to continue after you've closed this book, consider forming a writing group with a friend or two. You can rotate meeting locations, maybe meeting at each other's houses, or pick a central location. It's critical as well to decide when to meet. Bring a calendar to each meeting and select the next date before you leave. Don't rely on saying, "We'll call each other," because it's easier not to call.

What happens at the meetings? You'll have to decide this for yourselves, but here's a simple format. Someone writes an essay (or story or poem) and makes enough copies for everyone in the group. If the work is long, the writer delivers it to group members ahead of time so they can read it. If the work is short, the writer can bring it to the meeting and read it aloud to the group. Once everyone in the group is familiar with the work, discuss it. Be supportive and constructive. You can certainly mark errors in grammar or punctuation, but don't spend much time discussing them. Focus on ideas instead. When your own work is discussed, try to listen instead of participating. Otherwise, you may concentrate on defending your writing choices rather than being receptive to others' ideas. In fact, during discussion, you may want to busy yourself writing down some of their ideas.

While writing groups can be intense and invigorating, maybe you prefer not to discuss your work, or maybe you can't find others who are as committed to a group as you are. In either case, you may want to peruse *Poets & Writers* (online at www.pw.org), a magazine in which writers share ideas on their craft, covering much more than just poetry. Writers ultimately work alone, but such magazines provide a sense of community and remind us that our struggles are universal. As a bonus, the back of the magazine is filled with hundreds of addresses to which you can send your work.

Being a Writer

One limitation of the writing you do in school is that it frequently seems artificial. You compose much of your school writing in response to an assignment designed to provide practice with a particular rhetorical concept. Then your writing is read by a very small audience: your teacher and perhaps your classmates.

How will your writing change when you choose the assignment, decide on your own due date, and know your work will reach dozens, hundreds, thousands, or even more readers? Professional writers deal with this reality on a daily basis. They decide what they want to write about, how to develop it, and how best to put it in the hands of readers.

Now that you have a solid background in writing, and as you see the end of high school on the horizon, you should begin to think more like a writer and less like a *student* writer. Look for opportunities to write what *you* choose and then say what *you* want to say.

Earlier chapters of this book provided you with ideas, advice, and practice in dealing with numerous writing purposes. Implicit in this approach is that while you are a student, you should be learning. (Otherwise, going to school has very little purpose.) Becoming adept at using these various methods and approaches is an important part of becoming an effective writer and communicator, and being an effective writer and communicator is essential to being fully human. This chapter provides you with ideas and, ideally, inspiration for continuing to discover and use new dimensions to your writing voice. But this is really only a beginning.

Writers on Writing

In the richness of language, its grace, breadth, dexterity, lies its power. To speak with clarity, brevity and wit is like holding a lightning rod.

—*James Salter*

Practice

Your assignment for this chapter is to write a piece of creative nonfiction. Before beginning the Chapter Assignment, try the following exercises to practice writing creative nonfiction.

1. Think about a routine you perform nearly every day: getting ready for school, walking from class to class, meeting friends for lunch, or something similar. Write a paragraph on this routine that makes the behavior seem anything but routine. For instance, lunch with friends could be described in the form of an Academy Awards presentation: "The award for messiest eater goes to...."

2. Write a few sentences of satire intended to subtly criticize driving habits that annoy you. Recall that satire is usually more subtle than a direct attack or commentary. For instance, a direct account might include a brief description of various types of drivers. A satire, on the other hand, might depict various drivers as different breeds of dogs.

3. Create a public service announcement on friendship. Include information on the qualities one should possess to be a good friend.

4. Write two descriptions of one familiar place, adopting a different tone for each. For instance, you might describe a dentist's office using details that evoke admiration—then terror. In the first case, the dentist's drill might sound like a purr or hum; in the second case, the same drill might grind shrilly.

5. Spend about three minutes addressing this question: What makes people happy? Once you're done, think of a creative way to convey your answer to an audience of your peers. Sometimes a creative title will prompt ideas. Consider these titles for your creative nonfiction essay: (a) Happiness 101; (b) Happiness Is Like Building an Ice Cream Sundae; (c) How to Package Happiness.

Chapter Assignment

Prewriting

Use the following suggestions to help you select a topic and clarify the tone of your essay.

Selecting a topic and adopting a tone usually occur simultaneously. If you decide to write about injustice, for instance, your tone is probably going to be serious. Once you select a topic—and appropriate tone— keep an open mind and consider a different approach. If writing about injustice, consider satire or parody. In practical terms, try this: Write an opening paragraph that matches your initial inclinations toward your topic. Then write an alternate opening. You may ultimately decide to stick with your initial thoughts, but this is a useful exercise in exploring fresh approaches and seeing your material anew.

Writing Topics

Select one of the following suggestions to develop into an essay. Feel free to tailor these topics to suit your needs.

1. Imagine that your school newspaper wants to run an article outlining study tips. The editors are worried that a straightforward approach will bore readers. Think of a more novel and creative way to approach this article.

2. You are a museum tour guide. Highlight the damaging effects of smoking, drinking, or using other drugs by leading the reader from one museum "room" to another. You might begin with something like, "Welcome to the cancer exhibit. On the left are your lungs…"

3. Write your own *Newsweek* "My Turn" essay. To get a sense of how to approach writing this essay, read a few recent columns, two of which are included at the end of this chapter, Professional Model 13.3 and Student Model 13.1. In brief, you will state an opinion or share a personal experience. This is *your* turn to assert *your* voice, your turn to be heard.

4. Think about an issue that many people regard seriously, such as obeying rules, using "appropriate" manners, attending a good college, or dressing sharply. Write a satire on this issue in which you clearly suggest that people lighten up.

5. Write a parody poking fun at some famous book or person.

6. Write about an event that shaped your life. Instead of using the traditional approach of a narrative, try a different form: a newspaper column, a news bulletin, a movie review, a letter, and so on. You may consider comparing the personal event with some major historical event—or treating the personal event *as* historical.

7. Turn on talk radio or watch a few minutes of talking heads on television to find out the hot topic of the day. You'll probably discover that the same points are being made in the same stale way. Your task is to write about the topic from an original perspective. (If you have access to cable television, you might want to watch an episode of *The Daily Show* or *The Colbert Report* on Comedy Central for examples on how to do this. The newspaper *The Onion* or TheOnion.com, its online counterpart, are other good sources to study.)

8. If you like the previous suggestion but become stuck, consider writing a parody of talk radio or television. For instance, you can write about some topic of your choosing from the point of view of a talking head.

9. Henry David Thoreau once asserted that with the invention of the railroad, people lost the use of their feet. Write about a recent change or invention that, in your opinion, has caused more negative than positive consequences.

10. If you've ever had to wait in line for a driver's license or to be admitted to a hospital, you know how belittling this can be. Write a satire on the ways in which our lives are reduced by bureaucratic policies.

Revision

As you revise and edit your first draft, consider these suggestions.

1. Think about the tone you've adopted in your essay. Are there words or phrases that don't match or contribute to this tone? Select a few sentences and play around with different word choices to clarify your tone.

2. Pore through your essay and underline four or five verbs that could be replaced with more effective verbs. For each underlined verb, think of one or two substitutes.

3. Read your paper aloud to hear your transitions. Check two or three places where you believe the transitions are working well. Also, mark

all the places where smoother transitions are needed. Learn from the former and change the latter.

4. Reread your first paragraph. Is this the best way to engage your audience? How else might you begin this essay? Reread your conclusion. What is your purpose here and how do you achieve it? Describe another way in which you could end the essay.

Peer Review

Use these questions to help you evaluate another student's writing. Remember, specific suggestions and examples are most helpful.

1. Write down two or three questions you have for the writer.

2. What did you like most about this essay? Be specific.

3. What parts of the essay do you think could be more developed?

4. What other suggestions do you have for the writer?

"No Messages on This Server," and Other Lessons of Our Time

by Verlyn Klinkenborg

Meet the Writer

Verlyn Klinkenborg's essays and editorials have been published in many magazines. He lives in rural New York and writes a column for the *New York Times* on many subjects, but most often on the universal themes he sees operating within the tracts of his small farm.

I do not own a BlackBerry or a pager. I don't chat or instant-message or text-message. My cellphone could connect to the Web if I let it, but I don't. I don't gamble on the Internet nor do I game on it (or on any other electronic device). And yet I'm starting to twitch.

I have three everyday telephone numbers, not counting Skype and a calling card, and two fax numbers. I have six working e-mail addresses, as well as a few no longer in use. A couple of weeks ago I started writing a blog for *The Times*. Part of my job, as a blogger, is to read and approve the publication of readers' comments. That is the equivalent of another form of e-mail. There are probably half a dozen Really Simple Syndication tools on my computer, and one or another of them is always unfurling the latest ribbon of news in the background. It is astonishing how old the morning's headlines seem by evening.

Back in the dial-up days, computer users made brief forays onto a bulletin board or some outpost of the primitive Internet, all the while clocking connection time in order to keep costs down. Going online was like driving a Stanley Steamer—better for scaring horses and wowing the youth than for long-distance hauling. There was always a slightly neurotic edge to it. You could feel the seconds ticking away while nothing happened. But nowadays turning on the computer is synonymous with being online. Who turns the computer off? It's rarely worth severing that digital link. For some of us, the computer has become less and less a place to work and more and more a place to await messages from the ether, like hopeful spiritualists.

I thought I was a fairly temperate user of computers. But in the past year or so I have become addicted to e-mail. I confess it. You probably know the signs. Do you tell your e-mail program to check for messages automatically every two minutes—and then disbelieve it when it comes up empty? Have you learned to hesitate before answering a new message so it doesn't look as though you were hunched over the keyboard, waiting? Do you secretly think of lunch as a time for your inbox to fill up? But the clearest sign of e-mail addiction is simply to ask yourself, what is the longest you've gone without checking your e-mail in the past two months? Anything longer than a broken night's sleep is good.

I blame my e-mail addiction, in part, on the United States Postal Service. Seeing the mail lady pull up to our rural mailbox in her red station wagon with the flashing amber light on top is one of the high points of my day, whether there is anything "good" in the mail or not. (The "goodness" of mail is another question entirely.) When you think about it, the postal system is a remarkable thing, even in this new universe of instant-delivery systems. Its genius is this: The mail comes only once a day. All that expectation gathered into a single visit! And once-a-day-ness is built right into the system. I try to imagine the mail lady bringing every piece of mail to our mailbox as she gets it. In fact, that's exactly what she does, because the mail shows up only once a day at the local post office.

I suppose I could tell my e-mail program to check for mail on a postal schedule—once a day—although minutes are the only intervals the software understands. But that would defeat the logic of e-mail, which is meant to arrive seriatim—hence, its addictive punch. The principle of snail mail is infrequency; the principle of e-mail is frequency. The real question is, what is the frequency for?

I think of e-mail as a continuing psychology experiment that studies the effect on humans of abrupt, frequently repeated stimuli—often pleasurable, sometimes not, but always with the positive charge that comes from seeing new mail in the inbox. So far, the experiment has revealed, in me, the synaptic responses of a squirrel.

It is a truism of our time that we now have shorter attention spans than ever before. I don't think that is true. What we have now are electronic media that can pulse at the actual rate of human thought. We have the distinct discomfort of seeing our neural pace reflected in the electronic world around us.

Amid all that is wasteful, distracting, irrelevant and downright evil about e-mail, there is also this. We carry dozens of people, sometimes hundreds, around with us in our heads. They pass in and out of our thoughts as quickly as thought itself. E-mail is a way to gather these people—so many of them scattered across the globe—into the immediacy of our lives in a way that makes even a phone call feel highly formalized. It is the nearness of e-mail, the conversations it creates, that is addicting as much as the minute-by-minute stimuli. I try to remember that when I am getting twitchy, when I start wondering whether the mail server is down again. I tell myself that I'm just listening for a chorus of voices, a chorus of friends.

Discussion Questions

1. What is Klinkenborg's tone? What phrases, sentences, or paragraphs effectively convey this tone? What other possible tones could a writer adopt for this subject?

2. Klinkenborg seems to be writing only about himself. (In fact, six of the eight paragraphs begin with *I*.) Does Klinkenborg intend for this essay to have wider relevance? How do you know?

3. Describe Klinkenborg's method of developing this essay. How does each paragraph build upon the preceding paragraph?

4. Evaluate Klinkenborg's final sentence. What effect does it have?

5. Does Klinkenborg's essay remind you of anything in your own experience? Could you write about similar subject matter from your own perspective?

I Have Been Called a Luddite

by Kurt Vonnegut

Meet the Writer

Kurt Vonnegut was the beloved author of many novels and short stories. His themes centered on the dangers of rampant technology, the warnings about the advancement of scientific discoveries stripped of morality, and the need for human connection. He managed to convey all this in a whimsical and endearing style.

I have been called a Luddite. I welcome it.

Do you know what a Luddite is? A person who hates newfangled contraptions. Ned Ludd was a textile worker in England at around the start of the nineteenth century who busted up a lot of new contraptions—mechanical looms that were going to put him out of work, that were going to make it impossible for him with his particular skills to feed, clothe, and shelter his family. In 1813 the British government executed by hanging seventeen men for "machine breaking," as it was called, a capital crime.

Today we have contraptions like nuclear submarines armed with Poseidon missiles that have H-bombs in their warheads. And we have contraptions like computers that cheat you out of becoming. Bill Gates says, "Wait till you can see what your computer can become." But it's you who should be doing the becoming, not the damn fool computer. What you can become is the miracle you were born to be through the work that you do.

Progress has beat the heck out of me. It took away from me what a loom must have been to Ned Ludd two hundred years ago. I mean a typewriter. There is no longer such a thing anywhere. *Huckleberry Finn*, incidentally, was the first novel ever to be typewritten.

In the old days, not long ago, I used to type. And, after I had about twenty pages, I would mark them up with a pencil, making corrections. Then I would call Carol Atkins, who was a typist. Can you imagine? She lived out in Woodstock, New York, which you know was where the famous sex and drugs event in the '60s got its name from (it actually took place in the nearby town of Bethel and anybody who says they remember being there wasn't there.) So, I would call up Carol and say, "Hey Carol. How are you doing? How is your back? Got any blue-birds?" We would chit-chat back and forth—I love to talk to people.

She and her husband had been trying to attract bluebirds, and as you know if you have tried to attract bluebirds, you put the blue-bird house only three feet off the ground, usually on a fence along a property line. Why there are any bluebirds left I don't know. They didn't have any luck, and neither did I, out at my place in the country. Anyway we chat away, and finally I say, "Hey, you know I got some pages. Are you still typing?" And she sure is. And I know it will be so neat, it will look like it was done by a computer. And I say, "I hope it doesn't get lost in the mail." And she says, "Nothing ever gets lost in the mail." And that in fact has been my experience. I never have lost anything. And so, she is a Ned Ludd now. Her typing is worthless.

Anyway, I take my pages and I have this thing made out of steel, it's called a paper clip, and I put my pages together, being careful to number them, too, of course. So I go downstairs, to take off, and I pass my wife, the photo journalist Jill Krementz, who was bloody high tech then, and is even higher tech now. She calls out, "Where are you going?" Her favorite reading when she was a girl was Nancy Drew mysteries, you know, the girl detective. So she can't help but ask, "Where are you going?" And I say, "I am going out to get an envelope." And she says, "Well, you're not a poor man. Why don't you buy a thousand envelopes? They'll deliver them, and you can put them in a closet." And I say, "Hush."

So I go down the steps, and this is on 48th Street in New York City between Second Avenue and Third, and I go out to this news-stand across the street where they sell magazines and lottery tickets and stationery. And I know their stock very well, and so I get an enve-lope, a manila envelope. It is as though whoever made that envelope knew what size of paper I'm using. I get in line because there are people buying lottery tickets, candy, and that sort of thing, and I chat with them. I say, "Do you know anybody who ever won anything in the lottery?" And, "What happened to your foot?"

Finally I get up to the head of the line. The people who own this store are Hindus. The woman behind the counter has a jewel between her eyes. Now isn't that worth the trip? I ask her, "Have there been any big lottery winners lately?" Then I pay for the envelope. I take my manuscript and I put it inside. The envelope has two little metal prongs for going through a hole in the flap. For those of you who have never seen one, there are two ways of closing a manila envelope. I use both of them. First I lick the mucilage—it's kind of sexy. I put the little thin metal diddle through the hole—I never did know what they call them. Then I glue the flap down.

I go next to the postal convenience center down the block at the corner of 47th Street and Second Avenue. This is very close to the United Nations, so there are all these funny-looking people there from all over the world. I go in there and we are lined up again. I'm secretly in love with the woman behind the counter. She doesn't know it. My wife knows it. I am not about to do anything about it. She is so nice. All I have ever seen of her is from the waist up because she is always behind the counter. But every day she will do something with herself above her waist to cheer us up. Sometimes her hair will be all frizzy. Sometimes she will have ironed it flat. One day she was wearing black lipstick. This is all so exciting and so generous of her, just to cheer us all up, people from all over the world.

So I wait in line, and I say, "Hey what was that language you were talking? Was it Urdu?" I have nice chats. Sometimes not. There is also, "If you don't like it here, why don't you go back to your little tinhorn dictatorship where you came from?" One time I had my pocket picked in there and got to meet a cop and tell him about it. Anyway, finally I get up to the head of the line. I don't reveal to her that I love her. I keep poker-faced. She might as well be looking at a cantaloupe, there is so little information in my face, but my heart is beating. And I give her the envelope, and she weighs it, because I want to put the right number of stamps on it, and have her okay it. If she says that's the right number of stamps and cancels it, that's it. They can't send it back to me. I get the right stamps and I address the envelope to Carol in Woodstock.

Then I go outside and there is a mailbox. And I feed the pages to the giant blue bullfrog. And it says, "Ribbit."

And I go home. And I have had one hell of a good time.

Electronic communities build nothing. You wind up with nothing. We are dancing animals. How beautiful it is to get up and go out and do something. We are here on Earth to fart around. Don't let anybody tell you any different.

Discussion Questions

1. What is Vonnegut's thesis? Is it implied or explicitly stated? In your opinion, does he prove his thesis? Why or why not?

2. What is Vonnegut's tone? What phrases, sentences, or paragraphs effectively convey this tone? What other possible tones could a writer adopt for this subject?

3. Vonnegut begins this piece by discussing and defining the term *Luddite*. Then he never directly refers to it again. Is this an effective strategy? Why or why not?

4. Evaluate Vonnegut's final paragraph. Is it effective? Why or why not?

Professional Model 13.3

My Black Skin Makes My White Coat Vanish

by Mana Lumumba-Kasongo

Meet the Writer

Mana Lumumba-Kasongo is a freelance writer and board-certified emergency physician. She was born in the country of Zaire (now called the Democratic Republic of the Congo).

The first time it happened I was a brand-spanking-new M.D., filled with an intern's enthusiasm. Proudly wearing my pristine white coat and feeling sure that I was going to save the world, I walked into my patient's room.

"Hello, I'm Dr. Kasongo. How can I help you?" I asked cheerfully. The patient was a pleasant African-American woman whose chief complaint was abdominal pain. I spent the next 10 minutes taking her history, examining her thoroughly and doing a rectal exam to spot signs of internal bleeding. I explained that I'd treat her pain, check her blood work and urine samples, and go from there. "That's great," she said with a smile. "When is the doctor going to see me?"

I frowned. Hadn't she heard me? Hadn't I just administered an invasive exam on her posterior? "I *am* the doctor," I told her, making myself smile again. Did she sense my newness? Was it my lack of confidence that made it hard for her to believe I had a medical degree? I decided that even though I was a 30-year-old intern, it must be the youthful appearance I inherited from my ageless mother that was confusing her.

That was four years ago. There have been many such incidents since then, ranging from the irritating to the comical, and I no longer have much doubt that what baffled my patient was the color of my skin. Several months later, I was having dinner at an upscale hotel in Las Vegas with a friend, when she started choking on a piece of food. As she flailed her arms in obvious distress, frantic cries of "Is there a doctor in the room?" rang out from nearby tables. I assured everyone that I was a doctor and administered the Heimlich maneuver successfully. Even as my friend regained her bearings, people at the surrounding tables kept screaming for a physician. Once the "real doctors"—two white males—came to the table and saw that her airway was clear, they told the staff that it appeared that I was in fact a doctor and that my friend was going to be fine. Yet, far from comforting them, this information produced only quizzical looks.

Over the years, the inability of patients and others to believe that I am a doctor has left me utterly demoralized. Their incredulity persists even now that I am a senior resident, working in one of the world's busiest hospital emergency rooms. How can it be that with all the years of experience I have, all the procedures I've performed and all the people I've interacted with in emergency situations, I still get what I call "the look"? It's too predictable. I walk in the room and introduce myself, then wait for the patient—whether he or she is black, white or Asian—to steal glances at the ID card that is attached to my scrubs or white coat. (I've thought of having it changed to read something like: *It's true. I am a real doctor. Perhaps you've seen a black one on TV?*)

I remember talking to one of the white, male attending physicians in my training program after he witnessed one such encounter. "Listen," he said, trying to comfort me, "I can walk in wearing a T-shirt and jeans and I'll always be seen as the doctor, even without an introduction. You will not." My heart sank as I thought of Malcolm X's words, "Do you know what white racists call black Ph.D.'s? N----r!"

Only a small portion of the growing number of female doctors—not quite 4 percent—look like me. Perhaps that's why, for most people, "doctor" still doesn't fit the stereotypical image of a black woman in this country. Unfortunately, black children may be even more adversely affected by this than white ones. That point was driven home to me months ago, when a 6-year-old black girl refused to let me treat her when her mother brought her to the emergency room and left us alone. She insisted on being seen by a white doctor, leaving me feeling both embarrassed and humiliated.

Throughout the years, I've spoken to other female doctors about their experiences. While my white, female colleagues sometimes get "the look," it doesn't happen nearly as often as it does for black, female doctors. My African-American peers have their own ways of dealing with it; some even preempt suspicious patients by saying, "Yes, I am a doctor, and you can check online when you get home."

I've decided to try not to be bothered by my patients' attitudes. Like all doctors, I've worked hard to get to where I am. And occasionally I see that there is hope for humanity. A few months ago I treated a white, eightysomething man who had pneumonia. As I set up his IV line, I noticed that he was staring at me. Finally he said, "It must have been very hard for you to make it." After a pause, he added, "A woman—and black." We both laughed. Someone understood.

Discussion Questions

1. What is Lumumba-Kasonga's tone? What phrases, sentences, or paragraphs effectively convey this tone? What other possible tones could a writer adopt for this subject?

2. Lumumba-Kasonga relates four narrative episodes in her essay. What is the effect of each?

3. Lumumba-Kasonga begins with an ambiguous first sentence that leaves the reader guessing about what "it" is. What are the advantages and disadvantages of this strategy?

4. Evaluate the transitions at the beginning of each paragraph. How does each provide a link to the previous paragraph?

Nobel Prize Acceptance Speech, 1950

by William Faulkner

Meet the Writer

Acclaimed American author William Faulkner was raised in Oxford, Mississippi. His many novels, all set in his legendary and imagined Yoknapatawpha County, feature an entire world within a few square miles.

I feel that this award was not made to me as a man but to my work—a life's work in the agony and sweat of the human spirit, not for glory and least of all for profit, but to create out of the materials of the human spirit something which did not exist before. So this award is only mine in trust. It will not be difficult to find a dedication for the money part of it commensurate with the purpose and significance of its origin. But I would like to do the same with the acclaim too, by using this moment as a pinnacle from which I might be listened to by the young men and women already dedicated to the same anguish and travail, among whom is already that one who will someday stand here where I am standing.

Our tragedy today is a general and universal physical fear so long sustained by now that we can even bear it. There are no longer problems of the spirit. There is only the question: When will I be blown up? Because of this, the young man or woman writing today has forgotten the problems of the human heart in conflict with itself which alone can make good writing because only that is worth writing about, worth the agony and the sweat.

He must learn them again. He must teach himself that the basest of all things is to be afraid; and, teaching himself that, forget it forever, leaving no room in his workshop for anything but the old verities and truths of the heart, the old universal truths lacking which any story is ephemeral and doomed—love and honor and pity and pride and compassion and sacrifice. Until he does so he labors under a curse. He writes not of love but of lust, of defeats in which nobody loses anything of value, of victories without hope and worst of all without pity and compassion. His griefs grieve on no universal bones, leaving no scars. He writes not of the heart but of the glands.

Until he relearns these things he will write as though he stood among and watched the end of man. I decline to accept the end of man. It is easy enough to say that man is immortal simply because he will endure; that when the last ding-dong of doom has clanged and faded from the last worthless rock hanging tideless in the last red and dying evening, that even then there will still be one more sound: that of his puny inexhaustible voice, still talking. I refuse to accept this. I believe that man will not merely endure: he will prevail. He is immortal, not because he alone among creatures has an inexhaustible voice, but because he has a soul, a spirit capable of compassion and sacrifice and endurance. The poet's, the writer's, duty is to write about these things. It is his privilege to help man endure by lifting his heart, by reminding him of the courage and honor and hope and pride and compassion and pity and sacrifice which have been the glory of his past. The poet's voice need not merely be the record of man, it can be one of the props, the pillars to help him endure and prevail.

Discussion Questions

1. Consider Faulkner's rhetorical situation regarding his audience and purpose. He was receiving the most important literary award available to a living writer; he was speaking to a live audience in a foreign country; and he knew his remarks would be widely read. What phrases, sentences, and paragraphs did Faulkner intend for an audience wider than the one in the room at the time of the speech? How do you know?

2. Since this is a speech, rhythm is critical. Using two examples from this speech, explain how Faulkner achieves rhythm. Consider sound, repetition, and parallel structure.

3. What is Faulkner's thesis? Is it implied or explicitly stated? In your opinion, has Faulkner proven his thesis? Why or why not?

4. What does Faulkner say is the "duty" of a writer? Does this apply to you? Why or why not?

The Question

by Julia Kraus

Meet the Writer

Julia Kraus is from Wichita, Kansas. This essay was the top winner in the Kaplan/Newsweek "My Turn" Essay Competition.

It's a normal conversation, really.

It's the first day of the 11th grade. I've just met my biology lab partner. We talk casually. He mentions his brother. Then he asks me The Question.

The Question isn't earth-shattering. It isn't even unusual. The Question is: how many brothers and sisters do you have?

It isn't even an interesting question. He doesn't expect the answer I give him after a good ten seconds of silence. My answer is: I can't remember. I really can't. And The Question always throws me for a loop anyway. Does he mean right now, how many siblings I have at this moment in time? Or does he mean every sibling I've ever had in my life?

Because I honestly don't know the answer to how many siblings I have right now. When I left home this morning, I only had three. When I come home tonight, I could still have three. Or I could have another two. Or four. It depends. And as for all the siblings I've ever had, the tally is currently nearing 250.

I think.

Foster care is so hard to explain.

Every time someone asks The Question, it ends up becoming a whole conversation. There's no easy way to answer. I could say "two" and have that be the end of it, because I do have two, real, son-of-my-parents brothers, but that answer is incomplete. It doesn't tell the whole truth. I could say, "over 200," but that leads to blank looks and such witticisms as "what do you do, run a sweatshop?" I could just say we do foster care: and lead into the inevitable conversation straightaway. Any way I truthfully answer The Question sends me scores more.

How long have we been doing this? Almost eight years now. Yes, sometimes it's hard to give them up. No I don't usually mind them. I like kids. No, I'm not a foster kid myself. No, I'm not adopted. No, I don't know your cousin Rosie that got put in foster care last year. I couldn't tell you even if I did know her. Why? Not allowed. Against the law. No, I can't tell you stories about them.

I don't mind questions, usually.

The last thing was a lie, though. I could tell you stories if I wanted to, if I left off the names of the kids. But if you ask, I won't tell. Why would you want to know? Why would you care?

You'd tell me to stop talking if I started to tell you stories. You'd be shocked. You wouldn't want to hear.

There's the 3-year old girl that was stripped, doused with cold water and force-fed. In her front yard in January.

There's the retarded teenage mother who doesn't know who her daughter's father is. The young woman's stepfather swears up and down that it can't be him because he's had a vasectomy. Not because he's never had sex with his stepdaughter.

There's the 6-month-old boy, eyes goggling almost sightlessly, hooked up to God-knows-what machine, whimpering. He's been sent to us because he was shaken at a previous foster home, shaken hard, shaken fast, shaken violently until his brain slapped against his skull and his eyes popped out, whereupon his shaker pushed them back into their sockets with his thumbs. His vision will never exceed 20:100.

There's a 3-year-old boy with eyes swollen shut by a huge double shiner. His two bottom left ribs were broken. He had fist-sized bruises on his chin and cheeks. The only time he complained was once, when he was eating. He said his mouth hurt. My mom looked. His teeth were rotted through.

There's the baby we had for just a day or two. Not long after she went home, her father flew into a temper and killed her. She was less than a year, I do remember that.

Are you covering your ears? Are you screaming at me to stop? Good.

I want to.

That'll teach you to ask me to tell you stories.

I remember being 14 and being at a sleepover. I didn't know one of the girls well. Everyone else was talking animatedly about a TV show.

"Fill me in, guys," I said, "I've never heard of this show. What's it about?"

The girl I didn't know stared at me. "Never?"

I shook my head. "I don't really have time to watch TV...."

"You're pretty naïve, aren't you?" She interrupted. "Pretty sheltered." She said it casually.

I stared at her. "Naïve?"

"Well," she said. "I can just tell. You are."

I said nothing.

I wanted to. I wanted to stand up and scream at her, tell her stories that made her cringe and cry and beg me to stop. I wanted to shake her hard, shake her fast, shake her violently.

Instead, I said firmly, some time later, "I'm not naïve. You've never seen a newborn addicted to cocaine. I am not naïve."

She looked at me somewhat quizzically.

I'm not.

I think about them, all the kids. Pictures come, disparate, non-sequential pictures that tell no stories and give no names. My mother, sleeping in a rocker with our first foster baby. My father, checking the sprinklers in the backyard with a toddler clutching his hand. A baby squalling in the port-a-crib. A pair of sad, too-old eyes. A tiny hand curled around my finger.

Sounds come. Cries, mainly terrified, or resigned, or painful, or hungry, or angry. Laughs sometimes. The sighs of a sleeping newborn. Computerized toddler toys. Kiddie jingles galore.

Smells come. Formula. Lysol. Clean hair. Spit-up. Diapers. Lotion. Detergent. Dryer sheets. Lemony air freshener.

And names come. Brandon. Nique. Devonte. Isaiah. Kevin. Typani. Leticia. Rosa. Angel. Sometimes the name brings a picture, but usually not. I am not naïve.

I stopped being naïve the day after I turned 9 years old, the day our first baby arrived. I will never be naïve again.

See what one Question will do?

Discussion Questions

1. Kraus's piece begins with an ambiguous statement. Is this an effective strategy? Why or why not?

2. Describe Kraus's purpose. In your opinion, does she fulfill her purpose? Why or why not?

3. Kraus's writing includes paragraphs with only one or two words, any number of sentence fragments, and quite a few of her paragraphs begin with *I*. Many writing purists would criticize her for these usages. What do you think?

4. Notice how the ending of Kraus's essay connects to the beginning. What is the effect of this strategy?

5. Kraus uses imagery to offer the reader a vivid understanding of her life. List three examples of imagery and describe the effect of each use.

Student Model 13.2

Hope
by Samantha Schmaus

Meet the Writer

Samantha Schmaus plans to attend the University of Minnesota–Duluth to eventually become a psychiatrist. She'd like to thank her parents, brother, and grandparents for their love and support.

Hope. A four letter word. Webster says it's "to have confidence, trust; to wish for something with expectation of its fulfillment." Dashboard Confessional says that "hope dangles on a string, like slow spinning redemption." Emily Dickinson says that hope is a thing with feathers.

I don't think that hope is a thing spinning on a string, or a bird, or that it can be easily explained.

Hope is elusive.

I take a smooth piece of clay, and examine it in my hands. It is the perfect texture, not too hard, not mushy; perfect. I just spent the past half hour wedging it, so all the air bubbles are out of it. I sat at the wedging table, creating the perfect piece of clay so that I could throw the perfect pot.

I walk over to my favorite wheel, make sure that I have the good bucket, filled with warm, clean water and all the tools necessary.

I put the bat on the wheel, and slam my piece of clay onto it.

I kick the wheel, while dousing the clay with water. I kick harder and harder, until it reaches the perfect speed, and I dig in.

The most horrible events in history have been caused by the best intentions.

I once had a friend who was having some troubles with this boy. She had liked him, but he was a jerk to her and she fell out of "like." He did something to redeem himself, and she thought for a day or two that she liked him again, and they started going out. Each day, she found more and more things about him that annoyed her. Things that she had never before noticed. The way he smacks his food while he eats, the way he expected her to have her entire life revolve around him, the way he memorized her work schedule, the way he met her before each class. Each day she found she liked him less and less, not only as a boyfriend, she liked him less as a person. He did certain things she didn't agree with, such as trying to control how she spent her time and who she hung out with and being exceedingly clingy. She didn't want to break up with him and hurt his feelings. She knew it would ruin the friendship that they had worked for years to create. She wondered if it was already too late. In the end, she began to resent him. She knew it wasn't his fault; it was her own issues that she was dealing with. Regardless, she began to resent everything about him.

I center the clay, and I lose a big chunk of it.

"Oh, well," I say. "It's just a little piece."

I raise the clay up and smoosh it down three times, destroying any air bubbles that threaten the survival of my pot.

I had another friend who had this long time crush on this guy. She had liked him back when they were young, back in the good old days of note-passing middle school. She had hoped when they got to high school, and everyone started coupling off, that they would be the next in line. They would be the next ones that everyone "aww cute"-ed. She got over it, but she still felt a connection to him, not so much sexual or whatever, but a strong, platonic connection. She considered him one of her better friends, and felt that she could talk to him about anything. Their relationship was an odd one, but they understood it and that was all that mattered.

At least, that's what I thought.

He revealed to one person that he liked another girl. One of my friend's best friends.

She ended up finding out in a round about way, picking up on clues and little pieces of overheard sentences. She felt betrayed, humiliated, and blind. How could she not have seen it? How could he have done this? How long had it been going on? Had everyone known and just watched as she made a fool of herself?

In her heart of hearts, I think she had probably hoped that one day, he would finally open his eyes and see what a catch was sitting right in front of him. I think she still has reason to hope, but what do I know?

Finally, I dive in with my thumbs to the very center of the clay, opening it up. Preparing it to become a glorious vase. I start pulling the clay up, and it begins to take shape. The smooth feel of the clay under my hands is both relaxing and hypnotic. I blink and feel as though my pot has grown several inches higher in the blink of an eye. I start to get very excited; it's looking wonderful. I go to pull it up one more time, thinking I can get another couple of inches out of it, and I notice one side of my pot is very weak. I sigh, and quit pulling from there, rather pulling above it to preserve what thickness it had. It seems to work and I get a good inch or two out of the top, and smile in victory.

I have smiled too early, however. I go to flare the top of the pot out, and the entire top third of my clay rips off.

I remember watching a movie one time. There was a line in there that had something to do with good intentions. It went somewhere along the lines of, "Oooh you're bad I can't believe you did this." "But I had the best intentions..." "That's what Hitler said when he started the Holocaust."

I think it was *Jurassic Park*. I haven't seen that movie in forever.

It is a shock and I am disappointed, but I refuse to be discouraged. I keep going with what I have. I will still be able to make my pot; it just won't be as large as I would have liked. I pull some more out of the bottom, and begin to work on the bottom part of my project, squeezing the clay in to make a little stand, like a goblet. I am successful, and I look at my creation and feel proud of myself. However, the edges are a little rough, so I reach toward my bucket to get the sponge.

Alas, in reaching toward the sponge, I bump into my pot, simply yet effectively ruining it once more.

I stare at it and silently groan. *You've got to be kidding me.*

It's my junior year, and I'm trying out for the fall play. I am hoping that this year will be *my* year. That I will finally get my shot. That I will be rewarded for all my hard work and struggling, my never-ending commitment and determination. I walk into auditions with a cocky attitude and a strut in my step, giving off an air of "I got this in the bag."

My auditions go by wonderfully. I nailed every line. Every word I said was supersaturated with emotion and feeling. I am a golden goddess of acting. I feel like I got the role I want in the bag. I feel very confident in myself and my ability.

Samantha Schmaus .... Grandma

My confidence is shattered, my hopes destroyed, and my ego and self-esteem plummeted lower than it was before.

Maybe next time…

Not a problem. I take the needle tool and slice off the top portion that was affected. I am left with a little under a fourth of the clay I started out with. But that's okay. I can still create something wonderful.

I once heard that when you are a young child, you can rebuild your self-esteem every day. Doesn't matter how much you get picked on, you will wake up the next morning feeling *wonderful* about yourself.

However, when you get older, things start to add up. And your self-esteem doesn't grow back as much overnight. And little pieces start to not grow back.

I think hope is like that. Children hope for everything and feel that everything is possible. However the older you get, the more practical your hopes get. And you're less likely to think they will be realized.

But what do I know? That's just my theory.

So I try to make a low, flat dish. Seems like it'd be easy enough, just flatten it, open it, flatten it some more. Not a huge deal, right?

Maybe not so much.

Minutes later, I come to the realization that I am no longer creating a pot; I am mushing around clay, wet, uncooperative clay. And my "dish" is nothing more than a smear of clay across my bat.

You know that phrase, when life gives you lemons, make lemonade? Well, what if you don't have any sugar? Or water? Or ice cubes?

What happens when life gives you lemons and all you can make out of it is, well, lemons?

I stare at the lump of clay resembling a tumor sitting on the wheel.

I am amazed at how depressing this situation was. All I wanted to do was make something wonderful, and I worked so hard to prepare it, and I set up everything so it would be just right. When I failed, I kept going. I kept trying and trying. I tried to make the best out of every situation that came my way, and to not get discouraged. Through all the obstacles, I persevered. But in the end, it didn't matter. All my hard work, all my preparation, all my determination, was for naught. How symbolic. That really saddens me.

Discussion Questions

1. In your own words, describe Schmaus's thesis.

2. Is this essay an optimistic or pessimistic view of hope? Is it both optimistic and pessimistic? Explain and offer examples.

3. Hope is an abstract concept. In what ways does hope remain abstract in this essay? In what ways does Schmaus exemplify hope as a more tangible concept?

4. What do you think happens to hope as one gets older? Compare your answer to Schmaus's argument in this essay.

5. Schmaus divides her essay into several segments. If you wanted to add a segment, describe what you might add. Where would you put this new material?

6. Schmaus uses her own life as well as the experiences of her friends to build her argument about hope. In what way do her references to others' experiences improve or weaken the essay? Do you agree with her choices in this situation, or would you suggest that Schmaus limit the stories in the essay to anecdotes from her own experience? Explain your answer.

The Art of Applying: A Satirical Approach to the College Admissions Process

by Colleen Reding

Meet the Writer

Despite her protestations against the college admissions process, Colleen Reding was accepted to her first choice school and is looking forward to pursuing a major in political science.

Information for Candidates

Dear Prospective University:

I am very pleased to learn of your interest in applying to me. I look forward to receiving your application and seeing what you have to offer. Please use the following information to learn more about my admission requirements and about application procedures. It is important to realize that I am highly selective and that the caliber of the applicants is outstanding. Please fill out the application forms thoroughly and accurately; I am interested in finding out what separates you from all the other universities.

Your application materials must be received in exactly three weeks, seven hours, and forty-two minutes after receiving this letter. Any materials received after this date will be promptly and carefully discarded into a garbage receptacle. You will receive my decision on April 31. A thick, beige envelope will signify that you are accepted, while a thin, white envelope means "Sorry, you are not good enough." Therefore, you need not even bother to look in the envelopes as there is nothing enclosed inside.

I wish you the best of luck as you begin this exciting process. Undoubtedly, you will have a busy year as you embark on filling out applications. However, it is of the utmost importance that you continue to excel academically, to win championships in athletics, to make strides in research, and to achieve world peace. Your overall performance this year will weigh heavily on my decision.

Please feel free to contact me with any questions you may have. You may call between 8:13 and 8:27 A.M. on the first Tuesday of each month. You may also contact me via e-mail, and my little brother will send you a prompt and adequate response.

Sincerely,

Colleen Reding

Dean of Admissions

Application Instructions

In order to fairly and accurately determine which university is the most deserving of my attendance, I require that the prospective schools submit four personal essays, three series of standardized test scores, two letters of recommendation, and a partridge in a pear tree.

The selection criterion that will provide me with the most comprehensive view of your aptitude is the standardized test, the ACT (Amuse Colleen Test). You will be given forty minutes to complete five thousand and eighty questions. You must take the test three times so that I can be certain that a single high score was not the result of luck or dishonesty. The exam will test your knowledge on everything from obscure poets to the behaviors of equatorial lizards and from mathematical probabilities to my favorite movie quotes. This test spans a wide range of academic interests; I personally recommend that you hire an expensive tutor to help you prepare for the test that has been compared to the task of Sisyphus. (Yes, Greek mythology will be included in this exam.)

Another component of the application process is the optional interview. Prospective universities are invited to send a representative to visit me at my convenience, and I will conduct an interview. Although an interview is not required, I strongly encourage it (wink wink, nudge nudge). This informal and candid interview serves as an opportunity for me to make a personal connection with you. The representatives will simply be judged on everything from their taste in shoes to their political ideologies.

In addition to sending in your application, you are obligated to send an application fee of $75. (Along with this fee, you may choose to attach a monetary bribe.) The $75 is a standard processing fee as I will have to purchase a folder in which to place all of the applications as well as a trip to Hawaii so that I may relax after making these difficult decisions.

As previously mentioned, I require that you submit four essays. The essays serve as a means for me to get to know the "real" you.

The prompt for the first essay is "Why should I attend your university?" In other words, what makes you unique? Feel free to blatantly attack the reputations of other universities. Please limit your response to 398 words, and please refrain from using the letter *e*. For your next essay, grade the quality of the food in your cafeterias on a scale from one to ten. Then, compare yourself to your favorite dish, and be sure to include explanations for your comparisons. In the third essay, your objective is to describe in great detail your history as a university. Write in narrative form and fabricate your stories as much as possible. The final writing sample is designated as "topic of your choice." Your approach toward this essay should be to cleverly mention the names of every famous person who attended your fine institution. I am fairly confident that I will never read your mini-masterpieces just as many of you will fail to read this far into these instructions.

The final component of the application consists of the recommendations. You may choose two students to give their "unbiased" opinions on college life. When selecting these students, consider which students have an expert command of superlatives and have access to a ten-ton thesaurus. As soon as the students send me the recommendations, your application file will be complete. At this point, I will begin the coin toss that is the admissions process.

Thank you for your continued interest in me. It is important that you keep the application process in perspective. While completing this application may seem daunting, you need not worry. The outcome will only affect your entire future.

Discussion Questions

1. What is Reding's thesis? What is her strategy for proving her thesis? In your opinion, does she do so successfully?

2. Describe Reding's tone, her attitude toward this subject. What words, phrases, or paragraphs effectively convey this tone? What other possible tones could a writer adopt for this subject?

3. Describe Reding's purpose. In your opinion, does she fulfill her purpose? Why or why not?

4. As Reding satirizes the college application process, she reverses the traditional roles of applicant and college. Find specific examples of this reversal.

5. Find examples of exaggeration used by Reding. In your opinion, do they help her achieve her purpose? Why or why not?

Appendix A

Grammar, Usage, and Punctuation Handbook

The Sentence

The Basic Building Block of the English Language

From the time you entered school, you probably have been speaking and writing in sentences. In the English language, the sentence is the basic unit of meaning.

A **sentence** is a group of words that expresses a complete thought. Every sentence has two basic parts: a subject and a predicate. The **subject** tells whom or what the sentence is about. The **predicate** tells information about the subject—what the subject is, what the subject does, or what happens to the subject.

	subject	predicate
sentence	The impassioned scholar	brushed dust from the ancient parchment.

A group of words that does not have both a subject and a predicate is called a sentence fragment. A **sentence fragment** does not express a complete thought.

sentence fragment	Dr. Vollan. (The fragment does not have a predicate. The group of words does not answer the question What did Dr. Vollan do?)
sentence fragment	Quizzed the students. (The fragment does not have a subject. The group of words does not answer the question Who quizzed the students?)
sentence fragment	On quantum physics. (The fragment does not have a subject or predicate. The group of words does not tell what the sentence is about or what the subject does.)
complete sentence	Dr. Vollan quizzed the students on quantum physics.

Hint   When reading a sentence fragment, ask yourself, "What is missing?" A sentence fragment is usually missing either a subject, a verb, or both subject and verb.

Functions of Sentences

There are four different kinds of sentences: *declarative, interrogative, imperative,* and *exclamatory.* Each kind of sentence has a different purpose. You can vary the tone and mood of your writing by using the four different sentence types. Read the example sentences aloud and notice how your voice changes to express each sentence's different meaning.

- A **declarative sentence** makes a statement and ends with a period.

  Samuel is nearly finished with his novel.

- An **interrogative sentence** asks a question and ends with a question mark.

  Does he have an agent yet?

- An **imperative sentence** gives an order or makes a request and ends with a period or an exclamation mark. An imperative sentence has an understood subject, often *you.*

  (You) Tell Samuel not to compromise the artistic merits of his work.

  (You) Please remind him.

- An **exclamatory sentence** expresses strong feeling and ends with an exclamation mark.

> The book has been published!

Simple and Complete Subjects and Predicates

In a sentence, the **simple subject** is the key word or words in the subject. The simple subject is usually a noun or a pronoun and does not include any modifiers. The **complete subject** includes the simple subject and all the words that modify it.

> **Hint** Every word in a sentence is part of a complete subject or complete predicate.

The **simple predicate** is the key verb or verb phrase that tells what the subject does, has, or is. The **complete predicate** includes the verb and all the words that modify it.

In the following sentence, a vertical line separates the complete subject and complete predicate. The simple subject is underlined once. The simple predicate is underlined twice.

complete subject	complete predicate
A tawny <u>serpent</u> with bright orange eyes	<u>drank</u> from the shallow pond.

> **Hint** The complete subject can be replaced by a single pronoun—
> *I, you, he, she, it, we,* or *they.*

Sometimes, the simple subject is also the complete subject, and the simple predicate or verb is also the complete predicate.

> <u>Piranhas</u> <u>attacked</u>.

To find the simple subject and simple predicate in a sentence, first break the sentence into its two basic parts: complete subject and complete predicate. Then, identify the simple predicate by asking yourself, "What is the action of this sentence?" Finally, identify the simple subject by asking yourself, "Who or what is performing the action?"

In the following sentences, the complete predicate is in parentheses. The simple predicate, or verb, appears in boldface. Remember, verbs may have more than one word, and as many as four.

one-word verb   Two brightly colored hummingbirds (**flit** about the flower garden.)

two-word verb   Two brightly colored hummingbirds (**are flitting** about the flower garden.)

three-word verb   For hours, two brightly colored hummingbirds (**have been flitting** about the flower garden.)

four-word verb   Two brightly colored hummingbirds (**might have been flitting** about the flower garden.)

Compound Subjects and Predicates

A sentence may have more than one subject or predicate. A **compound subject** has two or more simple subjects that have the same predicate. The subjects are joined by the conjunction *and*, *or*, or *but*. A **compound predicate** has two or more simple predicates, or verbs, that share the same subject. The verbs are connected by the conjunction *and*, *or*, or *but*.

compound subject

<u>Monique</u> and <u>Gina</u> | <u>narrated</u> the play.

compound predicate

A large gray <u>whale</u> | <u>soared</u> into the air and <u>crashed</u> down into the ocean.

The conjunctions *either* and *or* and *neither* and *nor* can also join compound subjects or predicates.

compound subject

Either <u>David</u> or <u>Michael</u> | <u>washes</u> the pickup truck on Saturday.

Neither <u>snow</u> nor <u>sleet</u> | <u>discouraged</u> Kurt from making the trip.

compound predicate

<u>They</u> | either <u>lost</u> or <u>hid</u> the key to the lockbox.

The <u>colonel</u> | neither <u>sought</u> nor <u>accepted</u> the party's nomination.

A sentence may also have a compound subject and a compound predicate.

compound subject and compound predicate

Thomas and Noah | composed the lyrics and wrote the music for this production.

Sentence Structures: Simple, Compound, Complex, and Compound-Complex Sentences

A **simple sentence** consists of one independent clause and no subordinate clauses. It may have a compound subject and a compound predicate. It may also have any number of phrases. A simple sentence is sometimes called an *independent clause* because it can stand by itself.

Parliamentary government has its foundations in the thirteenth century.

Aristocrats forced King John to sign the Magna Carta in 1215.

The Plantagenet and Tudor Dynasties ruled England until the 1500s.

A **compound sentence** consists of two sentences joined by a semicolon or by a coordinating conjunction preceded by a comma. Each part of the compound sentence has its own subject and verb. The most common coordinating conjunctions are *and, or, nor, for, but, so,* and *yet.*

The English Renaissance started during the sixteenth century; it continued into the 1600s with the works of Milton and Newton.

England increased its military power during the seventeenth century, **but** the country was torn apart by a civil war from 1642 to 1649.

A **complex sentence** consists of one independent clause and one or more *subordinate clauses*. A **subordinate clause** has a subject and a verb but doesn't express a complete thought and can't stand alone. The subordinate clauses in the examples below are underlined.

If you study the American Revolution, be sure you also read historians who present the British perspective on the war.

As a scholar who does research, you have a duty to seek the objective truth.

If you combine a compound sentence and a complex sentence, you form a **compound-complex sentence**. This kind of sentence must have two or more independent clauses and at least one subordinate clause. In the following examples, the subordinate clauses are underlined.

Thomas Jefferson, <u>who wrote the Declaration of Independence</u>, could have been hanged for treason, or he might have been imprisoned <u>if the British had won the war</u>.

Americans often use the term "tyrant" <u>when they discuss King George III</u>, but he and most British subjects did not believe the colonies were being treated unfairly.

Run-on Sentences

A **run-on sentence** is made up of two or more sentences that have been run together as if they were one complete thought. A run-on sentence can confuse the reader about where a thought starts or ends.

Take a look at the following examples of run-on sentences. In the first run-on, called a **fused sentence**, no punctuation mark is used between two complete thoughts. In the second run-on, called a **comma splice**, a comma is used incorrectly to separate two independent clauses.

Castanets are a percussion instrument made of two small pieces of wood, hollowed out like shells clicked together by moving the fingers, they produce a short, sharp sound. (fused sentence)

A tuning fork is a small steel instrument shaped like a fork, musicians use it as a reference to tune their instruments. (comma splice)

You can correct a run-on by dividing it into two separate sentences. Mark the end of each idea with a period, question mark, or exclamation point. Capitalize the first word of each new sentence.

Castanets are a percussion instrument made of two small pieces of wood, hollowed out like shells. Clicked together by moving the fingers, they produce a short, sharp sound.

You can also correct a run-on by using a semicolon. The second part of the sentence is not capitalized. Use a semicolon to join two sentences only if the thoughts are closely related.

A tuning fork is a small steel instrument shaped like a fork; musicians use it as a reference to tune their instruments.

Wordy Sentences

A **wordy sentence** includes extra words and phrases that can be difficult, confusing, or repetitive to read. When you write, use only words necessary to make your meaning clear. Revise and edit your sentences so that they are not wordy or complicated. Review the following examples to learn about three different ways to correct wordy sentences.

Replace a group of words with one word.

wordy   Gloria can't use her mother's car **until such time as** she proves she can be responsible.

revised   Gloria can't use her mother's car until she proves she can be responsible.

Replace a clause with a phrase.

wordy   Students **who are acting in the play** must rehearse after school.

revised   Students **in the play** must rehearse after school.

Delete a group of unnecessary or repetitive words.

wordy   Without knowing the **surrounding** circumstances, I found his response puzzling **in nature**.

revised   Without knowing the circumstances, I found his response puzzling.

wordy   **The reason for** Betty's **decision** to visit Tuscany was **her desire** to take an Italian cooking class.

revised   Betty decided to visit Tuscany because she wanted to take an Italian cooking class.

revised   Betty went to Tuscany to take an Italian cooking class.

Do not confuse a wordy sentence with a lengthy sentence. Writers vary their sentence lengths to create rhythm and add variety and liveliness to their work. Note the lengthy sentence underlined in the following excerpt. Even though the sentence is long, it does not contain "extra words." The precise word choices in the long sentence make its meaning clear and vivid.

> Tribulation is treasure in the nature of it, but it is not current money in the use of it, except we get nearer and nearer our home, heaven, by it. Another man may be sick too, and sick to death, and this affliction may lie in his bowels as gold in a mine and be of no use to him; <u>but this bell that tells me of his affliction digs out and applies that gold to me, if by this consideration of another's danger</u>

I take mine own into contemplation and so secure myself by making my recourse to my God, who is our only security.

from Meditation 17
John Donne

Combining and Expanding Sentences

A series of short sentences in a paragraph can make your writing sound choppy and boring. The reader might also have trouble understanding how your ideas are connected. By **combining and expanding sentences**, you can connect related ideas, make sentences longer and smoother, and make a paragraph more interesting to read.

One way to combine sentences is to take a key word or phrase from one sentence and insert it into another sentence.

short, choppy sentences	The truck spun out of control. It was speeding.
combined sentence (with key word)	The speeding truck spun out of control.
short, choppy sentences	Janine is tutoring a new boy. He is **from Russia**.
combined sentence (with key phrase)	Janine is tutoring a new boy from Russia.

Hint   When you insert a key word from one sentence into another, you might need to change the form of the word.

The cat sprang onto the windowsill. The jump was **graceful**.
The cat **gracefully** sprang onto the windowsill.

Another way of combining sentences is to take two related sentences and combine them by using a coordinating conjunction—*and, but, or, so, for, yet,* or *nor.* By using a coordinating conjunction, you can form a compound subject, a compound verb, or a compound sentence.

| **two related sentences** | The speeding car spun out of control. It hit the median. |
| **combined sentence** | The speeding car spun out of control **and** hit the median. (compound verb) |

two related sentences	Emergency room doctors went out on strike. Nurses and lab technicians pledged their support.
combined sentence	Emergency room doctors went out on strike, and nurses and lab technicians pledged their support. (compound sentence)
two related sentences	Chrysanthemums dotted the flowerbeds. There were also asters and kale plants.
combined sentence	Chrysanthemums, asters, **and** kale plants dotted the flowerbeds. (compound subject)

Hint When combining two related sentences to form a compound sentence, you need to insert a comma before the coordinating conjunction.

Hint When you form a compound subject, make sure the compound subject agrees with the verb in number.

Making Passive Sentences Active

A verb is **active** when the subject of the verb performs the action. It is **passive** when the subject of the verb receives the action.

| **active** | The waves smashed the raft to pieces. |
| **passive** | The raft was smashed to pieces by the waves. |

Hint Overusing passive verbs in sentences makes your writing dull and weak. Active verbs engage your reader's attention and make your sentences sound more natural, alive, and interesting.

Achieving Parallelism

A sentence has **parallelism** when the same forms are used to express ideas of equal—or parallel—importance. Parallelism can add emphasis and rhythm to a sentence. Words, phrases, and clauses that have the same form and function in a sentence are called **parallel**.

not parallel	**To play handball** and **swimming** are Chet's ways of working off stress. (The infinitive phrase and gerund are not parallel.)
parallel	**Playing handball** and **swimming** are Chet's ways of working off stress.
not parallel	Much of the land was **arid** and a **large number of rocks**. (The highlighted words include an adjective and a complement.)
parallel	Much of the land was **arid** and **rocky**.

Hint When revising for parallelism, read your sentences aloud. Any errors in parallelism will sound awkward.

Varying Sentence Beginnings

Just as you probably wouldn't like to eat the same thing for breakfast every morning, your readers wouldn't enjoy reading the same sentence pattern in every paragraph. By **varying sentence beginnings**, you can give your sentences rhythm, create variety, and keep your readers engaged.

Sentences often begin with a subject. To vary sentence beginnings, start some sentences with a one-word modifier, a prepositional phrase, a participial phrase, or a subordinate clause.

subject	**The farmers** welcomed the evening breeze.
one-word modifier	**Tonight** the farmers welcomed the evening breeze.
prepositional phrase	**After a sweltering day**, the farmers welcomed the evening breeze.
participial phrase	**Welcoming the evening breeze**, the farmers sat on the back porch.
subordinate clause	**Because temperatures and humidity were high**, the farmers welcomed the evening breeze.

Incorrect Subject-verb Agreement

A subject and its verb must agree in number. Use singular verb forms with singular subjects and plural verb forms with plural subjects.

Intervening Words

A prepositional phrase that comes between a subject and a verb does not determine whether the subject is singular or plural.

> The northern **coast** of Siberia **lies** inside the Arctic Circle. (*coast lies*—singular)

> The **temperature** inside the Arctic Circle barely **rises** above freezing even in summer. (*temperature rises*, singular)

> The **seas** to the north of Canada **are** filled with islands and icebergs. (*seas are*, plural)

> The **Inuit**, people of northern Canada and Greenland, **carve** real and mythical animals from walrus ivory and caribou antlers. (*Inuit carve*, plural)

When the subject is an indefinite pronoun, the *object* of the preposition sometimes controls the verb. This exception is covered on page 473.

> Some of the **ground** has been tilled and planted.

> Some of the **grounds** have been tilled and planted.

Compound Subjects

Use a plural verb with most compound subjects connected by *and*.

> <u>Cinnamon</u> and <u>nutmeg</u> **add** flavor to hot chocolate.

> <u>Fish</u>, <u>caribou</u>, <u>seals</u>, <u>polar bears</u>, and <u>whales</u> **provide** the bulk of the Inuit diet.

Use a singular verb with a compound subject that refers to one person or thing or that generally conveys the idea of a unit.

> Ham and eggs is a new flavor of jellybean. (one dish)

> Peace and quiet descends on the valley. (one state of being)

Use a singular verb with a compound subject made up of singular nouns or pronouns connected by *or* or *nor*. Use a plural verb with a compound subject formed from plural nouns or pronouns.

singular	Neither the newspaper nor the television **forecasts** weather accurately.
	Either a bouquet of flowers or a plant **makes** a good gift for a friend in the hospital.
plural	Either the police or the firefighters **hold** their charity dance contest this weekend.
	Neither the beets nor the carrots **have** matured enough to harvest.

When a compound subject consists of a singular subject and a plural subject connected by *or* or *nor*, use a verb that agrees in number with the subject that is closer to it in the sentence.

Either the girls or Niles **feeds** the rabbit and the bird. (*Niles feeds*, singular)

Either Niles or the girls **feed** the rabbit and the bird. (*girls feed*, plural)

Indefinite Pronouns as Subjects

Indefinite pronouns are pronouns that refer to people or things in general. Some indefinite pronouns are always singular and take singular verbs: *anybody, anyone, anything, each, either, everybody, everyone, everything, much, neither, nobody, no one, nothing, one, other, somebody, someone, something.*

Everyone believes decisive action should be taken. (*everyone believes*, singular)

No one plans to express an opinion, however. (*no one plans*, singular)

Some indefinite pronouns are always plural and take plural verbs: *several, both, few, many.*

Many are inspired by the speaker's enthusiasm, but **few** join his organization. (*many are, few join*, plural)

Several have questions that he can't answer. (*several have*, plural)

Some indefinite pronouns can be either singular or plural, depending on their use in the sentence: *all, any, enough, more, most, none, plenty, some.* They are singular when they refer to a portion or to a single person, place, or thing. They are plural when they refer to a number of individual persons, places, or things. In some cases, the object of the preposition determines whether the verb is singular or plural.

All of the money is gone. (*All* refers to a single unit and therefore takes a singular verb.)

All of the jewels were stolen. (*All* refers to a collection of objects and therefore takes a plural verb.)

Inverted Word Order

In questions and in sentences beginning with *Here* or *There*, the verb usually appears before the subject. In these sentences with inverted word order, you must identify the subject and then make the verb agree with it in number. Saying the sentence to yourself in normal order often helps.

Here **sits** a model of Sir Francis Drake's flagship, the *Golden Hind*. (*model sits*, singular)

There **are** the doubloons that the pirates stole. (*doubloons are*, plural)

Where **does** the museum **display** its collection of pirate maps? (*museum does display*, singular)

Avoiding Double Negatives

Make sure that you use only one of the following negatives in each sentence: *not, nobody, none, nothing, hardly, scarcely, barely, can't, doesn't, won't, isn't, aren't*. A **double negative** is the use of two negative words together when only one is needed. Correct double negatives by removing one of the negative words or by replacing one of the negative words with a positive word.

double negative	Nobody had none of it left.
corrected sentence	Nobody had any of it left.
double negative	Joshua can't hardly pay his bills.
corrected sentence	Joshua can hardly pay his bills.
	Joshua can't pay his bills.

Avoiding Dangling and Misplaced Modifiers

Place modifying phrases and clauses as close as possible to the words they modify; otherwise, your sentences may be unclear or unintentionally humorous.

A **dangling modifier** has nothing to modify because the word it would logically modify is not present in the sentence. In the following sentence, the modifying phrase has no logical object. The sentence says that the firewood did the homework.

After doing his homework, the firewood was chopped.

You can eliminate dangling modifiers by rewriting the sentence so that an appropriate word is provided for the modifier to modify. You can also expand a dangling phrase into a full subordinate clause.

After doing his homework, Ethan chopped the firewood.

After Ethan did his homework, he chopped the firewood.

A **misplaced modifier** is located too far from the word it should modify.

The librarian announced that all fines on overdue books will be doubled yesterday.

You can revise a misplaced modifier by moving it closer to the word it modifies.

The librarian announced yesterday that all fines on overdue books will be doubled.

Yesterday the librarian announced that all fines on overdue books will be doubled.

Avoiding Split Infinitives

An **infinitive**, the base verb combined with *to*, should not be split under most circumstances. Infinitives such as *to save*, *to teach*, and *to hold* should not be interrupted by adverbs or other sentence components.

| **nonstandard** | Cal tried hard to neatly wrap the gift. |
| **standard** | Cal tried hard to wrap the gift neatly. |

In some cases, a modifier sounds awkward if it does not split the infinitive. In these situations, it may be best to reword the sentence to eliminate the split infinitive.

| **awkward** | Scientists hope to more than double their use of robots for dangerous tasks. |
| **revised** | For dangerous tasks, scientists hope to increase their use of robots more than 100 percent. |

In certain cases, you may want to use a split infinitive to express the exact meaning you intend.

> Neal decided to wave just to me as he walked by.

> Neal decided just to wave to me as he walked by.

> Neal decided to just wave to me as he walked by.

Commonly Misused Words

The following pages contain an alphabetic list of words and phrases that often cause usage problems.

a, an   Use *a* before words beginning with a consonant sound. Use *an* before words beginning with a vowel sounds, including a silent *h*.

> Debbie ordered Mongolian barbecue, called **a** "firepot."

> This salad dressing recipe is lower in calories because it doesn't have **an** egg in it.

> Kate didn't have **an** hour to spare on Thursdays.

accept, except   *Accept* is a verb meaning "to receive willingly" or "to agree." *Except* is a verb meaning "leaving out" or "excluding" or a preposition meaning "leaving out" or "but."

> The city council would not **accept** the proposal.

> Actors from the television show *The Sopranos* were **excepted** from the list of those invited to lead the Columbus Day parade.

> I like all herbs except cilantro.

affect, effect   *Affect* is a verb that means "to influence." The noun *effect* means "the result of an action." The verb effect means "to cause" or "to bring about."

> James Joyce's *A Portrait of the Artist as a Young Man* deeply **affected** my thinking.

> The novel had a strong **effect** on my reading for the next year.

> The new sales manager will **effect** major changes in the company's sales strategies.

ain't   This word is nonstandard English. Avoid using it in speaking and writing.

> **nonstandard**   Ain't that the best new show of the season?

> **standard**   **Isn't** that the best new show of the season?

all ready, already   *All ready* means "entirely ready or prepared." *Already* means "previously."

> The suitcases were packed and **all ready** to go.

> We discovered that tickets to Barrage had **already** sold out.

all right   *All right* means "satisfactory," "unhurt," "correct," or "yes, very well." The word *alright* is not acceptable in formal written English.

> **All right**, you win; we'll have pizza for dinner.

> Is your finger **all right** now that the cast is off?

a lot   *A lot* means "a great number or amount" and is always two words. Because it is imprecise, you should avoid it except in informal usage. *Alot* is not a word.

> It takes **a lot** of time and effort to persuade people that recycling is worth the effort.

> **A lot** of the books contributed to the library sale were brand new.

altogether, all together   *Altogether* is an adverb meaning "thoroughly." Something done *all together* is done as a group or mass.

> Millicent is **altogether** too passive for her own good.

> Our family was **all together** for the holidays.

anywheres, everywheres, somewheres, nowheres   Use these words and others like them without the *s: anywhere, everywhere, somewhere, nowhere.*

> Golden leaves fell **everywhere**.

> Jeannie left her sunglasses **somewhere** in the mall.

assure, ensure, insure   These words all mean "To make certain, safe, or secure." Generally, they may be used interchangeably. However, use *assure* when referring to people or setting a person's mind at rest. Use *insure* when referring to the guarantee of life or property against risk.

> After the coup, the military troops **assured** us that we would be safe.

> To **ensure** the show's success, the actors decided to hold a second dress rehearsal.

> He contacted an agent to discuss **insuring** the rare Ming vase.

at   Don't use this word after *where.*

> **Where** are you staying in Philadelphia?

bad, badly   *Bad* is always an adjective, and *badly* is always an adverb. Use *bad* after linking verbs.

> According to her mother, Merrie has a **bad** case of homesickness.
>
> The weather forecast looks **bad** for the weekend.
>
> If you do **badly** on one quiz, you can take it over.

beside, besides   *Beside* means "next to." *Besides* means "in addition to." *Besides* can also be an adverb meaning "moreover."

> Bart dropped his backpack **beside** his desk.
>
> No one **besides** Kara signed up for the science fiction lovers book club.
>
> I have too many papers to write this weekend; **besides**, I don't really feel like going.

between, among   Use *between* when referring to two people or things. Use *among* when you are discussing three or more people or things.

> We distributed the gifts **between** Gwen and Brian.
>
> We distributed the gifts **among** Gwen, Brian, and Kurt.

bring, take   Use *bring* when you mean "to carry to." It refers to movement toward the speaker. Use *take* when you mean "to carry away." It refers to movement away from the speaker.

> **Bring** me a glass of water, would you please?
>
> **Take** your jacket to school with you, Sonja.

bust, busted   Do not use these nonstandard words as verbs to substitute for *break* or *burst*.

> **nonstandard**   Reed thinks he may have **busted** his hand when he caught the ground ball.
>
>   Surely I will **bust** from having eaten so much pad Thai.
>
> **standard**   Reed thinks he may have **broken** his hand when he caught the ground ball.
>
>   Surely I will **burst** from having eaten so much pad Thai.

can, may   The word *can* means "able to do something." The word *may* is used to ask or give permission.

> Jessica **can** sing perfect harmony when she tries.
>
> Jaime, you **may** take home any leftovers.

choose, chose *Choose* is the present tense and *chose* is the past tense.

> Darryl **chooses** the members of his group by their willingness to share the burden.

> Darryl **chose** Harvey only once.

could of Use the helping verb *have* (which may sound like *could of*) with *could, might, must, should, ought,* and *would.*

> **nonstandard**   Tim might of lost the car keys.

> **standard**   Tim **might have** lost the car keys.

doesn't, don't *Doesn't* is the contraction of *does not.* It is used with singular nouns and the pronouns he, she, it, this, and that. *Don't* is the contraction of *do not.* Use it with plural nouns and the pronouns *I, we, they, you, these, and those.*

> The Shima-Marayuma Bridge **doesn't** have the look of a substantial structure.

> However, the Japanese **don't** want any of their bridges to collapse during earthquakes.

farther, further Use *farther* to refer to physical distance. Use *further* to refer to greater extent in time or degree or to mean "additional."

> Few bridges extend **farther** than San Francisco's Golden Gate.

> No **further** discussion is needed; Strauss was the most valuable player in this game.

fewer, less Use *fewer,* which tells "how many," to refer to things that you can count individually. *Fewer* is used with plural words. Use *less* to refer to quantities that you cannot count. It is used with singular words and tells "how much."

> **Fewer** salmon spawned this year because of the lack of water in Oregon streams.

> Businesses seem to be operating with **less** honor than they had in the past.

good, well *Good* is always an adjective. *Well* is an adverb meaning "ably" or "capably." *Well* is also a predicate adjective meaning "satisfactory" or "in good health." Don't confuse *feel good,* which means "to feel happy or pleased," with *feel well,* which means "to feel healthy."

> Joseph has a **good** sense of humor.

> Leslie felt **good** [pleased] about her involvement with the after-school children's program.

Newly baked bread makes a house smell **good**.

The cast performed **well** in the first act.

For someone with clogged sinuses, he smells quite **well**.

Caroline has not been looking **well** since her surgery.

had ought, hadn't ought   The verb *ought* should never be used with the helping verb *had*.

nonstandard	The roads are getting worse by the minute; you had ought to leave as soon as possible.
standard	The roads are getting worse by the minute; you **ought** to leave as soon as possible.
nonstandard	Someone with a delicate stomach hadn't ought to eat spicy Cajun food.
standard	Someone with a delicate stomach **ought** not eat spicy Cajun food.

hardly, scarcely   Since both of these words have negative meanings, do not use them with other negative words such as *not, no, nothing,* and *none*.

nonstandard	The poor old shepherd can't hardly walk the mountain anymore.
standard	The poor old shepherd **can hardly** walk the mountain anymore.
nonstandard	The Garcias hadn't scarcely gotten home when they left again.
standard	The Garcias **had scarcely** gotten home when they left again.

he, she, they   Do not use these pronouns after a noun. This error is called a double subject.

| nonstandard | My sister, she is twelve years older than I am. |
| standard | My sister is twelve years older than I am. |

hisself, theirselves   These are incorrect forms. Use *himself* and *themselves*.

| nonstandard | One of the job applicants talked to hisself as he filled out the necessary forms. |
| standard | One of the job applicants talked to **himself** as he filled out the necessary forms. |

nonstandard	The dancers watched theirselves in the mirror as they tried to achieve the perfect arabesque.
standard	The dancers watched **themselves** in the mirror as they tried to achieve the perfect arabesque.

how come Do not use in place of *why*.

nonstandard	Can anyone explain how come I always get a major pimple before an important occasion?
standard	Can anyone explain **why** I always get a major pimple before an important occasion?

in, into Use *in* to mean "within" or "inside." Use *into* to suggest movement toward the inside from the outside.

The bag of pretzels is **in** the kitchen.

Peewee reached **into** the bag of pretzels.

its, it's *Its* is a possessive pronoun. *It's* is the contraction for *it is*.

The bird, still in shock, barely opened **its** eyes.

It's difficult for a vet to treat a wild bird that has knocked itself out.

kind, sort, type Use *this* or *that* to modify the singular nouns *kind*, *sort*, and *type*. Use *these* and *those* to modify the plural nouns *kinds*, *sorts*, and *types*. *Kind* should be singular when the object of the preposition following it is singular. It should be plural when the object of the preposition is plural.

This **kind** of activity makes her knees hurt.

These **types** of cats are popular among people with allergies.

kind of, sort of Do not use these terms to mean "somewhat" or "rather."

nonstandard	It was sort of misty early this morning.
standard	It was **somewhat** misty early this morning.

lay, lie *Lay* means "to put" or "to place." *Lay* usually takes a direct object. *Lie* means "to rest" or "to be in a lying position." *Lie* never takes a direct object. (Note that the past tense of *lie* is *lay*.)

Please **lay** the afghan on the guestroom bed.

Mina **laid** the throw on the chair instead.

Lie down and rest before dinner, Aunt Gini.

Aunt Gini actually fell asleep when she **lay** down for a short rest.

learn, teach   *Learn* means "to gain knowledge." *Teach* means "to give knowledge." Do not use them interchangeably.

> Max **learned** how to play golf from his father.

> His best friend **taught** Max to putt.

like, as   *Like* is usually a preposition followed by an object. It generally means "similar to." *As, as if*, and *as though* are conjunctions used to introduce subordinate clauses.

> Miranda looks **like** her parents.

> That bracelet looks **as though** it is made of soda can pop tops.

> Francie threw the snowball just **as** Luke opened the window.

of   This word is unnecessary after the prepositions *inside, outside,* and *off*.

> Whenever the door slammed, the clock fell **off** the wall.

> The crowd **outside** the theater grew unruly.

> **Inside** the garage, wasps had started the construction of their nests.

precede, proceed   *Precede* means "to go or come before." *Proceed* means "to go forward."

> Senator Kant **preceded** his staff into the room.

> He **proceeded** to explain his views on the first strike.

quiet, quite   Although these words sound alike, they have different meanings. *Quite* is an adverb meaning "positively" or "completely," whereas *quiet* is an adjective that means "making little or no noise."

> Only cricket voices disturbed the **quiet** of the night.

> After a week of rain and fog, everyone in the cottage was **quite** ready for the return of beach weather.

real, really   *Real* is an adjective meaning "actual." *Really* is an adverb meaning "actually" or "genuinely." Do not use real to mean "very" or "extremely."

> Are these lilies **real**, or are they made of silk?

> We were **really** surprised to discover lupines growing amid the weeds.

reason . . . because   *Reason is because* is both wordy and redundant. Use *reason is that* or simply *because*.

> **nonstandard**   The reason they left early was because they were both tired.

standard	The reason they left early was that they were both tired.
standard	They left early because they were both tired.

regardless, irregardless   Use regardless, unmindful, heedless, or anyway. Irregardless is a double negative and should never be used.

nonstandard	Irregardless of your well-intentioned advice, I must do this my way.
standard	Regardless of your well-intentioned advice, I must do this my way.

rise, raise   *Rise* is an intransitive verb that means "to move upward." It is an irregular verb, and it does not take a direct object. *Raise* is a transitive verb that means "to lift or make something go upward." It is a regular verb, and it takes a direct object.

Many of the people Chuck works out with **rise** at five in the morning and are at the gym when it opens.

The work crew quickly **raised** the scaffold around the building.

scratch, itch   *Scratch* means "to scrape lightly to relieve itching." *Itch* means "to feel a tingling of the skin, with the desire to scratch."

Cats get into incredibly funny positions when they try to **scratch** their ears.

BiteStik will take away the **itch** of mosquito bites and prevent them from swelling.

set, sit   *Set* is a transitive verb meaning "to place something." It always takes a direct object. *Sit* is an intransitive verb meaning "to rest in an upright position." It does not take a direct object.

Maude **set** the table with her best china, crystal, and cutlery.

Emmett and Ellen **sit** on stools at the kitchen island and do their homework after school.

some, somewhat   *Some* is an adjective meaning "a certain unspecified quantity." *Somewhat* is an adverb meaning "slightly." Do not use *some* as an adverb.

nonstandard	Patrick is feeling some better this morning.
standard	Patrick is feeling **somewhat** better this morning.
standard	**Some** houseplants that flower should stay outdoors until the first frost.

than, then   *Than* is a conjunction used in comparisons. *Then* is an adverb that shows a sequence of events.

> Nothing tastes better on a brisk fall afternoon **than** a cup of warm apple cider.

> First we went to the movie and **then** we went to dinner at Bubba's Barbecue.

their, there, they're   *Their* is the possessive form of *they*. *There* points out a place or introduces an independent clause. *They're* is the contracted form of *they are*.

> **Their** roof has been reshingled recently.

> **There**, on the floor of the closet, lay the lost diamond earring.

> **They're** always first in line when the cafeteria opens.

them   *Them* is a pronoun. It should never be used as an adjective. Use *those*.

nonstandard	Claire enjoys **them** dance programs, such as *Stomp*, *Barrage*, and *River Dance*.
standard	Claire enjoys **those** dance programs, such as *Stomp*, *Barrage*, and *River Dance*.

this here, that there   Do not use. Simply say *this* or *that*.

nonstandard	This here color is perfect for the bedroom.
standard	**This** color is perfect for the bedroom.
nonstandard	That there is the largest spider I've ever seen!
standard	**That** is the largest spider I've ever seen!

to, too, two   *To* is a preposition that can mean "in the direction of." *Too* is an adverb that means both "extremely, overly" and "also." *Two* is the spelling for the number 2.

> Maria climbed **to** the top of Mount Morency.

> She has climbed in the Berkshires and New York, **too**.

> Climbing a mountain requires **too** much training.

> My **two** sports—scuba diving and race walking—are much easier.

try and   Use *try to* instead.

nonstandard	Frank will try and arrange several college interviews in the Boston area.
standard	Frank will **try to** arrange several college interviews in the Boston area.

use to, used to   Be sure to add the *d* to *used* to form the past participle.

nonstandard	Anitra use to live in Puerto Rico.
standard	Anitra **used** to live in Puerto Rico.

way, ways   Do not use *ways* for *way* when referring to distance.

nonstandard	The mall is still a ways down the highway on the right.
standard	The mall is still a way down the highway on the right.

when, where   When you define a word, don't use *when* or *where*.

nonstandard	*Hydrospeeding* is where participants, wearing helmets, flippers, and padded clothing, launch themselves down rapids holding on to a float.
standard	*Hydrospeeding* is a sport in which participants, wearing helmets, flippers, and padded clothing, launch themselves down rapids holding on to a float.

where, that   Do not use *where* to mean "that."

nonstandard	Tiffany read where her favorite team had lost two straight games.
standard	Tiffany read **that** her favorite team had lost two straight games.

which, that, who, whom   *Which* is used to refer only to things. Use it to introduce nonessential clauses that refer to things or to groups of people. Always use a comma before *which* when it introduces a nonessential clause.

Berbere, **which** combines chilies, pepper, ginger, cinnamon, cardamom, and cloves, is a spicy accompaniment to Ethiopian mutton dishes.

That is used to refer either to people or things. Use it to introduce essential clauses that refer to things or groups of people. Do not use a comma before *that* when it introduces an essential clause.

We learned a lesson **that we have never forgotten**.

Who or *whom* is used to refer only to people. Use *who* or *whom* to introduce essential and nonessential clauses. Use a comma only when the pronoun introduces a nonessential clause.

Captain James Buchanan Eads, **who** built the first permanent bridge across the Mississippi River, is commemorated with a giant portrait hung from the central arch.

Yuri Gagarin, **whom** you may remember from the early 1960s, was the first human to go into space.

who, whom The pronoun *who* has two different forms. *Who* is used when it functions as a nominative pronoun. *Whom* is used when it functions an objective pronoun.

Who did you say is calling? (nominative pronoun)

For **whom** were you asking? (objective pronoun)

who's, whose *Who's* is a contraction for *who is* or *who has*. *Whose* is the possessive form of *who*.

Who's got the tent poles?

Martha and Will are the ones **whose** house burned down last year.

without, unless Do not use the preposition *without* in place of the conjunction *unless*.

nonstandard	I will not go without you go with me.
standard	I will not go **unless** you go with me.
standard	I will not go **without** you.

your, you're *Your* is a possessive pronoun. *You're* is a contraction for the words *you* are.

Your nails are too long for typing and for throwing pottery.

I know this will make you unhappy, but **you're** going to have to trim them.

Punctuation

Editing for Punctuation Errors

When editing your work, correct all punctuation errors. Several common punctuation errors to avoid are the incorrect use of **end marks**, **commas**, and **semicolons**.

End Marks

An **end mark** tells the reader where a sentence ends. An end mark also shows the purpose of the sentence. The three end marks are the **period**, the **question mark**, and the **exclamation point**.

declarative sentence The albatross can glide on air currents for several days and sleep in flight.

imperative sentence	Take care.
interrogative sentence	Isn't that a perfect example of "playing 'possum'"?
exclamatory sentence	That's a spectacular view!

A **declarative sentence** makes a statement and ends with a period.

Ivory comes from the tusks of the elephant, the boar, and the walrus.

An **imperative sentence** gives a command or makes a request. Often, the understood subject of these sentences is *you*. An imperative sentence usually ends with a period. If the command or request is strong, the sentence may end with an exclamation point.

(You) Sign up now for a reduced-price membership.

(You) Stay away from the edge of the cliff!

An **interrogative sentence** asks a question. It ends with a question mark.

Have you ordered the cake for Isabella's birthday?

Hint   An indirect question ends with a period rather than a question mark.

Josh asked Mrs. Davidson what she thought of his college essays.

An **exclamatory sentence** expresses strong feeling and ends with an exclamation point.

Your work is amazing!

That's impossible!

Hint   Do not confuse imperative and exclamatory sentences. Whereas an exclamatory sentence always ends with an exclamation point, an imperative sentence may end with either a period or an exclamation point. Remember that an imperative sentence always gives a command or makes a request.

Other Uses of Periods

As you know, periods are used at the end of all declarative sentences and most imperative sentences. Periods can be used in other ways, too.

Abbreviations

Use a period at the end of most abbreviations or initials. An **abbreviation** is a shortened form of a word or phrase.

Personal Names

Use a period at the end of an abbreviated given name.

E. B. White   **T.** Peter Harris   George **K.** Anderson

Titles

Use a period after abbreviated social and professional titles and degrees.

Mr. Erik Marin	**Mrs.** Lucy Dove
Ms. Wexler	**Dr.** Minutez
Sen. Ella Wing	**Gov.** Marisa Aniskovich
Capt. Geoffrey Marvell	**Prof.** Leonard Maratolli

> **Hint**   When you use a professional title or degree after a name, do not include the title at the beginning of the name.
>
> **Dr.** Musa Habib or Musa Habib, **M.D.** (Not **Dr.** Musa Habib, **M.D.**)

> **Hint**   Spell out civil and military titles when they are used before last names alone.
>
> **Captain** Dolan   **Senator** Schweikert

Business Names

Use a period after abbreviated business names.

SandyEggo Pizza **Co.**   The Karma Kanic **Corp.**

Dilbert, Sons, and **Assoc.**

Addresses

Use a period after abbreviated addresses.

Hyacinth **Ave.** South Ocean **Blvd.** Kendall **Sq.**

Winding Hill **Rd.** Carson Pirie Scott **Bldg.**

Geographical Terms

Use a period after abbreviated geographical terms when you're using the abbreviated terms in notes, tables, and bibliographies.

Paris, **Fr.**

Little Rock, **Ark.**

Turks and Caicos, **B.W.I.** (British West Indies)

Hint Spell out the names of states and other geographical terms when you're using them in regular text.

The jazz festival is held in Newport, **Rhode Island.**

Time

Use a period after abbreviations for time and date designations in notes, tables, and footnotes.

a.d. 1323 72 **b.c.** 5:20 **a.m.**

12:00 **p.m.** 7 **hrs.** 34 **min.** **Sat.** morning, **Aug.** 3

When names of months and days appear in regular text, however, do not abbreviate.

Soccer practice is after school on **Wednesday** and **Friday**.

Labor Day in Australia is **October** 7.

Units of Measurement

Use a period after abbreviations of units of measurement used in tables and notes.

1 T. chili powder 8 in. x 10 in. baking pan

2 c. cooked ground meat 5 ft. 8 in.

4 oz. grated cheddar cheese 122 lbs.

When units of measurement appear in text, however, do not abbreviate. Spell out the names of units of measurement, whether they stand alone or follow a numeral.

> The recipe calls for a **cup** of apple cider.
>
> How many **liters** are in a gallon?
>
> The highway speed limit is sixty-five **miles per hour**.

Abbreviations without Periods

Some abbreviations do *not* use a period. Do *not* use periods with metric measurements, state names in postal addresses, or directional elements.

metric measurements	cc, ml, km, g, L
state postal codes	CA, TX, FL
compass points	N, NW, S, SE

Do *not* use periods with acronyms or abbreviations that are pronounced letter by letter. Capitalize all the letters, but use no periods.

Department of Motor Vehicles	**DMV**
Instant Messaging	**IMing**
Franklin Delano Roosevelt	**FDR**
Digital Versatile Disk	**DVD**

Commas

A **comma** separates words or groups of words within a sentence. Commas tell the reader to pause at certain spots in the sentence. These pauses help keep the reader from running together certain words and phrases when they should be kept apart.

Use commas to separate items in a series. The items in a series may be words, phrases, or clauses.

words in a series	Earl Lloyd, Nat Clifton, and Chuck Cooper were the first three African-American basketball players to join the NBA in 1950.
phrases in a series	Medical experts have noted that people who stutter rarely do so when they are talking to themselves, singing, or talking to a pet.
clauses in a series	The guard asked us who we were, where we had come from, and why we were there.

Use commas when you combine sentences using *and, but, or, nor, yet, so,* or *for*. Place the comma before these words.

Contrary to myth, hair does not continue to grow after death, **for** it requires nourishment from pumping blood.

A snake may have no ears, **but** its tongue is extremely sensitive to sound vibrations.

Hint Do not use a comma to separate the verb phrases of a compound predicate.

Cockroaches are opportunists and will eat wallpaper or TV cords.

Hint Make sure you use both a comma and a conjunction between independent clauses.

Great Britain was the first country in the world to issue postage stamps, and it is the only nation in the world today that doesn't use a national name on its stamps.

Use a comma after an introductory word or phrase.

Interestingly, piercing body parts, such as ears and navels, was once thought to release demons from the body.

During the reign of Peter the Great, any Russian man who wore a beard was expected to pay a special tax.

Use a comma to set off words or phrases that interrupt sentences. Use two commas if the word or phrase occurs in the middle of the sentence. Use one comma if the word or phrase comes at the beginning or at the end of a sentence.

Anne Boleyn, Henry VIII's second wife, wore gloves all her life to hide a sixth finger on one of her hands.

Yuma, Arizona, has the most sun of any locale in the United States, averaging sunny skies 332 days a year.

Taiwan, as I recall, was once known as Formosa.

Use a comma between two or more adjectives that modify the same noun.

Indian samosas are stuffed, deep-fried turnovers filled with meat or potatoes.

The diminutive, balanced, graceful bonsai is not difficult to grow.

Use a comma to set off names used in direct address.

Keisha, the word bonsai means "tray-planted."

Did you realize, Gary, that the eagle is a member of the hawk family?

Use commas to separate parts of a date. Do not use a comma between the month and the year.

On February 22, 1989, Barbara Jo Rubin became the first woman jockey to win a horse race.

Granddad came home from the war in March 1945.

Use commas to separate items in addresses. Do not use a comma between the state and the ZIP code.

The modern city of Istanbul, Turkey, was formerly known as Byzantium and then as Constantinople.

Send your check or money order to Wombats, Unlimited, 347 Wiggle Way, Tacoma, WA 87634.

Do not use unnecessary commas. Too many commas can make a sentence's meaning confusing and its rhythm choppy.

confusing After deciding that he could read two, but not all four of the library books, that had arrived at the same time, Eliot chose the most appealing ones, and returned the others.

clear After deciding that he could read two but not all four of the library books that had arrived at the same time, Eliot chose the most appealing ones and returned the others.

Semicolons

A **semicolon** joins two closely related sentences.

Neither of us spoke; we simply waited in silence to see what would happen.

Use a semicolon to join the independent clauses of a compound sentence if no coordinating conjunction is used.

Coordinating conjunctions such as *and, but, so, or, nor, for,* and *yet* can be used to combine two related sentences. A semicolon is a punctuation mark that also joins two closely related sentences. A semicolon used in place of a comma and conjunction adds emphasis to the second clause. The semicolon signals a pause that is longer than a comma's pause but shorter than a period's.

two separate sentences	The erratic forward scored infrequently. He also fouled too much and allowed too many shots.
joined with semicolon	The erratic forward scored infrequently; he also fouled too much and allowed too many shots.

Use a semicolon between independent clauses joined by a conjunction if either clause contains commas.

I want to write my term paper on Annie Peck Smith, Delia Akeley, Marguerite Harrison, or Louise Arner Boyd; but I can't decide which of these four women explorers fascinates me the most.

Use a semicolon between items in a series if the items contain commas.

The cruise itinerary included stops in Santo Domingo, Dominican Republic; San Juan, Puerto Rico; and Port of Spain, Trinidad.

Use a semicolon between independent clauses joined by a conjunctive adverb or a transitional phrase.

conjunctive adverb	I had driven all the way to East Haddam; unfortunately, Emily was waiting for me in Haddam.
transitional phrase	The audience rose to leave; in fact, there was a mad dash for the doors.

Colons

A **colon** is a punctuation mark that is used to mean "note what follows."

Use a **colon** to introduce a list of items.

A "palate cleanser" served before the entrée, sorbet was offered in these flavors: basil lemon, orange rosemary, or cilantro lime.

Miranda's favorite Yeats' poems include the following: "The Lake Isle of Innisfree," "Adam's Curse," and "The Second Coming."

Use a colon to introduce a long or formal statement or a quotation. The first word of the statement or quotation should be capitalized.

In the first lines of Ted Hughes's "Thistles," the poet displays some of his favorite themes in a collision of hard consonant sounds:
Against the rubber tongues of cows and the hoeing hands of men
Thistles spike the summer air
Or crackle open under a blue-black pressure.

When he says the following words, Professor Higgins pays Eliza the highest compliment, even if she doesn't realize it: "You and I and Pickering will be three old bachelors together instead of only two men and a silly girl."

Use a colon between two independent clauses when the second clause explains or summarizes the first clause. If the element following the colon consists of more than one sentence, then it should begin with a capital letter. If the second clause consists of only one sentence, then it may begin with a lowercase letter.

After weighing his alternatives, Kevin made a choice: he decided to postpone college for a year.

Tree shrews are like squirrels in two main ways: They are expert climbers that balance with their tails. They eat sitting up, holding their food in their hands.

Colons are also used between numbers that tell hours and minutes, after the greeting in a business letter, and between chapter and verse of religious works.

The matinee performance of "Moving Out" begins at 2:00 P.M.

Dear Sir or Madam:

Isaiah 26:3–10

In the following situations, do not use a colon: after a verb, between a preposition and its object(s), or after *because* or *as*.

after a verb

incorrect   The five fastest birds are: the peregrine falcon, the spine-tailed swift, the frigate bird, the spur-winged goose, and the red-breasted merganser.

correct	The five fastest birds are the peregrine falcon, the spine-tailed swift, the frigate bird, the spur-winged goose, and the red-breasted merganser.

between a preposition and its object(s)

incorrect	Birds use their beaks for: pecking at plants, poking in the earth for insects, feeding their young, cleaning their feathers, and building their nests.
correct	Birds use their beaks for a number of activities: pecking at plants, poking in the earth for insects, feeding their young, cleaning their feathers, and building their nests.
correct	Birds use their beaks for pecking at plants, poking in the earth for insects, feeding their young, cleaning their feathers, and building their nests.
incorrect	The bones of birds are a bit like inner tubes because: they are hollow and they are connected to air sacks throughout the body.
correct	The bones of birds are a bit like inner tubes because of these qualities: they are hollow, and they are connected to air sacks throughout the body.
correct	The bones of birds are a bit like inner tubes: they are hollow, and they are connected to air sacks throughout the body.

Ellipsis Points

Ellipsis points are a series of three spaced points. Ellipsis points are used to show that material from a quotation or a quoted passage has been left out. Read the following literature model, then note how the underlined material is omitted and replaced with ellipsis points in the second model.

> This may be true or it may be false—who can say?—but what is true in it, so it seemed to me, reviewing the story of Shakespeare's sister as I had made it, is that any woman born with a great gift in the sixteenth century would certainly have gone crazed, shot herself, or ended her days in some lonely cottage outside the village, half witch, half wizard, feared and mocked at. For it needs little skill in psychology to be sure that a highly gifted girl who had tried to use her gift for poetry would have been so thwarted and hindered by other people, so tortured and pulled asunder by her own contrary instincts, that she must have lost her health and sanity to a certainty.

> . . . any woman born with a great gift in the sixteenth century would certainly have gone crazed, shot herself, or ended her days in some lonely cottage outside the village, . . . feared and mocked at. . . . [A] . . . girl who had tried to use her gift for poetry would have been so thwarted and hindered by other people, so tortured and pulled asunder by her own contrary instincts, that she must have lost her health and sanity to a certainty.
>
> from *A Room of One's Own*
> Virginia Woolf

To use ellipsis points correctly, follow these guidelines:

- If material is left out at the beginning of a sentence or passage, use three points with a space between each point.

    . . . They would have spoken sharply but kindly, for they were substantial people who knew the conditions of life for a woman and loved their daughter—indeed, more likely than not she was the apple of her father's eye.

- If material is left out in the middle of a sentence, use three points with a space between each point.

    They would have spoken sharply but kindly, for they . . . knew the conditions of life for a woman and loved their daughter—indeed, more likely than not she was the apple of her father's eye.

- If material is left out at the end of a sentence, use an end mark after the three ellipsis points.

    They would have spoken sharply but kindly, for they were substantial people who knew the conditions of life for a woman and loved their daughter. . . .

Hint   Other punctuation may be used on either side of the ellipsis points if it helps the sense of the sentence or better shows what has been omitted.

I was at the mercy of savage predators! A pool of crocodiles seethed on one side of me and a ravening tiger approached on the other! I had reached the tragic end to a glorious existence.

. . . savage predators!. . . A pool of crocodiles. . . a ravening tiger!. . . I had reached the tragic end to a glorious existence.

Apostrophes

An **apostrophe** is used to form the possessive of nouns and pronouns; to form contractions; and to form the plurals of numerals, symbols, and words referred to as words.

> **Hint** To make pronunciation easier, add only an apostrophe after historical names of more than one syllable that end in *s*.
>
> Pegasus' wings, Perseus' adversary, Ulysses' companion, Archimedes' principle

- Use an apostrophe to form the possessive case of a singular or plural noun. To form the possessive of a singular noun, add an apostrophe and an *s* to the end of the word.

  an igloo's doorway   the mattress's indentations Max's band

The possessive of a plural noun is formed two different ways. If the plural noun does not end in *s*, you add an apostrophe and an *s* to the end of the word. If the plural noun ends in s, add only an apostrophe.

  dresses' styles   compasses' cases

  moose's antlers   children's hats

- Use an apostrophe to show joint or separate ownership. If two nouns are used to show joint ownership, form only the last noun in the possessive.

  William and Mary's reign   Lewis and Clark's mission

  Mom and Dad's goal   Simon and Garfunkel's hits

If two or more nouns are used to show separate ownership, form each noun in the possessive.

  Sheila's and Kim's memories   Keats's and Yeats's poetry

  dogs' and cats' personalities   cars' and trucks' motors

- Add an apostrophe and an *s* to form the possessive of an indefinite pronoun.

  someone's mistake   another's opinion

  everybody's efforts   somebody's key

- Use an apostrophe to form a contraction to show where letters, words, or numerals have been omitted.

I'm = I am	you're = you are
who's = who is	should've = should have
there're = there are	o'clock = of the clock
can't = cannot	we'd = we would
didn't = did not	they'll = they will
ma'am = madam	won't = will not

- Use an apostrophe to form the possessive of only the last word in a compound noun, such as the name of an organization or a business.

  my sister-in-law's career

  the National Council of Jewish Women's bylaws

- Use an apostrophe to form the possessive of an acronym.

  SAT's level of difficulty   IBM's new building   IRS's tax code

- Use an apostrophe to form the plural of letters, numerals, and words referred to as words.

  A's and B's   by 2's and 3's   too many ah's

- Use an apostrophe to show the missing numbers in a date.

  the Roaring '20s   Spirit of '76   '57 Chevy

- Use an apostrophe to form the possessive of time and money.

  a week's vacation   a penny's worth   two weeks' notice

Underlining and Italics

Italics are a type of slanted printing used to make a word or phrase stand out. In handwritten documents or in forms of printing in which italics are not available, underlining is used.

italics	In *Robinson Crusoe* and *Moll Flanders*, Daniel Defoe created fiction that appeared truer than autobiography.
underlining	In <u>Robinson Crusoe</u> and <u>Moll Flanders</u>, Daniel Defoe created fiction that appeared truer than autobiography.

- Use italics (or underlining) for the titles of books, plays, long poems, periodicals, works of art, movies, radio and television series, videos, computer games, comic strips, and long musical works and recordings.

books	*Tom Jones; Tristram Shandy*
plays	*School for Scandal; Macbeth*
long poems	*Elegy in a Country Churchyard; The Rime of the Ancient Mariner*
periodicals	*Fitness; Smithsonian; U.S. News and World Report*
works of art	*King and Queen; The Burning of the Houses of Parliament*
movies	*Greenfingers; October Sky; Gladiator*
radio/television series	*Antiques Roadshow; Morning Pro Musica; Biography*
videos	*Beauty and the Beast; Container Gardening: Root Pruning*
computer games	*Cruciverbalist; Robotech; SimsVille*
comic strips	*Dilbert; Hi and Lois; Peanuts*
long musical works/ recordings	*Swan Lake; Revolver; St. Matthew Passion*

- Use italics for the names of trains, ships, aircraft, and space-craft.

trains	*Shoreline Express*; *The Rocket*
ships	*Queen Elizabeth II*; *U.S.S. Saratoga*
aircraft	*Spirit of St. Louis*; *Enola Gay*
spacecraft	*Apollo 11*; *Sputnik*

- Use italics for words, letters, symbols, and numerals referred to as such.

  Howitzer is one of the few English words derived from the Czech language.

  Even though my name is spelled ***Nance***, it is pronounced the same as Nancy with a ***y***.

  The ***@*** has become a popular abbreviation because of the Internet.

- Use italics to set off foreign words or phrases that are not common in English.

  Tina suffered from the ***ennui***, or "apathy," of the typical teenager.

  Translated literally, the Latin ***De gustibus non est disputandum*** means "There's no accounting for taste."

Hint Borrowed words that have become part of the English vocabulary are not italicized.

Believing that his **karma** was bad, Alan made a habit of knocking on wood.

The gourmet chef prepared a marvelous **filet** of beef.

- Use italics to place emphasis on a word.

  I thought ***you*** had locked the door.

  Mr. Barnes didn't want just ***any*** answer; he wanted the ***correct*** answer.

Quotation Marks

Quotation marks are used to set off direct quotations, titles of short works, slang, and unusual expressions.

- Use quotations marks at the beginning and end of a direct quotation. When you use a person's exact words in your writing, you are using a **direct quotation.**

"If the cat heads to the cellar before a storm, I generally follow him," stated Miss King.

"I adore a nice, violent thunderstorm," said Jeanne, "but I have a morbid fear of tornadoes."

A direct quotation should always begin with a capital letter. Separate a direct quotation from the rest of the sentence with a comma, a question mark, or an exclamation point. Do not separate the direct quotation from the rest of the sentence with a period. When a quoted sentence is interrupted, the second part begins with a lowercase letter. All punctuation marks that belong to the direct quotation itself should be placed inside the quotation marks.

"How absurdly large your SUV is!" exclaimed Martin.

Letitia snapped, "Have you tried driving six teenagers to a soccer game in a regular car?"

"No!" Martin shouted in alarm. "I would rather eat worms than do such a thing!"

"Oh, Martin," sighed Letitia, "you are such an unbearable misanthrope."

Hint Use a lowercase letter when a quoted fragment of the original quotation is inserted in a sentence.

I hate to be impatient, but I get weary of Nana's constant references to "the good old days."

Place colons and semicolons outside the closing quotation marks.

Grandmother finds the following behaviors "beyond the pale": resting elbows on the table, using paper napkins, and saying "pardon."

Aunt Amy always calls me "honeybunch"; I think it's embarrassing but sweet.

Place exclamation points and question marks outside the closing quotation marks if the quotation itself is not an exclamation or a question.

What is the meaning of the proverb "Butter wouldn't melt in his mouth"?

When he stepped on your foot, I can't believe you said, "Excuse me"!

Place exclamation points and question marks inside the closing quotation marks if both the sentence and the quotation are exclamations or questions.

> Was it Shakespeare who wrote, "What's in a name?"

> Oh no, someone just screamed, "Fire!"

When a quoted sentence is interrupted, the second part begins with a lowercase letter, unless the first word of the second part begins a new sentence. Use quotation marks to enclose both parts of a divided quotation.

> "If you ever feel lonely or desperate," Mika told me, "you must promise to call me."

> "I will," I responded. "You must promise me to do the same."

Use only one set of quotation marks when a direct quotation of two or more sentences by the same speaker is not divided or interrupted.

> The ballet teacher addressed her new students. "I understand that as dancers you want to remain slender so as to show a beautiful line. However, I will not tolerate students who drive themselves to become emaciated. A dancer needs to be strong and healthy; he or she needs to eat a healthful diet with sufficient nutrients and calories. If I have worries about any of you, I will talk to your parents and send you to a nutritionist."

- Don't use quotation marks to set off an **indirect quotation**. An indirect quotation is a rewording of a person's exact words.

> | **direct quotation** | "Don't leave anything behind in the taxi," said the recording. |
> | **indirect quotation** | The recording reminded us not to leave anything behind in the taxi. |

- Use single quotation marks to enclose a quotation within a quotation.

> Mrs. Hemphill said, "I cry every time I read Churchill's words, '. . . we shall fight on the beaches, we shall fight on the landing grounds, we shall fight in the fields and in the streets, we shall fight in the hills; we shall never surrender.'"

- In dialogue, enclose each speaker's words in quotation marks, and begin a new paragraph every time the speaker changes.

> "I'm sorry, Mrs. Wilson," Ella stammered, rising. "But he asked me—"
> "He's just a foolish child and you know it!" Granny blazed.
> Ella bowed her head and went into the house.

"But, Granny, she didn't finish," I protested, knowing that I should have kept quiet.

She bared her teeth and slapped me across my mouth with the back of her hand.

"You shut your mouth!" she hissed. "You don't know what you're talking about!"

from *Black Boy*
Richard Wright

- Sometimes a direct quotation from an author's work may be several paragraphs in length. If so, place quotation marks at the beginning of each paragraph and at the end of only the last paragraph.

The Declaration of Independence gave a list of reasons why the colonists felt justified in throwing off the yoke of British governance:

"For quartering large bodies of armed troops among us;

"For protecting them, by a mock trial, from punishment for any murders which they should commit on the inhabitants of these States;

"For cutting off out trade with all parts of the world. . . ."

- Do not use quotation marks if you are quoting a long passage. Instead, set off the entire passage from the rest of the text by indenting and single-spacing it.

In this selection from The Autobiography of Benjamin Franklin, Franklin tells about an occasion in which his brother, a newspaper publisher, was imprisoned:

One of the Pieces in our Newspaper, on some political Point which I have now forgotten, gave Offense to the Assembly. He was taken up, censured, and imprisoned for a Month by the Speaker's Warrant. I suppose because he would not discover his author. I too was taken up and examined before the Council; but though I did not give them any Satisfaction, they contented themselves with admonishing me, and dismissed me, considering me perhaps as an Apprentice who was bound to keep his Master's Secrets. During my Brother's Confinement, which I resented a good deal, notwithstanding our private Differences, I had the Management of the Paper, and I made bold to give our Rulers some Rubs in it, which my Brother took very kindly, while others began to consider me in an unfavorable Light, as a young Genius that had a Turn for Libeling and Satire.

- Use quotation marks to enclose the titles of short works such as short stories, poems, articles, essays, parts of books and periodicals, songs, and episodes of TV series.

short stories	"The Garden-Party," "White Dump"
poems	"Sailing to Byzantium," "Sonnet XXX"
articles	"Unbuilding the World Trade Center," "Picking Up Terror's Trail"
essays	"Odysseus' Scar," "On Genius and Common Sense"
parts of books	"Novels of Detection, Crime, Mystery, and Espionage," "Life in an Early Castle"
songs	"Sweet Jane," "London Calling"
episodes of TV series	"Dagger of the Mind," "Bart the Genius"

- Use quotation marks to set off slang, technical terms, unusual expressions, invented words, and dictionary definitions.

> When asked to describe the crazy period of getting ready for work and/or school in the morning, Barbara Wallraff came up with "pandemornium" in an *Atlantic Monthly* article titled "Word Fugitives."

> According to *Webster's New World Dictionary*, the word gobo is an Americanism meaning "a black screen used to reduce light falling on a camera lens."

Hyphens and Dashes

Hyphens

Hyphens are used to make a compound word or compound expression.

compound nouns	eye-candy, name-dropper, know-how, trade-off
compound adjectives used before a noun	ill-advised decision, short-term investment, broken-down jalopy
compound numbers	forty-one years, eighty-five dollars
spelled-out fractions	one-half cord of wood, three-quarters cup of water

Hint Use a dictionary to find out if a compound word or expression is hyphenated or written as one word or two words.

If a word must be divided at the end of a line, a few rules will help you know when and how to hyphenate:

- Divide an already hyphenated word at the hyphen.

  Kira's nieces attended the celebration, but her **sister-in-law** was ill.

- Divide a word only between syllables. If you are uncertain of a word's syllables, look up the word in a dictionary.

  | **incorrect** | Our backyard resembled a miniat-ure forest |
  | **correct** | Our backyard resembled a minia-ture forest |

- Do not divide a one-syllable word.

  | **incorrect** | The cell is the smallest living unit capable of grow-th, movement, and reproduction. |
  | **correct** | The cell is the smallest living unit capable of growth, move ment, and reproduction. |

- Do not divide a word so that one letter stands alone.

  | **incorrect** | Muhammad Ali was once invited to lecture on p-oetry at Oxford University. |
  | **correct** | Muhammad Ali was once invited to lecture on poetry at Oxford University. |

- Use a hyphen with the prefixes *all–*, *ex–*, *great–*, *half–* and *self–* and with all prefixes before a proper noun or proper adjective.

ex-president	all-around nice guy
anti-American	self-concept
great-grandfather	half-baked idea
post-Renaissance style	pre-Columbian statuary

- Use a hyphen with the suffixes *–free*, *–elect*, and *–style*.

  salt-free pretzels   Texas-style barbecue

  secretary-elect Orthland

Dashes

A **dash** is used to show a sudden break or change in thought. Note that a dash is longer in length than a hyphen. Dashes sometimes replace other marks of punctuation, such as periods, semicolons, or commas.

In the example below, the first dash sets off a descriptive phrase that emphasizes the meagerness of the meal. In the second example, the dash shows a break in conversation. In both cases, the dashes illustrate Laura's level of distraction.

> The telephone. "Yes, yes; oh yes. Kitty? Good morning, dear. Come to lunch? Do, dear. Delighted of course. It will only be a very scratch meal—just the sandwich crusts and broken meringue shells and what's left over. Yes, isn't it a perfect morning? Your white? Oh, I certainly should. One moment—hold the line. Mother's calling."
>
> from "The Garden-Party"
> Katherine Mansfield

A dash can also be used to mean *namely*, *that is*, or *in other words*.

Picking up the pieces of his life, Henry turned to a new hobby—jigsaw puzzles.

Erika Harold talked with teenagers about abstinence—from drugs, sex, and alcohol—during her yearlong tour as Miss America 2003.

Parentheses and Brackets

Use **parentheses** around material that is added to a sentence but is not considered of major importance. This material might include explanations, facts, minor digressions, and examples that aid understanding but are not essential to the independent clause.

> Englishman William Oxberry (1784–1824) was known as "The Five P's" because he was a printer, poet, publisher, publican (keeper of a public house or tavern), and player (actor).

> Luanne (accurately sensing the mood of the crowd) skipped three of the four pages of her speech.

> We played all kinds of games that summer (for example, Risk, Clue, Candyland, Nertz, and Monopoly).

Parentheses are also used to punctuate a parenthetical sentence contained within another sentence. Do not capitalize the parenthetical sentence unless it begins with a word that should be capitalized. Do not end the parenthetical sentence with a period, but you may end it with a question mark or exclamation point.

> The author's latest work (it will never be a best seller!) is about corpse lilies and other parasitic plants.

> Ella was (she'd kill me if she heard me say this) really rather shy and humorless.

Commas, dashes, and parentheses may all be used to enclose words or phrases that interrupt the sentence and are not considered essential to the independent clauses surrounding them. Notice in the following sentences how each punctuation mark increases the emphasis.

> Olive oil, bread, and wine, foods that are the backbone of Greek gastronomy, were once held sacred. (a short pause)

> The foods that are the backbone of Greek gastronomy—olive oil, bread, and wine—were once held sacred. (a stronger break in the sentence)

Olive oil, bread, and wine, the backbone of Greek gastronomy, were once held sacred (and even had their own designated gods). (an additional pause containing a reinforcing detail)

Use **brackets** to enclose information that explains or clarifies a detail in quoted material.

"The architect's overcharges [$1,500] seem entirely legitimate," Janet Posvar, town councilperson, is quoted as saying.

According to the experts who write for Gardening in Small Spaces, "Espalier [a way of growing a tree in two dimensions] has become extremely popular."

Appendix

B

Graphic Organizers

When you sit down to write a first draft, there's no reason to be staring at a blank page or screen. Instead, you should be glancing at the wealth of notes you've taken during a rich prewriting session. Graphic organizers can guarantee that your prewriting process will be rich.

Graphic organizers are pictorial representations of ideas. They show connections and highlight relationships between concepts that you probably would not otherwise consider. Most graphic organizers are easy to use, but don't let that fool you into thinking that the results of using one will be simple or dull.

In this appendix, we will provide you with a variety of graphic organizers that you can tailor to your needs. One chart might work better for description; another might be more helpful for a comparison essay. You can even combine two methods or create your own. For instance, you might simply draw a square in the middle of your paper, write your topic in the square, branch out from there, and see what happens.

More important than the type of graphic organizer you use during prewriting is your attitude toward the process. Keep an open mind. Write—or draw—fast. Don't censor ideas you deem silly or stupid, or thoughts that don't completely fit within your original topic. You can always delete or ignore such ideas once you're done. And be inquisitive. Dig beneath the surface. Search for new ways to approach familiar subjects.

Cluster Chart

A cluster chart is easy to use. Place your main idea in the middle of a circle and think of as many related ideas as you can. You can also branch off from those related ideas, as shown in the following samples.

You might use a cluster chart to help you define a concept. Allow one question to generate other questions and branch out from there, as shown in the top cluster chart on page 533. You might branch out even farther than in the example shown to answer some of those questions.

You could also use a cluster chart to help you describe something, as shown in the second cluster chart on page 533.

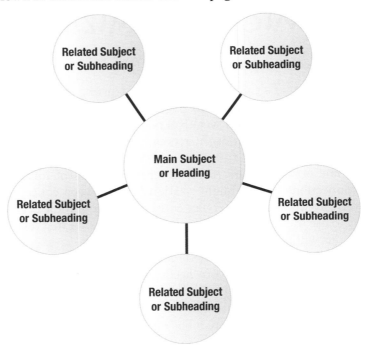

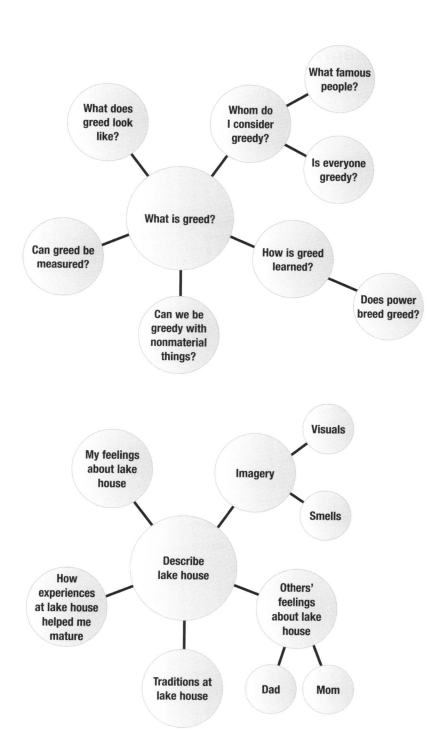

Venn Diagram

Use a Venn diagram to compare and contrast ideas. The overlap area in the middle shows commonalities between two subjects or ideas.

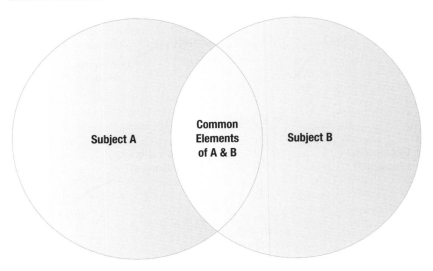

Subject A

Common Elements of A & B

Subject B

Topic 1: Basketball

Topic 2: Childhood Game

- many rules
- hard practices
- emphasis on winning

- competitive
- life lessons
- fun

- few rules
- no practices
- little emphasis on winning

Sensory Details Chart

When you need to describe a person or thing, appeal to the senses. Use this chart to help you brainstorm. After filling in the chart, you might circle or check the items you consider most important.

Sight	Smell	Sound	Taste	Touch

Purpose: Describe an old neighborhood

Sight	Smell	Sound	Taste	Touch
• houses • fences • doors • streetlights	• cooking • grass • certain buildings	• car horns • moms calling • dogs barking	• afternoon snacks • a blade of grass • a sleeve • a cut	• friend pulling my arm • stickiness of ice cream cone • asphalt

Figurative Language Chart

Use this chart to help you see beyond literal descriptions.

What I Want to Convey	Literal Description	Figurative Possibility

What I Want to Convey	Literal Description	Figurative Possibility
I want to show the physical and emotional strength of my grandfather.	• Large hands • Broad shoulders • Never complained	• His hands were as broad as the bottom of a bushel basket. • His shoulders filled the doorway. • A darkness descended upon him after he lost his job, but he refused to give in to that.

K-W-L Chart

K = What I **Know**. W = What I **Want** to Learn. L = What I **Learned**.

This chart is useful when using research in an essay. The chart can help direct your research and clarify your purpose. Fill in the first two columns before you begin your research. After your research, summarize your notes in the third column. Then you might loop back to the second column; based on what you've learned, do you have more questions? After all of this, you can begin to refine a purpose for your own writing.

What I Know About (Subject)	What I Want to Learn	What I Learned

What I Know About Depression	What I Want to Learn	What I Learned
• Affects mood • Affects eating and sleeping • Some people take medication	• Do all people suffer the same symptoms? • Do people eat more or less when depressed? • Do all people respond positively to medication?	• Different symptoms include crying, anger, insomnia, or sleeping all the time. • Some depressed people eat more; others have no appetite. • Everyone responds differently to different medications.

Time Line

Use a time line to help you highlight important events in a narrative or to help you find a narrative topic. In the time line sample below, you may notice that the last event is less physical than the previous two examples. Keep in mind that during the brainstorming phase, consistency is not as important as the ideas themselves. Jot down as many ideas as you can.

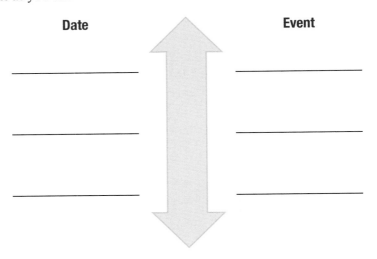

Purpose: Narrative about why I like risks

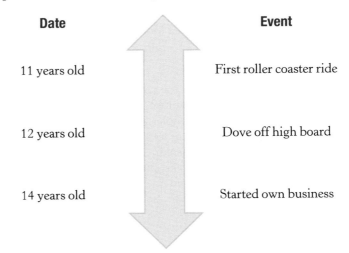

Writing for the ACT and SAT

L et's begin this appendix with a little history lesson on how the two primary college admission testing programs—ACT and SAT—have evaluated the writing skills of their customers. For decades, these tests have offered multiple-choice sections dealing with punctuation, grammar, spelling, parallel structure, and various rhetorical strategies. Those students who picked the right answers received high scores on the English parts of the tests. Although everyone involved understood that a better measurement of a student's composition aptitude would be derived from a direct sampling of the student's writing, it wasn't practical because of the sheer magnitude of the task of reading and consistently grading hundreds of thousands of essays each year.

Then the earth shifted. By 2005 technology had improved to the point where it became possible to efficiently deliver essays to graders in various locales and receive their evaluations in a timely manner. This made ACT and SAT happy because they could present an increasingly accurate composite of their test takers by including a more valid measure of them as writers. Colleges and universities were happy for two reasons: (1) they know that writing is important for success in college, and the new scores helped them better choose students who were most likely to achieve that success, and (2) in many cases, colleges were able to do away with their own on-campus writing tests for incoming students. (Many colleges still require application essays. That is a different matter covered in Chapter 11.) Even some prospective test takers were happy because they could demonstrate their writing competence in ways previously not possible.

Many students, however, were not so happy about the addition. They felt a new level of anxiety added to an already stressful situation. Those students who did not see themselves as strong writers were concerned that their college admission options would be affected by a factor not previously considered.

That brings us to you and your situation as you prepare for these examinations. The good news is that you already know the basics of effective writing, and that is really what the essay readers (and college admissions departments) are interested in seeing. Still, the specific purpose and target audience for standardized test essays are unlike any writing tasks you may have previously encountered.

In this appendix you will learn strategies and approaches that will serve you well for these and other similar test situations. You will also gain an understanding of how ACT and SAT present these tests.

The essay sections of both the ACT and SAT will demonstrate how well you fulfill the expectations of a competent college writer. Specifically, the testers want to know the following:

- Can you take a stance or position on an arguable topic?

- Can you fully develop a set of reasons or evidence for your position?

- Can you effectively organize your writing?

- Are you able to compose sentences with appropriate diction and usage and follow conventions such as correct spelling and punctuation?

Before delving into how to think about each of these expectations, let's take a look at how the concepts of audience and purpose apply to writing essays on standardized tests. Who is your audience? Your audience will be two or three experienced high school or college writing teachers. Each reader will spend about two minutes with your essay and give it a rating. In some cases, your essay may also be made available to the colleges where you are applying, but for all practical purposes, your audience is those two or three raters.

Let's not have any illusions about your writing purpose. Your purpose is to demonstrate that you have competence when it comes to writing. Even more specifically, your purpose is to show that you have enough writing competence to be a successful college student.

If you were given the opportunity to provide a portfolio of your best writing accumulated over several months or years, your purpose would still be the same, but that's not the situation here. You also do not have the luxury of several hours to write an essay. You have a half hour or less to write something, and it will be rated by a very small number of people who will actually spend very little time reading it.

So, now you understand the challenges and the playing field. Let's move on to the particulars.

Stance: The raters want to see if you can take a position and defend it. So, take a stand! Avoid becoming overly subtle when it comes to the position you are taking. Avoid taking a position that says, "Well, both sides of this argument have some pretty good points." Your readers already know that. State *your* position early and clearly. Also, be sure you are responding directly to the requirements of the essay prompt. Changing the prompt in order to suit your own preferences is not a good idea. The test-writers very carefully write those prompts so that certain rhetorical approaches are necessary. If you do not address the specifics of the prompt, your focus will be off, and it will affect your rating.

For example, the ACT writing prompts usually describe a con-troversial educational issue. Then the test taker is directed to take a particular stance on the issue and support it with "specific reasons and examples." Those are pretty clear directions, and you should approach the task in a particular way. If a test taker instead decides to address the prompt by writing a long narrative that he hopes will make his position clear, he is taking a huge risk. Or if a student simply chooses to discuss why this is "an interesting topic" without declaring a specific position, he also is not likely to score well.

Similarly, the SAT prompts give strong cues about how to develop your response. After a provocative quote or scenario is provided, you are directed to take a position on it, including examples from your own experience, knowledge, reading, or observations. Clearly, the raters are looking for an unequivocal stance and a satisfying number of supporting points drawn from a variety of sources. A student whose examples are all drawn from events in her social life will be at a disadvantage compared to a student who includes material from her friendships, her knowledge of a particular subject matter domain, and relevant books she has read.

Development: The raters want to see if you can develop a set of reasons or ideas that support your position. Your paragraphs should make a good first impression. Skimpy, one- or two-sentence paragraphs make a poor first impression, as do paragraphs that go on for longer than a page. A good gauge for whether or not you have sufficiently elaborated is to simply hold your thumb and forefinger as far apart as possible. The space in between is about how much space each paragraph should take up on a page. Of course, if you are one of those people with huge or miniscule handwriting, you will need to adjust that "rule of thumb."

One particular method of development that we suggest you include, if possible, is acknowledging the opposition argument. Raters reward you if you acknowledge one or more of the arguments held by those with opinions contrary to yours, and then *effectively and logically articulate why your opinion is more valid.* If you are able to include this approach in one or more of your body paragraphs, you will be rewarded.

Don't hesitate to use your own personal experiences as a way of providing examples or development. It's perfectly fine to use *I* or any other first-person perspectives in the development of your essay.

Organization: The raters want to know if you have a sense of how to organize an expository essay. The safest bet here is to not become overly intricate. If you have a compelling introduction, approximately three developed body paragraphs, and a satisfying conclusion, you will not be rated poorly on organization. On the other hand, if you immediately see a unique, sophisticated way to organize your essay, that can help your rating a little bit. Our advice though is to not spend precious minutes coming up with something that might not be immediately apparent to a reader on his three-hundredth essay of the day. If it's a great idea, and you're sure you can pull it off, go for it. Otherwise, put your energy into crafting a solid introduction and conclusion, and don't get too fancy.

Don't overlook the opportunity to somehow connect the beginning and ending. If your introduction has a particularly compelling phrase or example, refer to it again in your conclusion. Your raters will recognize your ability to control that aspect of your writing, and they will reward you for it.

Word Choice and Mechanics: Be honest with yourself about this one. Your vocabulary and usage skills are what they are. You will obviously write as well as you can on this essay. Keep in mind that your goal is to write clearly and convincingly, so write with words that you can control. You are better off using your everyday vocabulary than to throw in a thesaurus gem whose meaning and usage are beyond your control.

Obviously, you will not intentionally make grammatical, punctuation, or spelling mistakes. As you move quickly through the composition process, however, you might slip up. Some errors may be due to the fact that you are unaware of a spelling or usage rule. You cannot do anything about those errors at this point. Other errors, however, are simply due to thinking about another part of the writing process as you are composing the sentences. These errors can be found and cleaned up if you leave a few moments at the end to read over your essay at least once. The raters realize that your work is the result of writing within a limited amount of time, so an occasional usage or mechanical mistake is not a huge problem on this essay. Mechanical perfection is not the goal or standard.

Again, your raters are focusing on those few categories.: stance, development, organization, word choice and mechanics. They do not know your past grades or writing experiences, whether they are positive, negative, or mixed. They will deal with the essay you create, and they will deal with it quickly. With those dynamics in mind, here are some more bits of advice:

- Write as neatly as you can. Many students your age have poor penmanship because they have done much of the writing in their lives on computers. Maybe you are one of them. Do the best you can. In general, printing is easier to read than cursive. Unless it takes you much longer to print than to write in cursive, you should consider printing. Your writing has only a few seconds to make an impression. Do everything you can to make that first impression positive.

- Choose your stance quickly. The fate of the world does not depend on whether you choose stance A or stance B. The essay prompts are written so that any number of positions can be taken in response to them. The important issue is how you develop the one you choose.

- Spend a little time organizing. After choosing your position, jot it down right away, along with a few bullet points or some other informal outline format. Yes, your time is limited, but this is a good investment of a couple of minutes. Write down your development ideas, along with any thoughts you have about your introduction and conclusion. When you actually begin to write, you will then have a map to follow. You won't need to have it memorized or try to think it up as you go. It will already be there, ready for a glance whenever you need it.

- Leave a few minutes for editing. You won't have time to recopy or totally alter your approach; don't even try to do either of those. Instead, read carefully to see if you can catch any accidental errors. If you find something that needs to be changed, make the correction as neatly as possible. Fixing the error is more important than having a cross-out, so neatness can be compromised for correctness.

Specifics of ACT and SAT

The very fact that these tests now have essay portions is testament to how both ACT and SAT change their testing methods from time to time. Although the specifics noted here are accurate as of the time of publication, you should check with your school guidance counselor or the websites of ACT and College Board, the publisher of the SAT, for the latest information and advice about these tests.

ACT

The ACT exam is offered in two formats: ACT or ACT Plus Writing. All states offer both tests on all testing dates. (Not all colleges require the writing test, so whether or not it is in your best interests to take that writing portion is up to you. You may wish to consult your guidance counselor about your options. Our goal is to help you with this essay test, if you decide to take it.) Students taking the ACT Plus Writing test may be tested in a different room or area than students taking the ACT without the writing portion.

The ACT essay is written within a thirty-minute time limit. Students must compose their essays using a pencil on the lined paper provided by ACT, and the essays must be written in English.

The ACT Plus Writing test has been administered only since 2005. The essay prompts of the first few years were for persuasive writing, and they involved school-related topics or topics presumed to be of interest to high school students, such as fast food.

Your essay will be read by two raters, each of whom will rate it on a scale of one to six. If the ratings vary by more than one point, your essay will be read by a third rater who will decide which rating is more appropriate. A perfect score on the ACT essay is twelve.

The results of the ACT writing test are reported in two ways: as a writing subscore, and as part of a combined English/writing score. The writing test does not affect your ACT composite score or any of the subject area scores.

SAT

The essay portion of the SAT is not optional. It is now part of the writing section of the SAT. The twenty-five-minute essay portion is the first part of the SAT that you will take, followed by a thirty-five-minute multiple-choice writing test.

The SAT essay prompt follows a specific format. The first part of the prompt is an excerpt or short quote from a source that addresses a particular issue. The second part of the prompt directs you to explain your point of view on the issue, using your own experiences and perspectives, as well as material from other sources, such as books or articles that you have read.

You will be provided with lined paper on which to write the essay.

Your essay will be read by two raters, each of whom will rate it on a scale of one to six. Your essay score is the sum of their ratings with a twelve as a perfect score.

The best resource to take with you into either of these tests is confidence. You have learned from all of the writing experiences in your life. You know the basics of good writing. You have some specific strategies in mind to help you navigate the experience of writing a standardized test essay. You are as prepared as possible, and that should give you the self-assurance you need to write the best essay you can.

Appendix

D

Documentation Formats

This appendix gives examples of documentation formats for the Works Cited list and for internal documentation.

Works Cited List

The following citation examples for a Works Cited list are based on the format designed by the Modern Language Association (MLA). Please note that some teachers may prefer or require other formats. Also, please be aware that the MLA formats change occasionally to accommodate new technology or new approaches to documentation. Although the following examples do not reflect this, all entries must be double-spaced.

Print Sources

One Author:
Heffalump, Thomas. *The History of Stuffed Animals in the Late Twentieth Century*. New York: Shephard and Milne Publishers, 2006. Print.

Two Authors:
Wyrd, Iam Veri, and William Beriche. *Ten Ways to Fail in College Without Really Trying*. New York: Partian Books, 2010. Print.

Three or More Authors:
Wyrd, Iam Veri, et al. *Ten More Ways to Fail in College Without Really Trying*. Phoenix: Partian and Moore Books, 2009. Print.

Author(s) with an Editor:

Sever, Blanche. *Teens Who Need to Dress in Black Have Blue Thoughts.* Ed. John Inthecaan. New York: Shadow Press, 2011. Print.

One Editor:

Sleeper, Grace, ed. *Believe It or Not: People Who Sprinkle Salt on Watermelon and Wear Sandals with Black Socks While Cutting the Lawn.* New York: Best Practices Publishing, 1999. Print.

Edition of a Literary Work:

Shakespeare, William. *Romeo and Juliet.* Ed. Pamela Perfect. London: Lowe Classics, 1983. Print.

Newspaper Article (One Author):

Dootie, Howdie. "Man on Moon Meets Elvis in Crater." *Far West Tribune.* 30 June 2007: 12. Print.
(If no author is given, the title of the article is listed first.)

Magazine Article (One Author):

Let, Ham. "Son Taunts Stepfather Before Attending Play." *Weekly News.* 30 Sept. 2010: 35. Print.
(If no author is given, the title is listed first.)

Reference Article (One Author):

Pole, Thaddeus. "Frogs." *Encyclopedia Animalia.* 2007 ed. Print.
(If no author is given, the article title is listed first.)

Reference Series:

Bloom, Harold. "Changes in Romeo and Juliet." *The Myth of Love.* Alfred Knopf, 1966. *Twentieth Century Literary Criticism.* Eds. Dedria Bryfonski and Sharon K. Hall. Detroit: Gale Research Co., 1979. 2:297–298. Print.

Pamphlet:

Careers in Painless Dentistry. Chicago: Institute for Dental Research, 2001. Print.
(If author's name is given, list it first.)
(The date in parentheses is the date you accessed the information.)

Online Sources

Entire Web Site:

Access Excellence. The National Health Museum, 4 Dec. 2009. Web. 1 May 2011.
(The first date is the date of publication. The second date is when you accessed the site.)

Page on a Website

"Mitosis." *Access Excellence*. The National Health Museum, 4 Dec. 2009. Web. 1 May 2011.

(The first date is the date of publication. The second date is when you accessed the site.)

Database

"The Voice of Mockingjay." *Kirkus Reviews* 78.20 (2010): 12. *EBSCOhost*. Web. 1 May 2011.

(The first date is the date of publication. The second date is when you accessed the site.)

Other Sources

Broadcast Program:

"Marilyn Monroe." *Biography*. Arts and Entertainment. 23 Jan. 2001. Television.

Personal Interview:

Bieber, Justin. Personal Interview. 20 Mar. 2010.

Internal Documentation

Parenthetical documentation is the most widely used form of internal documentation. To use this method to document the source of a quotation or an idea, place in parentheses immediately after the borrowed material a brief note identifying the source. This type of note is called a parenthetical, or internal, citation, and the act of placing such a note is called citing a source. The first part of a parenthetical citation refers the reader to a source in your Works Cited list. The second part of the citation refers the reader to a specific page or place within the source. If the source is clearly identified in the text, omit it from the citation and give only the page number(s). Notice the punctuation in each case, especially the end period after the parentheses.

For works listed by author or editor, use the author's or editor's last name:

"It's unlikely the problem in East Timor will be solved militarily" (McGuinn 364).

For works listed by title, use the title, abbreviating if title is lengthy:

Indonesia's rule over East Timor is disputed by the United Nations ("East Timor" 632).

When the author's name is used in the text, cite only the page number:

McGuinn believes that military forces cannot end the problem in East Timor (80).

Index

A

Abbreviations
  in online writing, 411–412, 415
  with periods, 510, 511
  without periods, 512
Absolutes, avoiding in argument
  essays, 281
Academic writing, 172
Acronyms, 520
ACT essays, 539–545. *See also*
  Argument essays
    audience, 540
    choosing topic, 541
    first impressions, 543
    overview of, 544–545
    vocabulary used, 543
Action, putting description in, 48
Action/active verbs, 52–54
Active sentences, 492
Addresses, 511, 514
Adjectives, compound, 526
Ad populum, avoiding, 284–285
"Air Glory" (Rotter), 445–446
Allende, Isabel, "In Giving I Connect
  with Others," 259–260
"America: Made in China" (Wiemer),
  354–361
American Psychological Association
  (APA) format, 338, 345
Analogies, faulty, 283
Anderson, Gary, "Is This Heaven?
  No, It's Wrigley Field," 74–76
Anonymity of online writing, 413
Apostrophes, 518–520
Argument essays, 278–329
  for ACT / SAT exams, 541–543
  audience, 279–280
  avoiding fallacies, 282–285
  building valid arguments, 285–289
  choosing topic, 291–294
  conclusions, 291
  organizing, 289–294
  presenting evidence, 291
  thesis, 289–291
  using logic, 279, 280–282

Arguments
  building valid, 285–289
  circular, 282
Argument to the people fallacy,
  284–285
"Aria" (Richard Rodriguez), 105–111
Articles vs. essays, 279
"The Art of Applying: A Satirical
  Approach to the College Admissions
  Process" (Reding), 481–483
Assertions, 293–294
Assumptions
  making, 282–283
  pointing out false and
    unreasonable, 288
Audience
  for ACT/SAT essays, 540
  for argument essays, 279–280
  for creative nonfiction, 450
  for in-class essays, 371
  for journals, 453
  for literary essays, 362
  for online writing, 411, 412
  for process essays, 213
  remembering, 4
  writing for particular, 136

B

"Backwards Tumble" (Nimets),
  125–127
Banks, Anthony G., Jr., "Poetic
  Privacy," 272–274
Beata, Alex, "Personal Geography,"
  406–407
"Beauty Is in the Eye of the Beholder"
  (Veit), 163–166
"Becoming a Poet" (Williams),
  237–241
Bedell, Jack, "Physical and Social
  Laws in Ray Carver's 'Popular
  Mechanics'", 381–385
Begashaw, Noah, "In the Shoes of a
  True Ethiopian," 116–119
Begging the question, 282–283
Behaviors, defining meanings of, 243
Berg, Elizabeth, "Escaping Into the
  Open," 26–27

U

V

W

Z

Acknowledgements

American Honda Motor Company. American Honda Motor Company advertisement. Published in *Newsweek*, October 28, 1996. Copyright © 1996 American Honda Motor Co., Inc. Reprinted by permission of American Honda Motor Company.

The Atlantic Monthly. "She: Portrait of the Essay as a Warm Body" by Cynthia Ozick. Published in *Atlantic Monthly*, September 1998.

Sharon Begley. "Your Brain Online." *Newsweek.* January 8, 2010. Newsweek/ Daily Beast Company LLC. All rights reserved. Used by permission and protected by the Copyright Laws of the United States. The printing, copying, redistribution, or retransmission of the Material without express written permission is prohibited."

Stuart D. Bykofsky. "No Heart for the Homeless" by Stuart D. Bykofsky. Copyright © 1986, by Stuart D. Bykofsky. Published in *Newsweek*, December 1, 1986. Reprinted by permission of the author.

Dave Chappelle. "That's What I Call Funny" by Dave Chappelle. Published in *Time* January 17, 2005. Reprinted by permission of the author.

Daily Herald. "Maybe Your Inner Child is Comfy in Middle Ages" by Burt Constable. Copyright © *Daily Herald*, November 13, 1997. Reprinted by permission of the *Daily Herald*.

Joan Didion. "In Bed" by Joan Didion. Copyright © 1979 by Joan Didion. Originally published in *The White Album*. Reprinted by permission of the author.

Discover. "Attacking HIV" by Josie Glausiusz. *Discover*, August 1998. Reprinted by permission of *Discover* magazine.

Daniel Ferri. "Dancin' Circles" by Daniel Ferri. Copyright © 1999. Originally broadcast on Chicago Public Radio. Reprinted by permission of the author.

Mary Fons. "Running on Ice." Papergirl. November 6, 2010. Web. June 27, 2011. "On Being a 'Market Kid. '" Papergirl. November 12, 2010. Web. June 27, 2011

Norman German and Jack Bedell. "Physical and Social Laws in Ray Carver's 'Popular Mechanics'" by Norman German and Jack Bedell. Published in *Critique*, Summer 1988. Reprinted by permission of the authors.

David R. Godine, Publisher, Inc. "Aria" from *Hunger of Memory* by Richard Rodriguez. Copyright © 1982 by Richard Rodriguez. Reprinted by permission of David R. Godine, Publisher, Inc.

HarperCollins Publishers. From *Escaping Into the Open* by Elizabeth Berg. Copyright © 1999 by Elizabeth Berg. Reprinted by permission of HarperCollins Publishers. "Male-Female Conversation is Cross-Cultural Communication" from *You Just Don't Understand* by Deborah Tannen. Copyright © 1990 by Deborah Tannen. Reprinted by permission of HarperCollins Publishers.

Harvard University Press. From *One Writer's Beginnings* by Eudora Welty. Reprinted by permission of the publisher, pp. 3–6, Cambridge, MA.: Harvard University Press, Copyright © 1983, 1984 by Eudora Welty.

Ernest Hemingway. "When You Camp Out, Do it Right" by Ernest Hemingway. Copyright © The Hemingway Foreign Rights Trust. Reprinted with permission.

Henry Holt and Company. "In Giving I Connect with Others" by Isabel Allende. Copyright © 2005 by Isabel Allende. Copyright © 2006 by This I Believe, Inc. Reprinted by permission of Henry Holt and Company, LLC. "So You Want to Be a Writer?" by Donald M. Murray from *The Writer's Home Companion: An Anthology of the World's Best Writing Advice, from Keats to Kunitz*, edited and with an introduction by Joan Bolker, copyright © 1997 by Joan Bolker. Reprinted by permission of Henry Holt and Company, LLC.

Susannah Indigo. From "Bad Hemingway" by Susannah Indigo. From webpage: http://www.susannahindigo.com/si_hemingway.shtml. Copyright © 1997 by Susannah Indigo. Reprinted by permission of the author.

Garrison Keillor. "Leave Me Alone." Originally published as a syndicated column published by Tribune Media Services. Copyright © 2009 by Garrison Keillor. Reprinted by permission. All rights reserved.

Stephen King. "Now You Take 'Bambi' or 'Snow White'—That's Scary!" by Stephen King. Copyright © Stephen King. All rights reserved. Originally appeared in *TV Guide* (1981). Reprinted with permission.

Ellen Levine Literary Agency/Trident Media Group. "Sweet Like a Crow" by Michael Ondaatje. Copyright © 1982 by Michael Ondaatje. Reprinted by permission of Ellen Levine Literary Agency/Trident Media Group.

David Long. "The Power of the Tangible" by David Long. Published in *Poets and Writers*, September/October 2002. Reprinted by permission of the author.

William Morris Agency. From "Judy Blume Talks About Writing: A Personal View" by Judy Blume. Published by www.judyblume.com. Copyright © 2005 by Judy Blume. Reprinted by permission of William Morris Agency, LLC on behalf of the author.

Jean V. Naggar Literary Agency. "Involuntary Conversions, Preemptive Counterattacks, and Incomplete Successes: The World of Doublespeak" from *Doublespeak* by William Lutz. Reprinted by permission of the author.

New York Times. "'No Messages on this Server,' and Other Lessons of Our Time" by Verlyn Klinkenborg, from *Editorial Observer*. (New York Times) January 29, 2006. Reprinted by permission of *New York Times*.

Newsweek, Inc. "Don't Be Bland" by Bruce Poch, *Newsweek*, August 21-28, 2006 copyright © 2006, Newsweek, Inc. All rights reserved. Reprinted by permission. "A Gift in Disguise" by Ryan Patrick Kelley. Newsweek Education Program copyright © 2003, Newsweek, Inc. www.newsweekeducation.com. "Is This What Life's About?" by Elizabeth Shaw, *Newsweek*, May 5, 1997. All rights reserved. Reprinted by permission. "My Black Skin Makes My White Coat Vanish" by Mana

Lumumba-Kasongo, *Newsweek*, April 3, 2006 copyright © 2006, Newsweek, Inc. All rights reserved. Reprinted by permission. "The Nature of Things" by Ruth Cherry, *Newsweek*, March 3, 1997. All rights reserved. Reprinted by permission. "Once Unique, Soon a Place Like Any Other" by Abe Whaley, *Newsweek*, November 14, 2005. All rights reserved. Reprinted by permission. "Poetic Privacy" by Anthony G. Banks Jr. Newsweek Education Program copyright © 2005, Newsweek, Inc. www.newsweekeducation.com. "The Question" by Julia Kraus. Newsweek Education Program copyright © 2005, Newsweek, Inc. www.newsweekeducation.com. "Sidewalks Can Make a Town a Neighborhood" by Carolyn V. Egan, *Newsweek*, April 24, 2006. All rights reserved. Reprinted by permission. "The Siesta Solution" by Jennifer Ford. Newsweek Education Program copyright © 2005, Newsweek, Inc. www.newsweekeducation.com. "We Had the Love, But I Long for the Letters" by William Shaw, *Newsweek*, April 17, 2006. All rights reserved. Reprinted by permission. "Frightening—And Fantastic." by Anna Quindlen, Newsweek. September 18, 2006. Copyright © 2006. The Newsweek/Daily Beast Company LLC. All rights reserved. Used by permission and protected by the Copyright Laws of the United States. The printing, copying, redistribution, or retransmission of the Material without express written permission is prohibited.

Michele Norris. "Capture the Conversation." by Michele Norris. Grace Notes. September 17, 2010. Web. June 27, 2011. Moody, Neli. "Two Rivers." Michele Norris: Your Stories. June 8, 2011. Web. June 27, 2011. "Arleen-Birthday present: Are you black, sorta?" Michele Norris: Your Stories. June 8, 2011. Web. June 27, 2011.

Chris Offutt. "Home to the Hills" by Chris Offutt. Copyright © 1998 by Chris Offutt. Published originally in *New York Times Magazine*, October 25, 1998. Reprinted by permission of the author.

Robert Phillips. "Why I Write" by Robert Phillips. Published in *Poets and Writers*, March/April 1999. Copyright © 1999 by Robert Phillips. Reprinted by permission of the author.

Pif Magazine. Interview with Naomi Shihab Nye by Rachel Barenblat. Published in *Pif Magazine*, May 31, 2006 and *Pif Magazine* website: http://www.pifmagazine.com/SID/240/?page=4&. Reprinted by permission of *Pif Magazine*.

Random House, Inc. "A Country Road Song" from *Meditations from a Movable Chair* by Andre Dubus, Copyright © 1998 by Andre Dubus. Used by permission of Alfred A. Knopf, a division of Random House, Inc. "Popular Mechanics" from *What We Talk About When We Talk About Love* by Raymond Carver, Copyright © 1981 by Raymond Carver. Used by permission of Alfred A. Knopf, a division of Random House, Inc. "Upon Receiving the Nobel Prize for Literature, 1950" from *Essays, Speeches, Letters* by William Faulkner, edited by James B. Meriwether. Copyright © 1950 by William Faulkner. Used by permission of Random House, Inc.

St. Martin's Press. "On Dumpster Diving" from *Travels with Lizbeth* by Lars Eighner. Copyright © 1993 by the author and reprint by permission of St. Martin's Press, LLC.

Shambhala Publications, Inc. From *Writing Down the Bones* by Natalie Goldberg; Copyright © 1986, 2005. Reprinted by arrangement with Shambhala Publications, Inc., www.shambhala.com.

Mike Shannon. "The Spitball Interview: W.P. Kinsella" from *The Best of Spitball: The Literary Baseball Magazine*, edited by Mike Shannon. Published by New York Pocket Books, 1988. Reprinted by permission of the author.

Bonnie Smith-Yackel. "My Mother Never Worked" by Bonnie Smith-Yackel. Published in *Women: A Journal of Liberation*. Copyright © 1975 by *Women: A Journal of Liberation*. Reprinted by permission of the author.

Meredith Stewart. "Moderation, Guilt, and Social Media." In For Good. December 8, 2010. Web. June 27, 2011.

Tribune Media Services, Inc. "So Much to Hate, and So Little Time" by Mike Royko from *For the Love of Mike: More of the Best of Mike Royko*, foreword by Roger Ebert. Copyright © Tribune Media Services, Inc. All rights reserved. Reprinted with permission.

University of Chicago. "This Year's Essays" The University of Chicago: Admission & Financial Aid website, 2005. Http://collegeadmissions.uchicago.edu/level3.asp?id=376. From 2006–2007 Essays: Essay Option 2, Inspired by Aleksandra Ciric, Oyster Bay High School, Oyster Bay, NY; From 2005–2006 Essays: Essay Option 1, Based on a suggestion by Katherine Gold of Cherry Hill High School East, Cherry Hill, NJ; From 2003–2004 Essays: Essay Option 2, Inspired by Maximilian Pascual Ortega, a graduate of Maine Township High School South, Park Ridge, IL. Reprinted by permission of University of Chicago Admissions Office.

Kurt Vonnegut. "I have been called a Luddite" from *A Man Without a Country*. Copyright © 2005 by Kurt Vonnegut. Reprinted with the permission of Seven Stories Press, www.sevenstories.com.

Writers House LLC. "I Have a Dream" by Martin Luther King, Jr. Reprinted by arrangement with the Estate of Martin Luther King, Jr., c/o Writers House as agent for the proprietor New York, NY. Copyright © 1963 Martin Luther King, Jr., copyright renewed 1991 by Coretta Scott King.

We have made every effort to trace the ownership of all copyrighted material and to secure permission from copyright holders. In the event of any question arising as to the use of any material, we will be pleased to make the necessary corrections in future printings. Thanks are due to the aforementioned authors, publishers, and agents for permission to use the material indicated.